Moldova

Moldova

Arena of International Influences

Edited by Marcin Kosienkowski and William Schreiber

LEXINGTON BOOKS
Lanham • Boulder • New York • Toronto • Plymouth, UK

Published by Lexington Books
A wholly owned subsidary of The Rowman & Littlefield Publishing Group, Inc.
4501 Forbes Boulevard, Suite 200, Lanham, Maryland 20706
www.rowman.com

10 Thornbury Road, Plymouth PL6 7PP, United Kingdom

British Library Cataloguing in Publication Information Available

Library of Congress Cataloging-in-Publication Data
Kosienkowski, Marcin.
  Moldova : arena of international influences / Marcin Kosienkowski and William Schreiber.
      p. cm.
  Includes index.
  ISBN 978-0-7391-7391-6 (cloth : alk. paper) -- ISBN 978-0-7391-7392-3 (electronic)
  1. Moldova--Foreign relations--1991- I. Schreiber, William, 1990- II. Title.
  JZ1622.K67 2012
  327.476--dc23
                              2012008690

Printed in the United States of America

Contents

List of Abbreviations

AA	Association Agreement
AEI	Alliance for European Integration (Moldova)
AP	Action Plan
ATPs	Autonomous Trade Preferences
BMC	Bessarabian Metropolitan Church
BSEC	Black Sea Economic Cooperation Organization
CDU/CSU	Christian Democratic Party (Germany)
CEI	Central European Initiative
CFR	United States Senate Committee on Foreign Relations
CFSP	Common Foreign and Security Policy
CIB	Comprehensive Institution-Building
CIS	Commonwealth of Independent States
CSCE	Conference on Security and Cooperation in Europe
DCFTA	Deep and Comprehensive Free Trade Area
DfID	Department for International Development (United Kingdom)
DRA	Department for Romanians Abroad
EaP	Eastern Partnership
EC	European Commission
EDMs	"Early Day Motions" (United Kingdom)
EEAS	European External Action Service
ENP	European Neighbourhood Policy
ENPI	European Neighbourhood and Partnership Instrument
EU	European Union
EUBAM	European Union Border Assistance Mission to Moldova and Ukraine
EUSR	European Union Special Representative
FCO	Foreign and Commonwealth Office (United Kingdom)
FDI	Foreign Direct Investment
FDP	Free Democratic Party (Germany)
GATT	General Agreement on Tariffs and Trade
IMF	International Monetary Fund
IRI	International Republican Institute (United States)
MCC	Millennium Challenge Corporation (United States)
MFN	Most-Favored-Nation
MICOM	Moldovan Initiative Committee of Management (United Kingdom)
MSSR	Moldavian Soviet Socialist Republic

NAC	National Administration for Citizenship (Romania)
NATO	North Atlantic Treaty Organization
ODA	official development assistance
ODIHR	OSCE Office of Democratic Institutions and Human Rights
OECD	Organization for Economic Co-operation and Development
OIF	l'Organisation internationale de la francophonie (International Organization of the Francophonie)
OSCE	Organization for Security and Cooperation in Europe
PCA	Partnership and Cooperation Agreement
PCRM	Party of Communists of the Republic of Moldova
PEP	Peacekeeping English Project
PiNF	People in Need Foundation (Czech Republic)
PIPA	People in Peril Association (Slovakia)
PLDM	Liberal Democratic Party of Moldova
PMR	Pridnestrovian Moldavian Republic or Transnistria or the left bank of the Dniester River
PPCD	Christian Democratic People's Party (Moldova)
RCI	Romanian Cultural Institute
SFPA	Slovak Foreign Policy Association
SPD	Social Democratic Party (Germany)
TACIS	Technical Assistance for the Commonwealth of Independent States
TIKA	Turkish Agency for International Development and Cooperation
UfM	Union pour la Méditerranée (Union for the Mediterranean)
UNDP	United Nations Development Programme
UNESCO	United Nations Educational, Scientific and Cultural Organization
USSR	Union of Soviet Socialist Republics
WTO	World Trade Organization

Foreword

Moldova boasts a proud history, rich in culture and diversity. Today's Moldova is still young—it recently celebrated its twentieth birthday—but throughout history this piece of land has provided a beautiful mosaic of many ethnic groups, and many religions.

I am by no means the first person to acknowledge this. One of Poland's most famous writers—Jozef Ignacy Kraszewski—described the cosmopolitan charm, the energy that he discovered in nineteenth century Chisinau. Kraszewski describes street signs written in French, Russian, German and Polish. Chisinau was truly a European microcosm.

An enduring characteristic throughout the nation's history is its European heartbeat. Since regaining independence in 1991, Moldova has again shown this well-founded European identity. This can be felt when one is driving down the streets of Chisinau, but more importantly it can also be sensed when meeting and interacting with Moldova's people.

The two decades since Moldova's independence have been challenging. Conflict and economic perils have taken their toll. We must never forget the hundreds of Moldovans who tragically lost their lives in the fighting that ravaged the country in the early 1990s. It is due to this history, not despite it, that Moldova finds itself at a fundamental crossroads. The country's future hinges, more than ever, on what happens in the coming years.

I was very happy to visit Moldova in December 2010 and I witnessed how open and sensitive the Moldovan people are. I was truly grateful for the very friendly welcome that I received on my arrival.

During the visit, I encouraged the country's political leaders to stick together to overcome the institutional deadlock that has crippled Moldova's political system for too long. I delivered the strong message that the EU is the best bet for Moldova's future. We have to break with the politics of the past because they do not benefit Moldova's citizens.

The second message of my visit was that Moldova needs stability above all else. Moldova is the spearhead in our Eastern partnership with a very important position in our common neighborhood. In terms of democratic credentials, I can say that it leads the way for other Eastern Partnership countries to follow.

Although Moldova is now on the right path, it still has some way to go. Consequently, my third message stressed the importance of continuing economic reforms and social progress. Today, European integration is no longer a fairytale fantasy for Moldova—it is achievable, but only through hard work and concrete measures. However, as with all things which require hard work, the Moldovan people must continue to show patience and undergo sometimes painful sacrifices to reach this goal.

Politicians have already started to implement structural reforms necessary for closer European ties. Though reforms in the field of justice and internal affairs have shown progress, they must still continue. Moldova has important work ahead, not only in strengthening democracy and the rule of law, but also fighting corruption and tackling the problem of poverty.

These reforms will not be easy, and there is a risk that the feelings of both people and politicians may be bruised. Nonetheless, the goal of entering the EU should be the goal of all Moldovans regardless of political color. One thing is clear: remaining united during this transition process is crucial.

I understand the need for this unity from personal experience. In this respect, the Republic of Moldova's current situation has strong parallels with my country—Poland. Ten years ago, as Prime Minister, I introduced a string of comprehensive reforms to get Poland on track for EU accession. My government pushed through four painful reforms: in education, healthcare, local administration and pensions. We closed down 22 of our 60 coal mines. Within a matter of months, one hundred thousand miners in my constituency were made unemployed. At first, many of my fellow citizens were afraid of the reforms we introduced because they did not understand them. Eventually, though, they yielded significant, tangible benefits. Importantly, the reforms were also made possible because of the strong support for EU accession from the main opposition parties.

Without these reforms Poland would not be what it is today: a confident and secure country as well as an important member of the European Union and NATO. Last year, Poland was the only EU country showing positive economic growth. This can also be Moldova's future.

Moldovans are not alone; we are here to help. The European Union has shown that it is ready to support its reform efforts through technical and financial assistance. The European Parliament has approved €90 million worth of macro-financial assistance for Moldova. Institutional ties between Chisinau and Brussels are becoming stronger. For example, the EU-Moldova Action Plan plays a very important role both in deepening mutual co-operation and helping Moldova to meet EU standards. Moldova is also a key player in our joint Danube strategy, grouping 14 countries together to find common solutions to the macro-region's challenges. It is this kind of step-by-step approach which will help Moldova along its road of reform.

The European Parliament is encouraging a "people to people" approach. I welcome the European Commission's action plan for visa liberalization. We also fully support the ongoing talks on the Association Agreement and look forward to the start of the negotiations on a deep and comprehensive Free Trade Area.

I welcome the plans to relaunch fully-fledged international talks on the Transnistrian conflict settlement. Dialogue is the main tool to solve long-standing disputes. The EU is strongly committed to the settlement of the conflict. A stable, democratic and prosperous Moldova will be more successful in reuniting the country.

The international nature of this book serves to underline Moldova's growing importance in Europe and Moldova's significance and commitment to the European Union as a key partner in the region.

Europe stands on the side of Moldova. Its success is important to us. Each Moldovan citizen has a crucial role to play helping to maintain the correct course of their country.

Professor Jerzy Buzek
President of the European Parliament

Preface

This book is devoted to the Republic of Moldova, a former Soviet republic situated in Eastern Europe. For international actors, Moldova functions as an arena of influences—in other words, a sphere of intersecting interests, activities and, occasionally, competition. The volume seeks to analyze the policy of nineteen selected players in the Moldovan arena since the country's independence at the end of August 1991.

Among these actors are Belarus, Bulgaria, China, the Czech Republic, the European Union, France, Germany, Hungary, Italy, Lithuania, Poland, Romania, Russia, Slovakia, Turkey, Ukraine, the United Kingdom, and the United States of America. This group includes Moldova's neighbors, global players with stakes in the region, and other states with interests in Moldova. Finally, Transnistria is also included, taking into account that it conducts its own external activity and bears a great importance for Moldova. Transnistria, a quasi-state which detached from Moldova at the beginning of the 1990s, is completely outside the control of Moldovan authorities, although it still belongs to the Republic of Moldova under international law. The Dniester River is as an internal border dividing Moldova into right-bank under rule of Chisinau and left-bank where Transnistria is located.

Each chapter of the book is devoted to one of these actors, with the exception of the Czech Republic and Slovakia, which are grouped together. The chapters are listed in alphabetical order with one exclusion in the case of Transnistria, which—as a quasi-state—differs from other actors and is included at the end of the volume. The title of each chapter describes the chapter's main thesis analyzing a given actor's policy toward Moldova. The structure of chapters is not standardized and authors were free to organize their papers as they liked. This allowed them to focus on the central elements and time periods of their actor's policy toward Moldova and to skip over those less important.

The contributors are academics, experts and practitioners of different nationalities. Crucially, each chapter has been written by a person either directly from or somehow tied to the international actor of his or her chapter. We believe this is the book's strongest asset: chapters are more reliable, because each author has a first-hand understanding of policy conducted by his or her actor, and access to primary and original sources in their original language. By providing these chapters together in a common language, we hope the volume contributes to a greater understanding of the country's complex international landscape.

Regarding sources used by authors, titles of these written in less popular languages, other than German, French, Italian and Russian, are translated into

English in order to familiarize readers with them. A comment should be made also on statistical data concerning Moldova's foreign economic activity used in the book. Statistics of the National Bureau of Statistics of the Republic of Moldova cover only the territory under the control of the Moldovan authorities. Whereas statistics provided by national and EU statistical offices include all foreign economic activity of Moldova, including Transnistria. This information is also provided where relevant in chapters using such data, but only when trade with Transnistria constitutes a substantial portion of the actor's trade with Moldova.

The chapters were written between June and October 2011, and they reflect the situation up to this date. Readers should note that in December 2011 a change of power took place in Transnistria. Its previously unshakable leader, Igor Smirnov, lost power in elections and was replaced by Yevgeniy Shevchuk. Additionally, the Moldovan parliament finally managed to choose a president, Nicolae Timofti, in March 2012, after almost three years of attempts.

We could think of no more appropriate author than Professor Jerzy Buzek, the President of the European Parliament, to write the preface of this volume. Professor Buzek, as a representative of the European Union, was perhaps the only possible contributor seen by the majority of authors as a positive force in the region.

We would like to thank our authors for their diligence; Justin Race, Sabah Ghulamali and the people at Lexington Books; professors Sharon L. Wolchik and Ryszard Zięba; our friends and family, particularly Ernest Schreiber for his tireless editing.

We hope this book will offer an important contribution to the narrow bibliography on Moldova. It should be emphasized that it is the only work of such broad international scope. We hope that it will prove useful for state officials, academics, journalists, students and others interested in Moldova and the region. Finally, we hope that the book will help promote awareness of Moldova and the international actors shaping its future.

Marcin Kosienkowski   William Schreiber
Lublin, Poland   Washington, DC

Chapter One

Belarus: A Pragmatic Approach toward Moldova

Vladislav V. Froltsov

Relations with the Republic of Moldova in the 1990s and 2000s exemplified the pragmatic orientation of modern Belarusian diplomacy. First of all, it focused on forming beneficial economic relations between Belarus and its foreign partners, with a focus on sustainable interaction. Political instability in Moldova, as well as its inter-ethnic contradictions and its difficult relationship with both Russia and Ukraine, were not an obstacle for the development of close bilateral relations. In this framework, both countries could achieve a mutually advantageous trade balance, as well as maintain their friendship against a background of differing and contradicting political processes within the Eastern European region.

During the preparation of this chapter, information and materials were used from the foreign affairs ministries of Belarus and Moldova, as well as the Embassy of Belarus in Chisinau. Finally, publications and some statistical data from the mass media were used. It should also be noted that in the early 2000s, there was significant research interest in the bilateral relationship between these two countries. From 1999 to 2009, a detailed article about the history and current cooperation was prepared by the Belarusian ambassador in Moldova, Vasiliy Sakovich. In 2010, it was published in a collected volume of research papers, *Moldoscopie (Probleme de analiză politică)* (Moldoscopie [Problems of political analysis]).[1] In December 2004, Andrey Yermolovich, counselor of the Belarusian embassy, delivered his PhD thesis "Belarusian-Moldovan Relations: The present situation and development trends (a political analysis)" at Moldovan State University. He managed to give a quite exhaustive picture of the early years of relations between Belarus and Moldova as independent states.[2]

In addition, the Belarusian Embassy in Chisinau regularly organized scientific-practical conferences devoted to various aspects of bilateral relations. Some researchers presented very interesting reports and publications considering historical aspects of communications between Belarusians and Moldovans. For example, the Belarusian historian Sergey Lashkevich described aspects of diplomatic relations between the Grand Duchy of Lithuania and Moldavian Principality from the fourteenth to the sixteenth centuries (at that time the modern Belarusian lands were part of the Grand Duchy of Lithuania).[3]

1

Nevertheless, an analysis revealing the primary directions of Belarusian foreign policy toward Moldova, as well as a definition of Belarusian interests in Moldova and a history of their evolution during twenty years of the Belarusian-Moldovan interaction is still relevant. It would allow for the consideration of the most prominent aspects of bilateral cooperation and give a detailed forecast regarding their further development. Namely this paper seeks to trace:

- the establishment of political dialogue between Belarus and Moldova in the early 1990s, its evolution in the late 1990s and early 2000s, as well as its apparent crescendo from 2008 to 2010;
- notable features of foreign trade between the two countries;
- cooperation with Gagauzia within bilateral relations;
- cultural and humanitarian interaction;
- and perspectives on Belarusian-Moldovan relations.

It is also necessary to explain the considerable attention this chapter devotes to the development of economic relations between the two countries—in particular to the volume and structure of foreign trade. For post-Soviet republics, in which the economy is essentially supervised and coordinated by the state, the promotion of foreign trade is an extremely important, if not defining, feature of political interaction. As such, the expansion of export opportunities is one of the highest priority issues for modern Belarusian diplomacy. Trade opportunities largely determine the significance of different countries and regions for Belarus.

Finally, it is important to mention the position of the Republic of Belarus concerning the self-proclaimed and internationally unrecognized Pridnestrovian Moldavian Republic. Throughout twenty years of political interaction, Transnistria was not put on the agenda by the Belarusian government, out of respect for the territorial integrity of Moldova. One example of this approach was a situation in October 2006, when the so-called parliament of Transnistria addressed a request to the legislatures of Belarus and Ukraine to recognize its independence. In reply, Head of the Standing Committee of the House of Representatives of Belarus for International Affairs and Ties with the Commonwealth of Independent States Vadim Popov emphasized that his country recognizes the territorial integrity of Moldova, part of which is Transnistria. Therefore Belarus maintains diplomatic relations with Moldova, and the question of PMR recognition has been shelved.[4]

The Political Dialogue

Diplomatic relations between the two countries were established on November 19, 1992. The Embassy of Moldova started its work in Minsk in 1993. The Moldovan Ambassador in the Republic of Belarus simultaneously represents his country in Lithuania, Latvia and Estonia. The Belarusian Embassy was opened in Chisinau two years later. First Ambassador of the Republic of Belarus in the Republic of Moldova Nikolay Grinev officially started his duties in May 1995.[5]

The signing of the Treaty on Friendship and Cooperation between the Republic of Belarus and the Republic of Moldova in 1992 was also important for the development of bilateral cooperation. It entered into force in August of 1994 and formed the basis of the further Belarusian-Moldovan relations.

President of the Republic of Belarus Alexander Lukashenko visited Moldova in September 1995. During this official visit, both countries defined the main directions of their cooperation. The basis for sustainable interaction at the highest political level between Belarus and Moldova was established. In 1999, Vasiliy Sakovich was appointed Belarusian ambassador to Moldova. He was head of the diplomatic mission for the next ten years. Earlier Sakovich headed the (financial) Control Chamber of Belarus and was a Member of Parliament.

An official visit of Moldovan President Petru Lucinschi to Belarus took place in June 2000. The countries signed twelve agreements and international treaties, and accepted a long-term program of economic cooperation between Belarus and Moldova for a period of ten years.[6]

In late August 2001, Moldovan Prime Minister Vasile Tarlev made an official visit to Belarus. In December 2001, Moldovan Parliamentary Chairman Eugenia Ostapciuc officially visited Belarus. In January 2003, Belarusian Chairman of the Council of the Republic of the National Assembly Alexander Voytovich, made an official visit to Moldova. During his visit to Moldova, a Cooperation Agreement between the parliaments of both countries was signed. In October 2005, a working visit of Moldovan Prime Minister Tarlev to Belarus took place.[7]

In the second half of the 2000s, the intensity of bilateral contact in the political sphere decreased. The only activity was an exchange of parliamentary delegations. In June 2006, Alexander Sayko, head of the Working Group on Cooperation with the Moldovan Parliament, led a Belarusian parliamentary delegation to Moldova. During this visit there were a few meetings between the Belarusian Parliamentarians and Chairman of the Moldovan Parliament Marian Lupu, Chairman of the Moldovan Parliamentary Friendship Group with Belarus Iurie Eriomin, and other Moldovan MPs and representatives of the executive branch. In November 2006, Eriomin, head of the Friendship Group with the National Assembly of Belarus, and committeeman on the Agriculture and Food Industry of the Moldovan Parliament, led a Moldovan Parliamentary delegation to Belarus.[8]

The Foreign Trade[*]

Against the background of declining intensity of bilateral political contacts in the late 2000s, interaction in the economic sphere blossomed. While commodity

---

[*] Belarusian statistics include indicators for all Moldova (including Transnistria).

circulation between the two countries failed to exceed $110 million in the 1990s and early 2000s, steady growth was observed from 2004 to 2009. It is visible in table 1.1.

Table 1.1. Commodity circulation between Belarus and Moldova from 2003–2010

Year	Volume, in mil. USD	Growth, in %
2003	104.0	—
2004	142.2	36.7
2005	174.5	22.9
2006	176.7	1.3
2007	226.5	28.2
2008	334.9	47.7
2009	255.0	-23.6
2010	249.2	-2.0

Source: Posol'stvo Respubliki Belarus' v Respublike Moldova, "Torgovo-eko-nomicheskoye sotrudnichestvo," http://www.moldova.belembassy.org/rus/belmol /ecsotr/ (accessed March 24, 2011).

Therefore, it is quite important to analyze the correlation between export and import within the framework of the Belarusian-Moldovan commodity circulation, which explains its fundamental growth between 2007 and 2008, and its fall from 2009 to 2010. Until 2007 the volume of Belarusian exports to Moldova and Moldovan exports to Belarus were, as a rule, comparable. A negligible excess of Belarusian exports existed due to the character of bilateral foreign trade exchange. From Belarus to Moldova, hi-tech goods were delivered: tractors and motor vehicles for the transport of goods, parts and accessories, road and building equipment, tires, refrigerators and deep-freezers, etc. From Moldova came fruits, vegetables, and other agricultural products, including wine.[9] About a quarter of all Moldovan wine exports went to Belarus.[10] The difference in market prices for these kinds of goods predetermined a positive trade balance in favor of Belarus. Since 2007 the situation changed considerably. It is visible in table 1.2.

Thus, in 2007 Belarusian exports increased by 51.1 percent, and in 2008—by 1.7 times. But in 2009 its volume decreased almost by a quarter, and in 2010—it fell to 2 percent. The official Web site of the Belarusian Embassy in Chisinau explained this decline in exports to Moldova by the negative influence of the world financial and economic crisis on the dynamics of bilateral trading and economic relations worldwide.[11] Nevertheless, these circumstances did not prevent Moldovan agricultural producers from maintaining exports into Belarus at the pre-crisis level.

Table 1.2. Export and import volumes in Belarusian trade with Moldova from 2005–2010

Year	Export to Moldova, in mil. USD	Import from Moldova, in mil. USD
2005	102.2	72.3
2006	95.7	81.0
2007	144.6	81.9
2008	242.2	92.7
2009	170.4	84.6
2010	165.3	83.9

Source: Posol'stvo Respubliki Belarus' v Respublike Moldova, "Torgovo-eko-nomicheskoye sotrudnichestvo."

It is important to consider the commodity structure of Belarusian exports to Moldova. Within the framework of this analysis, it is necessary to pay special attention to the sensitivity of the total cost of Belarusian exports from the cost of oil products (petroleum oils, other than crude) supplied to Moldova.

This interdependence is illustrated in table 1.3.

Table 1.3. Petroleum oils, other than crude, exported to Moldova and their share in the total cost of the Belarusian exports to the country from 2005–2010

Year	Whole export, in mil. USD	Share of oil products in the whole export cost, in mil. USD and in %
2005	102.2	50.1 mil. (49.0%)
2006	95.7	39.4 mil. (41.2%)
2007	144.6	73.7 mil. (51.0%)
2008	242.2	155.0 mil. (64.0%)
2009	170.4	108.7 mil. (64.0%)
2010	165.3	93.0 mil. (57.3%)

Source: Posol'stvo Respubliki Belarus' v Respublike Moldova, "Torgovo-eko-nomicheskoye sotrudnichestvo;" National Statistical Committee of the Republic of Belarus, *Foreign trade of the Republic of Belarus. Statistical book* (Minsk: National Statistical Committee of the Republic of Belarus, 2010), 126, http://belstat.gov.by/homep/ru/publications/ftrade/2010/main.php (accessed March 31, 2011).

Note: Figures include petroleum bitumen and coke, with the exception of 2010.

Having increased the delivery of oil products from 2007 to 2008, the Belarusian side managed to achieve a total increase of total exports to Moldova. This commodity group brought Belarus almost two-thirds of income from trade with Moldova. However, the falling prices for production also led to a reduction in total cost of Belarusian exports from 2009 to 2010, as well as to a total decrease of commodity circulation between the two republics.

As declared on the official Web site of the Belarusian Embassy in Chisinau, a commodity circulation decrease in 2010 was connected to the reduction of oil product deliveries from Belarus at 12.9 percent.[12] Besides the falling cost of oil and petroleum products throughout world and regional markets, a negative influence on exports of this kind could also be caused by a change in favorable conditions of purchase of Russian oil for Belarusian oil refineries. Because of this variable, it is quite difficult to predict the final volume and structure of foreign trade turnover between the two countries in 2011, as the dynamics of Belarusian exports depend on some external factors. Moldovan imports to Belarus will likely remain at their former level, considering the real demand for Moldovan agricultural products in the Belarusian market.

The Belarusian government also promoted an export increase of agricultural commodities from Moldova that could not be produced in Belarus. As Vasiliy Sakovich pointed out, special decrees from the president of Belarus were published on the creation of favorable conditions for the delivery of Moldovan fresh fruit and vegetable products, and on the stimulation of Moldovan still and sparkling wine sales within the Belarusian market. As a result, from 1999 to 2002, the commodity circulation doubled.[13]

Cooperation with Gagauzia

In its promotion of Belarusian products in Moldovan markets, the Embassy of Belarus did not exclude the Gagauzian autonomy. In February 2007, Vasiliy Sakovich visited Comrat. A local newspaper, *Yedinaya Gagauziya*, characterized the arrival of the ambassador as "a visit of the head of the Belarusian Manufacturers' Delegation," thus underlining the importance of the meeting of the head of the Belarusian diplomatic mission with the Chairman of the People's Assembly of Gagauzia Stepan Esir and *Bashkan* (or *head*) Mihail Formuzal. In turn, the *Bashkan* characterized the visit of the ambassador as "an important meeting of friends." He also recalled the Cooperation Agreement between the Autonomous Territorial Unit of Gagauzia (Gagauz Yeri) and the Mogilev Regional Executive Committee of Belarus signed in 2000.[14]

In his address, Sakovich noted a success not only in bilateral cooperation, but also listed a number of problems that Belarusian enterprises faced in Moldova. The ambassador expressed concern regarding the reconstruction of the Chisinau tractor factory, Tracom, where a joint release of tractors was planned. It also involved the joint release of trolley buses. On the eve of Sakovich's visit to

Gagauzia, an Agreement of Intent to this effect was signed in Chisinau. In early February 2006 the implementation of this manufacturing project was coordinated with the Moldovan Minister of Industry and Trade Vladimir Antosii.[15]

In response, Formuzal promised to study and adopt Belarusian experience in agriculture. It was decided to open a trading house of Belarus in Comrat, and a Gagauzian trading house in Belarus.

The Russian information agency *Regnum*, which specializes in post-Soviet issues, quoted *Yedinaya Gagauziya*. The newspaper reported the questions discussed by Gagauzian businessmen and representatives of Belarusian enterprises. The inability to serve as dealers of Belarusian products was a problem for Gagauzians, as many such contracts are signed with firms in Chisinau. In turn, the visiting Belarusians pointed out that it was difficult to organize purchases of Gagauzian wine products, although Russia—the biggest market for wine from Moldova—had refused its import. *Yedinaya Gagauziya* blamed Chisinau, as the government of Moldova prohibited the export of wine-making materials (considered raw materials), in an effort to support the manufacture of finished products such as wine in Moldova.[16]

Cultural and Humanitarian Bilateral Interaction

Besides economic relations, the Belarusian Embassy in Chisinau paid much attention to interaction with representatives of the Belarusian diaspora in Moldova, numbering approximately 20,000 at the declaration of Moldovan independence. When the new independent state of Moldova was declared, Belarusians established their own cultural organizations. In 1992, the first Belarusian association was created in Chisinau. In 2004, the first Congress of Belarusians in Moldova took place, in which representatives of the various organizations participated.[17]

As Vasiliy Sakovich noted, on the whole, Belarusian-Moldovan relations in the economic, scientific, and cultural spheres have an active and mutually advantageous character. As an example for successful economic cooperation, he cited the complementary rather than competitive nature of the national economies, the geographical proximity of the countries, and the bilateral flow of goods. In the areas of science, culture, and education, a good fellowship between peoples had formed during the Soviet period, and it was especially in the interest of both states to preserve and develop cooperation along these lines.[18]

At the same time, Sakovich ascertained a less than favorable trend developing in the framework of Belarusian-Moldovan political relations—namely, the prolonged pause in the exchange of top-level officials since October 2005.[19]

Dialogue Activation in 2008–2010

Nevertheless, the situation started to change by mid-2008, as Belarus began to dialogue with the EU. In late May, Polish Foreign Minister Radosław Sikorski announced the Eastern Partnership program with the support of Sweden. Both Belarus and Moldova were invited to take part in it. The presence of new common interests stimulated an increase in bilateral interaction at the political level.

In early June of 2008, Moldovan President Vladimir Voronin officially visited the Republic of Belarus. During his visit, several aspects of bilateral cooperation were discussed.[20] In November 2008, the heads of the two countries' governments, Sergey Sidorskiy and Zinaida Greceanîi, took part in the opening of a new Belarusian Embassy building in Chisinau. During the celebrations, both prime ministers stated the presence of a mutual interest in strengthening bilateral communications. Belarusian Ambassador Vasiliy Sakovich paid special attention to the considerable success in the development of economic cooperation. From 1998 to 2008, commodity circulation between the two countries grew six-fold. Belarusian exports to Moldova increased eight times over during the same period.[21] Bilateral meetings of the prime ministers were also held in May of 2008 and 2009 during two meetings of the Summit of the Heads of the CIS governments. Some questions of economic cooperation were discussed there. In November 2008, the Belarusian Chairmen of the Council of the Republic, Boris Batura, and the House of Representatives of the National Assembly, Vladimir Andreychenko, met with the Chairman of the Moldovan Parliament Marian Lupu, during the Inter-Parliamentary Assembly of the CIS in St. Petersburg.[22]

The new ambassador of Belarus in Moldova, Vyacheslav Osipenko, presented his credentials to Moldovan Minister of Foreign Affairs and European Integration Andrei Stratan on July 9, 2009. During this meeting they discussed the expansion of Belarusian-Moldovan cooperation in the economic sphere as well as attracting Belarusian investments to the Moldovan economy.[23] Before his appointment as the ambassador in Moldova, Osipenko held the position of deputy chief of the Division for Foreign Economic Activity Coordination and director of the Department for Foreign Economic Activity in the Belarusian Foreign Ministry.[24] A changing of the ambassador to Belarus occurred three months after the parliamentary elections in Moldova, which had resulted in the formal victory of the ruling Communist party, but also in a strengthening of the liberal and democratic parties. Sending Chisinau such a highly professional Belarusian diplomat, with experience in the spheres of foreign trade policy coordination, confirmed the basic priorities of the Belarusian policy toward Moldova, namely the enlargements of exports, mutually advantageous trade and further political dialogue.

This approach did not significantly shift after the change in Moldova's government in September 2009. Interaction at the highest political level proceeded. It may even be said that the dialogue became considerably more active after the so-called pro-European coalition came to power in Chisinau. This trend was largely due to the striving of both countries to take part in the ambitious EU Eastern Partnership program.

In October 2009, Belarusian President Alexander Lukashenko made a working visit to the Republic of Moldova to participate in a session of the Council of Heads of CIS States. During this visit, the Belarusian President held a bilateral meeting with Acting President of Moldova and Chairman of Parliament Mihai Ghimpu. In March 2010, another working meeting between the President of Belarus and the Acting President of Moldova took place in Kiev. In July 2010, a meeting of the Belarusian Chairman of the Council of the Republic of the National Assembly Anatoliy Rubinov with Acting President Ghimpu was held during the World Conference of Speakers of Parliaments in Geneva.[25] By August 2010 some ninety-seven agreements were concluded between the two countries, sixty of which entered into force.[26]

Following the results of the presidential election in Belarus in December 2010, the Moldovan Foreign Ministry issued a statement urging the Belarusian government to continue the democratic reforms necessary to bring its electoral process into accordance with international standards.[27] There were no statements from top officials in Moldova. In early April 2011, Minsk was visited by a delegation of Moldovan MPs, led by Chairman of the Commission of Foreign Policy and European Integration, and Vice-President of the Democratic Party of Moldova Igor Corman. He underlined that Belarus is an important trade and economic partner for Moldova, and is seventh among economic partners in volume of commodity circulation. He expressed confidence in continuing effective dialogue between the two countries and their parliaments.[28]

All of these facts testified to the aspirations of the leadership of Chisinau's new ruling coalition to continue dialogue with Minsk along the same mutually advantageous lines. Belarus' unchanged support for the territorial integrity of Moldova also promoted further dialogue between the two countries, and an increase in high-level political exchanges in the late 2000s.

Conclusion

This chapter has reviewed Belarusian policy toward Moldova in several stages. Each stage was characterized by a certain change in the vision of Moldova's role in Belarusian foreign policy interests and priorities.

It is possible to distinguish the following stages:

- *1992–1995*—establishment of diplomatic relations and the maintenance of existing communications in place since the Soviet period. Chronologically: the establishment of diplomatic relations in November 1992, an official visit of Belarusian President Alexander Lukashenko to Moldova in September 1995;
- *1995–2005*—an increase in political interaction arrives against the background of the sustainable development of economic cooperation. The end of this stage could be marked October 2005, when Moldovan Prime Minister Vasile Tarlev visited Belarus. By the mid-2000s, a political and legal base for the interaction of two countries had been formed, steady commercial relations were established;

- *2005–2008*—a period of low intensity in political contact (as former Belarusian Ambassador Vasiliy Sakovich noted) arrives against the background of a considerable increase in Belarusian exports to Moldova, due to an increase in the share and cost of oil products. This boosts Belarusian exports to Moldova by 2.5 times;
- *2008–2010*—a renewal of the active political dialogue occurs, especially after the liberal and democratic coalition comes to power in Chisinau, which is interested in interaction with Belarus within the framework of cooperation with the EU and the realization of the Eastern Partnership program. An increase of political dialogue between the two countries was not prevented by falling trade turnover, after Russia changed its delivery terms of oil to Belarus.
- *2010*–at present, relations are largely defined by the EU's policy toward Belarus. This factor will certainly be considered by the current Moldovan government, which aspires to the closest possible integration with the European Union. In turn, trade between the two countries also depends on external factors, taking into account the dominating proportion of oil products made from Russian petroleum supplies in the structure of Belarusian exports to Moldova.

Analyzing Belarusian policy within the framework of these stages allows us to distinguish the following groupings of Belarusian interests toward Moldova, ranked according to their importance:

- Economic and foreign trade interests. First of all, increasing Belarusian exports to Moldova. The Republic of Belarus is interested in expanding its share of high-technology product export to Moldova (motor vehicles, machinery, and mechanical appliances, etc.), as well as including placing their manufacture within Moldovan territory. This takes into account the difficulty of predicting the future situation of oil products.
- Interest in political dialogue. Friendly relations with top officials in Chisinau, regardless of their political views, allow Belarus to strengthen its position within the framework of interaction with both Russia and the EU. Therefore, the very sensitive issue of Transnistria (for every government in Chisinau), is not mentioned in Belarusian-Moldovan political interactions in any regard. This is in contrast to the relations of Moldova with Russia and Ukraine.
- Cultural and humanitarian interests, including the support of the small Belarusian diaspora in Moldova, and the even smaller Moldovan diaspora in Belarus. Informal communications and contacts left over from the Soviet period played a considerable role in this regard. It was necessary only to assist this cooperation at the state level.

It is possible to assume in conclusion that despite some external factors, Belarusian-Moldovan cooperation will safely continue its present course and priorities, placing importance on political dialogue, the development of foreign trade, and the extension of commodity markets for both countries. For the Republic of Belarus, maintaining friendly relations with any government in Chisinau will be as important as it was during the past twenty years of interaction with the various political forces of the country. The markets of Moldova, small as they may be, nevertheless provide annual income totaling some hundreds of millions of dollars for Belarusian industry, which is important under conditions of increasing economic competition in the post-Soviet territory.

For the Republic of Moldova, Belarus remains a solid partner that does not try to interfere with its internal affairs, and provides a market for Moldovan agricultural products. These constants will be taken into account by any future government of Moldova—regardless of its foreign policy preferences.

Notes

1. Vasiliy Sakovich, "Belorussko-moldavskiye otnosheniya v kontekste formirovaniya moldavskoy gosudarstvennosti," *Moldoscopie (Probleme de analiză politică)* 49, no. 2 (2010): 156–66.
2. Andrey Yermolovich, "Belorussko-moldavskiye otnosheniya: sostoyaniye i tendentsii razvitiya (politologicheskiy analiz)" (PhD diss., Moldovan State University, 2004), http://www.cnaa.md/files/theses/2004/3191/andrei_ermolovici_abstract_ru.pdf (accessed March 23, 2011).
3. Sergey Lashkevich, "Iz istorii diplomaticheskikh otnosheniy mezhdu Velikim knyazhestvom Litovskim i Moldavskim knyazhestvom (ser. XIV–XVI vv.)," in *Belarus'–Moldova: vzglyad molodezhi v tret'ye tysyacheletiye: materialy mezhdunarodnoy nauchno-prakticheskoy konferentsii, 28–29 aprelya 2004 g.* (Chisinau: Vector, 2004), 54–61.
4. "Belorussiya ne priznayet Pridnestrov'ye nezavisimym gosudarstvom," *Newsinfo.ru*, October 12, 2006, http://www.newsinfo.ru/news/2006-10-12/item/672089/ (accessed March 30, 2011).
5. Posol'stvo Respubliki Belarus' v Respublike Moldova, "Istoriya dvustoronnikh otnosheniy," http://www.moldova.belembassy.org/rus/belmol/ (accessed March 24, 2011).
6. Sakovich, "Belorussko-moldavskiye otnosheniya," 159–60.
7. Posol'stvo Respubliki Belarus' v Respublike Moldova, "Istoriya;" Ministry of Foreign Affairs and European Integration of the Republic of Moldova, "Bilateral cooperation. Republica Belarus. Principalele vizite bilaterale," August 2010, http://www.mfa.gov.md/bilateral-cooperation-en/#visits (accessed March 27, 2011).
8. Posol'stvo Respubliki Belarus' v Respublike Moldova, "Istoriya."
9. National Statistical Committee of the Republic of Belarus, *Foreign trade of the Republic of Belarus. Statistical book* (Minsk: National Statistical Committee of the Republic of Belarus, 2010), 125–27, http://belstat.gov.by/homep/ru/publications/ftrade/2010/main.php (accessed March 31, 2011).
10. Posol'stvo Respubliki Belarus' v Respublike Moldova, "Torgovo-ekonomicheskoye sotrudnichestvo," http://www.moldova.belembassy.org/rus/belmol/ecsotr/ (accessed March 24, 2011).

11. Ibid.
12. Ibid.
13. Sakovich, "Belorussko-moldavskiye otnosheniya," 160.
14. "Komrat-Minsk: 'Gotovy razvivat' sotrudnichestvo...' Gagauziya za nedelyu," *IA REGNUM Novosti*, February 23, 2007, http://www.regnum.ru/news/787013.html (accessed March 23, 2011).
15. "Posol Belorussii vstretilsya s ministrom promyshlennosti i torgovli," *IA REGNUM Novosti*, February 8, 2006, http://www.regnum.ru/news/586642.html (accessed March 23, 2011).
16. "Komrat-Minsk."
17. Sakovich, "Belorussko-moldavskiye otnosheniya," 158.
18. Ibid., 162–65.
19. Ibid., 165.
20. "Prezident Moldavii posetit Belorussiyu s ofitsial'nym vizitom," *IA REGNUM Novosti*, May 14, 2008, http://www.regnum.ru/news/1083561.html (accessed March 23, 2011).
21. "Poluchiv kredit ot Rossii, Belorussiya obeshchayet obespechit' protsvetaniye Moldavii," *IA REGNUM Novosti*, November 14, 2008, http://www.regnum.ru/news/1083561.html (accessed March 23, 2011).
22. Posol'stvo Respubliki Belarus' v Respublike Moldova, "Istoriya."
23. "Belorussiya naznachila novogo posla v Moldavii," *IA REGNUM Novosti*, July 9, 2009, http://www.regnum.ru/news/1184577.html (accessed March 23, 2011).
24. Posol'stvo Respubliki Belarus' v Respublike Moldova, "Posol Belarusi," http://www.moldova.belembassy.org/rus/ambbellat/ (accessed March 24, 2011).
25. Posol'stvo Respubliki Belarus' v Respublike Moldova, "Istoriya."
26. Ministry of Foreign Affairs and European Integration of the Republic of Moldova, "Bilateral cooperation. Republica Belarus. Cadrul juridic bilateral," August 2010, http://www.mfa.gov.md/bilateral-cooperation-en/#visits (accessed March 27, 2011).
27. "Moldaviya prisoyedinilas' k pozitsii ES po vyboram v Belorussii," *IA REGNUM Novosti*, December 22, 2010, http://www.regnum.ru/news/fd-abroad/moldova/1359600.html (accessed March 23, 2011).
28. "Parlamentarii Belarusi i Moldovy namereny sodeystvovat' razvitiyu sotrudnichestva mezhdu dvumya stranami," *Novosti Belarusi. BelTA*, April 4, 2011, http://www.belta.by/ru/all_news/politics/Parlamentarii-Belarusi-i-Moldovy-namereny-sodejstvovat-razvitiju-sotrudnichestva-mezhdu-dvumja-stranami_i_548530.html (accessed April 4, 2011).

Chapter Two

Bulgaria: Relations with Moldova under the Influence of the Bulgarian Diaspora

Nicolai Ţveatcov

Historically, relations between Bulgaria and Moldova have always been inten-sive, due to a variety of factors. The first reason is that this region was an area of geopolitical concurrence between three Empires: the Russian Empire, the Otto-man Porte and the Austro-Hungarian Empire.

A second factor is the diaspora of ethnic Bulgarians primarily in the South-ern region of Moldova. The appearance of Bulgarian settlements in Moldova began in the early nineteenth century, when the Russian Empire spread into the region. The modern population of so-called "Bessarabian Bulgarians" settled in the region of southern Bessarabia at the end of the eighteenth and the beginning of the nineteenth centuries. Particularly large waves of immigrants arrived after the Russo-Turkish Wars of 1806 and 1828. The settlers came primarily from what is now Eastern Bulgaria, but many of them were also descendants of Bul-garians from the western part of the country, who had moved east before the eighteenth century.[1] From the late 1980s, the Bulgarians of Moldova improved relations with their homeland, and the Bulgarian minority in Moldova became the subject of bilateral cooperation between the two countries.

Another very important basis of practical cooperation is the international activities of both states. Mutual relations are described by the Bulgarian Embas-sy to Moldova in this way:

> The development and intensification of both friendship and partnership with the Republic of Moldova feature very prominently among the foreign policy priori-ties of the Republic of Bulgaria. No problems of a political or other nature exist between the two countries. Fruitful cooperation is maintained both in the sphere of bilateral relations and within the international organizations of which the two countries are members. Bilateral political relations have progressively devel-oped in recent years, with a growing tendency to include political dialogue at the official level, as well as the highest level.
>
> Cooperation in the field of European and Euro-Atlantic integration is an im-portant element in relations between the two countries. As a member state of the European Union, Bulgaria has contributed to the development of relations

13

between the EU and Moldova under the European Neighbourhood Policy and the 1998 Partnership and Cooperation Agreement, the specific ENP manifestation regarding Moldova. Bulgaria supports the reforms of the Moldovan government and its pro-European orientation. Bulgaria considers Moldova a priority state in the context of international cooperation for development.[2]

Nevertheless, there is reason for tension—namely the Alliance for European Integration, which came to power in Moldova in 2009, replacing the Communist party, which had strong ties to the development of Bulgarian policy toward the Moldovan state.

The Development of Political Relations

Relations between the Bulgarians and the Moldovans have a long history. Many consider them to have started with the transfer of Eastern Orthodox Christianity and culture from Bulgaria to Moldova. During one historical period (around the fifteenth century), the two countries even shared a common border. These links were maintained over the centuries, and they led to the recognition of Moldovan independence by Bulgaria on December 28, 1991, and the establishment of diplomatic relations between the states on February 5, 1992. Evgeniy Ekov, the ambassador of Bulgaria to Moldova from 2001–2005, noted that centuries of cooperation between Moldova and Bulgaria contributed to the development of modern relations in both bilateral and multilateral formats; he added that cooperation in the region was crucial.[3]

Both countries support and promote regional cooperation in the socio-economic and cultural spheres. Issues in energy, transportation, infrastructure, the environment, border security, migration, etc., are often discussed at joint meetings.[4] Solving these problems maintains stability and development in the East European region. In recent years, the interests of Bulgaria in Moldova have significantly increased.

In January 2008, during a working visit to Bulgaria, Vladimir Voronin, the president of Moldova, met with Georgi Parvanov, the president of Bulgaria. The two discussed the current status of bilateral relations and the prospects of cooperation between Moldova and Bulgaria. Voronin invited Parvanov to visit Moldova the following year. Parvanov accepted this invitation and visited Moldova in March 2009.[5]

After the 2009 change of power in Moldova, ensuring a continuity of the previous Moldovan government's policies has become a top priority for Bulgaria. This concern is not accidental. In the 2009 parliamentary elections, residents of the Taraclia district—populated largely by Bulgarians—voted en masse (80 percent) for the Party of Communists, which was defeated by the opposition. Bulgaria fears that the political choice of the Bulgarian diaspora in Moldova will have a negative impact on the cultural autonomy and socio-economic development of the Taraclia district.

Economic Cooperation

Tourism is the foremost area of economic cooperation between Bulgaria and Moldova. Bulgarian-Moldovan relations are developed through tourism organized by travel agencies (every summer more than thirty thousand Moldovan tourists visit Bulgaria). Organizations and government agencies affiliated with the tourism industry share information and promotional materials. Both sides also find it necessary to work together in attracting investments and creating joint ventures to boost the tourism industry.

The second most important area of cooperation is in transport and communications. The two countries exchange ideas on the organization of direct lines of communication between them by road, rail, and air. The Intergovernmental Bulgarian-Moldovan Commission for Economic Cooperation decided to examine the possibilities of opening direct rail and flight connections between Bulgaria and Moldova.

Cooperation in agriculture is a third factor in economic relations. Moldovan agricultural production is well known in Bulgaria and this form of economic cooperation is traditional for both states. Bulgaria and Moldova keep each other informed about the path of agriculture reform within their respective countries, the restoration of private land ownership and changes in agricultural laws and regulations.

Finally, energy is an important field of cooperation. The two sides are discussing the possibility of bringing power lines from the city of Vulcăneşti (in Moldova) to the Dobrudja region (Bulgaria), for the transmission of electricity from Moldova to the Balkan countries, with the participation of the energy system in Bulgaria.[6]

The Bulgarian Diaspora in Moldova:
The Basis of Bulgarian-Moldovan Relations

Despite the importance of these economic ties, the Bulgarian minority in Moldova has been, and continues to be, the most important subject of bilateral cooperation between the two states. The issue requires that Moldovan-Bulgarian bilateral relations be kept cordial, aimed at the further development of bilateral and multilateral formats, and representative of both countries' interests.

Since 1991, relations between the two sovereign states were characterized by several trends. First of all, throughout this period of cooperation, Chisinau and Sofia were guided by mutual interests, which also coincided with the goals of the European integration processes. Following the recommendation of most experts and international organizations, the Moldovan government adopted an inclusive citizenship law and granted extensive rights of cultural autonomy to all minorities shortly after the country's independence. It is difficult to find a better example in the former Soviet Union of a new elite and government in a country dominated by an ethnic majority that was more accommodating to minorities in general—and to the Russian minority in particular—than the government that took power in the Republic of Moldova in 1991. In contrast with some post-Soviet countries, like the Baltic republics, citizenship was immediately granted to all, language policy was both moderate and patient, education was supported in a variety of languages including Ukrainian, Bulgarian, and Turkish (during the Soviet period there were only two languages taught in schools—Moldovan and Russian), and political representation was available to all groups.[7]

This policy was carried out regardless of the political leadership in either capital. In Moldova, foreign policy is the constitutional prerogative of the president. The presidents of modern Moldova were Mircea Snegur, Petru Lucinschi, and Vladimir Voronin. Their Bulgaria counterparts were Zhelyu Zhelev, Petar Stoyanov, and Georgi Parvanov.

The Bulgarian diaspora in Moldova has played an active role in establishing friendly relations between the two countries. Supporting the Bulgarian diaspora of Moldova, including Bulgarians in Transnistria, is an important task of Bulgarian foreign policy in Moldova.

It is important to note that the establishment of diplomatic relations and the opening of the Bulgarian Embassy in Chisinau, were initiated by representatives of the Bulgarian diaspora from Moldova.[8]

With the opening of the Bulgarian Embassy in Moldova, cooperation between the education ministries expanded: Moldovan students started studying in Bulgarian high schools, researchers were trained in Bulgaria, the list goes on.

The authorities in Chisinau and Sofia recognize that the Bulgarian diaspora has been a stabilizing factor in a period of political instability for Moldova that has lasted since 1991, and this stabilizing factor plays an important role in developing cooperation between two independent states. This was clear to all of the modern presidents, prime ministers, and parliamentary chairmen of both Moldova and Bulgaria.

Accidental or deliberate infringement of cultural or other rights of the Bulgarian ethnic group in Moldova could ruin the architecture of inter-ethnic relations in this country and simultaneously ruin international relations between Bulgaria and Moldova.[9]

Cultural Issues

Ethnic and cultural problems of the Bulgarian population in Moldova were carefully monitored by the Moldovan authorities, regardless of the political authorities in power at the time. The Moldovan government adopted a set of measures to promote Bulgarian culture in 1992–1995, which were elaborated by the State Department on National Issues, created in 1991. The State Department on National Issues was created as a permanent body independent of executive authority, exercising state policy in the field of ethnic relations and language.

The Bulgarian language was introduced in the schools of ethnically Bulgarian villages in Moldova. In Tvardiţa a Bulgarian music school was opened, and in Taraclia a Bulgarian college was started. There are now Bulgarian primary schools in Taraclia, and the village of Valea-Perjei, and a Bulgarian school in Chisinau. Under the auspices of the Institute of Cultural Heritage of the Academy of Sciences of Moldova, a Department of Bolgaristika (Bulgarian Studies) was formed. Broadcasts in the Bulgarian language via central television and radio were also permitted.

Ultimately, the Moldovan government kept the Taraclia region as a national center of Bulgarian culture, and Moldova opened Taraclia State University as a center for training personnel knowledgeable in the Moldovan language, the official language of the country, to serve the Bulgarian community.[10]

Taraclia's "Political Crisis"

From 1994 to 1999 the so-called Taraclia political crisis took place. It derived its name from a region populated largely by Bulgarians in the southern part of Moldova. According to the most recent census, about 45,000 inhabitants live in the Taraclia region. Slavic Bulgarians represent about 66 percent of the population. According to official figures, they number around 28,000. Because of this, Taraclia is a culturally autonomous region of the Slavic Bulgarian minority. (Historically, several different types of Bulgarian people existed: a) Slavic Bulgarians, which represent the majority of people in Bulgaria; b) Islamic Bulgarians, living mostly on the bank of the Volga river in the Russian Federation and c) Gagauz people—a Christian Bulgarian ethnic group that speaks the Gagauz language, which is similar to the Turkish language.)[11] By comparison, the region is also home to Moldovans—14 percent, Gagauz—8 percent, Ukrainians—6 percent, Russians—5 percent, Romanians—1 percent.

The apex of tensions between central and local authorities came with a decision adopted in October 1999, granting county status (*judeţ*) to the Taraclia region, changing the administrative and territorial reform introduced in 1998. This decision took into account the interests of the Bulgarian population concentrated in the South. In January 1999, the Bulgarians of the Taraclia region, where about half of all Moldovan Bulgarians live, protested against administrative boundary changes made in 1998. The changes abolished the Taraclia district (a Soviet-era *raion*) and attached the area to neighboring Cahul County, in the process transforming the Bulgarian population from a two-thirds local majority to a 16-percent minority. The principal fear of local Bulgarians was a potential loss of state subsidies for local Bulgarian language education resulting from the fact that they no longer held a local majority. In May 1999, Taraclia's population boycotted local elections, and Bulgarians in the local administration refused to relinquish posts officially abolished under the territorial reform.[12]

In 2002, the upcoming administrative-territorial reform forced the national Bulgarian ethnic and cultural organizations to bring up the issue with the country's leadership time and time again. Under these reforms, the Taraclia County was transformed into the Taraclia district (since 2003).[13]

The Bulgarian language is taught in schools that are located in areas of concentrated Bulgarian settlement. During a visit to Bulgaria in 2004, President Vladimir Voronin pledged to establish a university for Moldova's Bulgarians. In 2004, Taraclia State University was opened. In 2009, during an official visit of the Bulgarian president to Moldova, this university was named in honor of the well-known Bulgarian religious figure, Metropolitan Gregory Tsamblak.

It must be noted that all Moldovan measures fit the ratified Council of Europe Framework Convention on National Minorities, as well as a number of national laws On National Minorities of the Republic of Moldova and the Legal Status of Their Organizations[14] and The National Policy of the Republic of Moldova.[15] It can be argued that in shaping relations between Moldova and Bulgaria, Chisinau authorities sought a policy of continuity with the Bulgarian minority.

In instances of political strife between the Bulgarian diaspora and the authorities in Chisinau, Sofia has not interfered in the internal affairs of Moldova directly, but nevertheless has demonstrated its concerns for the welfare of the Bulgarian minority on the basis of bilateral agreements on domestic legislation and European legal standards on minority rights. The Bulgarian government defended by diplomatic means (such as official declarations, a working meeting between the Bulgarian Ambassador and official representatives of Moldovan government) the rights of the Bulgarian diaspora in Taraclia County from 1998 to 1999, and Bulgaria has since provided material, financial and human resource assistance to Taraclia State University "G. Tsamblak." Bulgaria also showed its concern for the bombing of Parkany village in 1992, during the so-called military phase of the Transnistrian conflict (this village has 10,500 people, of whom about 80 percent are Bulgarians). In 1991, this village hosted the first Congress of Transnistrian Deputies of All Levels. This congress recognized the utility of proclaiming the Transnistrian Autonomous Soviet Socialist Republic within the Moldavian Soviet Socialist Republic.[16]

Bulgaria not only cares about ensuring the rights of the Bulgarian minority in Moldova, but also seeks constructive collaboration with forces in Chisinau to solve minority issues. Bilateral policy in Chisinau and Sofia is accompanied by a desire for mutually acceptable solutions regarding the diaspora issues. In one particular example, the Bulgarian side wanted Taraclia University to have the status of a joint Moldovan-Bulgarian university, but as a result of negotiations, another acceptable solution was achieved, in accordance with Moldovan legislation.

In general, friendly relations and mutual understanding were established between the two capitals, accompanied by sustained and multilateral Moldovan-Bulgarian cooperation.[17]

However, at present, there are a number of issues that will influence the further development of bilateral relations, particularly concerning objectives like visa liberalization for Moldovan citizens, trade cooperation, and others.

Moldovan Policy toward Taraclia University:
A Potential for Damage

There is one last important factor in bilateral relations: the European Union. In the context of its declared European aspirations, Moldova's new government may be planning to continue close cooperation with Bulgaria. If Moldova continues to move toward the European Union, Bulgaria's role will only increase.

However, policy documents of the new government lack any mention of Bulgaria. This could be seen as deliberately ignoring Bulgaria as one of Moldova's priority partners for European integration. Perhaps Bulgaria is not a country of strategic importance in the eyes of the political forces that came into power after July 2009, but if this is the case, it is an area of departure from the foreign policy of previous administrations.

Also, the program of the new government does not mention Taraclia as a university center of Moldova. Several other university centers of Moldova were officially listed, but Taraclia was not mentioned.

Taraclia's University "G. Tsamblak" is only five years old and, as a result, it is inferior in all regards to the other universities in Moldova. However, the university has potential to develop the Taraclia district. This university was created to reform the education and training of Bulgarian students in Moldova, to provide them with an ethnic and cultural identity, and to promote the community's integration with the Moldovan language, culture, economic, socio-economic and political environment.

Slighting or ignoring this university, such as in its omission from the governmental program is an unambiguous gesture, which will complicate the situation of the Bulgarian minority in Moldova. Taraclia University helps Moldova meet international standards for the training and education of national minorities.

These standards include the development of education systems in countries with multi-ethnic populations, which allow them to retain their cultural identity. At the same time, these institutions allow students to be integrated into the majority, enabling them to move in an era of globalization, which requires popular worldwide European languages.

Ignoring Taraclia's university indicates that the new Moldovan government erroneously interprets the meaning of the European legal norms and laws in the field of national minorities. If this is the case, then there is a risk that the Bulgarian government might reconsider its policy toward Moldova.

Chisinau's attitude to Taraclia University tests the strength of relations between Bulgaria and Moldova. This university is a modern product of cooperation between the two states, and it should be properly developed.

Conclusion

Relations between ethnic groups in Moldova are generally good, and policy toward the Bulgarians must be recognized as particularly liberal. The Moldovan political elite should understand that the support of modern Moldovan society, with all of its ethnic and identity components, cannot be won by the policies and ideas of any party or group. The national idea of a sovereign, democratic and neutral Moldova must become true for all citizens and ethnic groups. Only when this happens will the Moldovan state have a clear future for its European aspirations.

Sofia's political elite are increasingly providing aid and assistance to the Bulgarian diaspora abroad regardless of the political factors associated with their location.[18]

Until the present day, Taraclia did not have full status as a national-cultural center of the Bulgarian diaspora in Moldova. The political struggle from 1998 to 1999 for the formation of Taraclia as a Moldovan administrative-territorial center with a Bulgarian ethnic majority continued well over the next decade, and later became an objective for Taraclia County's political representatives, as well as the Bulgarian diaspora organizations.

For Sofia and Chisinau, it should be taken for granted that national and cultural issues for Bulgarians in Moldova do not stop at the borders of Taraclia, but rather they should become the basis of fruitful cooperation between both states.

These issues could become a guarantee of further improving Moldovan-Bulgarian cooperation, and may become a key part of Bulgaria's policy in support of Moldova's European aspirations.

Notes

1. See Ivan Grek and Nikolay Chervenkov, *Bŭlgarite v Ukrayna i Moldova. Minalo i nastoyashte* [Bulgarians in Ukraine and Moldova. Past and Present] (Sofia: Khristo Botev, 1993).

2. See Bulgarian Embassy to Moldova, "Political relations," http://www.mfa.bg /en/52/pages/view/4340 (accessed August 20, 2011).

3. Evgeniy Ekov, "Ya vizhu ogromnyy potentsial v razvitii otnosheniy mezhdu Bolgariyey i Moldovoy," interview with *Welcome Moldova*, http://www.welcome-moldova.com/ru/articles/bulgarian-ambassador-rus.shtml (accessed July 22, 2011).

4. "Protokol pyatogo zasedaniya Mezhpravitel'stvennoy moldavsko-bolgarskoy komissii po torgovo-ekonomicheskomu i nauchno-tekhnicheskomu sotrudnichestvu,"

Chisinau, February 27, 2009, http://www.ms.gov.md/_files/4761-Prot%2520CM-bulgara .pdf (accessed July 24, 2011).

5. Bolgarskaya Obshchina Respubliki Moldova, "Vizit prezidenta Respubliki Bolgarii gosp.Pyrvanova," http://borm-md.org/node/210 (accessed July 25, 2011); "V khode rabochego vizita v Respubliku Bolgariya sostoyalas' vstrecha prezidenta Respubliki Moldova Vladimira Voronina i prezidenta Bolgarii Georgi Pyrvanova," Moldova: Photo Gallery, January 28, 2008, http://www.photo.md/news_info.php?news_id=1183& lang=rus (accessed July 24, 2011).

6. Ekov, "Ya vizhu ogromnyy potentsial;" see "Protokol pyatogo zasedaniya."

7. Eiki Berg and Wim van Meurs, "Borders and Orders in Europe: Limits of Nation- and State-Building in Estonia, Macedonia and Moldova," *Journal of Communist Studies and Transition Politics* 18, no. 4 (2002): 65.

8. Ministerstvo na vŭnshnite raboti na Republika Bŭlgarie [Bulgarian Foreign Ministry], "Republika Moldova" [The Republic of Moldova], http://www.mfa.bg/bg /pages/view/4338 (accessed July 26, 2011).

9. Ivan Grek, "Bolgarskiye grabli," *Gagauziya v novostyakh*, April 27, 2010, http://info.gagauzia.ru/news/bolgarskie_grabli/2010-04-27-800 (accessed July 26, 2011).

10. "Voprosy integratsii ostayutsya v povestke dnya," *Nezavisimaya Moldova*, January 30, 2009, http://www.nm.md/daily/article/2009/01/30/0307.html (accessed July 26, 2011).

11. It should be noted that the ethnic origin of the Gagauz people is subject to different theories. See Claus Neukirch, "Autonomy and Conflict Transformation: The Case of the Gagauz Territorial Autonomy in the Republic of Moldova," in *Minority Governance in Europe*, ed. Kinga Gal (Budapest: Open Society Institute, 2002), 105–23.

12. Minority Rights Group International, "Moldova: Bulgarians," http://www .minorityrights.org/5028/moldova/bulgarians.html (accessed July 27, 2011).

13. Byuro mezhetnicheskikh otnosheniy Respubliki Moldova, "Stranitsy istorii," www.bri.gov.md/files/files/isctoria_BRI(rus).doc (accessed July 27, 2011).

14. Zakon o pravakh lits, prinadlezhashchikh k natsional'nym men'shinstvam, i pravovom statuse ikh organizatsiy, no. 382, July 19, 2001, http://lex.justice.md/viewdoc .php?action=view&view=doc&id=312817&lang=2 (accessed July 28, 2011).

15. Lege privind aprobarea Concepţiei politicii naţionale a Republicii Moldova [Law on the approval of the Concept of National Policy of the Republic of Moldova], no. 546, December 19, 2003, http://lex.justice.md/index.php?action=view&view=doc&lang= 1&id=312846 (accessed July 28, 2011).

16. Ivan Grek, "Moldavsko-bolgarskiye otnosheniya i deyatel'nost' pravitel'stva," Ava.md, November 15, 2009, http://ava.md/034-kommentarii/03307-moldavsko-bolgarskie -otnosheniya-i-deyatelnost-pravitelstva-vladimira-filata.html (accessed July 28, 2011).

17. "Georgiy Pyrvanov: 'Bolgariya podderzhit yevropeyskuyu integratsiyu R. Moldova,' " *Moldova azi*, March 12, 2009, http://www.azi.md/ro/print-story/1740 (accessed July 30, 2011).

18. Rosen Ivanov, "Kandidat·stvaneto za bŭlgarsko grazhdanstvo v Moldova e izklyuchitelno ulesneno" [Applying for citizenship in Moldova is very easy], interview with *Radio "Fokus,"* June 20, 2011, http://www.focus-news.net/?id=f18015 (accessed July 30, 2011).

Chapter Three

China: Policy toward Moldova under the Influence of Socialism

Lingqi Meng

As the only European country in which the Communist Party still plays a significant role on the domestic political stage, Moldova draws more attention than other small post-Soviet states in China's foreign policy agenda. Especially in the period after 2001, when the Moldovan Party of Communists took full power in Moldova, the relationship between Beijing and Chisinau developed rapidly. Recently exchange and cooperation has not been restricted only to politics and economics as in the 1990s, but also extended to areas like military and culture. A similarity of ideology—if not the most important variable in the development of the relationship between the two countries in this period—has at least advanced relations considerably. Through an examination of Moldova's position in China's diplomatic strategy and the concrete development of the relationship between the two countries, this chapter will devote itself to determining the variables that influence Chinese foreign policy toward Moldova. It should be emphasized that the main focus of this chapter concentrates on Sino-Moldovan relations before 2009, when the Moldovan Party of Communists fell out of power. The developments afterward will be briefly discussed in the conclusion.

Moldova in China's Foreign Policy

The role of Moldova in China's foreign policy was from the very beginning linked to China's general policy toward the post-Soviet states. In the early 1990s, China experienced the most difficult phase in its diplomacy since the period of reform and opening in 1979. The repression of a students' democratic movement at Tiananmen Square in 1989 provoked a wide range of sanctions imposed by Western countries, and to some extent caused the isolation of Beijing in international society. As Qian Qichen, the former Chinese foreign minister, puts it, the years from the end of the 1980s to the beginning of the 1990s are "the most difficult period in China's diplomacy."[1] Breaking the isolation and winning more support on the international stage were top priorities in Chinese foreign policy at that time. Therefore, Beijing adopted an active diplomatic stance toward all of the post-Soviet states. As one of those states, Moldova established official diplomatic relations with China on January 30, 1992—just five months after Moldova declared its independence.

The successful establishment of diplomatic relations could be attributed in large part to the international environment confronting China at that time. It does not necessarily mean that Moldova plays a significant role in China's foreign policy strategy. Indeed, two or three years after the protests in Tiananmen Square, relations between China and the other Western powers got back on a normal track and continually gain importance for foreign policy decision making in China.

In the past two decades, the structure of China's diplomatic interests and the priorities of China's foreign policy have gradually stabilized. Diplomacy with the great powers, neighboring countries, and the third world are considered the three most important pillars in China's foreign policy strategy. For China, Moldova is neither a great power nor a neighboring country. At the most it could be regarded as a member of the third world category. But considering the long-standing tradition of Chinese diplomacy—in which the third world countries are primarily defined as the developing countries in Asia, Africa, and Latin America—Moldova does not play a significant role in this category either.

Moldova's insignificant role is reflected in official government papers about foreign policy in China. Both in the speeches of Chinese government officials and in the annually published white paper on China's foreign policy, discussions of Moldova are very difficult to find. Even in academic circles, Moldova has never become a lively discussed issue. At the end of 1991, Qian Qichen mentioned the post-Soviet countries in his report at the twenty-third meeting of the Seventh National People's Congress standing committee: "from the disintegration of the Soviet Union onwards, the Chinese government will insist on the principle of non-interference in the internal affairs of the other counties,[2] respect for the people's choice in these countries, and at the same time continue to maintain and develop friendly and cooperative relations with them."[3] This is one of few guiding instructions the Chinese government issued to establish relations with the new states that appeared after the collapse of the Soviet Union. Originally, this policy did not aim to deal with small countries such as Moldova, but to pave the way for developing Beijing's relations with great powers (like Russia) and neighboring countries (like Kazakhstan). Relations between China and Moldova are also treated according to this guiding principle, but Moldova cannot be considered the main target of this policy.

In summary, the establishment of diplomatic relations with Moldova is more a product of China's general policy toward all the post-Soviet states than an actively pursued initiative of the Chinese government. Whether concerning China's national security, its search for political support, or the possibilities of cooperation in the field of economics and energy, Moldova plays only a limited role in China's foreign policy strategy. This situation has not changed during the past two decades.

Relations between China and Moldova

The limited role of Moldova in China's foreign policy has not necessarily led to the underdevelopment of relations between the two countries. In the past two decades, the relationship between China and Moldova can be described as both stable and progressive. Not only in the political realm, but also in economic and other areas, this trend is clear.

Political Relations

The development of political relations between the two countries is manifested primarily through two aspects of this relationship.

The first aspect is the frequent high-level visits between the two states. Table 3.1 summarizes the most important visits since 1992, during which the official diplomatic relationship between the two states was established.

Table 3.1. The high-level visits between Moldova and People's Republic of China

Moldovan visits to China	Chinese visits to Moldova
November 1992: Mircea Snegur (President)	September 1993: Xu Wenbo (Vice Minister of Culture)
February 1993: Ion Botnaru (first Deputy Minister of the Foreign Ministry)	October 1993: Tian Zengpei (Vice Foreign Minister)
September 1994: Alexandru Burian (Deputy Foreign Minister)	October 1994: Qian Zhengying (Vice Chairman of Chinese People's Political Consultative Conference)
March 1996: Petru Lucinschi (Parliament Chairman)	April 1995: Qian Qichen (Vice Premier and Foreign Minister)
September 1996: Mihai Popov (Foreign Minister)	August 1996: Wu Jieping (Vice Chairman of the Standing Committee of National People's Congress)
November 1998: Ghenadie Ciobanu (Minister of Culture)	October 2000: Wei Jianxing (member of the Standing Committee of the Political Bureau and member of the Secretariat of the Communist Party of China Central Committee)
June 2000: Petru Lucinschi (President)	July 2001: Jiang Zemin (President)
November 2001: Vasile Tarlev (Prime Minister)	October 2001: Sun Fuling (Vice Chairman of Chinese People's Political Consultative Conference)

Table 3.1. (*continued*)

Moldovan visits to China	Chinese visits to Moldova
June 2002: Victor Gaiciuc (Minister of Defense)	July 2002: Ma Xiaowei (Vice Minister of Ministry of Health), Li Zhaoxing (Vice Foreign Minister)
August–September 2002: Eugenia Ostapciuc (Parliament Chairman), Victor Puşcaş (Chairman of the Constitutional Court)	September 2002: Long Yongtu (Vice Minister of Commerce and Foreign Economic Cooperation)
November–December 2002: Ion Pacuraru (Minister of Culture)	November 2002: Cheng Siwei (Vice Chairman of the Standing Committee of National People's Congress)
February 2003: Vladimir Voronin (President)	September 2003: Luo Gan (member of the Standing Committee of the Political Bureau)
December 2004: Mihail Camerzan (Deputy Chairman of Parliament)	June 2004: Li Meng (Vice Chairman of Chinese People's Political Consultative Conference)
November 2005: Valeriu Pleşca (Minister of Defense), Anatolie Gorodenco (Minister of Agriculture and Food Industry)	June 2005: Liu Qi (member of the Political Bureau)
January 2006: Ion Ababii (Minister of Health and Social Protection)	May 2006: Wu Bangguo (Chairman of the Standing Committee of National People's Congress)
October 2006: Andrei Stratan (Deputy Prime Minister and Foreign Minister)	
December 2006: Igor Dodon (Minister of Economy and Commerce)	
October 2008: Marian Lupu (Parliament Chairman)	

Sources: Moldovan Embassy to China, "Bilateral relations," http://www.china .mfa.md/bilateral-relations-en/ (accessed July 10, 2011); Ministry of Foreign Affairs and European Integration of Moldova, "Bilateral cooperation," http:// www.mfa.gov.md/bilateral-cooperation-en/ (accessed July 10, 2011).

State visits between Moldova and China are not only at a comparatively high level, but they also cover a wide range of working areas. The President of China, Jiang Zemin, paid a state visit to Moldova personally in 2001; besides exchanges in the political area, visits of officials working in other areas, such as military and culture, can also be seen between the two countries.

A second aspect of the political relationship lies in mutual support and co-operation based on bilateral agreements between the two countries. Since 1991, there have been four important bilateral agreements signed between Beijing and Chisinau. The four agreements include two Joint Communiqués signed in November 1992 and February 2003, and two Joint Statements signed in June 2000 and July 2001. It is noteworthy that not only general principles like "mutual respect for sovereignty and territorial integrity" are mentioned in these agreements, but they also emphasize cooperation in terms of economics, agriculture, non-governmental organizations and even military affairs. Especially after 2000, issues like anti-separatism and anti-terrorism began to play an increasingly significant role in mutual agreements between the two states.[4]

Political relations between China and Moldova developed smoothly after the establishment of official diplomatic relations. In some cases, the range of exchange and cooperation between Beijing and Chisinau exceeds the one between Beijing and other states, which play apparently more significant roles in world politics than Moldova. This trend was evident after 2001, when the Party of Communists of the Republic of Moldova came into power. Jiang Zemin paid a state visit exactly three months after the leader of the Communists, Vladimir Voronin, was elected president of Moldova.

Economic Relations

Although the absolute amount of foreign trade between Beijing and Chisinau is small, a positive development trend has existed since the first contact in foreign trade between the two countries in 1992, when Liu Shan, Chinese assistant foreign trade minister, visited Moldova to sign an economic and trade agreement.[5]

The volume of foreign trade between China and Moldova was only about $0.35 million in 1992. Thereafter in the 1990s, this figure hovered at around $1.00 million. A rapid growth of trade volume occurred after 1999.[6] This growth followed the establishment of the Economic and Trade Cooperation Committee between China and Moldova in the same year. The regular meeting of this committee has brought about many concrete policies and projects promoting the development of trade between the two states. Table 3.2 shows the development trend of the two countries' trade volume since 2000.

As can be seen from table 3.2, despite occasional fluctuations, the trend of overall trade between China and Moldova is moving upward. At the same time, because the absolute trade volume between the two countries is quite small and there is no stabilized trading system between them, the structure of exports and imports is not stable enough. In 2000, China's imports from Moldova accounted for about 97.5 percent of the total foreign trade volume between Moldova and China, while this proportion dropped to 4.3 percent in 2009. In 2009 the trade volume between the two countries ($75.83 million) made up 5.4 percent of the total foreign trade volume of Moldova. That made China Moldova's sixth largest trading partner. But this figure only accounted for 0.00345 percent of total foreign trade volume of China in that year.

Table 3.2. China's trade with Moldova in the period of 2000–2009 (mil. USD)

Year	Total	Export	Import
2000	8.12	0.20	7.92
2001	14.79	2.15	12.64
2002	5.90	1.69	4.21
2003	14.74	6.72	8.02
2004	24.10	23.91	0.19
2005	51.63	51.49	0.14
2006	32.19	31.63	0.56
2007	51.39	49.98	1.41
2008	73.82	71.21	2.61
2009	75.83	72.57	3.26

Source: Chinese Foreign Ministry, "Zhongguo tong Mo'erduowa Gongheguo de guanxi" [The relations between China and Moldova], March 25, 2011, http://www.fmprc.gov.cn/chn/gxh/cgb/zcgmzysx/oz/1206_29/1206x1/t7045.htm (accessed July 10, 2011).

With regard to the structure of trading goods, wine is almost the only Moldovan product imported by China. In contrast, China's exports to Moldova cover a wide range of goods such as household appliances, building materials and textile products. In recent years, Chinese communication equipment, furniture, and cars have increasingly gained importance in trade between the two countries in terms of China's exports.[7]

Besides foreign trade, China has also provided Moldova a significant number of low-interest loans and economic assistance. During the working visit of Chinese Vice Premier and Foreign Minister Qian Qichen in 1995, China provided humanitarian aid in value of approximately $60,000 to Moldova. After Moldova provided China $0.1 million humanitarian aid because of an earthquake in southwest China in May 2008, China paid back twice as much—$0.2 million—in order to help Moldova cope with the consequences of floods in August of the same year. In July 2009, China and Moldova signed a memorandum of understanding, in which China agreed to provide Moldova $1 billion in loans.[8] This amount comprises about one-sixth of the total GDP of Moldova in 2008.

As in the political field, the rapid development of economic relations between China and Moldova also emerged after 2001. Both with regard to China's foreign trade with Moldova and China's foreign aid to Moldova, growth in the first decade of the twenty-first century was much faster than the growth in the 1990s.

Relations in Other Areas

Cooperation and exchange between China and Moldova are not only restricted to the fields of politics and economics, but also extend to areas such as military and culture.

Military cooperation between the two countries is reflected in China's military aid to Moldova. The Chinese Foreign Ministry has reported this kind of aid twice from the year 2000 to 2009. The first occurred in June 2004. According to reports, Moldova received military goods in value of approximately $846,000 from China.[9] The second time was in May 2009, and the amount of aid was not disclosed by the Chinese government.[10] The frequent high-level visits between the armies of the two countries since 2000 are further proof of the military cooperation between them. Deepening this kind of cooperation was explicitly emphasized in the Joint Communiqué between Beijing and Chisinau in 2003.[11]

Cooperation between China and Moldova in the cultural realm has also drawn more and more attention in relations between the two countries. Only ten months after the establishment of diplomatic relations, the Chinese and Moldovan governments signed a cultural cooperation agreement, which laid the foundation for later cultural exchanges between the two countries.

An exchange of students and experts began in 1997, when six Moldovan students received scholarships from the Chinese government and began their studies in China.[12] In 2001, an agreement concerning cooperation in the field of education was also signed by the two governments. The first Confucius Institute was established in Chisinau in 2009, in order to promote Chinese language and culture.[13]

Relations between China and Moldova were described as "exemplary" by Moldovan President Petru Lucinschi during his visit to China in 1996.[14] From a political point of view, high-level visits between the two states are frequent and reach a substantial depth; from an economic point of view, the trade volume of the two countries maintains a rising trend; furthermore, cooperation in the form of low-interest loans and humanitarian aid also plays a significant role in economic relations between the two countries. Moreover, military cooperation and cultural exchange between Beijing and Chisinau also show a smooth development. Especially in the first decade of the twenty-first century, relations between China and Moldova have experienced rapid development.

China's National Interest and
Sino-Moldovan Relations

The history of Sino-Moldovan relations and their development raises two important questions. How could a country like Moldova, which neither has significant influence in the international political arena, nor is rich in natural resources, draw an incommensurately high degree of attention from the Chinese government? And why have relations between China and Moldova developed so rapidly, especially during the first decade of the twenty-first century? In order to answer these questions, it is necessary to conduct a concise analysis of Chinese national interests and examine to what extent the development of Sino-Moldovan relations serves these interests.

For China, the development of relations with Moldova can contribute to the realization of the following four national interests (at a minimum):

1) The so-called "core interests" of China. Maintaining the political system and national security, protecting state sovereignty and territorial integrity, and sustaining stable economic and social development are defined as "core interests" of China.[15] The inviolability of sovereignty and territorial integrity always serves as the most important principle of Chinese diplomacy. In the eyes of the Chinese government, both Moldova and China are suffering from separatism in their own country. The problem of Transnistria in Moldova is considered by the Chinese government as the same problem as separatist movements in Tibet, Xinjiang and Taiwan. While Western countries do not always share China's point of view on these issues, Moldova has been a strong supporter of the one-China policy from the very beginning. In high-level meetings between the two countries, Chinese government officials have emphasized repeatedly that there is no core conflict of interest between the two countries, and China appreciates Moldova's attitude toward issues concerning the core interests of China.

2) Political support. Winning increased political support in the international arena is one of the most important goals pursued by the Chinese government in foreign policy since the People's Republic of China was founded. After the end of the Cold War, the Western democratic countries begin to play a dominant role in arranging the rules of the game in world politics. In this context, China emphasizes diplomacy with the so-called third world, once again in order to gain support from the countries not in the "Western camp." Chinese policy in Moldova could be considered as one such effort. Cooperation between Moldova and China in the United Nations was described as "fruitful" in the Joint Communiqué between the two countries in 2003.[16] Moldova shares China's viewpoints not only in the United Nations, but also on many other issues. Certain ideas advanced by the Chinese government, such as multi-polarization, the democratization of international relations, and independent choice of development models, have all won support from Moldova.

3) Regional strategic interests. Shortly after China agreed to provide Moldova $1 billion in loans, *Reuters* published an article analyzing the reasons for

China's behavior. As the author of the article puts it, for China, the loan is "not devoid of commercial potential . . . it could be a way to establish a clientele in the European Union's backyard as well as Russia's."[17] In making this connection, the author attributes to Moldova considerable geopolitical importance. Good relations with Moldova increase the influence of China, especially in dealing with Russia: "By strengthening its hand in Russia's backyard, as it were, China gives itself more leverage in overall negotiations with Moscow."[18] Although it is still questionable whether Moldova is important enough to serve as a bargaining chip in the eyes of the Chinese government, this analysis is logically tenable. With the advance of the Chinese economy, China is also beginning to pursue more political influence in regional and world politics. Gaining support from small countries like Moldova could lead to a positive breakthrough in the realization of this diplomatic strategy.

4) Ideological interests. After the end of the Cold War, China gradually realized the significance of ideological interests in the pursuit of its economic interests. Non-acceptance of Chinese political values in the international community has increasingly become a bottleneck restricting China's influence in world politics. The goal of promoting China's own political values—an ideology that differs from the liberal, democratic values of the West—in the rest of world has in recent years acquired increasing importance in China's foreign policy agenda. There is no doubt that supporting Moldova, or more precisely speaking supporting the Party of Communists in Moldova, would strengthen the forces that do not accept Western values. The rapid development of Sino-Moldovan relations after 2001 is not unrelated to the fact that the Party of Communists came to power in Moldova the same year. The Memorandum of Understanding, in which China agreed to provide Moldova $1 billion in loans, was signed right before Moldovans repeated national elections in July 2009. This can be considered indirect support from the Chinese government to the then-ruling Moldovan Party of Communists.[19]

Conclusion

China has maintained good relations with Moldova since its founding as an independent state in 1991. During the past two decades, the development of Sino-Moldovan relations reached a relatively high degree in almost every respect. This is supported not only by the frequent high-level visits and economic cooperation between the two countries, but also by a wide range of exchanges in areas like military and culture. Analysts of China's diplomacy frequently question why the Chinese government is interested in such a small country as Moldova, which has neither natural resources nor political influence. A definitive answer cannot be given even today. The discussion above has tried to enumerate the most significant possible answers to this question, but because of the opacity of decision making in China, nobody can definitively judge whether the points listed above have in fact been taken into consideration by policymakers in China. The only plausible conclusion may lie in the notion that ideological proximity does affect China's foreign policy toward Moldova, because the development of Sino-Moldovan relations changed before and after the Party of Communists came to power in Moldova in 2001.

Since 2009, when the Alliance for European Integration came to power in Moldova, there have been areas of both continuity and change in the country's relations with China. On one hand, foreign trade between the two countries continues to develop post-2009. As Fang Li, the Chinese ambassador to Moldova, put it, China imported seven times more wine from Moldova in 2010 than the previous year;[20] China also continues to support Moldova after 2009. In November 2010, $500,000 in aid was provided by the Chinese government for Moldovan victims of floods that summer.[21] Military aid was also provided by China in May 2011.[22] In cultural matters, a cooperation protocol for 2011 to 2014 was signed during a working visit of Yang Zhijin, the Chinese deputy minister of culture, to Moldova.[23] On the other hand, in the political realm, relations between Beijing and Chisinau have not been as close as during the rule of the Moldovan Communist party. This is demonstrated not only by Beijing's lack of high-level contacts with the new Moldovan government after 2009, but in continued contact with former statesmen from the Moldovan Party of Communists by the Chinese side. In September 2010, Chinese Ambassador Fang Li visited Vladimir Voronin and expressed his wish to deepen the relationship between the two Communist parties.[24] In February 2011, Petru Lucinschi, another formerly prominent member of the Communist Party of the Soviet Union, received a warm reception in the Chinese embassy in Chisinau.[25] All of these incidents may substantiate the claim that ideology does play a significant role in determining the course of Sino-Moldovan relations.

Notes

1. Qian Qichen, *Waijiao shiji* [Ten stories of a diplomat] (Beijing: Word Affairs Press, 2003), 165.
2. "Other countries" refer to the post-Soviet states.
3. Qian Qichen, *Waijiao shiji*, 224.
4. "Joint Communiqué between the People's Republic of China and the Republic of Moldova on establishing diplomatic relations," Moscow, January 30, 1992, http://news .xinhuanet.com/ziliao/2003-09/06/content_1066289.htm (accessed July 10, 2011); "Joint Statement between the People's Republic of China and the Republic of Moldova on continuously strengthening comprehensive cooperation in the 21st century," Beijing, June 7, 2000, http://news.xinhuanet.com/ziliao/2003-09/06/content_1066460.htm (accessed July 10, 2011); "Joint Statement between the People's Republic of China and the Republic of Moldova," Chisinau, July 20, 2001, http://www.fmprc.gov.cn/chn/gxh/zlb/smg/t5354.htm (accessed July 10, 2011); "Joint Communiqué between the People's Republic of China and the Republic of Moldova," Beijing, February 24, 2003, http://www.fmprc.gov.cn/chn /gxh/zlb/smgg/t23816.htm (accessed July 10, 2011).

5. Gu Zhihong, *Mo'erduowa* [Moldova] (Beijing: Social Science Academic Press, 2004), 274.

6. Economic and Commercial Counsellor's Office of the Chinese Embassy to Moldova, "Shuangbian jingmao hezuo" [Bilateral economic and trade cooperation], June 24, 2010, http://md.mofcom.gov.cn/aarticle/zxhz/hzjj/201006/20100606986490.html (accessed July 10, 2011).

7. Ibid.

8. Olesya Dmitracova, "China's new foreign policy takes shape in Moldova," *Reuters*, February 2, 2010, http://www.reuters.com/article/2010/02/02/us-china-moldova-idUSTRE61140D20100202 (accessed July 10, 2011). The $1 billion loan was not paid in the end. The official reason was that Moldova was not able to absorb this loan because of International Monetary Fund limits.

9. Chinese Foreign Ministry, "Xu Zhongkai dashi chuxi Zhongguo yuanzhu Mo'erduowa junshi wuzi jiaojie yishi" [Ambassador Xu Zhongkai attends the ceremony to hand over the military aids to Moldova], June 2, 2004, http://www.fmprc.gov.cn/chn/pds/gjhdq/gj/oz/1206_29/1206x2/t126513.htm (accessed July 10, 2011).

10. Chinese Foreign Ministry, "Zhongguo yuan Mo'erduowa wuzi jiaojie yishi zai mo juxing" [Ceremony to hand over China's aid to Moldova is held in Moldova], May 22, 2009, http://www.fmprc.gov.cn/chn/pds/gjhdq/gj/oz/1206_29/1206x2/t564047.htm (accessed July 10, 2011).

11. "Joint Communiqué," February 24, 2003.

12. Gu Zhihong, *Mo'erduowa*, 275.

13. Chinese Foreign Ministry of China, "Mo'erduowa guojia gaikuang" [General situation in Moldova], March 25, 2011, http://www.fmprc.gov.cn/chn/gxh/cgb/zcgmzysx/oz/1206_29/1207/t182190.htm (accessed July 10, 2011).

14. Gu Zhihong, *Mo'erduowa*, 274.

15. Dai Bingguo, "Zhongguo de hexinliyi you san ge fanchou" [China's core interests have three aspects], *ifeng.com*, December 7, 2010, http://news.ifeng.com/mainland/detail_2010_12/07/3379812_0.shtml (accessed July 10, 2011).

16. "Joint Communiqué," February 24, 2003.

17. Dmitracova, "China's new foreign policy."

18. Ibid.

19. Marc Champion, "In Moldovan Vote, It's East vs. West," *The Wall Street Journal*, July 29, 2009, A9.

20. Chinese Embassy to Moldova, "Zhu Mo'erduowa dashi Fang Li jieshou Mo guojia dianshitai caifang wenda" [Questions and answers in the interview of Moldovan National TV-Station with Fang Li, the Chinese ambassador to Moldova], http://md.china-embassy.org/chn/xwdt/t833365.htm (accessed July 10, 2011).

21. Chinese Embassy to Moldova, "Fang Li dashi he Feilate zongli chuxi Zhongguo yuan Mo shuizai kuan yishi" [Chinese ambassador Fang Li and Moldovan Prime Minister Filat attend the donation ceremony for flood aid], http://md.china-embassy.org/chn/xwdt/t766684.htm (accessed July 10, 2011).

22. Chinese Embassy to Moldova, "Zhongguo junshi yuanzhu wuzi jiaojie yishi zai Mo'erduowa juxing" [The ceremony to hand over China's military aid is held in Moldova], May 28, 2011, http://md.china-embassy.org/chn/xwdt/t826002.htm (accessed July 10, 2011).

23. Chinese Embassy to Moldova, "Zhongguo zhengfu daibiaotuan fangwen Mo'erduowa" [Cultural delegation of the Chinese government visits Moldova], http://md.china-embassy.org/chn/whjl/t738345.htm (accessed July 10, 2011).

24. Chinese Embassy to Moldova, "Zhu Mo'erduowa dashi Fang Li baihui Mo gong zhuxi, qian zongtong Woluoning" [Chinese ambassador in Moldova Fang Li visits the President of Moldovan Party of Communists, former President of Moldova Voronin], http://md.china-embassy.org/chn/xwdt/t752831.htm (accessed July 10, 2011).

25. Chinese Embassy to Moldova, "Zhu Mo'erduowa dashi Fang Li huijian qian zongtong Bide Luqinsiji" [Chinese ambassador in Moldova Fang Li visits the former President of Moldova Petru Lucinschi], http://md.china-embassy.org/chn/xwdt/t794989.htm (accessed July 10, 2011).

Chapter Four

The Czech Republic and Slovakia: Partnership with Moldova for Transformation and Europeanization[*]

Juraj Marušiak

Immediately after the proclamation of Moldovan independence in 1991 and the dissolution of Czechoslovakia in 1992, the intensity of both the Czech Republic and Slovakia's bilateral relations with Moldova was at nearly nonexistent levels. Since Moldova was not a European Union candidate country, political contacts were mainly in the bilateral framework of pan-European institutions (Council of Europe, Organization for Security and Cooperation in Europe), or in the framework of regional organizations such as the Central European Initiative and annual meetings of the presidents of Central European states. Moldova was outside Czech and Slovak attention in the post-Soviet area, overshadowed by relations with Russia, Ukraine and later Belarus. During the 1990s, neither the Czech Republic nor Slovakia considered opening embassies in Chisinau.

A new view on Moldova has taken shape in the context of the EU accession of the Visegrad Group countries (Czech Republic, Hungary, Poland and Slovakia) and Moldova's involvement with the European Neighbourhood Policy. The first document concerning the Eastern Policy of the EU was spelled out by a community of experts from Visegrad countries—including Czech and Slovak experts—on the eve of EU accession in 2003. It assumed an increase of interest toward Moldova, although it postponed the elaboration of a specific national strategy for the country until after the accession of Romania.[1] In spite of this fact, the main focus of both Czech and Slovak Eastern policy was still Russia, due to the depth of economic relations and both countries' energy dependency on Russian oil and natural gas. Secondly, the policy focused on Ukraine, especially after the Orange Revolution, and on Belarus, in support of the democratic opposition there. "Moldovan" issues did not in fact become part of the daily agenda of Czech and Slovak diplomacy and media. Thus the EU enlargement in

* The author wants to express his thanks to the officers of the Czech and Slovak Foreign Ministries for their comprehensive consultations and willingness to help with the research and preparation of this article.

2004 did not affect the interest in Moldova of the Czech Republic and Slovakia to any large extent. The situation changed after the parliamentary election in 2005, when the then-ruling Party of Communists of the Republic of Moldova confirmed (at least verbally) its commitment to policies focused on integration with the EU. The next milestone was the Moldovan parliamentary elections in 2009, and the establishment of the governmental coalition of pro-European parties. Although Moldova does not represent a priority in the foreign policy of either country, and the intensity of official contact with Moldova does not reach the level of certain Visegrad Group countries like Poland and Hungary, the character of bilateral Czech and Slovak relations with Moldova is significant from the point of view of their main actors and their bilateral agendas.

The Czech Republic and Moldova

Political Agenda

The first official bilateral visit at a high level took place in spring 1999, when Moldovan Deputy Prime Minister Alexandru Muravschi paid a visit to Prague. Later, Czech Foreign Minister Jan Kavan visited Chisinau in September 2000, and Andrei Stratan, Moldova's head diplomat, visited Prague in October 2004. In February 2005, Czech Deputy Prime Minister Martin Jahn visited Moldova. Afterwards, Moldovan Justice Minister Ion Paduraru (1998) and Interior Minister Gheorghe Papuc (2003) visited Prague. Sporadic contacts were maintained on the parliamentary level as well. For example, in March 2003 a Czech parliamentary delegation led by Vice-Chairman Vojtěch Filip visited Chisinau, accompanied by a group of businessmen. In September 2004, Moldovan Parliamentary Chairman Eugenia Ostapciuc visited Prague.[2]

A breakthrough in bilateral relations took place during Jahn's visit to Chisinau in February 2005, when representatives of the Moldovan government officially asked the Czech Republic for assistance in its preparation for EU-accession, mainly in the field of legislation. Moldovan Prime Minister Vasile Tarlev also requested a liberalization of the visa regime for Moldovan citizens, and he expressed interest in the training of Moldovan experts at Czech ministries, mainly in the transportation, communication and energy sectors.[3] A joint delegation of the parliamentary committees for EU affairs from both Czech chambers of government, the Parliamentary Senate and the Chamber of Deputies, visited Chisinau in September 2005. Following Jahn's visit and the positive Czech response to the Moldovan request for transformation aid, the European agenda became a crucial issue in bilateral relations. The Europeanization of bilateral relations contributed to an unprecedented intensification of political relations and to an upgrade of their institutional framework. The result was the opening of the Czech Embassy in Chisinau on December 19, 2005, and reciprocally the first ambassador of the Moldovan Republic in Prague was appointed on March 1, 2007.

European Union integration and economic cooperation were the main topics of Moldovan Prime Minister Tarlev's visit to Prague in April 2006. His counterpart, Jiří Paroubek, confirmed the Czech Republic's willingness to provide assistance to Moldova by the transposition of *acquis communautaire* to its national legislation.[4] Czech Deputy Foreign Minister Tomáš Pojar visited Moldova from June 26 to 28, 2006. A presidential meeting between Václav Klaus and Vladimir Voronin took place on September 13, 2006, in Prague. Klaus and Voronin met a second time on May 25, 2007, in the framework of the meeting of presidents of Central European countries in Brno. Former president of Moldova Vladimir Voronin (2001–2009) regularly spent his holidays in the Czech Spa Karlovy Vary.[5] He met Václav Klaus during his private stay in the Czech Republic on September 13, 2006.[6]

Economic cooperation, the Transnistrian conflict, and the creation of a new bilateral agreement on developing cooperation were the main topics of Moldovan Prime Minister Zinaida Greceanîi's visit on September 2, 2008.[7] During her visit, the Promotion and Mutual Protection of Investments Agreement was signed, and Greceanîi took part in the official opening of the Moldovan Embassy in Prague. In 2008, a parliamentary delegation led by Vojtěch Filip, Czech vice-chairman of the Chamber of Parliamentary Deputies, and a delegation of the chamber's Human Rights Committee visited Moldova. Consultations on the ministerial level were held during a visit of Stratan to a meeting of Visegrad Group foreign ministers on November 24, 2007, and the Moldovan finance minister attended a meeting of EU ministers for development cooperation in Prague in the framework of the 2009 Czech EU Council Presidency.

The Eastern Partnership and the further enlargement of the EU are key priorities of foreign policy for the Czech Republic. This sense of priority is compounded by the fact that since 2009, the new EU Commissioner of the Enlargement and ENP is a Czech diplomat, Štefan Füle. On the other hand, Czech President Vaclav Klaus expressed his reservations in May 2007 about Moldova's EU membership prospects before the solution of the Transnistrian conflict, but as the Czech Republic has a parliamentary form of government, the role of the president in shaping foreign policy is low.[8]

The Czech Presidency of the EU Council played an important role during the political crisis of Moldovan parliamentary elections in April 2009. Czech Foreign Minister Karel Schwarzenberg tackled issues related to the demonstrations and unrest by placing a phone call to Moldovan Foreign Minister Stratan, who reiterated the desire to deepen relations between Moldova and the EU, and recognized his country's European aspirations.[9] Acting Czech Prime Minister Mirek Topolánek paid a visit to Chisinau as the head of an EU delegation. After bilateral talks with Moldovan President Voronin, Topolánek expressed concern on behalf of the European institutions regarding the situation in Moldova. Following the 2009 elections, opposition protests against the falsifications of parliamentary elections gave way to violent clashes between the opposition and pro-governmental forces. The Moldovan government and President Voronin threatened prosecution and created a political conflict with Romania. The Czech prime minister reiterated the importance of Moldova's pro-European orientation and stressed the EU's interest in a swift solution to stabilize the social and political situation in Moldova, emphasizing that the European institutions were willing to support the Moldovan authorities' efforts in this direction. He appreciated the political will required to launch this dialogue between parties. Topolánek emphasized the EU's willingness to collaborate with Moldova, referring particularly to the opportunities presented by the Eastern Partnership. The EU's commitment to the preservation of democratic procedures was also indicated by the fact that Topolánek met with representatives of the Moldovan opposition before consultations with Voronin.[10] President Voronin expressed the Moldovan leadership's intentions to act further to normalize the situation in Moldova by means of dialogue and consensus.[11] The actions of the Czech EU Council Presidency contributed to a peaceful and democratic solution during one of Moldova's most serious political crises since the country's independence in 1991.

After the August 2009 establishment of a new pro-European government in Moldova, brief bilateral consultations of foreign ministers took place during the Central European Initiative summit in Bucharest on November 13, 2009, and during the Visegrad Group summit on March 2, 2010, in Budapest. Czech Foreign Minister and Deputy Prime Minister Schwarzenberg paid a visit to Chisinau on September 30, 2010, to attend the third informal meeting of the Friends of Moldova Group, which was also attended by European Commissioner Füle.

Subsequently, Schwarzenberg met with the Moldovan head of diplomacy, Iurie Leancă. The Czech minister expressed support for reform efforts and the pro-European direction of Moldova. The Moldovan representatives appreciated his pronouncement, because, according to his statement, Moldova is not on its way into Europe; it is already part of Europe—EU accession is the task at hand. Conversely, Schwarzenberg stressed this process requires clear commitment and compliance with all conditions.

The ministers agreed on joint interests in the development of bilateral cooperation, including the intensification of trade and the creation of favorable conditions for Czech investors. Finally, they signed the Memorandum of Cooperation for European Integration. According to Iurie Leancă "the signed memorandum will back Moldova as it advances on its European path, help it overcome challenges and current problems, and create new prospects in the Eastern Partnership."[12] Schwarzenberg and Moldovan Education Minister Leonid Bujor signed an agreement concerning education, culture, youth, and sport. The document assumes cooperation in these areas, including exchanges of students and teachers, as well as the training of highly skilled specialists for the two countries' national economies. The Czech Republic will provide assistance to Moldova in its implementation of the Bologna Declaration provisions. The agreement also stipulates the promotion of scientific and cultural collaboration between universities, as well as academic mobility for joint projects launched within the European Union, UNESCO, the Council of Europe and the Stability Pact for South Eastern Europe.[13]

Cooperation of Moldova with the EU, development aid and the priorities of the upcoming Czech Visegrad Group presidency were the main topics of Iurie Leancă's working visit to Prague and his consultations with Schwarzenberg from May 16 to 17, 2011.[14]

Development and Transformation Aid

Human rights issues and transformation assistance play a very important role in the foreign policy of the Czech Republic. Both for center-left and center-right governments, these issues are considered priorities and distinctive components of the Czech Republic's identity in the international arena. In Czech foreign policy, democracy and transformation assistance is separated from official development aid. Transformation cooperation has, since 2007, been coordinated by the Department of Human Rights and Transformation Policy in the Czech Foreign Ministry.

Moldova is among the most important recipient countries of Czech humanitarian, development and transformation aid. On the grounds of resolution no. 302, adopted by the Government of the Czech Republic on March 31, 2004, Moldova has been recognized as a program country receiving Czech development aid with the aim of developing long-term cooperation. Development aid is focused on migration issues as well as on increasing the export potential for Czech products and technologies on the Moldovan market. Further aid is focused on environmental issues, with particular concern to water management, waste management systems, support for education, social infrastructure, and the service and capacity building of Moldovan state administration (police, border security, etc.). Moldova remained a territorial priority[15] of Czech international development cooperation even after the adoption of the new Concept of Foreign Development Cooperation of the Czech Republic, 2010–2017.[16] The Czech Republic plays the role of an EU support facilitator, charged with the coordination of donors' policy toward the Moldovan government. Since 2010, the key priority of Czech development aid is the transfer of Czech experience with political and economic transformation.

Activities aimed at the prevention of illegal migration are some of the most important projects of Czech development aid, provided with support from the Czech Ministry of Interior, International Organization for Migration and Czech Catholic Charity. The transfer of Czech environmental technologies is also given importance.[17] Czech Agricultural University in Prague coordinated an initiative aimed at the development of the Moldovan countryside, and in cooperation with Moldovan State University, the project focused on the approximation of the educational process to the EU standards (2006–2008). Czech NGOs are actively involved in a project focused on abandoned Moldovan children. In 2010, the Czech Republic sent $4 million in development aid to Moldova.

The People in Need Foundation is one of the most active Czech NGOs involved in transformation cooperation in Moldova. Since 2003, the foundation focused on building the capacity of NGOs in Transnistria. PiNF arranged for Moldovan representatives of local administration to visit the Czech Republic and study the Czech experience with local government reform. The political education of young experts in Moldova, with the aim of sharing the Czech experience in several fields of political and social transformation, was the aim of a common project between the Prague Security Studies Institute and the Institute for Development and Social Initiatives "Viitorul" in Moldova. Capacity building in the entrepreneurial sector was the main goal of a project launched by technological agency CzechInvest, the NGO Agora Central Europe and the Czech Catholic Charity, which provided projects supporting the democratization of municipal administration and civic participation at the local level.[18] Additionally, the Czech Republic actively provides humanitarian aid to Moldova. In 2008 it was the first country to respond to the droughts of 2007 and the following year's floods. This support was mentioned with much appreciation by Moldovan Prime Minister Greceanîi during her visit to Prague.[19]

Labor Migrations

The Czech Republic is a destination for migrant workers from Moldova. According to official data there were 2,969 Moldovans working in the Czech Republic on June 30, 2006.[20] This number increased to 4,475 in 2010, making Moldovans the second-largest foreign labor force in the Czech Republic after Ukrainians (43,755).[21] The Czech Republic is interested in the inflow of labor from Moldova, and has participated in a project titled Active Selection of Qualified Foreign Employees together with citizens from other, mostly Slavic, countries— Bulgaria, Kazakhstan, Croatia, Belarus, Serbia, Montenegro, Canada, Ukraine, Russia and Bosnia and Herzegovina.[22] On the other hand, the Czech Republic still maintains a tough and restrictive visa regime for Moldovan citizens. In 2010, local Czech labor offices were instructed to take a tougher line on permits for foreigners seeking work in the country, or those wanting to prolong their existing permits[23] due to the consequences of the economic crisis and the increasing unemployment rate in the Czech Republic. In reality, there is some question as to whether the official data reflects the real situation; Moldovan citizens are the largest group of illegal immigrants in the Czech Republic. In 2009, Moldovan citizens accounted for a total number of 4,267 violations of the rules of residence in the Czech Republic (3 percent of all cases). Thus, Czech development aid is very much concerned with the prevention of illegal migration.[24]

Role of the Czech Republic in the Solution of the Transnistrian Conflict

The Czech Republic supports the territorial integrity of Moldova. Therefore it did not recognize the Transnistrian government or its official acts, such as elections. Before EU accession, the Czech Republic was involved in the solution of the Transnistrian conflict mainly in the framework of the OSCE. In 2000 and 2001, the country participated in the creation of a voluntary fund designed to finance projects for the transformation and liquidation of the former Soviet ammunition and small-arms depot in Transnistria. The Czech contribution was $10,000 in 2000 and €50,000 in 2001. Since 2005, the Czech Republic has participated in the European Union Border Assistance Mission to Moldova and Ukraine by sending one police officer.[25]

Foreign Trade and Economic Cooperation between the Czech Republic and Moldova

The volume of foreign trade between the Czech Republic and Moldova is rather low; Moldova never belonged on the Czech list of important trade partners. The dynamics of bilateral trade are increasing since the Czech EU accession in 2004. In 1998, the total turnover of bilateral trade amounted to $10.2 million, but in 1999 it fell to $8.7 million as a result of the Russian financial crisis. In 2006, overall trade between the Czech Republic and Moldova was three times above the level of 1998.[26] This rapid growth was recorded after the EU accession of the Czech Republic. While in 2004 the turnover of bilateral trade was €35.5 million, in 2008, before the global financial crisis, it increased to €51.5 million. In 2009 it dropped to €32.1 million, but in 2010 it increased again to €42.3 million. A positive trend in the bilateral trade turnover has been recorded in the first quarter of 2011 as well; it is 21.2 percent higher than in the same period of 2010. The trade balance of the Czech Republic with Moldova shows a positive trend over the long term. The trade balance in 2004 was €3.5 million, and in 2010 it had already risen to €26.5 million. The weakness of the Moldovan economy and the very slow process of its restructuring are two reasons why its share of bilateral trade with the Czech Republic is still at a low level. In 2010, Moldova was ranked seventy-three among the export partners of the Czech Republic and ninety-two among Czech import partners. In overall Czech foreign trade, Moldova was ranked seventy-eight. In 2009, the Czech Republic was nineteenth among importers to Moldova and was twenty-six among export partners of Moldova.[27] Czech exports to Moldova are represented mostly by vehicles, TV sets, products of machine engineering, glass, lamps, plastic products, paper, medicaments, etc. Czech imports from Moldova were dominated by metallurgical products (iron and steel bars, rods, metal threads, and fibers) until 2005. Later imports were shoes, wine, fruit products (dried fruit, fruit jams and marmalades, and wine grapes), clothing, etc.

The most successful Czech exporter in the Moldovan market is Škoda Auto, with an important share in the distribution of foreign cars in Moldova. The cars Škoda Octavia and Škoda Superb are used by the Moldovan government as well. Another company present on the Moldovan market is Škoda Electric, exporting trolley buses. The Czech company Sor Libchavy exported 350 buses to Moldova in 2005.[28]

Several Czech companies are in the process of considering investments in Moldova. Hamé Babice formerly produced pates for the Moldovan, Russian and Ukrainian market in Bălți, but after a conflict with the new owner of a factory, it withdrew from the Moldovan market. The Czech energy company ČEZ unsuccessfully negotiated involvement in the reconstruction and modernization of one of Chisinau's power plants, and the Czech and Slovak company J&T signed a 2009 memorandum on construction of the power plants in Ungheni. The Czech company Elektrizace železnic Praha is interested in the electrification of the railway corridor Ungheni-Bendery-Kuchurhan-Rozdil'na and Sigma is interested in the modernization and reconstruction of irrigation systems in Moldova. In 2006 Moldovan Prime Minister Vasile Tarlev and his Czech counterpart Jiří Paroubek were rather optimistic about the prospects of Czech investments in Moldova. They discussed the construction of complete industrial plants, waste purifying plants, etc., in Moldova by Czech companies. But Czech investments did not increase significantly due to the lack of transformation progress in Moldova until 2009, and the global financial crisis thereafter.[29]

Slovakia and Moldova

Political Agenda

As with the Czech Republic, bilateral relations between Slovakia and Moldova were, until the 2004 EU enlargement, at a low level and in the shadow of relations with Russia and Ukraine. Bilateral diplomatic relations were provided since the independence of both countries by the Slovak embassy in Bucharest and by the Moldovan embassy in Vienna. Slovakia is the only Visegrad Group country without a diplomatic mission in Chisinau, and Slovakia is represented only by an honorary consulate.

The first official contact on a high political level took place on the eve of Slovakia's EU accession in 2003, after an official visit of Slovak Foreign Minister Eduard Kukan to Chisinau. The state secretary of the Slovak Foreign Ministry, József Berényi, and the head of the Foreign Affairs Committee of the National Council of the Slovak Republic, Ján Figeľ, met Iurie Roșca, the leader and founding member of the Moldovan Christian Democratic People's Party on June 18, 2003, in Bratislava. His trip was organized during a tour of several countries (the United States, Italy, Czech Republic), where he informed listeners about violations of democracy by the ruling Communist party, which had gained a constitutional majority in the Moldovan parliament, and about the poor situation of the Moldovan media.[30]

State Secretary of the Slovak Foreign Ministry Oľga Algayerová attended a workshop in 2006 focused on potential cooperation between the Visegrad Group and Moldova. The mutual interest of Slovakia and Moldova in improving and strengthening the bilateral relationship rose from Slovakia's active engagement in favor of the continuation of EU enlargement, and Moldovan interest in Slovak methods of transformation. In 1998 Slovakia, an outsider to European integration prospects after years of stagnation during the rule of Vladimír Mečiar (1994–1998), was able to quickly catch up with its Visegrad neighbors and to join the EU together with them in 2004.

The first official visit of Slovak President Ivan Gašparovič to Moldova took place on June 19, 2007, accompanied by a delegation of Slovak businessmen. He met Moldova President Vladimir Voronin, Prime Minister Vasile Tarlev and Chairman of the Moldovan Parliament Marian Lupu. Bilateral consultations were focused on the Slovak transition process, strengthening economic and political cooperation, and support for Moldova in search of a solution of the Transnistrian conflict. State Secretary Algayerová and minister of interior of Moldova Gheorghe Papuc signed an intergovernmental agreement on combating organized crime.[31] Gašparovič confirmed Slovak support for Moldova's integration into the EU. According to him, Moldova needs to meet all the criteria for EU integration, but conversely, the European community should not block this progress or impose additional requirements. Voronin mentioned the importance of Slovakia's European experience for Moldova. Slovakia, during its 2007 presidency of the Visegrad Group, tried to develop cooperation between this organization and GUAM, which was a topic of consultations between Slovak Foreign Minister Ján Kubiš and the ambassadors of GUAM-countries.[32]

But in fact, for the next two years after Gašparovič's visit to Chisinau, a period of stagnation in both bilateral relations and in Moldovan-EU relations took place. This was caused partially by the growing political tensions in Moldova before the April 2009 parliamentary elections and the rapprochement of President Voronin with Russia initiated in the second half of 2006, which was intensified after the Georgian-Russian war in 2008. This situation changed after the creation of a pro-European coalition in Moldova following the July 2009 parliamentary elections.

While the distinguishing mark of foreign policy for the Czech Republic is commitment to human rights, for Slovakia it is the transformation agenda. For that reason, Foreign Minister Miroslav Lajčák offered help in the framework of the Eastern Partnership, including providing development aid and transformation know-how to Moldovan Foreign Minister Iurie Leancă at the ministerial meeting of the OSCE in Athens on December 1, 2009.[33] Slovakia and Moldova shared a common position regarding refusal to recognize Kosovo's independence; Slovakia—as an opponent of ethnically based separatism and the violent change of state borders, supports the territorial integrity of Moldova. The Slovak position is motivated mainly by the fear of territorial revisionism on the part of Hungary and the potential separatist tendencies of the Hungarian minority living in southern regions of Slovakia.

Following the invitation of Deputy Premier Lajčák, Foreign and European Integration Minister Iurie Leancă paid an official visit to Slovakia on February 9, 2010. Slovakia has, according to Lajčák, "much sympathy for Moldova, which creates a very favorable foundation for the development of dynamic bilateral cooperation in various sectors." He stressed Slovak understanding of Moldova's difficulties, because Slovakia too had transitioned from authoritarian to democratic government. He declared active Slovak support for Moldova at a meeting of donors due in Brussels on March 24, 2010. Lajčák also supported cooperation between the authorities and civil society, and announced a trip of Slovak NGO representatives to Moldova to jointly identify needs in the European integration process with Moldovan partners.[34]

Thus, as in the case of the Czech Republic, transformation and development aid became crucial agenda points of bilateral relations between Slovakia and Moldova. An analogous agreement was signed during the visit of Lajčák to Chisinau on May 7, 2010. An early step in Slovak official development assistance was providing €100,000 for the modernization of Moldovan public service TV by the Slovak government. Lajčák's visit was accompanied by a workshop with forty Moldovan NGOs, organized by the Slovak NGO Pontis Foundation. The representative of Pontis Foundation, Milan Nič, stressed that Moldova is the most vulnerable Eastern neighbor of the EU, and at the same the most dynamic Eastern Partnership country.[35] Lajčák, together with other ministers from the informal Friends of Moldova Group met Moldovan Prime Minister Vlad Filat and Leancă at the EU ministerial meeting in Luxembourg on June 14, 2010. Lajčák confirmed EU support of Moldovan transformation and its approximation to the EU and stressed the necessity of continuing the reform process.[36]

The new Slovak government created after parliamentary elections in June 2010 confirmed its commitment to the Eastern Partnership program and to increasing Slovak support of democratization and modernization in the countries of the former Soviet Union. The first meeting of the new Slovak Foreign Minister Mikuláš Dzurinda with Leancă took place at the conference "GLOBSEC 2010" in Bratislava. Later Dzurinda visited Chisinau in November 2011. He approved the first Slovak visa at the Common Visa Application Centre at the Hungarian embassy in Chisinau.[37] Issues of bilateral relations and development assistance were discussed in consultations between State Secretary of the Slovak Foreign Ministry Milan Ježovica and State Secretary of Moldovan Ministry of Foreign Affairs and European Integration Andrei Popov on October 1, 2011. Slovakia confirmed support of Moldova's integration path to the EU before the upcoming early elections in the country. Ježovica presented support of the integration ambitions of the new Moldovan government after the November 2010 early elections at the conference "Democratization and the European Future of

Moldovan Republic," organized by the Visegrad Group countries on February 18, 2011.[38]

Slovakia is actively involved in the operation of EUBAM and, according to the Slovak Foreign Ministry, will continue its participation in the mission. Currently Slovakia is represented in the mission by five experts—three policemen and two customs officers. Appreciation for Slovak involvement in the EU Eastern Partnership program, which concerns Moldova as well, was confirmed by the decision of Catherine Ashton, Chief of the European External Action Service, when on December 14, 2010, she appointed Slovak diplomat Miroslav Lajčák (a former Slovak foreign minister) as the head of the EEAS department for relations with the Western Balkans, Eastern Partnership and Russia.[39]

Foreign Trade and Economic Cooperation between Slovakia and Moldova

The volume of bilateral trade is rather small and, due to the economic crisis, it has declined significantly from €71.0 million in 2008, to €28.7 million in 2009, and €28.6 million in 2010. Slovak exports to Moldova consist mainly of vehicles (19.4 percent), copper (12.6 percent), paper and cartons (12.4 percent), electric devices (12.1 percent), and optical tools and instruments (9.0 percent). Slovak imports from Moldova are represented mainly by clothing (47.7 percent), furniture and mattresses (37.2 percent), non-alcoholic and alcoholic beverages, and vinegar (5.5 percent). The balance of Slovak trade with Moldova is currently positive (€9.5 million in 2009; €15.6 million in 2010). It has been so in all previous years, except for 2007 (€2.6 million), when it was negative.[40] Just as in the Czech Republic, due to the low size of bilateral trade, this balance can be very easily influenced by even a single significant transaction.[41]

Currently the Slovak wine company Vinárske závody Topoľčany, s.r.o., is interested in investing in the production and processing of Moldovan wines. Agro CS Slovakia is distributing fertilizers in Moldova; SD-spoločnosť is trading in Moldova with non-ferrous metals. There are also other companies present on the Moldovan market—Matador Púchov (tires), Tatra Textil (sport clothes), U.S. Steel Košice (steel products), Slovmag Lubeník, Slovnaft Bratislava (fuel), etc.[42]

Slovak Development Aid to Moldova

Moldova has been included among the territorial priorities of Slovak development cooperation in 2009 as a project country, according to the National Programme of Official Development Assistance for the Year 2011, and it belongs among the priority countries.[43]

Together with other countries of the Western Balkans and the Eastern Partnership, Moldova has been included in a new scheme of technical assistance—the Centre for the Transfer of Experience of Integration and Reforms, aimed at communicating the transformation, reform, and integration experience of Slovakia. The main objective of this program is strengthening the reform effort, fulfilling the European perspective and promoting good governance in the selected countries. Since 2010, the Slovak Foreign Policy Association has implemented a project called the "National Convention on the EU in Moldova." The aim of this project is the institutionalization of the public debate on EU-related issues based on the partnership of governmental, non-governmental and business organizations in Moldova, strengthening Moldovan expert capacity in negotiation of the Association Agreement and the Deep and Comprehensive Free Trade Area, and finally public involvement in national policy making on EU-related issues through the establishment of sectorial EU communities in Moldova based on the model of the National Convention on the EU Working Groups. This project, conceived as an interactive and permanent information channel for all segments of Moldovan society, is based on the Slovak experience with the organization of permanent expert dialogue and public debate on EU affairs in Slovak society. The Moldovan partners of the SFPA think tank are the Institute for Development and Social Initiatives "Viitorul," the Foreign Policy Association of Moldova and the independent think tank Expert Grup.[44]

The previously mentioned Pontis Foundation, in cooperation with a Moldovan partner, the East Europe Foundation, started in December 2010 to implement a project titled, "Slovakia and the European Future of Moldova: building capacities of the Moldovan NGO sector for dialogue with the state administration on the European future of Moldova." The main aim of the project is to build organizational, human and expert capacities. Pontis Foundation is organizing trainings and study visits to Bratislava and Brussels for ten NGO leaders grouped in the National Participation Council with Moldova, which provides for communication between thirty local NGOs and Moldova's government. The project will go on until July 2012, and is supported with funds from Slovak Aid.[45]

The Slovak embassy in Bucharest provides Moldovan NGOs small grants in the framework of a special micro-grant scheme, mainly focused on the poorest regions of Moldova. The main aim of this scheme is to provide assistance in the field of education (the reconstruction of schools and kindergartens), the improvement of administrative structures, and the reconstruction of water supplies. There have been nine micro-grants supported by the Slovak embassy to the total sum of €35,000 in the year 2009. One year later there were already 19 micro-grants with a total amount of €93,200 and in 2011 there are expected to be 47 micro-grants with a total cost of €230,000. One of the projects built a dormitory for the Union of Visually Handicapped People. A Slovak lecture hall was also opened at the Free International University of Moldova.

One of the oldest Slovak NGOs operating in Moldova is the People in Peril Association (a close partner of the People in Need Foundation in the Czech Republic), which in 2003 invited Iurie Roşca, the leader of the Moldovan opposition PPCD party, to Slovakia.[46] In 2008, PIPA, in cooperation with a local partner, Saint George Peasants, delivered humanitarian assistance to 1,012 peasants in the twenty-one most drought-affected regions of Moldova. Material aid consisted of corn seeds, fertilizers, and petrol for agricultural machinery. PIPA carried out a monitoring visit to the project areas to assess the distribution of the material aid in two of the affected regions—Strǎşeni and Anenii Noi.[47]

Conclusion

Moldova's bilateral relations with the Czech and Slovak republics, and the dynamic development since the year of 2003, show that a relatively few official contacts at the highest level, as well as a low level of bilateral trade and investments, does not necessarily mean the lack of a positive agenda. The Czech and Slovak example shows how the Europeanization of foreign policy in terms of promoting the EU value system, and the countries' experience of European integration, can shape the political, ideological, and territorial priorities of individual EU member states. Conversely, both the Czech Republic and Slovakia are able to promote themselves to EU institutions as responsible partners bringing their own contribution to the EU agenda.

The Slovak example shows that large amounts of financial resources and the direct diplomatic presence of an embassy are not essential conditions of effective bilateral policy and the promotion of the country's soft power. Slovakia, as well as the Czech Republic, chose the "low-cost" way of promoting their countries' agendas. Their main message is the promotion of a successful model of transformation and European integration, and "advocacy" for Moldova within European institutions. Therefore, their activities are appreciated by the Moldovan government and NGOs, in spite of the fact that the amount of Slovak or Czech transformation and development assistance is, obviously, lower than the aid provided by donors like the US or Germany.

The Czech and Slovak case is innovative in other regards as well. In both of these cases, actors of so-called "public diplomacy"—non-governmental organizations, were present in Moldova before official representatives of the state, and these NGOs prepared the proper foundations for a qualitative shift in relations on the governmental level. Even after the establishment and acceleration of relations on the official level, Czech and Slovak NGOs continue to be the main actors in bilateral cooperation.

Notes

1. Katarzyna Pełczyńska-Nałęcz et al., *Eastern Policy of the EU: The Visegrad Countries' Perspective. Thinking about an Eastern Dimension* (Warsaw: Centre for Eastern Studies, 2003), 29, 33–34, http://www.osw.waw.pl/sites/default/files/punkt_widzenia 4.pdf (accessed August 3, 2011).

2. Zastupitelský úřad ČR v Kišiněvě [Czech Embassy in Chisinau], "Moldavsko. Souhrnná teritoriální informace" [Moldova. Comprehensive Territorial Information], BusinessInfo.cz, June 27, 2011, http://services.czechtrade.cz/pdf/sti/moldavsko-2011-06-27.pdf (accessed August 3, 2011).

3. "Moldavsko požádalo ČR o pomoc při vstupu do EU" [Moldova asked the Czech Republic for assistance in the EU-accession], *Zahraniční politika České republiky*, no. 2 (2005): 21.

4. Jiří Paroubek and Vasile Tarlev, "Tisková konference předsedy vlády ČR Jiřího Paroubka a předsedy vlády Moldavské republiky Vasile Tarleva v Praze" [Press-conference of the Prime Minister of Czech Republic Jiří Paroubek and the Prime Minister of Moldova Vasile Tarlev in Prague], April 21, 2006, *Zahraniční politika České republiky*, no. 4 (2006): 12–15.

5. "Politika i ekonomika. Vladimir Voronin nakhoditsya v Chekhii s chastnym vizitom," *Logos Press*, no. 12 (2004), http://dlib.eastview.com/browse/doc/6120207 (accessed August 3, 2011).

6. "Prezident přijal moldavského prezidenta" [President met president of Moldova], *Zahraniční politika České republiky*, no. 9 (2006): 3.

7. Média centrum [The Media Center of the Czech Government], "Premiér přijal předsedkyni vlády Moldavské republiky Zinaidu Greceanii" [Prime Minister met the Prime Minister of the Republic of Moldova Zinaida Greceanii], September 2, 2008, http://www.vlada.cz/scripts/detail.php?id=40861 (accessed August 3, 2011).

8. Petr Kratochvíl, "Země východní dimenze Evropské politiky sousedství v české zahraniční politice" [The Eastern dimension of European Neighbourhood Policy countries in Czech foreign policy], in *Česká zahraniční politika v roce 2007* [Czech foreign policy in 2007], ed. Michal Kořán (Praha: Institute of International Relations, 2008), 238.

9. Moldovan Embassy to the Czech Republic, "Minister Andrei Stratan had a phone conversation with his Czech counterpart Karel Schwarzenberg," April 13, 2009, http://www.ambasadamoldova.cz/en/news/press-releases/minister-andrei-stratan-had-a-phone-conversation-with-his-czech-counterpart-karel-schwarzenberg (accessed August 3, 2011).

10. Petr Štefan, "Moldavská opozice chce mezinárodní přepočítání voleb, slyšel Topolánek" [Moldovan opposition wants the international recount of elections, heard Topolánek], *iDNES.cz*, April 22, 2009, http://zpravy.idnes.cz/kazdy-ctvrty-moldavan-chce-emigrovat-hasit-spory-priletel-i-topolanek-1mm-/zahranicni.aspx?c=A090422_070839_domaci_jw (accessed August 3, 2011).

11. Moldovan Embassy to the Czech Republic, "President Vladimir Voronin today met acting Czech Prime Minister Mirek Topolanek," April 22, 2009, http://www.ambasadamoldova.cz/en/news/press-releases/president-vladimir-voronin-today-met-acting-czech-prime-minister-mirek-topolanek (accessed August 3, 2011).

12. Moldovan Embassy to the Czech Republic, "Moldova to benefit from Czech support in EU integration," September 30, 2010, http://www.ambasadamoldova.cz/en/news/press-releases/czech-supports-moldova (accessed August 3, 2011).

13. Ministerstvo zahraničních věcí České republiky [Czech Foreign Ministry], "Ministr Schwarzenberg se setkal se svým moldavským protějškem" [Minister Schwarzenberg met his Moldovan counterpart], September 30, 2010.

14. Czech Foreign Ministry, "Ministr Schwarzenberg příjal ministra zahraničních věcí Moldavské republiky" [Minister Schwarzenberg met the minister of foreign affairs of the Republic of Moldova], May 16, 2011.

15. Together with Afghanistan, Bosnia and Herzegovina, Ethiopia and Mongolia.

16. Česká rozvojová agentura [Czech Development Agency], *Koncepce zahraniční rozvojové spolupráce na období 2010–2017* (Prague, 2010), http://www.czda.cz /download.php?group=stranky3_soubory&id=4 (accessed August 3, 2011).

17. Czech Foreign Ministry, "Ministr Schwarzenberg navštívil v Moldavsku rozvojové projekty" [Minister Schwarzenberg visited the development projects in Moldova], October 2, 2010.

18. Czech Foreign Ministry, "Prioritní země a projekty transformační spolupráce" [Priority countries and the projects of transformation cooperation] http://www.mzv.cz /jnp/cz/zahranicni_vztahy/lidska_prava/prioritni_zeme_a_projekty_transformacni/moldav sko/index.html (accessed August 3, 2011).

19. Média centrum "Premiér přijal."

20. Milada Horáková, *Zahraniční pracovní migrace v České republice dva roky po vstupu ČR do EU* [The foreign labour migrations in Czech Republic two years after the EU-accession] (Prague: VÚPSV, 2006), 22.

21. Moldovan Embassy to the Czech Republic, "Czech Republic tightens work permits procedures for foreigners," March 12, 2010, http://www.ambasadamoldova.cz/en /consular-services-and-information/consular-announcements/czech-work-permits (accessed August 3, 2011).

22. Ondřej Hofírek and Michal Nekorjak, "Neregulérní práce imigrantů v Ceské republice" [Irregular labor of immigrants in the Czech Republic], *Sociální práce/Sociálna práca*, no. 2 (2007): 78–90.

23. Moldovan Embassy to the Czech Republic, "Czech Republic tightens."

24. Czech Ministry of the Interior, *Zpráva o situaci v oblasti vnitřní bezpečnosti a veřejného pořádku na území České republiky v roce 2009 (ve srovnání s rokem 2008)* [Report on the situation in the field of internal security and public order at the territory of the Czech Republic in 2009 (comparing to 2008)] (Prague, 2010), 35, http://www.mvcr .cz/soubor/zprava-komplet-2009-pdf.aspx (accessed August 3, 2011).

25. Czech Ministry of the Interior, *Report on Public Order and Internal Security in the Czech Republic in 2008 (compared with 2007)* (Prague, 2009), http://www.mvcr .cz/soubor/bezp-situace2008-eng-pdf.aspx (accessed August 3, 2011); Czech Foreign Ministry, *Zpráva o zahraniční politice České republiky, leden – prosinec 2009* [Report on the foreign policy of the Czech Republic, January–December 2009] (Prague, 2010), http:// www.mzv.cz/file/592100/Zprava_o_zahranicni_politice_2009__CZ_FINAL_po_vymene _Korey.pdf (accessed August 3, 2011).

26. Michal Mejstrik et al., *Analysis of the Moldovan-Czech Economic Relations: Hindrances and Opportunities for Increasing Bilateral Trade and Investment* (Chişinău– Prague: EXPERT-GRUP – EEIP, 2007), 29, http://www.eeip.cz/download/7_analyza _moldavsko-ceskych_hospodarskych_vztahu_en.pdf (accessed August 3, 2011).

27. Zastupitelský úřad ČR v Kišiněvě, "Moldavsko."

28. Czech Foreign Ministry, "Do Moldavska by mělo zamířit 350 českých autobusů" [350 Czech buses should be heading to Moldova], February 28, 2005.

29. Paroubek and Tarlev, "Tisková konference."

30. People in Peril, "Visit of the Moldovan opposition politician (2003)," http:// www.peopleinperil.sk/index.php?option=com_content&view=article&id=388:visit-of-the -moldovan-opposition-politician-2003&catid=131:moldavsko&Itemid=323 (accessed August 3, 2011).

31. "Ivan Gašparovič dnes popoludní odcestuje do Moldavska" [Ivan Gašparovič will today travel to Moldova], *SITA*, June 19, 2007.

32. Ministerstvo zahraničných vecí Slovenskej republiky [Slovak Foreign Ministry], "J. Kubiš prijal veľvyslancov štátov GUAM" [J. Kubiš met the ambassadors of the GUAM member states], March 2, 2007.

33. Slovak Foreign Ministry, "Slovensko ponúka Moldavsku pomoc pri európskych ambíciách" [Slovakia proposes help with European ambitions to Moldova], December 1, 2009.

34. "Slovakia vows support for Moldova's EU aspirations," *Moldpres*, February 11, 2010, http://politicom.moldova.org/news/slovakia-vows-support-for-moldovas-eu-aspirations-206039-eng.html (accessed August 3, 2011).

35. Slovak Foreign Ministry, "Moldavsko ďakuje Slovensku za pomoc a podporu" [Moldova appreciates Slovakia for the help and support], May 7, 2010; Pontis Foundation. "Moldavsko chce byť štandardnou európskou krajinou" [Moldova wants to be a standard European country], May 12, 2010, http://www.nadaciapontis.sk/15040 (accessed August 3, 2011).

36. Slovak Foreign Ministry, "Podpora SR a EÚ Moldavsku" [Support of Slovakia and EU to Moldova], June 14, 2010.

37. There has been discussed the presence of the Slovak officer in the Hungarian embassy in Chisinau.

38. Slovak Foreign Ministry, "Milan Ježovica na návšteve Moldavska" [Milan Ježovica paid visit to Moldova], February 18, 2011.

39. "Ashton Appoints Lajcak EU Diplomacy Head for Balkans and Eastern Europe," *TASR*, December 14, 2010, http://www.slovenskecentrum.sk/en/news/read/177 30/ashton-appoints-lajcak-eu-diplomacy-head-for-balkans-and-e-europe (accessed August 3, 2011).

40. Slovak Foreign Ministry, "Informačný materiál. Moldavsko" [Informatory material. Moldova], May 2011.

41. See Zastupitelský úřad ČR v Kišiněvě, "Moldavsko."

42. Slovak Foreign Ministry, "Informačný materiál."

43. Slovak Aid, *Národný program oficiálnej rozvojovej pomoci SR na rok 2011* (Bratislava: Slovak Agency for International Development Cooperation – SAIDC, 2011), http://www.slovakaid.sk/wp-content/uploads/2011/02/NP-ODA-2011.pdf (accessed August 3, 2011). The other priority countries of Slovak development aid in 2011 are Kenya, Sudan, Afghanistan, Bosnia and Herzegovina, and Montenegro.

44. National Convention on the EU in Moldova, "About the project," 2011, http://conventia.md/about-the-project/ (accessed August 3, 2011).

45. Pontis Foundation, "Slovakia and the European Future of Moldova," February 17, 2011, http://www.nadaciapontis.sk/en/15627 (accessed August 3, 2011).

46. People in Peril, "Visit of the Moldovan."

47. People in Peril, "Droughts in Moldova (2008)," http://www.peopleinperil.sk/index.php?option=com_content&view=article&id=449:droughts-in-moldova-2008&catid=159:moldova&Itemid=440 (accessed August 3, 2011).

Chapter Five

The European Union: From Ignorance to a Privileged Partnership with Moldova[*]

Natalia Shapovalova and Jos Boonstra

The European Union has changed significantly over the past twenty years. The union enlarged from twelve member states in the early 1990s to twenty-seven in 2007. Established in 1992 by the treaty of Maastricht, the union was created alongside the existing European Communities. In 2009, the union acquired a legal personality after the Lisbon Treaty entered into force. Integration spread to new policy areas: The European Monetary Union and the border-free Schengen zone were established, hugely impacting perception of the EU abroad.

Significant institutional changes took place in foreign policy, security and defense, and core domains of national state sovereignty, which EU member states were reluctant to integrate. The introduction of a Common Foreign and Security Policy through the treaty of Maastricht (1992), has been an important step in this regard, as well as the creation of the Secretary General/High Representative for CFSP by the treaty of Amsterdam (1997). Following the Franco-British Saint Malo Declaration, the Cologne European Council in 1999 agreed on establishing the European Security and Defence Policy, which enabled the development of an EU role in conflict prevention and crisis management. The institutional strengthening of the EU's foreign policy was further developed through the Lisbon Treaty (2007), which created the permanent President of the European Council and the High Representative of the Union for Foreign Affairs and Security Policy as permanent chair of the EU's Foreign Affairs Council and the Vice President of the European Commission. On the basis of the Lisbon Treaty, the European External Action Service was created in 2010, and Commission delegations around the world became EU delegations.[1]

During this lengthy process, the EU also increasingly developed foreign and security policies with respect to specific regions. Ahead of the Eastern enlargement of 2004, the EU started to develop its neighborhood policy so as to bundle the countries to the south and the east of the EU into one comprehensive pro-

[*] The authors would like to thank Leonid Litra, Stanislav Secrieru and Dinu Toderascu for their comments on an earlier draft of this chapter. The authors are grateful to Silvia Mosneaga for her research assistance.

51

gram. The European Neighbourhood Policy is the main overarching framework for relations with neighboring countries, and it was further deepened through a specific approach for the south, the Union for the Mediterranean (2008) and for the six countries to the EU's east, the Eastern Partnership (2009).

Relations between Moldova and the European Union have taken substantial time to develop. Moldova has not ranked high on the EU's foreign policy priority list and European integration policy has not developed in Moldova at the same pace as in the Baltic States or the Balkans during the 1990s. Contractual relations were developed on the basis of a Partnership and Cooperation Agreement, but intensification of political dialogue across a broad range of policy areas came only in the mid-2000s through ENP and EU engagement in the resolution of the Transnistria conflict. From the EU's point of view, Moldova became geographically closer after 2004, and especially after the 2007 EU enlargement that included Romania. Although Moldova did not represent many economic opportunities for the EU, concerns over security and stability issues did increase in Brussels. The EU felt a growing sense of discomfort with the unresolved Transnistrian dispute so close to its borders. More broadly, the union took a keen interest in seeing its neighbors develop into stable democracies with market economies, to form a ring of stability around the EU.

From Chisinau's perspective, interest in the EU also grew substantially in the mid-2000s, for the same reasons of geographic proximity, as well as a growth in knowledge about the EU, and support for integration. The EU was suddenly closer than Russia, which had formerly been Moldova's main partner. The leadership in Chisinau hoped that good relations with the EU would help counterbalance Russia's influence in Moldova, particularly in Transnistria.

This chapter offers an overview of the development of EU-Moldova relations since the latter's independence in 1991. It explores the development of the EU's influence on Moldova, but also Moldova's views on the EU and its adherence to "European standards" through economic and democratic reform. Central themes in the analysis are political engagement, EU assistance and conditionality.

The chapter is divided in three parts that follow a chronological trajectory. The first part looks at the period from Moldova's independence to 2001. In this period, Moldova was developing as an independent state while the EU was slowly establishing itself as a foreign policy actor with unfolding interests in the newly independent states to its east. The second part explores the period of consecutive Communist-led governments in Moldova from 2001 to 2009. This period was characterized by Moldova's declared turn toward the EU in mid-2000 as its priority foreign policy direction, as well as the EU's engagement in the region through the ENP. The third part begins in the aftermath of the so-called "Twitter revolution" in April 2009, when contested parliamentary elections led to street riots in Chisinau and snap elections in July brought a change of government. A new government led by the Alliance for European Integration prioritized relations with the EU. This coincided with the launch of the EU's Eastern Partnership initiative aimed at boosting ties with six East European and

South Caucasus countries, among them Moldova, that had taken an active role by working with the EU through this initiative.

EU Policy toward Moldova in the 1990s: On the Margins

The European Union's policy toward Moldova in the early 1990s developed in the context of Europe's approach toward the post-Soviet space. The European Communities saw little distinction between the newly independent states which emerged from the dissolution of the Soviet Union. All of them—apart from the Baltic States, which along with Central European countries took an accession path to the EU—were entitled to the European Commission's technical assistance under the TACIS program. They negotiated a Partnership and Cooperation Agreement with the EU. In the eyes of Brussels, Moldova was insignificant compared to Russia or even, to a lesser extent, Ukraine. Moldova was the third country to sign a PCA with the EU in November 1994, which entered into force in 1998 after ratification by EU member states. The European Communities and its member states were not directly involved in conflict mediation during or immediately after the war, but through regional institutions, primarily the Organization for Security and Cooperation in Europe and its American[2] ambassador in Chisinau.[3] This lack of engagement can be explained by a low threat perception from the European member states in comparison with other conflicts (e.g. in the Western Balkans and the Middle East) and an unwillingness to interfere in Russia's sphere of influence.[4] At the time, European foreign and security policy had not been developed, and there was neither the opportunity nor the expertise needed within the EU for a unified approach to post-Soviet conflicts. Meanwhile, there was also little demand coming from Chisinau, which relied on Moscow's involvement.

Signed for a ten-year period, the PCA aimed at establishing a framework for political dialogue and the promotion of trade and investment. It also served as the basis for legislative, economic, social, financial, and cultural cooperation, as well as support for Moldova's transition to democracy and a market economy.[5] Although this agreement points to a normative partnership between the European Communities and Moldova by referring to respect for democracy, principles of international law, and human rights, its main focus is trade and economic cooperation. The accord envisioned an approximation of Moldova's legislation to that of the community and the prospect of a free trade area.[6] Offering minor economic and financial incentives, the PCA did not foresee any negative consequences in the case of non-compliance. While Moldova aligned its legislation to some EU norms, mostly in areas connected to trade facilitation, the agreement as a whole was not implemented. One Moldovan expert argued that "while Moldova had few incentives to implement the PCA, the EU had no real leverage over its partner, neither enough interest nor will for more active involvement in the implementation process of the PCA."[7]

Although the PCA did not envision the prospect of full integration in the EU, unlike the Association Agreements signed with Baltic and Central European states, the agreement gave impetus to Moldova's European integration. It institutionalized political dialogue between the EU and Moldova, introducing such mechanisms as the Cooperation Council (ministerial level meetings once a year); the Cooperation Committee (with frequent meetings and work in sub-committees including senior-level representatives of the European Commission, the EU Council and the Moldovan government); and the Parliamentary Cooperation Committee (to exchange views and make recommendations to the Cooperation Council). Unlike Russia and Ukraine, regular meetings at the highest political level (summits) between Moldova and the EU were not envisioned.

The idea of Moldova's integration into the EU was raised for the first time in 1995, when the Moldovan Parliament adopted the Foreign Policy Concept of the Republic of Moldova, in which relations with the EU were envisioned as part of regional and sub-regional cooperation. The parliament, underlining the need for a flexible and balanced foreign policy, outlined a plan with the gradual integration of Moldova into the EU as a major goal, and it saw the PCA as a first step.[8]

In 1996, the second Moldovan president, Petru Lucinschi, was the first to express integration aspirations to European officials. He sent letters to the president of the European Commission and leaders of EU member states, expressing Moldova's will to become an associate member of the EU by 2000, and to start negotiations on an Association Agreement. Additionally, in December 1997, Prime Minister Ion Ciubuc met the prime minister of Belgium and the European commissioner for external relations in Brussels, asking for support in granting Moldova association member status. A year later, after parliamentary elections in 1998, a new government led by the same prime minister declared European integration of Moldova a foreign policy strategic goal.[9]

From 1999 onwards, Moldova tried to ride the momentum of the Western Balkans enlargement by seeking membership in regional initiatives for South-Eastern Europe, foremost the Stability Pact for South Eastern Europe, an EU initiative to coordinate international efforts in strengthening peace, security and democracy in the Balkans. Finally, Moldova was admitted to the Stability Pact in 2001, the only ex-Soviet country in this club. The Moldovan authorities hoped that this might offer a short-cut toward EU integration with this group of potential candidate countries: Some hoped it would eventually lead to a Stabilisation and Association Agreement and inclusion into the substantial assistance programs for the Balkans.[10] Eventually, the stability pacts' focus shifted from the broader Balkans to the Western Balkans, since Bulgaria and Romania were firmly *en route* to membership, and in the end, this strategy went nowhere for Chisinau.

Meanwhile, the need for democratic and economic reforms to foster closer ties with the EU had not impressed itself upon Moldovan politicians. There was little understanding within the elite that integration with the EU meant domestic transformation and did not concern only foreign policy. The PCA commitments were not met and there was little internal or external EU pressure to make the necessary changes. The government led by the Democratic Agrarian Party and supported by the Socialists—the former Communist leadership that came to power in 1994—wasted international assistance provided to support economic reform in Moldova. As the outcome of this "reform," Moldova became one of the poorest regions in Europe.[11] The pro-European coalition of political parties (the Alliance for Democracy and Reforms) that ruled during 1998–2001 was marked by political divisions and appeared unable to carry out any substantial reforms.[12] Moreover, in 1998, Moldova's economy was severely affected by the negative impact of Russia's financial crisis. In 2001, the Party of Communists of the Republic of Moldova that came first into power during the 1998 elections won the majority of seats in the Parliament. Its leader Vladimir Voronin became the third president of Moldova. During the election campaign, the Communists promised prosperity based on a Soviet-style economy and welfare state, as well as accession to the Russia-Belarus Union, and the settlement of the Transnistrian conflict through increased cooperation with Russia.

During this moment of uncertainty over a Communist-ruled Moldova, the EU's policy toward Moldova was about to enter a new phase provoked by its eastward enlargement.

The EU and Moldova in the 2000s: A European Flag with Hammer and Sickle

In the early 2000s, EU policy toward Moldova, as well as the other post-Soviet countries, began to change. The eastern enlargement that made the EU an immediate neighbor of European post-Soviet countries was the main driving force behind this change. In Moldova, the Communist government turned to a more balanced foreign policy, embarking on EU integration to boost its legitimacy within Moldovan society and to obtain benefits from engagement with the EU.

Promoting Stability and Prosperity in the New Neighborhood

Starting in the late 1990s, the then-candidates for EU accession, in particular Poland, started to advocate the idea of an eastern dimension of the EU, a framework for enhanced cooperation with Eastern European countries. This call found support among some old member states, such as the United Kingdom and Sweden, which advocated for a specified policy toward new EU neighbors, in particular Belarus, Moldova and Ukraine, from the Commission as well as the newly installed EU High Representative for Common Foreign and Security Policy.[13]

In 2003, the European Commission adopted a Communication called Wider Europe Neighbourhood: A New Framework for Relations with our Eastern and Southern Neighbours that established a conceptual framework for European Neighbourhood Policy. The new policy aimed at "sharing the benefits of the EU's 2004 enlargement with neighboring countries in strengthening stability, security and well-being for all concerned."[14] The ENP included a wider geographical area by incorporating Eastern and South Mediterranean neighbors. It set aside the question of EU accession, which caused disappointment among the eastern neighbors with EU accession ambitions—Ukraine and Moldova—but did offer an upgraded toolbox and resources to the EU's relations with the neighborhood.

In February 2005, the EU and Moldova signed an ENP Action Plan, a political document outlining the list of strategic objectives and commitments taken by both parties to intensify political, security, economic, and cultural relations. Though the AP does not mention a membership prospect and merely acknowledges Moldova's European aspirations, the Moldovan government saw it as a step toward an associate membership in the EU.[15]

While based on the principle of joint partnership, the AP introduced the principle of conditionality in EU-Moldova relations, making the intensity of the relationship dependent "on the degree of Moldova's commitment to common values as well as its capacity to implement jointly agreed priorities."[16] The AP also envisioned a mechanism for monitoring progress achieved in implementation to be carried out by the bodies established by the PCA and the European Commission.

Binding for three years,[17] the AP formulated eighty objectives and 294 measures across seven areas: political dialogue and reform; cooperation for the settlement of the Transnistrian conflict; economic and social reform, as well as development; trade-related issues, market and regulatory reform; cooperation in justice and home affairs; transport, energy, telecommunications, environment, and research, development and innovation; and finally people-to-people contacts. Since the number of measures and actions to be taken by Moldova outweighs those to be taken either by the EU or jointly,[18] the document has often been referred to as a reform list or a roadmap to be followed by Moldova in order to come closer to the Union.

In October 2005, the European Commission finally inaugurated its Delegation to Moldova (before EU-Moldova affairs were dealt with by the delegation in Kiev). One year earlier, in October 2004, Moldova established a diplomatic mission to the EU, separate from its earlier established embassy to Belgium.

From 2003, the EU began taking the first steps to facilitate a resolution of the Transnistria conflict, such as imposing a travel ban on Transnistrian officials blocking negotiations, and mediating negotiations on customs and border agreements between Ukraine and Moldova.[19] In accordance with the objective of cooperation on the Transnistria conflict settlement in the EU-Moldova AP, the EU appointed an EU Special Representative for Moldova in 2005, and along with the United States it joined the five-sided negotiations (consisting of the OSCE, Russia, Ukraine, and the two conflicting parties) as an observer.

Crucially, on November 30, 2005, the EU Border Assistance Mission to Moldova and Ukraine was deployed to the Ukraine-Moldova border. EUBAM aims to assist Ukraine and Moldova in bringing their border management practices in line with European standards and in enhancing the professional capacities of border and customs officials. EUBAM has aimed to contribute to the Transnistria conflict settlement by helping to end smuggling, trafficking, and customs fraud, and to reduce the flow of illicit income to Transnistria, which is considered a source of economic support for the separatist regime. The mission's work has been assessed mainly positively.[20] Notwithstanding the technical character of its assistance, the mission's impact is often seen as extending into the political dimension.[21] One of its major achievements, with an impact on the Transnistria conflict settlement, has been its support for implementation of the Joint Declaration of a Customs Regime on the Common Border, which was signed in 2005 by Ukraine and Moldova. Due to this agreement, more than seven hundred Transnistrian-based companies registered with the customs authorities in Chisinau and became eligible for the EU trade preferences granted to Moldova.[22] EUBAM also played a role in the resumption of the Chisinau-Odessa passenger railway line that goes through Transnistria, in 2010.[23]

While the EU decided against sending a peacekeeping mission to Moldova, an option widely circulated in the EU in 2003 and 2006,[24] its "work in 'the low politics' of conflict resolution has made the EU increasingly influential in the economic, social aspects, and soft security dimensions of the Transnistrian conflict."[25] On one hand, eastern enlargement, the ENP tool box, and the EU's growing security capabilities and peacekeeping experience created an environment for a more comprehensive and proactive EU policy. On the other hand, the pro-Western regime change in Ukraine and President Vladimir Voronin's own turn to the West in 2004, made the EU's engagement more welcome and effective.[26]

Since 2008, the EU has been engaging Transnistria through confidence-building projects between the left and right banks of the Dniester River and aid to Transnistria in social affairs, healthcare, education, transport, or environmental issues.[27] The EU also launched a program to support civil society development in Transnistria. Representatives of the EU delegation and of member states' embassies began to visit Transnistria, and information about these visits was frequently published in the local press.[28] This engagement is deemed important to addressing the imbalance of EU relations with Chisinau and Tiraspol. As a Tiraspol-based analyst pointed out, in right bank Moldova, European integration is an official foreign policy supported by political and social consensus in support of the Europeanization of Moldova. In Transnistria, he argues, "the European picture is absolutely different." From Tiraspol's point of view, relations with the EU are seen only in the framework of the settlement process, while "the notion of Europeanization is unknown to Transnistrian society and, as a term, it does not carry a positive charge."[29] The latter is no surprise considering the amount of official anti-Western and anti-European propaganda there.

For all of Moldova, including Transnistria, the EU is the most important trading partner, with a 52.0 percent share of external trade in 2010. Trade of all Moldova with the EU grew consistently from €766 million in 2001, reaching its peak of €2.45 billion in 2008, before the economic crisis hit trade volumes.[30] If one looks at Transnistria's trade abroad separately, the EU is the main destination of Transnistrian goods. In the first quarter of 2011, exports to the EU constituted 58.3 percent, whereas exports to CIS countries—only 25.7 percent.[31]

In 1999, the EU granted preferential access to its markets for Moldovan goods under the General System of Preferences regime. It allowed for up to a 10 to 30 percent reduction of tariffs, depending on the category of exported good. Nevertheless, use of the GSP was of limited advantage to Moldova, since most of its production fell into the sensitive category.[32] In 2006, the EU granted Moldova trade preferences under the GSP+ regime. This allowed 7,200 commodities duty-free access to the EU market, about 3,000 more than in 2006.[33]

In 2008, the EU introduced Autonomous Trade Preferences for Moldova, which gave unlimited and duty-free access to the EU market for all products originating in Moldova, except for certain agricultural products (e.g. sugar, meat, wine, fruits and vegetables, dairy). For these products, specific tariff rates and quotas were applied. The EU conditioned the ATPs on Moldova's improvement of its certification and customs controls systems.[34]

The EU's assistance to Moldova grew significantly in the 2000s. From 1991 to 2006, Moldova received €320.0 million of technical assistance under TACIS, macro-financial assistance and humanitarian aid, plus assistance in the food security program, and small funds to promote civil society and work on human rights and democracy promotion. In 2007, a new technical assistance tool—the European Neighbourhood and Partnership Instrument—was introduced when the TACIS projects concluded. The ENPI envisaged €209.7 million for Moldova from 2007 to 2010. Moldova became the top recipient of EU aid per capita among the eastern neighbors, being second worldwide only after Palestine. Through budgetary support and technical assistance, the ENPI aims at assisting the implementation of Moldovan reforms within three priority areas: democracy and good governance; regulatory reform and strengthening of administrative capacity; and economic growth and poverty reduction. In 2007, the EU granted Moldova €45.0 million of macro financial aid to alleviate the negative impact of price increases of energy imports from Russia and the latter's embargo of Moldovan wine.[35]

Following the AP objective, in October 2008, the EU and Moldova signed a visa facilitation agreement along with an agreement on the readmission of illegal migrants. The visa facilitation lowered the visa fee from €60 to €35, and provided an exemption from the visa fee for certain categories of applicants. Procedures of applying for a visa have become easier for certain categories of travelers (e.g. businessmen, students and journalists), while issuance of long-term multi-entry visas for frequent travelers has also been arranged. Holders of diplomatic passports have been entitled to travel without a visa.[36] Moldova was the first country in which the EU established a Common Visa Application Centre in 2007. The center facilitated applicants' access to the Schengen visa issuance procedure, since many EU states did not have consular representations in Chisinau, and Moldovan citizens had to travel to other countries to obtain the visa.

In June 2008, Moldova became one of the first countries to sign a Mobility Partnership with the EU, a non-legally binding tool to promote and manage labor migration policy with the EU.[37] Moldova's interest in such a partnership stems from the large number of Moldovan citizens working in Europe. Italy is the second most significant destination country of Moldovan migrants (after Russia), with Spain, Portugal, Greece, and Romania among other popular EU labor markets.[38]

In May 2008, Poland and Sweden put forward an initiative to strengthen the EU's policy toward its eastern neighbors, and to counterbalance the French-led Union for the Mediterranean. The initiative obtained greater importance after the five-day war between Russia and Georgia in August 2008. Following the Commission's Communication of December 2008, the European Council issued a declaration on the Eastern Partnership. The EaP offered a number of "carrots" to eastern neighbors, such as association agreements, free trade, visa liberalization, energy cooperation, and aid for institution-building and regional cohesion, all subject to progress in democratization and in establishing the rule of law and human rights. The EaP also introduced multilateral structures to foster regional integration among the six partner countries.

Echoing developments in the EU's relations with Ukraine, which was the first country in the region to start negotiations on a new agreement to substitute its expired PCA, the Moldovan president declared in June 2008 that Moldova would also seek an Association Agreement with Brussels stipulating its membership perspective.[39] In October 2008, the EU Council stated its readiness to negotiate a new and ambitious agreement with Moldova, which would include free trade and visa liberalization.[40] As in the case with Ukraine, the EU conditioned the future agreement on Moldova passing a test of democratic elections in spring 2009.

Voronin's Overnight Change from East to West

Moldova's foreign policy, under Communist leadership, was not unambiguously pro-Russian, and its domestic policies were seldom inspired by Communism. After an initial period of courting Russia and a failure to agree upon the solution of the Transnistrian conflict, the Communist government picked up the rhetoric of European integration. The Moscow-initiated Kozak Memorandum[41] on the settlement of the Transnistrian conflict was averted at the last moment, thanks to EU and OSCE advisers who persuaded President Voronin not to sign. The pressure of the Moldovan opposition and street protests also had some bearing on the President's rejection of the deal. At the 2004 Istanbul NATO summit, the Moldovan president called for the first time for the departure of Russian troops from Transnistria. This "overnight" change of direction turned Moldovan foreign policy 180 degrees from East to West.

While in June 2000 the Communists were the only parliamentary party that did not adhere to a document signed by 23 political parties declaring Moldova's EU integration as the country's main strategic priority, by November 2003 the Communists, together with all parliamentary factions, endorsed a common declaration on European integration. Moreover, according to a presidential decree, the Concept for the Integration of the Republic of Moldova in the EU was drafted in 2003 (although it was never published). The first deputy minister of foreign affairs declared that Moldova could file an application to join the EU, and by 2007 it would have the chance to get the status of EU associate member.[42] In 2005, the European Strategy of the Republic of Moldova was developed (however, never endorsed by the parliament) with the goal of preparing Moldova for EU membership.

During the Communist government's rule, the institutional framework for EU-Moldova relations was established.[43] First, in 2001, a unit dealing with economic adjustments in the process of European integration was created in the Ministry of the Economy. In 2002, the president set up the National Commission for European Integration, which was tasked with developing and submitting to the parliament a European integration strategy for Moldova, with developing an action plan for implementing this strategy, and with coordinating its implementation.

In 2003, a European integration department was created within the Ministry of Foreign Affairs. After the 2005 parliamentary elections, the ministry was renamed the Ministry of Foreign Affairs and European Integration. Moreover, the foreign minister was also nominated deputy prime minister. In 2004, during the negotiations of the ENP's AP between Moldova and the EU, the Moldovan cabinet established four inter-ministerial coordination commissions aimed at working out details and implementing the future plan.

As one Moldovan expert pointed out, the paradox was that all these changes were "promoted by the Party of Communists of the Republic of Moldova, a political formation which was pleading in 2001 . . . for a privileged relationship with the Commonwealth of Independent States, and for assessing the issue of Moldova's membership in the Russia-Belarus Union."[44] Sergiu Bușcaneanu explained the decrease of Euro-skepticism among the ruling elite by external factors, such as Moldova's dependence on international aid; increased criticism from the Council of Europe; lack of progress on the Transnistrian conflict settlement and new insight into Russia's role in this process.[45] Meanwhile public support for European integration was on the rise. As surveys show, a majority of the population supported Moldova's accession to the EU, and from April 2003 to April 2008, support grew from 61 to 71 percent.[46]

However, Moldova's Europeanization remained an idea only, as the pro-European rhetoric did not transfer into performance. As independent civil society assessments of the AP implementation (as well as the Commission's progress reports) show, little or no progress was registered in the development of democratic institutions, and laws adapted to promote positive change in this field were not enforced by the government. Greater progress was noted in the economic dimension, as well as in border management due to EUBAM.[47] Generally, the EU was more effective in cooperation with Moldova in areas where preferences of both parties converged, and where the EU made a number of minimal concessions (trade preferences, aid, visa facilitation and engagement in conflict resolution).[48]

The EU's Involvement in the Post-Electoral Crisis in Moldova

As the parliamentary elections of 2009 were approaching, the political situation in Moldova became tenser and society more polarized. The Communists were losing popularity. This trend became apparent in the 2007 local elections and was further confirmed by pre-election polls in 2008 and in early 2009. Meanwhile, Voronin, who was finishing his second term as president, looked for a way to stay in power. Hoping to re-legitimize his regime, Voronin turned to Russia for support.[49]

The pre-election year was marked by the authorities' efforts to curtail space for political competition. A series of steps was undertaken by the government, including amendments to the electoral law aimed at weakening the position of opposition parties, allowing the criminal prosecution of the opposition, and the manipulation of voters' lists. These moves raised suspicions about potential election fraud.[50] The 2009 campaign saw many breaches of legislation, namely the use of administrative resources by the governing party, unequal access of candidates to the media outlets, limitation of the right of assembly, and the destruction of opposition campaign posters.[51] During the election campaign, the EU representatives and member states' ambassadors made several statements expressing their concerns and calling on the authorities to fix these problems.

After the Central Electoral Commission indicated the victory of the Communist party, citizens' protests broke out on the streets of Chisinau on April 7, 2009. The protesters alleged the elections were fraudulent and called for a recount of votes, new elections or the government's resignation. The Communists suggested this was an attempted *coup d'état* inspired by Romania and it launched a series of arrests against protesters and opposition activists.

The EU failed to give a strong and coherent response to the April events. The EU representatives recognized the official election results, since the OSCE and other Western election observers concluded that the Moldovan parliamentary elections met "many of the OSCE and Council of Europe commitments."[52] When the crisis started, the EU, followed by the US, called primarily for dialogue between the government and the opposition.

Confronted with a wave of arrests, Brussels' attitude toward the Moldovan government gradually grew tougher. High-level visits by Mirek Topolánek, the head of the Czech government, which held the rotating EU Council presidency and Javier Solana, EU High Representative, on April 22 and 24 were instrumental in reducing the scale of arrests and harassment, which nevertheless continued. The EU urged an independent investigation, incorporating the opposition and EU experts, into the allegations of the government's abuse of power against protesters. However, none of these demands were accepted by Moldova's government, which left Brussels in a weak political position.[53]

The European Parliament took a more critical stance when it issued a resolution on May 7, 2009, condemning the massive campaign of harassment and grave violations of human rights by the Moldovan government.[54] However, the EP's call for stronger democratic conditionality in EU-Moldova relations was watered down by the EU Council in its conclusions of June 15, where it ambiguously mentioned that negotiations on a new enhanced agreement between the EU and Moldova would start "as soon as circumstances allow."[55] Similarly, EU member states did not respond to the parliament's appeal for a more active EU engagement by establishing a rule of law mission and strengthening the portfolio of the EU Special Representative to Moldova.[56]

Deepening EU-Moldova Relations in the 2010s: A Success Story?

EU-Moldova relations have deepened as a result of the Eastern Partnership and the installment of a new government formed by the four-party Alliance for European Integration after snap elections on July 29, 2009. Another election, held on November 28, 2010, due to parliament's inability to elect a president, renewed the mandate of the AEI, this time with three former-opposition parties.[57] The AEI drastically changed Moldova's foreign policy in the direction its name implies.

Moldova has been applauded for its reform efforts and activism in the EaP. This satisfaction was emphasized on July 2011, when Herman Van Rompuy, president of the European Council, visited Chisinau. When meeting Parliamentary Chairman (and acting President) Marian Lupu and Prime Minister Vlad Filat, he praised Moldova and stated that Europe's new "more for more" principle is likely to apply to the country's efforts in fighting corruption, judicial and law enforcement reform, development of anti-discrimination legislation, strengthening of the investment climate, and entrance into negotiations on a Deep and Comprehensive Free Trade Agreement.[58] The EU has allocated €550 million of assistance to Moldova from 2011 to 2013.

In May 2011, the commission and the EEAS released annual evaluation reports on the implementation of the ENP, including a country report on Moldova.[59] Of the six Eastern Partnership countries, Moldova received the best marks and seems to have surpassed Georgia (and earlier Ukraine) as the best student in the class. This ranking is unlikely to change, unless the current government gets in trouble over the stalemate in electing a president or tensions upset the three-party coalition. The EU reported that political uncertainly and a lack of re-sources could stave reform, but basically Brussels is keen to report a success story in the Eastern Partnership. So far, the initiative has not brought about sub-stantial reforms in the Eastern Neighbourhood countries, where a trend of demo-cratic reversion has emerged.[60] The EaP regional approach has not taken hold due to a lack of resources and the limited interest of the six recipient countries. In that sense, more is expected from the bilateral aspects of the Eastern Partner-ship, especially the Association Agreements, the Comprehensive Institution-Building program, the visa liberalization process, and the DCFTA. These are all linked to bringing Moldova and others into the EU's orbit without offering a direct perspective of membership.

The EU assessment of Moldova's democratic progress is generally in line with independent reports. For example, Freedom House's *Nation in Transit* project, which monitors the dynamics of democratic performance in post-Com-munist countries, slightly improved the overall democracy score of Moldova from 5.07 in 2008 to 4.96 in 2010.[61] Minor to moderate positive developments were noted in the electoral process, ensuring independence of media and judici-ary, and national democratic governance. In comparison to 2008, significant changes happened with regard to civil society's involvement in policy making and the government's openness to civil society.[62] Moldova also appeared as one of the top ten reformers in the World Bank's report on Doing Business.[63] How-ever, no progress was registered in the areas of local democratic governance and the fight against corruption since the mid-2000s. While the Moldovan govern-ment is good at adopting regulations, the will to implement these changes has been rather disappointing.

The Eastern Partnership's Bilateral Offers: Toward Long-Term Reforms

In January 2010, negotiations between Moldova and the EU started and ad-vanced quickly on an Association Agreement. The AA aims "to promote politi-cal association and economic integration between the Parties based on common values."[64] The agreement will be legally binding, and will go much further in substance and scope than the PCA, with a stronger monitoring and evaluation system, though it will likely stop short of a clear membership perspective.

In order to assist Moldova in meeting its new obligations under the AA, the CIB program is offered within EaP. In November 2010, a framework document was concluded for the period of 2011 to 2013, and the EU made over €41 mil-lion available. The funding will include twinning projects and technical assis-tance, administrative internships and specialized training, as well as the provision of equipment necessary to help Moldova meet EU norms and standards in various sectors.[65] In addition, Moldova was offered the chance to participate in EU internal programs (e.g. Customs-2013). This assistance is seen to boost Moldova's bureaucratic capacity to implement reforms, though the difficulty of attracting and keeping professional cadres in the underpaid civil service of Moldova will remain a challenge.

The institution-building assistance should also have a positive bearing on preparations for the negotiations of a Deep and Comprehensive Free Trade Area with the EU, which seems to be largely underpinning the reform agenda. Trade between the EU and Moldova has, over the last few years, benefited from the Autonomous Trade Preferences regime, further extended in 2011. Only a few agricultural products are currently restricted from entering the EU market by tariff rate quotas; however, slow adoption of standards and technical regulations and the difficulty of coping with sanitary and phytosanitary standards are the key obstacles to exporting to the EU.[66] The DCFTA, combined with EU assistance, is widely seen as helping Moldova comply with EU standards. In December 2009, Moldova adopted an action plan for the implementation of recommendations formulated by the European Commission in order to start free trade negotiations at the end of 2011. Moreover, Moldova sees the benefit of the DCFTA in increasing the country's attractiveness to European investors.

In May 2010, Moldova became a full member of the European Energy Community, an initiative established between the EU and a number of countries in South-Eastern Europe to foster market convergence through an extension of EU internal energy market legislation beyond the EU's borders. Membership in the community enables Moldova to reform its energy sector and improve energy security. In July 2011, the EU and Moldova started negotiating a Common Aviation Area Agreement that will increase flight connections and approximate Moldova to EU aviation rules.

The EaP has also launched a process of visa liberalization that should lead toward a visa-free regime in the long term. It is an extremely important issue for Moldova, which feels isolated after the Central European countries (especially Romania) joined the EU and were obliged to introduce a visa regime with Moldova.[67] This is why the Moldovan government has sought a proactive approach, also labeled as "pre-emptive," in the sense that Moldova started working on reform before establishing cooperation tools with the EU.[68] For example, the Moldovan State Border Service has been under reform, transformations of the Ministry of Interior are ongoing,[69] and in February 2008, Moldova was the first EaP country to introduce biometric passports.

In January 2011, Moldova was granted an Action Plan on Visa Liberalization. This plan lists four sets of reforms that Moldova needs to fulfill before the abolition of a visa regime with the EU. By the end of 2011, Moldova aspires to adopt the necessary legislative changes to conclude the first phase of the action plan implementation. The plan signed with Moldova (three months earlier than a similar agreement was signed with Ukraine) draws on the visa roadmaps which led to the abolition of the visa regime with the Western Balkan countries. However, in the case of the Eastern European countries, the conditions set by the EU are tougher and require a higher degree of compliance, which shows the reluctance of a number of EU states to agree on visa-free travel.[70]

Clearly the EU is not in a hurry to lift the visa regime with regard to Moldova soon after the Western Balkan countries obtained visa-free travel to the EU and several EU member states were inclined to create new barriers for non-EU citizens instead of opening up borders. Yet next to funding, visa liberalization is the strongest carrot the EU has at its disposal.

A €550 million EU aid package was dispersed through several EU instruments and mechanisms, between 2010 and 2013. The ENPI was the largest with €273 million, and it has the potential to substantially impact reform in Moldova.[71] The ENPI funding focuses on three priorities—good governance, rule of law, and fundamental freedoms; social and human development; trade and sustainable development. The largest portion of the funds is used for twinning projects, sectional budget support and technical assistance. But other mechanisms also have a strong focus on governance, the rule of law and human rights, foremost funding (especially for civil society) through the European Instrument for Democracy and Human Rights and the Non-State Actors and Local Authorities in Reform mechanism.

Support to Moldova from within the EU

Lack of support for further enlargement within the EU is a major challenge for the EU's policy toward Moldova. The accession prospect has been the most powerful carrot for encouraging the transformation and Europeanization of the EU's neighborhood.

Romania has the strongest bilateral relationship with Moldova and it is an important supporter of Moldova's membership in the EU. The special character of Romania-Moldova relations is based on common language and history as well as trade links, common border, energy cooperation and regional cooperation in the Balkans. More than a hundred thousand Moldovans hold Romanian passports.

Moldova-Romania relations received a fresh start under the AEI government in Moldova. In 2010, both countries established a strategic partnership for Moldova's European integration and Romania granted €100 million of aid over a four-year period. Romanian President Traian Băsescu declared that Moldova should be included in the next wave of the EU enlargement (into the Western Balkans group),[72] though this message has not found support in Brussels so far. In January 2010, Romania also initiated the European Action Group of the Republic of Moldova (also known as the Group of Friends of Moldova), an informal group open to all EU member states with the aim of coordinating efforts and conducting a dialogue to support the democratization and European integration of Moldova. The initiative was supported by many EU member states, as well as the European Commissioner for Enlargement and ENP.[73]

Generally, new member states support Moldova's European aspirations. Moldova signed European partnership agreements (memoranda of understanding on cooperation in European integration) with Bulgaria, the Czech Republic, Lithuania, Latvia, Slovakia, Hungary and Croatia as a future EU member.[74] These member states offer their advice and assistance to Moldova in carrying out the reforms agreed on with the EU. These countries are more in favor of EU enlargement than "old" member states which, with few exceptions, are against new enlargement commitments.

Poland advocated opening the prospect of EU membership to Moldova (and other Eastern European states) since 2003.[75] Since the change of government in Moldova, Poland's policy toward Chisinau has intensified because Moldovan success is deemed to be important for the success of the EaP, an initiative co-authored by Poland.[76]

The role of Hungary has been important in the establishment of the EU Common Visa Application Centre, which is housed in the premises of the Hungarian embassy in Chisinau. Hungary issues visas for fourteen Schengen states and Croatia.[77] The first head of the EUBAM, Ferenc Bánfi, and the second (and the final) EUSR to Moldova, Kálmán Mizsei, were Hungarians.

Among the EU member states, Bulgaria, the Czech Republic, France, Germany, Hungary, Lithuania, Poland, Romania, Sweden, the UK, and Italy have embassies in Chisinau, which indicates their interest in developing bilateral relations with Moldova.

The "old" member states such as Sweden, Germany, and the UK are important donors to Moldova. After Romania, Germany, Italy, the UK, and Poland are important trading partners for Moldova.[78] Germany's role, backed by France, was evident in the Transnistrian conflict settlement. From 2010 to 2011, high-level bilateral contacts between Moldova and Germany grew, with Moldova's prime minister meeting the German chancellor twice within this period. Chisinau, however, sees Germany's diplomatic efforts as an instrument in the German-Russian dialogue on security issues.[79] Despite Germany's substantial assistance to Moldova and its engagement in the conflict settlement, Moldova "has never been a high priority within Germany's Eastern Policy."[80]

The European Parliament, while its role in EU foreign policy is only consultative, supports the recognition of a prospect on membership. In the 2011 resolution on negotiations between the EU and Moldova on the Association Agreement, the Parliament called on the EU institutions "to base the EU engagement and ongoing negotiations with the Republic of Moldova on the assertion that the EU perspective, including Article 49 of the Treaty on the European Union . . . is both a valuable lever in the implementation of reforms and a necessary catalyst for public support of these reforms."[81] In another resolution, the parliament also urged the European Council and the Commission to make a visa liberalization offer to EaP countries "at least as generous as those proposed to the other countries with which they share a border," and called on the high representative and the EEAS "to step up their involvement in finding a solution to the protracted conflict in Transnistria."[82] Jerzy Buzek, president of the European Parliament, has been particularly outspoken in his support for Moldova, calling it "the spearhead of the Eastern Partnership, the good pupil of the class"[83] and "the hope for the region."[84]

Transnistria: In Moldova's Waiting Room?

Over the past two years, solving the Transnistrian conflict seems to have gained more priority in EU circles and somewhat less priority in Moldova. In June 2010, German Chancellor Angela Merkel and Russian President Dmitry Medvedev discussed a deal where the EU would establish an EU-Russia Committee as a forum for European security affairs, while Russia would agree to cooperate with Europe on the Transnistrian conflict settlement. It is noteworthy that Germany and not the EU structures themselves took the initiative for new talks and worked closely with Russia toward negotiations.[85] Little came of these plans, because the talks about increased involvement of Russia in Europe's security architecture have not evolved and are still dealt with through traditional EU and NATO channels of dialogue with Moscow. Nonetheless, Germany's mediation was helpful to unblock the 5+2 negotiations (Moldova, Transnistria, Ukraine, Russia and the OSCE plus the EU and US as observers): In September 2011, the decision to resume the official talks was announced. The result remains to be seen. Importantly, Russia, which stands behind the preservation of the Transnistrian regime, is hardly interested in changing a status quo that allows it to influence Moldova.[86]

Since March 2006, negotiations over Transnistria have been in shambles and there was little for the EU to "observe." The EUSR could do little as long as Russia seemed happy with the status quo, Ukraine went through a turbulent political process, the OSCE's role in general declined, and Chisinau and Tiraspol were less inclined to meet each other half way. The mandate of EUSR Kálmán Mizsei ended in February 2011 and was not renewed. His portfolio was integrated into the EU Delegation in Moldova. With the creation of the new EEAS, it was decided to limit the number of EUSRs, and the position in Moldova was not regarded as substantial enough. Meanwhile, the work of EUBAM will continue. A shortcoming is that the mission does not have direct contact with Transnistrian border guards, which limits possibilities to decrease the illegal movement of goods.

Whereas EU-Moldova relations have developed substantially over the last few years, the EU has not been able to leave a heavy footprint in Transnistria. This is not surprising taking into account that Transnistria's leadership is reluctant to work with the EU and sees Russia as its patron, while the EU considers Transnistria as part of Moldova, so any direct talks or programs engaging the Transnistrian leadership are not in the cards. From 2009 to 2011, the EU allocated €3.7 million to humanitarian and social projects, business development projects, and civil society capacity-building projects under "confidence-building measures" aimed at both banks of the river Dniester.[87] The amount increased to €12.0 million in 2011.[88] While Transnistrian NGOs have seen little of these funds, this initiative advances their involvement in European projects and in working with their counterparts in Chisinau.

The AEI government has taken a different stance to the Transnistrian settlement than its Communist predecessor. For former President Vladimir Voronin, the failure to solve the conflict with Russia's help ended in frustration and a hard-line position in Chisinau. The AEI government seeks to build trust internationally, but also with the regime in Tiraspol. Basically, the government has aligned its European vocation with seeking a solution and it knows that both will likely be long-term projects.[89] Since the government cannot deliver quickly on the settlement, it has chosen to strengthen the attractiveness of Moldova in the eyes of Transnistrians, which includes a good business environment, a growing economy, as well as democratization and the prospect of European integration.

Conclusion

The EU's policy toward Moldova has developed within the EU's regional approach: in the 1990s toward the CIS countries and in the 2000s toward the EU's (eastern) neighbors. Due to challenges to European security and stability in the Balkans and a "Russia first!" policy in the post-Soviet region, the EU ranked Moldova low on its external relations agenda. The PCA and TACIS aid were the main ties in the 1990s.

In the 2000s, driven by eastern enlargement, the EU adopted a proactive and comprehensive policy toward its neighborhood aiming at the creation of a zone of stability, security and prosperity on its borders. The Moldovan Communist government turned its initially pro-Russian policy on a course toward eventual EU accession. Due to this, Moldova was able to benefit from the EU's new offers to the neighborhood, such as intensified political dialogue, increased aid, trade and visa liberalization, as well as the EU's involvement in the Transnistria conflict resolution process. Despite growing linkage between the EU and Moldova, the Europeanization of Moldova achieved only limited results. The Communist government in Chisinau was not ready to pursue genuine democratic reforms, and most objectives undertaken in the EU-Moldova Action Plan remained unfulfilled. The EU had limited leverage to press for democratic change in Moldova. First, the prospect of Moldovan Europeanization was weakened due to the lack of an EU accession perspective. Second, the EU took into consideration Russia's role in the country.

The establishment of the Eastern Partnership as the EU's (Europeanization) policy toward its Eastern European neighbors and the arrival of a pro-European government in Chisinau have started a new era in EU-Moldova relations. Moldova aspires to be the privileged partner of the EU in the Eastern Neighbour-hood and the EU needs a "success story" in the region, where prospects of democratic reform are elusive.

So far, there is a risk that on one hand success will be measured by the pro-European intentions of the Moldovan government, and on the other, by the number of negotiation rounds and actions plans signed with the EU. The "success story" will hold only if Moldova, making a good use of the substantial international assistance, curbs corruption, reforms its judiciary and police, and improves human rights and living standards for the population.

Transnistria has been regarded by many experts as the easiest dispute to resolve of the four protracted conflicts in Eastern Europe and the South Caucasus, because of the lack of ethnic strife. The EU stepped up conflict resolution efforts in 2005 by becoming an observer to the mediation mechanism, appointing a special representative, and starting a border assistance mission for Ukraine and Moldova. While Transnistria is firmly on the radar of the EU and some member states, Moldovans themselves have understood that this issue might take longer to resolve. While remaining open to negotiations and suggestions, they understand that economic and democratic development (with EU support) is the best strategy for the eventual reintegration of Transnistria.

Full integration of Moldova in the EU will not be in the cards in the next decade, but further approximation is likely. Political stability and the will to implement reform and EU regulations are the main factors driving Moldova's Europeanization. Most likely, the EU will want to go as far as possible to bring Moldova into its orbit, while simultaneously excluding accession negotiations for the time being. In the end, the EU is interested in a stable and prosperous Moldova, while Moldova needs the EU to expand trade, boost its economy and improve its governance.

Notes

1. For an overview see Sophie Vanhoonacker, "The Institutional Framework," in *International Relations and the European Union*, ed. Christopher Hill and Michael Smith (Oxford: Oxford University Press, 2011), 75–100; Stephan Keukeleire and Jennifer MacNaughtan, *The Foreign Policy of the European Union* (Houndmills: Palgrave Macmillan, 2008), 35–65.

2. The OSCE mission to Moldova has been led by an American since 1995 (mission was established in 1993).

3. Marius Vahl, "The EU and Moldova: a Neglected Relationship," in *The EU and Moldova: On a Fault-line of Europe*, ed. Ann Lewis (London: The Federal Trust, 2004), 173.

4. See Marcin Kosienkowski, *Naddniestrzańska Republika Mołdawska. Determinanty przetrwania* [The Pridnestrovian Moldavian Republic. Survival Determinants] (Toruń: Wydawnictwo Adam Marszałek, 2010), 187–91.

5. Partnership and Cooperation Agreement between the European Union and the Republic of Moldova, Brussels, November 28, 1994, http://eur-lex.europa.eu/LexUriServ /LexUriServ.do?uri=CELEX:21998A0624(01):EN:NOT (accessed July 11, 2011).

6. In fact, the EU envisioned the prospect of free trade in its PCAs with Russia, Ukraine and Moldova, but not with the South Caucasus and Central Asia countries, which suggests the EU foresaw differentiation in relations with the CIS countries.

7. Sergiu Bușcaneanu, "The Relations of Moldova with the EU: Achieved Progress, Encountered Problems, and Future Prospects," in *Integration Perspectives and Synergic Effects of European Transformation in the Countries Targeted by EU Enlargement and Neighbourhood Policies: Moldova*, ed. Igor Munteanu and Sergiu Bușcaneanu (Budapest: Central European University, 2008), 133, https://cens.ceu.hu/sites/default /files/publications/cens-integrationperspectivesmoldova.pdf (accessed July 11, 2011).

8. Ibid., 118.

9. Ibid., 122.

10. Andrei Neguța and Alexandru Simionov, "Moldova and the EU: A View from Chisinau," in Lewis, *The EU and Moldova*, 185–94.

11. Igor Munteanu, "The Political Transformation Process in Moldova," in Munteanu and Bușcaneanu, *Integration Perspectives*, 28.

12. Ibid., 29.

13. See Elisabeth Johansson-Nogués, "The EU and its Neighbourhood: An Overview," in *Governing Europe's Neighbourhood. Partners or periphery?* ed. Katja Weber, Michael Smith, and Michael Baun (Manchester: Manchester University Press, 2007), 21–35.

14. European Neighbourhood Policy Strategy Paper. Communication from the Commission of the European Communities, Brussels, May 12, 2004, COM(2004) 373 final.

15. See "Republic of Moldova-EU Action Plan," *Democracy and Governing in Moldova* (e-journal) 2, no. 33 (2004), http://www.e-democracy.md/en/e-journal/20040630/ (accessed July 11, 2011).

16. EU-Moldova Action Plan, Brussels, February 22, 2005, http://ec.europa.eu /world/enp/pdf/action_plans/moldova_enp_ap_final_en.pdf (accessed July 11, 2011).

17. Later, the AP was prolonged by mutual agreement beyond February 2008.

18. See Sergiu Bușcaneanu, *How Far is the European Neighbourhood Policy a Substantial Offer for Moldova?* (Leeds, 2006), http://www.e-democracy.md/files/enp-moldova.pdf (accessed July 11, 2011).

19. See Marius Vahl, "The Europeanisation of the Transnistrian Conflict," *CEPS Policy Brief*, no. 73 (2005), http://aei.pitt.edu/6613/1/1227_73.pdf (accessed July 11, 2011); Kosienkowski, *Naddniestrzańska Republika Mołdawska*, 179–87.

20. George Dura, "EUBAM Moldova–Ukraine. The EU Border Assistance Mission to the Republic of Moldova and Ukraine," in *European Security and Defence Policy: The First Ten Years (1999–2009)*, ed. Giovanni Grevi, Damien Helly, and Daniel Keohane (Paris: EU Institute for Security Studies, 2009), 275–85.

21. Xymena Kurowska and Benjamin Tallis, "EU Border Assistance Mission: Beyond Border Monitoring?" *European Foreign Affairs Review* 14 (2009): 47–64.

22. MAEIE al Republicii Moldova [Moldovan Ministry of Foreign Affairs and European Integration], "Comentariul pe marginea declarațiilor reprezentantului oficial al MAE al Federației Ruse" [Comment on the official statements of the MFA of the Russian Federation], July 22, 2011, http://www.rusia.mfa.md/news-from-moldova-ro/?news= 487628 (accessed August 16, 2011).

23. European Union Border Assistance Mission to Moldova and Ukraine, "EUBAM Impact," http://www.eubam.org/en/quick/impact (accessed July 11, 2011).

24. In 2003, the Dutch OSCE Chairmanship-in-Office proposed the deployment of an OSCE peace support operation in Moldova. The operation would be led by the EU with possible Russian and Ukrainian contributions. However, Russia opposed any change of its peacekeeping mission in Transnistria. In 2006, the then-EU special representative to Moldova, Adriaan Jacobovits de Szeged, promoted an idea within the EU of inclining Russia toward a joint EU-Russia operation in Moldova, but a significant number of EU member states opposed the initiative, not least because of an unwillingness to spoil relations with Russia. See Nicu Popescu, "EU and the Eastern Neighbourhood: Reluctant Involvement in Conflict Resolution," *European Foreign Affairs Review* 14 (2009): 463–65.

25. Ibid., 465.

26. Jos Boonstra, "From a Weak State to a Reunified Moldova: New Opportunities to Resolve the Trasndniestria Conflict," *NATO Defence College Research Paper*, no. 23 (2005): 2–7.

27. Kosienkowski, *Naddniestrzańska Republika Mołdawska*, 183.

28. Alyona Getmanchuk et al., *Scenarios for the Development of the Transnistria Conflict: Challenges to European Security* (Kiev: Institute of World Policy, 2011), 91.

29. Sergey Shirokov, "European integration policies in the context of Transdniestrian conflict settlement," in *Moldova–Transdniestria: Working Together for a Prosperous Future Negotiation Process*, ed. Denis Matveev et al. (Chisinau: Cu drag, 2009), 211.

30. Małgorzata Jakubiak, ed., *Prospects for EU-Moldova economic relations*, CASE Report 67 (Warsaw: CASE, 2006), 39; European Commission, "EU Trade Statistics: Moldova," http://trade.ec.europa.eu/doclib/docs/2006/september/tradoc_113419.pdf (accessed July 12, 2011).

31. "Exportul din regiunea transnistreană s-a redus cu 14%" [Transnistrian exports fell by 14%], *Infotag*, April 27, 2011, http://www.azi.md/ro/story/17990 (accessed August 15, 2011).

32. Jakubiak, *Prospects for EU-Moldova*, 38.

33. Ibid.

34. European Commission, "European Commission proposes additional autonomous trade preferences (ATPs) for Moldova," press release, Brussels, November 14, 2007, http://trade.ec.europa.eu/doclib/docs/2007/november/tradoc_136747.pdf (accessed July 12, 2011).

35. Andris Spruds et al., *Analysis of the EU's Assistance to Moldova*, briefing paper, Directorate-General for External Policies of the Union (Brussels: European Parliament, 2008), 9.

36. Agreement between the European Community and the Republic of Moldova on the Facilitation of the Issuance of Visas, Brussels, October 10, 2007, http://www.chisinau.diplo.de/contentblob/1840194/Daten/142306/Acord_facilitare_eng.pdf (accessed July 12, 2011).

37. "Joint Declaration on a Mobility Partnership between the European Union and the Republic of Moldova," Luxembourg, June 5, 2008, http://www.iom.md/attachments/086_EU-MD%20Mobility%20Parntership%20Declaration.pdf (accessed July 12, 2011).

38. As for 2006, approximately one-quarter of the economically active population of Moldova worked abroad. Remittances are one of the most important sources of income for many Moldovan households, while it also helps to shorten the country's trade account deficit. See Alin Chindea et al., *Migration in Moldova: A country profile* (Geneva: Inter-

national Organization for Migration, 2008), http://www.iom.md/materials/moldova _migration_profile_april_2008.pdf (accessed July 12, 2011).

39. Igor Botan, "Republic of Moldova shall join EU one day, somehow..." *Democracy and Governing in Moldova* (e-journal) 6, no. 120 (2008), http://www.e-democracy .md/en/monitoring/politics/comments/200806301/ (accessed July 13, 2011).

40. Council of the European Union, "Council Conclusions on the Republic of Moldova," 2896th General Affairs Council meeting, Luxembourg, October 13, 2008, http:// www.consilium.europa.eu/ueDocs/cms_Data/docs/pressData/en/gena/103287.pdf (accessed July 13, 2011).

41. According to this plan, named after Dmitriy Kozak, a senior advisor to then-Russian President Vladimir Putin, the settlement of the conflict was conditioned on the Russian military presence in Transnistria until 2020 and Transnistria's (and the Gagauz autonomy) equal status in the federation.

42. Buşcaneanu, "The Relations of Moldova with the EU," 119.

43. Ibid., 105–11.

44. Ibid., 110.

45. Ibid., 111.

46. Institute of Public Policy, "Barometer of Public Opinion. The Dynamic," April 2008, http://www.ipp.md/public/files/Barometru/2008/BOP_March_April_2008_dynamic .pdf (accessed July 12, 2011).

47. Sergiu Buşcaneanu, ed., *Moldova and EU in European Neighbourhood Policy Context: Implementation of EU-Moldova Action Plan (February 2005–January 2008)* (Chisinau: ARC, 2008), http://www.expert-grup.org/library_upld/d64.pdf (accessed July 21, 2011); Dumitru Mînzărari, "EU-Moldova Action Plan: An unfinished job or a complete failure?" *IDIS "Viitorul" Discussion paper* 2 (2008), http://www.viitorul.org /public/1113/en/DP_2+ENG.pdf (accessed July 21, 2011).

48. Giselle Bosse, "The EU's Relations with Moldova: Governance, Partnership or Ignorance?" *Europe-Asia Studies* 62, no. 8 (2010): 1306–7.

49. Theodor Tudoroiu, "Structural factors vs. regime change: Moldova's difficult quest for democracy," *Democratization* 18, no. 1 (2011): 241.

50. Cristian Ghinea and Sergiu Panainte, "The Political System from the Republic of Moldova and its Evolution," in *Moldova. At the Crossroads*, ed. Sergiu Panainte (Bucharest: Soros Foundation Romania, 2009), 104–5.

51. Ghinea and Panainte, "The Political System;" Civic Coalition for Free and Fair Elections and League for Defense of Human Rights of Moldova, *Reports regarding the monitoring of the electoral process: 2009 Parliamentary elections*, 4 vols., 2009, http:// www.ladom.org.md/en/?p=rapoarte&id=0 (accessed July 24, 2011).

52. International Election Observation Mission, "Parliamentary Election, Republic of Moldova – 5 April 2009. Statement of Preliminary Findings and Conclusions," Chisinau, April 6, 2009, http://www.osce.org/odihr/elections/moldova/36823 (accessed July 13, 2011).

53. Balazs Jarabik, "Moldova between Elections: Europe or Isolation?" *FRIDE Policy Brief*, no. 16 (2009), http://www.fride.org/download/PB16_Moldava_eng_jul09 .pdf (accessed July 13, 2011).

54. European Parliament, Resolution, "On the situation in the Republic of Moldova," May 7, 2009, http://www.europarl.europa.eu/sides/getDoc.do?pubRef=-//EP//TEXT +TA+P6-TA-2009-0384+0+DOC+XML+V0//EN (accessed July 13, 2011).

55. Council of the European Union, "Council conclusions on the Republic of Moldova," 2950th General Affairs Council meeting, Luxembourg, June 15, 2009, http://

www.consilium.europa.eu/uedocs/cms_data/docs/pressdata/en/gena/108465.pdf (accessed July 13, 2011).

56. Jarabik, "Moldova between Elections."

57. The EU demonstrated its support for the coalition's renewal through the post-electoral visits of Polish, Swedish and German ministers, as well as the president of European Parliament to Moldova, whereas Russia supported a coalition that would include the Communist party.

58. Herman Van Rompuy, "Remarks by Herman Van Rompuy President of the European Council following the meeting with Vladimir Filat Prime Minister of the Republic of Moldova," Chisinau, July 6, 2011, http://europa.eu/rapid/pressReleasesAction.do ?reference=PRES/11/228&format=HTML&aged=0&language=EN&guiLanguage=en (accessed July 15, 2011).

59. European Commission and the High Representative of the European Union for Foreign Affairs and Security Policy, *Implementation of the European Neighbourhood Policy in 2010. Country report: Republic of Moldova*, Joint Staff Working Paper (Brussels, 2011), http://ec.europa.eu/world/enp/pdf/progress2011/sec_11_643_en.pdf (accessed July 15, 2011).

60. In 2010, the only "free" country in the region—Ukraine—has been downgraded to "partly free," according to the Freedom House report *Freedom in the World*.

61. The ratings are based on a scale of 1 to 7, with 1 representing the highest and 7 the lowest level of democratic progress. See *Nations in Transit 2011* (Washington, DC: Freedom House, 2011), http://www.freedomhouse.org/images/File/nit/2011/NIT-2011-Tables.pdf (accessed July 26, 2011).

62. William Crowther, "Moldova," in *Nations in Transit*, 371, http://www .freedomhouse.org/images/File/nit/2011/NIT-2011-Moldova.pdf (accessed July 26, 2011).

63. World Bank/IFC, *Doing Business 2010. Reforming through difficult times* (Washington, DC: IBRD/World Bank, 2009), http://www.doingbusiness.org/~/media /FPDKM/Doing%20Business/Documents/Annual-Reports/English/DB10-FullReport.pdf (accessed August 1, 2011).

64. "Second Joint Progress Report. Negotiations on the EU-republic of Moldova Association Agreement," Chisinau, April 11, 2011, http://www.eeas.europa.eu/moldova /docs/2011_05_aa_joint_progress_report2_en.pdf (accessed July 16 2011).

65. EU Delegation to Moldova, "Framework Document for the Comprehensive institution Building Programme 2011-2013 for the Republic of Moldova is signed," November 24, 2010, http://eeas.europa.eu/delegations/moldova/press_corner/all_news/news /2010/20101124_01_en.htm (accessed July 17, 2011).

66. Evghenia Sleptsova, "Shedding light on the ongoing EU-Moldova trade liberalisation," *Moldova's Foreign Policy Statewatch*, no. 13 (2010), http://www.viitorul.org /public/3111/en/Policy_Statewatch13_en.pdf (accessed 18 August, 2011).

67. Cristian Ghinea and Victor Chirilă, *EU-Moldova negotiations. What is to be discussed, what could be achieved?* (Bucharest–Chisinau, 2010), 21.

68. Raül Hernández i Sagrera, "Moldova: Pioneering Justice and Home Affairs Co-operation with the EU in the Eastern Partnership," *Moldova's Foreign Policy Statewatch*, no. 30 (2011), http://www.viitorul.org/public/3466/en/Policy%20Statewatch30_en.pdf (accessed July 17, 2011).

69. Ibid.

70. Raül Hernández i Sagrera, *'Mission Impossible'? Visa Liberalization Seen From Within the EU*, EaP Community, June 13, 2011, http://www.easternpartnership.org /community/debate/mission-impossible-visa-liberalization-seen-within-eu (accessed August 16, 2011).

71. For more information on EU funding to Moldova see the website of the State Chancellery of Moldova http://www.ncu.moldova.md/en/section/20.

72. "Basescu push for Moldova in next EU accession wave," *The Diplomat Bucharest* 6, no. 1 (2010), http://www.thediplomat.ro/articol.php?id=792 (accessed July 25, 2011).

73. By July 2011, four meetings of the group took place: The first meeting was held in January 2010 in Brussels, the second—on June 2010 in Luxembourg, the third—on September 2010 in Chisinau attended by a majority of EU member states, and the fourth took place on April 2011 in Luxembourg.

74. Eduard Tugui, "Republic of Moldova-Romania: Streamlining Strategic Partnership for European Integration," *Moldova's Foreign Policy Statewatch*, no. 22 (2011), http://www.viitorul.org/public/3353/en/Policy%20Statewatch22_en.pdf (accessed July 25, 2011).

75. Polish Foreign Ministry, "Non-paper with Polish proposals on a future shape of the policy of the enlarged EU towards its Eastern neighbours," January 2003, http://www .msz.gov.pl/Non-paper,with,Polish,proposals,concerning,policy,towards,the,new,Eastern ,neighbours,after,EU,enlargement,2041.html (accessed July 25, 2011).

76. In December 2010, foreign ministers of Poland and Sweden visited Moldova to encourage the renewal of the AEI government after the November snap election. Their visit was followed by that of President of the European Parliament Jerzy Buzek, who is also a Pole. In March 2011, the Polish prime minister made an official visit to Moldova for the first time, to participate in the EU-Moldova Forum organized under the aegis of the Polish government.

77. Official webpage of Common Visa Application Centre, http://www.cac.md /about_en.html (accessed August 11, 2011).

78. Alexandru Fala, "Economic Cooperation with the EU – A Prerequisite for Development of the Republic of Moldova," *Moldova's Foreign Policy Statewatch*, no. 28 (2011), http://www.viitorul.org/public/3443/en/Policy%20Statewatch28_en.pdf (accessed July 25, 2011).

79. Leonid Litra and Dumitru Rusu, "Opportunities in Moldovan-German Relations," *Moldova's Foreign Policy Statewatch*, no. 15 (2010), http://www.viitorul.org/public /3156/en/Policy_Statewatch15_en.pdf (accessed July 25, 2011).

80. Iris Kempe, "The German Impact on the European Neighbourhood Policy," *Foreign Policy in Dialogue* 7, no. 19 (2006): 33, http://www.deutsche-aussenpolitik.de /newsletter/issue19.pdf (accessed July 25, 2011).

81. European Parliament, Resolution, "The European Parliament's recommendations to the Council, the Commission and the EEAS on the negotiations between the EU and the Republic of Moldova on the Association Agreement (2011/2079(INI))," September 15, 2011, http://www.europarl.europa.eu/sides/getDoc.do?pubRef=-//EP//TEXT+TA +P7-TA-2011-0385+0+DOC+XML+V0//EN&language=IT (accessed October 19, 2011).

82. European Parliament, Resolution, "On the review of the European Neighbourhood Policy – Eastern Dimension," April 7, 2011, http://www.europarl.europa.eu /sides/getDoc.do?pubRef=-//EP//TEXT+TA+P7-TA-2011-0153+0+DOC+XML+V0//EN (accessed July 26, 2011).

83. Delegation of the European Union to Moldova, "President Buzek concludes official visit to Moldova," press release, December 11, 2010, http://www.eeas.europa.eu /delegations/moldova/press_corner/all_news/news/2010/20101211_01_en.htm (accessed July 26, 2011).

84. Jerzy Buzek, "Integrating the wider Europe after the Lisbon Treaty. Speech delivered at the Wider Europe Conference," Brussels, February 3, 2011, http://www.europarl

.europa.eu/president/view/en/press/speeches/sp-2011/sp-2011-February/speeches-2011-February-2.html (accessed July 26, 2011.)

85. Vladimir Socor, "German Diplomacy Tilts Toward Russia On Transnistria Negotiations," *Eurasia Daily Monitor*, June 6, 2011, http://www.jamestown.org/programs/edm/single/?tx_ttnews[tt_news]=38017&cHash=1d459b5f429bd05b6407b4d991087e1e (accessed July 17, 2011).

86. Theodor Tudoroiu, "The European Union, Russia, and the Future of the Transnistrian Frozen Conflict," *East European Politics and Societies*, published online before print, April 15, 2011:16, doi: 10.1177/0888325411404885.

87. Getmanchuk et al., *Scenarios for the Development*, 89.

88. "Annexes. Annual Action Programme 2011 Republic of Moldova," in *Commission Implementing Decision of 13/07/2011 on the Annual Action Programme 2011 in favour of the Republic of Moldova to be financed under Article 19 08 01 03 of the general budget of the European Union*, accessed 29 July, 2011, http://ec.europa.eu/europeaid/documents/aap/2011/af_aap_2011_mda.pdf

89. For an overview of the AEI's policy on Transnistria see Marcin Kosienkowski, "The Alliance for European integration and the Transnistrian conflict settlement," *Sprawy Narodowościowe–Nationalities Affairs* 38 (2011): 23–32.

Chapter Six

France: Unfulfilled Potential as a Major EU Partner of Moldova

Florent Parmentier

There is a paradox in French relations with Moldova: Despite strong connections in culture and to a lesser extent in economic ties, France is not seen as a major political partner for Moldova, falling behind other countries in this regard. Yet as a key European Union member state in the decision-making process, France was instrumental in supporting Romania's quest to achieve a membership perspective. The reason France supported Romania's bid to the European Union was founded on close cultural relations based on common Latin roots, roots that are largely shared by a majority of the Moldovan population. Indeed, France certainly has a political role in Moldova, but so far it has not been the vocal EU partner for Moldova that it was for Romania.

The study of French foreign policy making generally focuses attention on the French presidency (as a part of the *domaine réservé*, i.e., "presidential prerogative") and the foreign affairs minister (the *quai d'Orsay*).[1] Other actors are also relevant to understanding French foreign policy, but to a lesser extent (e.g. parliament). These actors may have a different set of priorities or partners abroad, and their relative engagement in various issues does shape the outcome of French foreign policy.

Indeed, the very question of a specific "French Moldovan policy" should be raised: How do we define it? What are French national interests in this country? To what extent is this policy specifically "Moldovan" in its content?

French foreign policy toward Moldova must be conceived in accordance to four dimensions of French foreign policy: its bilateral relationship with Moldova, Russia, Romania and the rest of Europe. These four relationships shape French policy by helping to define precise positions across a comprehensive range of Moldovan issues.

Bilateral Relations: Culture, Economy and Politics

As in other countries, Moldova has only a limited place in the headlines of the French press. News reports are generally focused on wide-ranging trafficking, the Transnistrian conflict, and European integration. But Moldova is generally not paid a great deal of attention, resulting in a lack of knowledge about the country. Still, bilateral relations have developed between France and Moldova since the independence of the latter.

Bilateral relations often result from the activities of a vibrant diaspora, which drives close relations, such as the French-Armenian community of around four hundred thousand descendants, who established themselves after the massacres of 1915. The impact of a diaspora is determined by three factors:[2] the material, cultural, and organizational resources available to them; the opportunity structures in the host country; and the diaspora's motivation to maintain solidarity with their home country. Unfortunately, a significant portion of the estimated twenty thousand Moldovans living in France are not legal residents. This limits the Moldovan community's possibilities. Moreover, this relatively new community has been unable to establish strong links with immigrants from Moldova who arrived several decades earlier.[3] Finally, there are some NGOs involved in the Moldovan-French relationship, but their size is still limited.

In this context, the role of culture as a bridge between the two countries, and more precisely the role of language, has been crucial to the development of bilateral relations. Language has often been regarded as a burning issue in internal politics in Moldova,[4] but the language question also has some international ramifications, particularly as regards the French-speaking world. As early as 1989, the first committee for the Alliance française was launched in Moldova, thanks to a local group of professors, two years before the end of the Soviet Union. Since 1991, the Alliance française has played a key role in fostering cultural, scientific and technical cooperation.[5] For example, the first Tempus programs in Moldova drew on expertise from French universities in agro-industrial development, like the University of Bordeaux on wine-making processes. These developments correspond with an official report of the French Senate issued in 1999. It placed a priority on higher education and training, offering scholarships to Moldovan students and training to high civil servants (mainly in the health and agricultural sectors).[6] In 2010, it was estimated that around 50 percent of Moldovan students studied the French language in school, and around 1,200 pursued their higher education in France.[7]

Beyond these well-established linguistic relations, *la Francophonie*[8] also concerns multilateral institutions, which emerged in the second half of the twentieth century. Chisinau was accepted in l'Organisation internationale de la francophonie (International Organization of the Francophonie) as a full member in 1997, during the Francophone Summit in Hanoi. Moldova was the third country from Central and Eastern Europe to integrate into this multilateral organization, following Romania and Bulgaria. The OIF has expanded throughout Central and Eastern Europe, both for historical reasons (French influence throughout various periods of the region's history), and pragmatic ones (a will for rapprochement between European partners).[9] A Maison des savoirs ("House of knowledge"), sponsored by the OIF and a network of associations opened in Chisinau in January 2010, only the second in the world. Its presence helps explain why the Moldovan authorities have repeatedly been in favor of organizing a Francophone Summit in Chisinau, first in 2012 and currently in 2014.

Economic actors can play a major role in the development of bilateral relations, be it as exporters or foreign investors. France, a key economic partner of Romania, has nevertheless had a limited impact in Moldova. The main sectors targeted by French firms for investment are industry, technology, banking and agro-industry. In industry, Lafarge, a major French industrial company that specializes in cement, has invested since 1999 in the Rezina plant, one of the largest in Moldova. Telephone services provider France Telecom invested in the local market in 1998, under the name of Voxtel; this market leader was rebranded as Orange in April 2007. In the banking sector, Société Générale acquired Mobiasbancă in January 2007, one of the largest commercial banks, with a very large network across the entire Moldovan territory. In agro-industries, Lactalis and Via Lacta (dairy groups), Bargues (nuts processing), and Beten (a service company) are major French investors in Moldova. Finally, some small and medium enterprises have invested in call centers or outsourcing activities. The visibility of French investors needs to be considered relative to the small size of the domestic market. As a trading partner, France is ranked fourteenth for Moldovan exports (1.3 percent market share) and tenth for imports (2.0 percent).[10] The Moldovan market is not crucial for these major French firms, and while opportunities for French investment exist, they cannot be considered priorities for many economic actors.

On the diplomatic and political levels, France was among the first EU member states to establish an embassy in Chisinau, at a time when many countries preferred to manage Moldovan affairs through their diplomatic services in Moscow, Bucharest or Kiev.[11] Political bilateral relations can be evaluated through various dimensions: official visits at a high level, cooperation between different official bodies or links between civil societies. Until 2011, Jacques Chirac was the first and only French president to visit Moldova on his trip to Ukraine in September 1998. Mircea Snegur (January 1993), and Petru Lucinschi (September 1997) went to Paris as presidents of Moldova. In the meantime, several visits have taken place at the ministerial level. Beyond a tiny circle, French politicians have only a limited knowledge of Moldova. Senator Josette Durrieu, who for fifteen years (1994–2010) wrote the Moldova reports of the Council of Europe, is a remarkable exception.[12] At the level of local authorities, several agreements have established twin cities, among others Grenoble and Chisinau since the mid-1970s), Villefranche-sur-Saône and Călăraşi, Greater Lyon and Bălţi, Marcy l'étoile and Holercani. Yet, the relative density of twin city networks between France and Moldova is much weaker than between France and Romania.[13] As regards political parties, the Democratic Party of Marian Lupu and the Liberal Democratic Party of Vlad Filat have established partnerships with the French Socialist Party[14] in 2002 and the Union for a Popular Movement[15] in 2011. Two foundations close to these parties, the Fondation Jean Jaurès and the Fondation Robert Schuman, have already started initiatives with Moldovan partners,[16] since French NGO activity in Moldova is limited.

The French View through a Russian Prism?

Russia has a major influence in the post-Soviet space in general, including Moldova, through various means (political influence, foreign investments, Transnistria, etc.). To some extent, French foreign policy toward Moldova is determined by larger relationships, such as that with Russia.

France is sometimes accused by Central Europe of being largely influenced by Russian foreign policy in the region, and maintaining a low political profile vis-à-vis the post-Soviet states. Some analysts openly favor a much closer relationship with Russia, rather than one of competition.[17] As a matter of fact, France and Russia share a long tradition of good relations over the past century, dating back to the French-Russian alliance prior to WWI, which was maintained by Charles de Gaulle, François Mitterrand, and Jacques Chirac. In Mitterrand's view, Russia remains an essential partner on the European continent in order to balance rising German power. In accordance with this policy, Jacques Chirac took a strict stance against the Iraq war in 2003, alongside Gerhard Schröder and Vladimir Putin.

During his electoral campaign in 2007, Nicolas Sarkozy was considered a more pro-American and less Russian-leaning leader than his predecessors. His criticism of human rights and the Chechen conflict during the election campaign were often noted.[18] Yet, the Georgian-Russian war of August 2008 marked a U-turn in Sarkozy's foreign policy.[19] A new policy of rapprochement toward Russia was initiated, including economic relations, (where France was largely outdistanced by Germany) and even in military affairs. Hence, in June 2011, despite fierce opposition from Central and Eastern European countries, France agreed to sell two Mistral-class assault warships, the largest ever military deal between a NATO country and Russia.

This generally good level of cooperation does not mean, however, that French and Russian diplomacy are a zero-sum game in Moldova—good relations with Russia are not always at the expense of other regional actors, such as Moldova. France may agree on many levels with Russia, and seek its support or neutrality on major international issues (e.g. Kosovo, Iran), while disagreeing with it on other issues. For instance, France has never recognized nor encouraged Transnistrian independence, and has supported Moldovan sovereignty. A policy of engagement with Russia does not mean that other Eastern European partners are simply marginalized. After all, Germany has taken the lead in discussions with Russia about the Transnistrian issue, notably in the French-German-Russian Deauville Summit,[20] while at the same time being the largest EU partner for Russia. France shares the German position, which assumes that Russia should ultimately withdraw its troops from Moldova's territory and allow Moldova to reunify with Transnistria, while Russia may receive compensation, including a major role in European security affairs.[21]

The Romanian Factor: A Driver in French Policy toward Moldova?

France has been a major source of inspiration for Romania since the mid-nineteenth century, when it became independent from the Ottoman Empire, notably thanks to Napoleon III's actions. Common Latin roots explain the cultural affinity between the two countries, and their often-close relations. This role was well described by Romanian historian Nicolae Iorga,[22] and summarized by the most famous Romanian diplomat, Nicolae Titulescu, founder of the League of Nations: "When it comes to Romania and France, it is difficult to separate sentiments from reason."[23] After WWI, French geographer Emmanuel de Martonne, a close adviser to Georges Clemenceau, played a crucial role in the integration of Bessarabia[24] into the Romanian territory, by advocating in advance of the peace treaties. The interwar period was the climax of this special relationship, which was reinvigorated only after the demise of Nicolae Ceaușescu in 1989.

Starting from the 1990s, France intensively lobbied in favor of Romania's membership in the European Union (and to a lesser extent for Bulgaria), in order to counterbalance what was perceived as "the recreation of a Mitteleuropa" under German aegis. Although Romania had more difficulties than many other countries in meeting European standards, it fulfilled its membership in 2007. At the end of 2008, France was the third investor in this country, behind Austria and Germany, and it held strong positions in the automobile industry, banking, agro-industry, etc. The French economic presence in Romania might lead some investors in the medium term to break into Moldovan markets (e.g., Société Générale, well implanted in Romania through its local branch BRD, subsequently purchased Moldovan bank Mobiasbancă). The economic development of Romania will probably encourage this process.

Politically, bilateral cooperation has flourished through regular top-level official visits and grassroots activities, both from local governments and NGOs. Nicolas Sarkozy signed a strategic partnership with Romanian President Traian Băsescu in 2008, in order to develop cooperation and restore France's political profile after several misunderstandings. He then declared at a press conference that the partnership "reinforces [his] conviction that all Balkan countries, with the addition of Moldova, have a perspective, in due time, to integrate with the European Union."[25] This declaration shows how the Romanian-French relations may have a decisive impact on French policy toward Moldova. In this regard, Romanian credibility as a leader of the Black Sea region remains crucial. Unfortunately, French-Romanian relations soured after the "Roma crisis"[26] in August 2010: For domestic political reasons, Sarkozy started to loudly criticize his Romanian counterpart, and oppose Romania's accession to the Schengen area. Laurent Wauquiez, then-French minister for European affairs, pointed to the fact that the Romanian and Bulgarian borders were a zone of regional instability, suggesting that it originates roughly 75 percent of illegal immigration in Europe.[27] The low credibility of Romania as a coherent and consistent European actor clearly limits its capacity to influence EU partners.

In conclusion, Romania might be a political driver for French foreign policy toward Moldova, but so far its limited place in the European decision-making process has limited this role.

France's Neighborhood Policy and the Eastern Partnership

French foreign policy toward Moldova is determined by its relations with other relevant actors of the region (Russia, Romania), but also by the EU integration process, which leads to adaptation and change in its national foreign policy.

France has developed its own concept of the European Neighbourhood Policy, by insisting on strong human and cultural links with the Southern Mediterranean countries. It sought to integrate these countries in the ENP at the beginning of the process (in 2003), and it has been a strong advocate of the Union pour la Méditerranée (Union for the Mediterranean). In this sense, France has paid much less attention to Eastern Europe than Germany and Poland, the two leading countries in the region. Moreover, France has generally been reluctant with regard to new EU enlargements, as it implies a complete change of the project the EU founding fathers envisioned.[28] While France was a central force in the realization of the UfM, Nicolas Sarkozy did not attend the Prague Summit in May 2009, when the Eastern Partnership was launched, unlike several other European heads of state and government.[29]

French diplomacy is not convinced that the Eastern Partnership should lead to the recognition of a European perspective for the countries concerned, for domestic as well as geopolitical reasons. With regard to the former, the policy of enlargement has lost support in French public opinion, a fact confirmed by the negative results of the referendum on the European Constitution in 2005. As Maxime Lefebvre stated concerning the latter, the French position can be summarized as follows:

> As long as a European (membership) perspective for the Eastern neighbors is not the issue, France is willing to strengthen this relationship while also strengthening the strategic partnership with Russia. The choice for the EU is not between Russia and its neighbors. By the same logic, the choice for these countries is not to be either in the European or the Russian *sphère d'influence*.[30]

In spite of this opposition to enlargement, France and Moldova try to cooperate pragmatically on European integration, a top priority for bilateral relations, notably through training and expertise. In April 2011, French Prime Minister François Fillon stated that Moldova should be a part of the enlarged Europe.[31] Yet, when it comes to the details, negotiations on EU integration are more difficult. Some French lobbies, notably in agro-industry, are not especially happy to see new competitors, since the EU wants to conclude a deep and comprehensive free trade agreement with Moldova, a wine producing and agricultural country. Similarly, French leadership is currently very reluctant on visa liberalization issues, which strains relations with Moldova. Consequently, in October 2010, French diplomacy was very reluctant to conclude a visa-free Action Plan with Moldova at the level of European foreign ministers. According to the French position, if the European Commission prepares this kind of agreement, the initiative should need approval from the member states.[32]

In short, French involvement in the EaP is limited, but its cooperation with Moldova trends more pragmatically toward concrete actions of rapprochement rather than abstract discourses on long-term European perspectives.

Conclusion

French foreign policy is characterized by a strong emphasis on cultural links, a will to develop economic relations and relative weakness in the political sphere. A significant cultural presence, due to historical and linguistic heritage, has helped strengthen bilateral relations. The limited size of the internal market cannot attract very many French economic actors, but bilateral relations are developing—more in terms of investments than trade. In political terms, France does not have well-funded political foundations comparable to those of Germany or the US; French political parties have only limited relations with their Moldovan counterparts, due to the relative weakness of French political parties.

European integration constitutes a major factor in the evolution of French foreign policy. For now, French diplomacy is not very desirous of proceeding with additional EU enlargements. Yet European integration has become a central focus of Moldovan politics, and French policy has tried to adapt by proposing cooperation in the relevant fields of European integration. French foreign policy toward Moldova lacks political consistency, but the country could potentially be a major partner for European integration, Moldova's declared goal.

Notes

1. The *domaine réservé* is particularly relevant in some areas, such as African affairs or international negotiations. Beyond the *quai d'Orsay*, there is the Ministry (or the Secretary of State) of European Affairs, which may also have a say in neighborhood policy.

2. Milton J. Esman, "Diasporas and International Relations," in *Modern Diasporas in International Politics*, ed. Gabriel Sheffer (New York: Saint Martin's, 1986), 336.

3. Several thousand people from Moldova, notably Jews, who fled the 1903 and 1905 pogroms, settled in France. However, they do not identify themselves with the currently existing Moldova, since the territory they fled was either under Romanian, Russian or

Soviet influence. Among these people, Robert Badinter is probably the most famous, a former minister of justice who obtained the end of the death penalty in France (1981).

4. Debates on Moldovan identity, which have been paid much attention by social scientists, focus on language questions, e.g. the nature of a so-called "Moldovan language" or competition between the Russian and Romanian languages.

5. See Ion Gutu, "La francophonie moldave après 1991," *La francopolyphonie: langue et identité* 1 (2007): 72–78. Stella Ghervas, arguably the most famous Moldovan historian abroad, was awarded the prix Guizot from l'Académie française in December 2009 for a book she wrote in French.

6. André Dulait, André Boyer, and André Rouvière, *La Moldavie: bâtir les fondements de l'identité nationale*, Sénat: Rapport d'information no. 102, November 29, 1999, http://www.senat.fr/rap/r99-102/r99-1020.html (accessed July 4, 2011).

7. "L'Europe fait rêver la Moldavie," *Toute l'Europe*, April 15, 2011, http://www.touteleurope.eu/index.php?id=2778&cmd=FICHE&uid=5235&no_cache=1&display%5Bfiche%5D=5235 (accessed April 21, 2011).

8. In French, there is a distinction between *Francophonie* and *francophonie*: the former refers to the multilateral institutions created in the early 1970s, while the latter refers to the community of speakers using French. See Dominique Wolton, *Demain la francophonie* (Paris: Flammarion, 2006).

9. Alexandre Wolff, "Francophonie et Europe Centrale et Orientale: les logiques d'une alliance," *Le courrier des pays de l'Est*, no. 1011 (January 2001): 9–39.

10. Biroul Național de Statistică al Republicii Moldova [National Bureau of Statistics of the Republic of Moldova], "Activitatea de comerț exterior a Republicii Moldova în ianuarie–mai 2011" [Activities of foreign trade of the Republic of Moldova in January–May 2011], July 11, 2011, http://www.statistica.md/newsview.php?l=ro&idc=168&id=3457 (accessed July 12, 2011).

11. The country was managed from Moscow by Pierre Morel, then French Ambassador in Russia, between 1992 and 1996. Serge Smessow was the first French Ambassador to settle in Chisinau, in 1996. He was at the time *Ambassadeur itinérant*, which means he was not on a full-time basis in Chisinau, sharing his time between Chisinau and Paris (he was appointed French ambassador for the EaP in April 2011). The first full-time ambassador in Chisinau was Edmond Pamboukdjian in 2003.

12. Moreover, several French institutions have developed ties with their Moldovan counterparts, e.g. Conseil économique, social et environnemental (the Economic, Social and Environmental Council). One of the council members, Evelyne Pichenot, wrote a report on civil society in Moldova for the Brussels-based European Social and Economic Committee in 2007. The first twinning of parliamentarian activities has been realized by a French and Hungarian consortium, including the parliaments of both countries.

13. It can be estimated that the density of relations is proportionally fifteen times less between Moldova and France in comparison with Romania and France. See Florent Parmentier, *Moldavie. Les atouts de la francophonie* (Paris: Non Lieu, 2010), 78–79.

14. The French Socialist Party started in 2002 to cooperate with the Democratic Party of Moldova.

15. The agreement was signed on June 13, 2011, in Chisinau, in the presence of Thierry Mariani, secretary of state for transport.

16. Fondation Jean Jaurès has focused its cooperation on electoral training and co-operation. It co-organized, along with the French NGO "Les Moldaviens," the first French-Moldovan Summit in the Moldovan parliament in July 2007. Fondation Robert Schuman has worked with the Moldovan parliament on other occasions, and has developed several activities—training, political cooperation with parliamentarians, etc.

17. Henri de Grossouvre, "La révision du traité de l'Elysée, l'Europe et la Russie," *Revue défense nationale*, no. 2 (2003): 67–77.

18. Jolyon M. Howorth, "Le nouveau Président et la politique étrangère et de sécurité," *Annuaire Français des Relations Internationales*, 2008, 360.

19. Marcel H. van Herpen, "The Foreign Policy of Nicolas Sarkozy: Not Principled, Opportunistic and Amateurish," *Cicero Foundation Great Debate Paper*, no. 1 (February 2010), http://www.cicerofoundation.org/lectures/Marcel_H_Van_Herpen_FOREIGN_POLICY_SARKOZY.pdf (accessed August 25, 2010).

20. In the final declaration, the French-German-Russian Deauville Summit (October 18–19, 2010) proposed to start closer cooperation on security issues, notably by attempting to solve the Transnistrian conflict. See "Déclaration finale à l'occasion de la rencontre tripartite Allemagne-France-Russie," Deauville, October 18–19, 2010, http://www.delegfrance-osce.org/spip.php?article286 (accessed May 11, 2011).

21. Vlad Socor, "Meseberg Process: Germany Testing EU-Russia Security Cooperation Potential," *Eurasia Daily Monitor*, October 22, 2010, http://www.jamestown.org/single/?no_cache=1&tx_ttnews%5Btt_news%5D=37065 (accessed May 11, 2011).

22. See Nicolae Iorga, *Histoire des relations entre la France et les Roumains* (Paris: Payot, 1918).

23. Quoted in Daniela Ghinea and Jean-Thomas Lesueur, "La Roumanie essaye-t-elle de séduire la France dans le nouveau contexte de son adhésion à l'Union Européenne?," *Synergies Roumanie*, no. 2 (2007): 118, http://ressources-cla.univ-fcomte.fr/gerflint/Roumanie2/daniela.pdf (accessed September 22, 2010).

24. Bessarabia was the name given by the Russian Empire to the territory of the Principality of Moldavia situated between the rivers of Prut, Dniester, the Chilia arm of the Delta, and the Black Sea when it was acquired in 1812. In 1918, in the aftermath of the Russian Revolution of 1917, Bessarabia as a whole joined Romania, before its annexation by the Soviet Union in 1940. It was the core of the Moldavian Soviet Socialist Republic, which became independent in 1991.

25. Nicolas Sarkozy and Traian Băsescu, "Conférence de presse conjointe," Bucharest, February 4, 2008, http://www.elysee.fr/president/les-actualites/conferences-de-presse/2008/conference-de-presse-conjointe-m-traian.5904.html (accessed June 5, 2011).

26. The "Roma crisis" broke out in Summer 2010, when President Sarkozy launched a crackdown on crime, targeting the Roma population emigrated in France. Starting with domestic considerations, the crisis strongly affected French-Romanian relations, when France openly criticized Romania for not integrating the Roma population.

27. "Schengen: les frontières roumaines et bulgares trop poreuses, affirme Paris," *LCP Assemblée nationale*, December 23, 2010, http://www.lcp.fr/actualites/politique/105 81-schengen-frontieres-roumaines-et-bulgares-trop-poreuses-affirme-paris (accessed January 17, 2011).

28. See, for instance, Christian Lequesne, *La France dans la nouvelle Europe. Assumer le changement d'échelle* (Paris: Sciences Po Les Presses, 2008).

29. He was replaced by his prime minister, François Fillon.

30. Maxime Lefebvre, "France and the European Neighbourhood Policy," *Foreign Policy in Dialogue* 7, no. 19 (July 2006): 123, http://www.deutsche-aussenpolitik.de/newsletter/issue19.pdf (accessed September 23, 2007).

31. "French premier to visit Moldova," *allmoldova.com*, April 14, 2011, http://www.allmoldova.com/en/moldova-news/1249050125.html (accessed April 16, 2011).

32. Valentina Pop, "EU gives green light to visa-free talks with Moldova," *EUobserver*, October 22, 2010, http://euobserver.com/9/31104 (accessed December 21, 2010).

Chapter Seven

Germany: Increased Attention toward Moldova?[*]

Dareg A. Zabarah

This chapter is dedicated to German-Moldovan relations since 1991. Three factors influence these relations: First is the unattractiveness of Moldova as a trade partner for Germany. Lack of strong mutual trade between the two countries, and thus the absence of lobbies in the political sphere, affected the agenda-setting priorities of political actors, leaving them free to address humanitarian issues. Second is Germany's own peculiar foreign and security policy. This policy is determined by delegations of foreign policy and security issues to supra-national and multinational organizations, such as the European Union and the North Atlantic Treaty Organization, and its special relationship with the former Soviet Union and later with Russia.[1] The third factor is German security concerns resulting from the unresolved legal status of the breakaway Pridnestrovian Moldavian Republic.

Setting the Agenda on Moldova: Humanitarian or Trade Issues?

As an export-oriented economy, Germany values trade relations. The centrality of trade relations has often led to concessions in human rights toward states with poor human rights records. In its external relations, Germany must always maneuver between trade issues (German jobs) and issues of human rights and democracy (general public concern, self-perception). In its relationship toward Moldova, such maneuvering is not necessary. As tables 7.1 and 7.2 show, the trade volume between Germany and Moldova is rather marginal.

* Thanks to Sabine Bär of the German Bundesbank, Stefan Kägebein of the Federation of German Industry, Stefan Sarter at the Press and Information Office of the Federal Government, Martin Sieg of the German-Moldovan Forum, Sonja Schueler of the Federal Ministry for Economic Cooperation and Development, and Regina Wippler of German Trade and Invest, for providing me with crucial information and answering my lengthy questions.

Table 7.1. Main external trade partners of Moldova from 1999–2009

Moldovan exports to:	in mil. USD	in %	Moldovan imports from:	in mil. USD	in %
Total	**1,028.26**	**100**	**Total**	**2,331.59**	**100**
Russia	291.14	28	Ukraine	426.64	18
Romania	141.67	14	Russia	317.34	14
Italy	107.62	10	Romania	260.17	11
Ukraine	92.82	9	*Germany*	*194.58*	*8*
Belarus	61.28	6	Italy	164.29	7
Germany	*60.82*	*6*	Belarus	86.32	4

Source: Ten-year arithmetic mean calculated from the National Bureau of Statistics of the Republic of Moldova, "External Trade," http://statbank.statistica.md /pxweb/Database/EN/21%20EXT/21%20EXT.asp (accessed June 30, 2011).

Table 7.2. Development of total bilateral trade between Moldova and Germany from 1999–2009 (mil. USD)

Year	Exports	Imports
1999	33.5	61.4
2000	36.2	87.7
2001	40.0	84.0
2002	46.1	85.7
2003	56.2	135.6
2004	71.3	150.2
2005	47.4	191.1
2006	51.9	214.1
2007	86.3	319.3
2008	63.8	364.5
2009	75.5	252.3

Source: Calculated from the National Bureau of Statistics of the Republic of Moldova, "External Trade."

While Germany has been Moldova's sixth largest trade partner in terms of exports to Germany and its fourth largest partner in terms of imports, Moldova ranked 91 in terms of German exports and 104 in terms of imports. The *yearly* average of imports and exports with Moldova totaled €296.3 million in 2009 and equaled roughly the *daily* trade turnover between Germany and the Netherlands of around €298.0 million during the same year. While imports from Germany increased strongly in recent years, export of Moldovan products to Germany did not witness a significant increase. The data clearly shows the asymmetric character of trade relations between Germany and Moldova.[2]

Compared to that of other European countries, Germany's foreign direct investment in Moldova is low. In 2009, FDI of German companies in Moldova equaled around 7.1 percent of the total FDI in the country. Other countries such as France and Italy make up 10.9 percent and 9.3 percent respectively. For details, see table 7.3.[3]

Table 7.3. German yearly net direct investment in Moldova from 1996–2010 (mil. EUR)

	1996	1997	1998	1999	2000	2001	2002	2003	2004	2005	2006	2007	2008	2009	2010
yearly net-direct investments	1	2	9	3	0	5	1	-1	2	3	-6	23	11	6	5
of which real estate services	1	1	3	1	-1	1	0	-1	1	4	-1	23	8	0	10
of which industrial production	0	0	5	3	0	3	1	0	0	0	-6	-1	2	5	-6

Source: Deutsche Bundesbank, *Zahlungsbilanzstatistik. Deutsche Netto-Direktinvestitionen im Ausland. Transaktionswerte nach Wirtschaftszweigen lt. Zahlungsbilanzstatistik: Land: Republik Moldau*, February 24, 2011.

Note: Figures less than 1 are rounded.

German investment in Moldova began only in 1996, initially in real estate services. This sector continues to attract the largest portion of German capital and it is characterized by fast returns on investment and low capital costs. Investment in Moldovan industry began two years later, in 1998, with the sugar beet producer Südzucker, which has been followed by a few other firms engaged mostly in non-capital-intensive sectors that promise fast returns. Direct investment remains at an overall low level. The disinvestment shows that German companies are still reluctant to maintain long-term commitments in Moldova. Long-term engagement is further hampered by the unfavorable investment climate characteristic of most post-Soviet states, which includes the usual challenges of corruption, lack of legal security and bureaucratic hurdles. The unresolved status of Transnistria is a further security concern for German investors. Unlike Russia or Ukraine, where similar conditions are often compensated by the vast natural resources of these countries, such resources are scarce in predominately rural, agrarian Moldova. Furthermore, a strong business lobby to advocate German trade interests in Moldova at the political level is largely absent, although the Foreign Investors' Association, which counts several German investors among its members and has been headed by Germans, is among the top lobbyists for a better political investment climate.

In Germany, Moldova is largely unknown. Unlike the larger Moldovan diaspora in Italy or France, only around 12,200 Moldovans live in Germany.[4] Of the approximately 7,500 people that declared themselves "ethnic" Germans in Moldova in 1989, around 6,992 left for Germany between 1992 and 2008.[5] Thus cultural ties between Germany and Moldova are not very strong. Newspaper articles published in the German media on Moldova are sporadic and mainly concentrate on the issues of poverty and economic hardship that the country and its people face. Human trafficking and forced prostitution are common subjects in the German press on Moldova.[6] The conflict in Transnistria is also infrequently discussed in the German media. Portrayed as the last "Soviet open-air museum," the image of the region is largely negative. Lawlessness, illicit trade of humans and drugs, and a repressive autocratic regime are the main public perceptions of the breakaway state.[7]

Compared to other countries in Europe and worldwide, German official development assistance to Moldova has been very low. Although aid increased since 2005, Moldova remains among the lowest aid-receiving countries in Europe. Moldova is not on the list of partner countries for ODA, which means that it does not receive regular bilateral development assistance, but profits from programs and disbursements from regional programs. This is why disbursements change from year to year. For details, see table 7.4.

Table 7.4. German bilateral and multilateral ODA to Moldova from 2000–2008 (mil. EUR)

Year	2000	2001	2002	2003	2004	2005	2006	2007	2008
Total ODA	6.55	4.27	5.74	8.00	9.30	21.50	13.20	24.40	21.80

Sources: Compiled from Bundesministerium für Wirtschaftliche Zusammenarbeit und Entwicklung, *Bi- und multilaterale ODA-Leistungen nach Ländern 2000–2004*, March 17, 2011 and Bundesministerium für Wirtschaftliche Zusammenarbeit und Entwicklung, *Bi- und multilaterale ODA-Leistungen nach Ländern 2004–2008*, March 17, 2011.

German Foreign Policy: A Strong Partner within Strong Multinational Structures

German foreign policy witnessed significant changes after the country's unification in October 1990 and its attainment of full sovereignty by the 2+4 Agreement.[8] The post-unification German leadership was eager to disperse the fears of its European partners—mainly France and the United Kingdom—of a strong Germany with hegemonic ambitions. Therefore the integration of Germany into EU and NATO structures was considered as one of the priority objectives of Chancellor Helmut Kohl's administration (1982–1998). The political elite believed that only through a strong economic interdependence between the states, and thus shared common interests, could long-term peace be achieved. The Kohl government was also highly sympathetic to the eastward expansion of the EU and supported the fast inclusion of the former Eastern bloc countries into the union. A favorable attitude toward the Soviet Union under Mikhail Gorbachev and later towards Russia under Boris Yeltsin, was characteristic of German policy. This was attributable not only to the friendly personal relationship between Kohl and the two Russian statesmen, but it also reflected positive German public sentiment toward the Soviet Union and Russia, resulting from the widespread opinion among the public in general, and the political elite in particular, that without the help of Gorbachev, a unification of East and West Germany would not have been possible. Thus, any policy toward the post-Soviet republics would have to be viewed within the context of relations with Russia. During Chancellor Gerhard Schröder's administration (1998–2005), this trend continued. Schröder and the Social Democratic Party were equally conciliatory towards Russia—especially toward Vladimir Putin. This trend changed after Chancellor Angela Merkel from the Christian Democratic Party took over in 2005. Merkel has openly criticized Putin for increasing authoritarianism and has adopted a critical stance on the Russian government's confrontational foreign policy, while at the same time consistently trying to maintain a dialogue and foster a partnership with Russia. Germany was the first country to offer a "modernization partnership," a concept later adopted by the entire EU toward Russia.

Despite being an important driving force behind the EU's enlargement toward the East in the past, Germany is now rather reluctant to continue this policy. In recent years, debates about the "absorption capacity" of the EU have been ongoing in the German public, which led to the skepticism of many conservative politicians regarding the benefits of any future eastward enlargement that would include poorer countries—such as Moldova—or countries that for some conservatives are not part of Europe—such as Turkey. Although Germany remains committed to full integration in the EU and NATO structures, German conservatives have been pleading in recent years for a stronger pursuit of German interests in the international arena, while left-leaning political actors still maintain the position that it is Germany's post-WWII obligation to surrender a degree of its sovereignty for the benefit of the common European interest. Policy toward Moldova must be viewed within the context as well.

The Phases of the Moldovan-German Political Relationship: From Poorhouse Unknown to Role Model for the EU Partnership?

Moldovan-German relations can be divided into four phases characterized by the intensity of their mutual relationship. By examining German parliamentary debates[9] where Moldova was discussed, and by analyzing reports from the main bilateral meetings that occurred between German and Moldovan politicians, this section will carve out the main issues of concern for German politicians when dealing with Moldova.

Phase I: Moldova, the Poorhouse Unknown, 1991–2002

During the first years of Moldova's independence, the German public was—if at all interested in the country—mainly concerned with the humanitarian issues there. This was reflected in the attitude of German lawmakers toward Moldova.

Although Germany was one of the first Western European countries to establish diplomatic relations with Chisinau in April 1992, Moldova did not constitute a priority on Germany's foreign policy agenda. The first meeting at a high diplomatic level occurred only in October 1995, when Moldovan President Mircea Snegur paid a visit to Germany and met with Chancellor Helmut Kohl to sign—inter alia—a joint statement defining the basis of the mutual relationship between the two countries. In the meeting, Snegur raised the issue of Russian troops stationed in Transnistria and asked the German Chancellor to support the withdrawal of these troops from Moldovan territory. Kohl responded that he would raise this issue with Boris Yeltsin, stating that "it would be a good thing if Russia would act in other places as it did in Germany."[10]

Until 2003, German lawmakers made only two inquiries to the government on Moldova. Both motions were filed by Deputy Egon Jüttner, a member of the ruling CDU/CSU. The first motion filed in 1994 inquired about the cultural, scientific and economic cooperation between Germany and Moldova, and the second motion filed in 1997 asked about planned steps for deepening German-Moldovan cultural relations.[11] In fact, only the first inquiry was answered, as Jüttner was absent from parliament when his second motion was handled.[12]

Phase II: Skeptical Approaches, 2003–2005

Between 2003 and 2005, Moldova appeared frequently on the agendas of the German lawmakers and government. The failure of the Kozak Initiative—a plan elaborated by Russia to regulate the Transnistrian conflict, which was launched behind closed doors and without consulting Western parties involved in mediating the conflict—did not lead only to a conflict between the EU and Russia, but also caused dismay in Chisinau and ultimately led to the administration of President Vladimir Voronin turning away from Russia and toward Europe.[13] This "turn to Europe," combined with strong mutual relations between the main political opposition party, the Moldovan Christian Democratic People's Party, led by Iurie Roşca, and the CDU/CSU party in Germany, brought increased awareness of Moldova to German parliamentarians.

In April 2003, two inquiries were made by another CDU/CSU lawmaker, Hermann Gröhe, in which he expressed concern over the Moldovan authorities' attempts under Voronin to hinder the activities of the PPCD and to strip its party leader, Roşca, of his immunity for organizing demonstrations. In his second inquiry, he asked about the stance of the German government regarding the planned introduction of Russian as a second official language in Moldova.[14] In its answer, the German government emphasized that it considered the suspension of the PPCD's activity and the stripping of three of its deputies of their immunity as "an illegitimate intervention in the democratic structure of the country."[15] In a diplomatic note of protest sent on January 29, 2002, to the Moldovan government, the German government expressed its concerns for pluralism and freedom of opinion in Moldova. The German government spokesperson further noted that on February 8, 2002, the Moldovan Ministry of Justice canceled the party's suspension. The immunity of Roşca was restored later the same year. On the language issue, the German government emphasized that due to the efforts of both the EU and the Council of Europe, it was possible to reach a compromise between the government and the opposition. As a result, a moratorium was imposed on the introduction of Russian and—according to the estimates of the German government—the issue was not on the political agenda.

Later in the course of that year, the entire parliamentary group of the CDU/CSU filed a detailed inquiry on the situation in Moldova. The inquiry included sixteen detailed points and was thus the longest on German-Moldovan relations. Its signatories, which included current Chancellor Angela Merkel, raised concerns about the political and economic situation in the country. The inquiry began with the following preamble:

> The political, economic and social situation in the Republic of Moldova is very tense. Poverty, social pauperization of wide parts of the population, human trafficking, and corruption provide cause for concern. The conflict between Moldova and Transnistria has not been resolved since 1990 despite international mediation efforts. Great numbers of Moldovans live outside of their country in the EU and other countries. Furthermore, many Moldovans hold a Romanian passport. In anticipation that the EU will soon have an external border with Moldova, it ought to be a concern of German policy to work toward democratic and market economic development and toward the improvement of the human rights situation in that country.[16]

The points addressed in the inquiry in fact mirrored the concerns stated in the preamble. While the first four points addressed democracy, human rights issues and bilateral Moldova-German contacts, the next four points were dedicated to the situation in Transnistria and its effect on EU security (drug trade and human trafficking). Here the lawmakers inquired about the efforts of the German government to ensure Moldova's internal stability and the role of Russia and Ukraine in the conflict. The next two points were dedicated to German engagement within the EU to ensure cooperation with its future neighbors, Moldova, Ukraine and Belarus, in order to avoid lines of division developing between the EU and those countries. The last five points addressed Moldova's dire economic situation and asked about the previous and future development of German aid policies toward Moldova.

In answer to the inquiry, the German government mentioned progress achieved in building a constitutional state in Moldova, but emphasized that the pace has been slow and that there were setbacks under the Voronin administration. These setbacks also concerned human rights, and the government cited the obstruction of the PPCD and other parties (such as the Braghiş Alliance) by the government and the curbing of press freedom as examples. On Transnistria, the German government raised its concern about ongoing illegal activities. According to the report, the regional elite around Igor Smirnov personally profited from such transactions and was highly entrenched with criminal activities. The position on Transnistria was summarized as follows: "As long as Transnistria is not de facto under control of the government in Chisinau, ready and able for efficient action, and as long as the region defies international control mechanisms, a clear amelioration of the situation cannot be expected. Transnistria will then remain a welcome field of operation for drug dealers and human traffickers."[17]

The German government shared the deputies' concerns about the economic hardships of Moldova and its people. It confirmed that due to inadequate political and social conditions, which reduce the possibility of cooperation, Moldova has been receiving the lowest aid per capita from the international community. With an average of $27.3 of ODA per capita for the years 1999 to 2001, it was by far the lowest-ranking beneficiary in Europe, where the quotas range between $201.0 (Bosnia and Herzegovina) and $56.0 (Armenia). In comparison internationally, it even scored lower than Eritrea, which received an average of $49.0 for the same period.

In reaction to these responses, the CDU/CSU deputies later filed a twelve-point motion to be voted on in parliament. The motion foresaw that the German Bundestag would request the German government to "develop an extensive concept to further consolidate Moldova's link to Europe."[18] In the motion, the German government was asked to exercise influence on the Moldovan government to ensure the development of democracy and human rights in that country. It further requested that the engagement of Germany should exceed the suggestions of the EU Neighborhood Concept of April 17, 2003, and it pled for a more active role on the part of the international community in providing development aid. The German government should further urge Moldova and its neighbors to actively fight organized crime, money laundering, the drug trade and human trafficking. In this context, the German government should offer to provide

German and European help. On the Transnistrian issue, it was suggested Germany exert influence on Russia to fulfill its obligation to the Organization for Security and Cooperation in Europe regarding the planned withdrawal of Russian troops from the region, and to constantly put the unification of Moldova on the agenda in bilateral talks with Russia. Finally it was suggested Germany advocate at the EU level the installation of an EU representative who would—together with the OSCE field mission—function as moderator in negotiations to unite Moldova and Transnistria, and who would actively campaign for the values, norms and rules of the EU in Moldova. Apart from the CDU/CSU, another opposition party, the Free Democratic Party, filed a motion in which it—inter alia—explicitly requested the German government to advocate at the EU level for the possibility of Moldova to become an EU member.[19] The motion was, however, later overturned in parliament by all other parties.[20]

The CDU/CSU motion was discussed in parliament on January 29, 2004. Twelve years after the country's independence, this was the first time that Moldova was discussed in the plenum of the German parliament. The country designee of the Bundestag for Moldova, CDU/CSU politician Claudia Nolte, who presented the motion, reminded the deputies of the difficult situation Moldova and its people undergo. While criticizing Voronin's administration for its ambivalent position between the EU and Russia, Nolte acknowledged the lack of EU engagement in providing viable alternatives for Moldova. The government's position was defended by Gert Weisskirchen (SPD) and Marianne Tritz (Alliance '90/The Greens), who pointed out that despite German engagement, the Moldovan side often lacks its own significant initiatives. Weisskirchen emphasized that Moldova should also take its own significant steps to ensure that the "way to Brussels" begins in the country itself.[21] The marginal engagement of Germany toward Moldova was also criticized by deputy Rainer Stinner (FDP) who expressed his dismay about the delay in the withdrawal of Russian troops from the east of Moldova and the soft stance of the German government.

The motion was edited to accommodate the input of the other parties who all supported the final document, which was later passed on for voting in parliament. The general tenor of the new motion was basically the same as that suggested by the CDU/CSU. Unlike the previous motion, the edited document foresaw the delegation of many of the planned initiatives to the EU. The changes reflected the ongoing accession talks between Romania, Bulgaria and the EU, which were in their final phase. Thus, instead of developing "an extensive concept to further consolidate Moldova's link to Europe,"[22] it was now suggested that the German government should "submit with emphasis German concepts to the Moldovan action plan within the 'wider Europe' concept, in order to contribute to the strengthening of Moldova's link to Europe."[23] The suggestion for increased engagement in development aid to Moldova that would exceed the suggestions of the Neighborhood Concept was dropped. The idea of an EU delegate was also abolished, and instead it was recommended to suggest the opening of an EU commission in Chisinau and to explore the possibility of wider EU engagement within the OSCE in order to solve the Transnistrian conflict.

Help in fighting criminal activities should also be provided only at the EU level. The edited motion was approved unanimously by all the deputies of the Bundestag on May 6, 2004. Apart from Nolte, critical remarks on the Voronin administration came also from Markus Meckel (SPD) and Stinner, who criticized the backward steps in human and civil rights, and the attempts to undo previous economic reforms, such as the re-collectivization of the agrarian sector. The speakers also addressed the problem of Transnistria, and the dangers resulting from its undefined status were highlighted.[24] The Transnistrian conundrum was also tackled in a later inquiry of Nolte in November of the same year, in which she asked about the new foreign policy concept adopted by the so-called Supreme Council of the PMR.[25] In its answer, the German government representative evaluated the results as being a further burden on bilateral relations between Tiraspol and Chisinau and stated—inter alia—that the German government would continue its efforts to find a peaceful solution to the conflict based on the territorial integrity of Moldova.[26]

In February 2005 the German government reported to parliament about the "development and results of the efforts for a stronger linkage of Moldova to Europe."[27] The report summarized various activities in Moldova, which included the planned opening of an EU-delegation office in 2005, German efforts in fighting criminal activities, Moldova's continued poverty and the stimulation of investments.

Phase III: From Praise to Disillusionment, 2006–2008

While Moldova was hailed as a "model pupil" for implementing EU neighborhood policy suggestions at the beginning of 2005, disillusion soon followed, due to the half-hearted reforms of the Voronin administration in its later years.

Moldova, however, continued to be a topic on the agenda of the German parliament with security issues (Transnistria) and humanitarian issues (poverty and human trafficking) dominating the agenda.

The next high-level visit of a Moldovan official, which occurred eleven years after Snegur's visit to Germany, was a visit of Voronin to Chancellor Merkel in Berlin in 2006. Besides a general discussion of bilateral relations, the Transnistrian issue was also present on the agenda.[28]

The Transnistrian conundrum was subject to an inquiry made by the opposition party FDP in June 2006. In the document, the deputies addressed their concerns about criminal activities originating from the region and the human rights violations of the Transnistrian regime against the population. The deputies requested the government to report in detail on twenty-five points. Except for the first point, which inquired about the concrete steps taken by the German government toward Moldova as foreseen in the motion of May 2004, the other questions touched on security issues in connection with Transnistria such as the evaluation of the EU Border Assistance Mission to Moldova and Ukraine, Ger-

man influence on Russian troop withdrawal, the production of weapons in Transnistria, and other similar topics.[29]

In its answer, the German government gave a positive assessment of the
EUBAM mission and mentioned the cooperation of all sides. Information on the
production or smuggling of weapons in Transnistria was not provided. The
German government indicated that such information—which it received from
intelligence sources—was classified and thus not for public disclosure.[30]

Moldova was brought up on the agenda again in March 2007 by the Alliance '90/The Greens party, now on the opposition benches. In connection with
an inquiry on the developments in Russia, the deputies asked about Russian
support of Transnistria and the delay of the Russian troop withdrawal. It further
raised its concerns over Russia's double standard of supporting separatists in
Transnistria and bringing the solution of the conflict to an international level,
while simultaneously refusing a similar approach in Chechnya.[31] The Russian
troops in Moldova were further discussed in the October 2007 parliamentary
session in connection with the Treaty on Conventional Armed Forces in Europe
(CFE). The speaker from the CSU/CDU party, now part of the government,
Karl-Theodor Freiherr zu Guttenberg, mentioned that although Russia has not
completely withdrawn all armed forces from the eastern parts of Moldova, the
number of soldiers did not exceed a few hundred who were mainly guarding an
ammunition depot, which should not be left unattended. The FDP speaker also
emphasized the need to show flexibility to Russia, since the dispute is over older
ammunition.[32]

Almost a year later another opposition party, the left-wing die Linke/PDS,
sent an inquiry on Moldova to the German government, in which it asked about
the effects of the EU Neighbourhood Policy on the economic and social development in Moldova. The inquiry addressed a variety of aspects, including questions on the settlement of the Transnistrian conflict, the combating of human
trafficking, German-Moldovan bilateral trade and aid, as well as a potential
long-term perspective of Moldova joining the EU.[33] On the latter question, the
German government stated that—depending on the pace of reform in Moldova—it would be discussed within the EU whether further cooperation would be
possible in excess of current efforts. Together with Ukraine, Moldova would
have the prospective of being closely connected to the EU within the framework
of the European Neighbourhood Policy.[34] A clear perspective to join the EU was,
however, not given.

A month later, the Alliance '90/The Greens filed a motion to the German
parliament in which it requested the lawmakers vote in support of the integration
of Moldova into Europe since the former now had a direct border with the EU as
a result of Romania joining the community in 2007. The document pointed out
"significant developments on the path to convergence with the EU."[35] Unlike in
previous documents, the critical tone toward the Voronin administration was
largely absent. Taking into consideration the existing threat stemming from the
unresolved status of Transnistria and the economic hardships of the Moldovan
population, which led to massive illegal immigration, the signatories pled for

more engagement in Moldova. Besides the usual human rights and security issues in connection with Transnistria found in previous motions, the second point of this motion contained a request to the German government to support a long-term perspective for Moldova to join the EU. After the motion was transferred to the relevant committees, a new paper—now signed by the CDU/CSU, FDP, SPD and the Alliance '90/The Greens—was presented for discussion in parliament. The new document did not contain, however, a perspective of Moldova joining the EU. In its preamble, which was much more critical toward the Moldovan government than the previous document, it mentioned that despite the reforms, many shortcomings remain, and that the country is still not in compliance with EU standards.[36] The motion further included a request to plead for the avoidance of electoral hurdles against candidates and parties by the Moldovan government in the upcoming 2009 elections. The motion, which was not debated in parliament, passed with the votes of the signatory parties. Despite general agreement with the substance of the document, the Linke party abstained from the vote as it was not able to express its concerns with regard to certain points due to its exclusion from the consultations.[37]

Phase IV: New Government, New Hopes?

After Moldovan-German relations reached a near nadir at the beginning of 2009, the government change in April 2009 brought new factors into the relationship. The new Prime Minister Vlad Filat was able to portray himself as highly pragmatic and effective in conducting Moldovan foreign policy. Working-level political contacts increased sharply between Germany and Moldova in recent years.[38] In a meeting between Merkel and Prime Minister Filat in May 2010, mutual cooperation between Moldova and the EU were discussed along with—as always—the Transnistrian question.[39] The Transnistrian issue was raised by Merkel in her meeting with Russian President Dmitry Medvedev in Meseberg in June 2010. The German Chancellor described the Transnistrian conflict as a possible practical case for deepening relations between Europe and Russia on security policy.[40] In fact, a German settlement initiative, which was not backed by an official EU endorsement, caused Moscow to pressure Tiraspol to resume negotiations in the 5+2 format on June 21, 2011, after their suspension in 2006. Support for resuming the 5+2 talks was emphasized by Merkel during the second visit of Filat to Berlin in May of the following year. In her statement, the German Chancellor emphasized Germany's "great compassion" and "great sympathy" with the fate of Moldova, resulting from the unresolved status of Transnistria, especially since "Germany itself experienced such a division."[41] Merkel explicitly refused to express her preference for either a unitarian or a federal solution, stating that this should be left to the negotiation process. While it is out of the scope of this chapter to analyze the details of the Transnistrian settlement initiative, Germany's engagement in the peace process is indeed noteworthy. While security concerns resulting from the region's unresolved status are surely driving this increased engagement, the increased attention toward Moldova must be seen in the context of German-Russian relations. Moldova serves as a test case in mending fences, not only between Russia and Germany, but also between Russia and the EU. It is, however, still too early to fully assess the extent of German influence on the peace settlement process.

Conclusion

The sections above show that Moldovan-German relations have been characterized by a long-time disinterest of Germany in Moldova. Apart from humanitarian issues, the main point of concern for parliamentarians seems to be one of security, resulting out of the unresolved status of Transnistria. The predominance of humanitarian issues on the political agenda is a logical consequence of an image of Moldova as the "poorhouse of Europe" cultivated in German public opinion. The lack of investment and trade opportunities, and thus the absence of other agendas in the two countries' relationship, further facilitated the dominance of humanitarian agendas. It took Germany more than ten years to increase its ties with Moldova.

During the second phase, from 2003 to 2005, increased political ties indeed translated into concrete economical figures. German exports to Moldova increased significantly.[42] German direct investment remained, however, at a low level—showing the reluctance of German investors to engage in Moldova. The global financial crisis of 2008, which was felt also in Moldova in 2009 and 2010, resulted in setbacks for German exports to Moldova. German investors still remain unwilling to commit to long-term engagements as the disinvestment of €6 million in 2010 in Moldovan industrial production has shown. It is unlikely that Moldova will evolve into a significant trade and investment partner for Germany in the near future.

The political rapprochement between Germany and Moldova occurred at a time when the political elite of Moldova distanced themselves from Russia. In fact, every move away from Moscow brought Chisinau closer to Brussels, and thus to Berlin. This trend continued after the ousting of Vladimir Voronin and the replacement of the Moldovan political leadership with pro-Western personnel. While German politicians seem interested in Moldova pursuing economic and political reforms, and bringing the country "closer to Europe," it seems that German leadership is keen on making sure that these processes occur without additional German expenses. This consideration is reflected not only in the low level of German development aid, but also in the reluctance of the German government to provide Moldova with a genuine perspective to join the EU. Unlike Moldova's integration into the European Neighbourhood Policy, a perspective of Moldova joining the EU would involve significant political and economic costs that Germany is not willing to undertake. This sentiment is especially strong in light of the debate surrounding the EU's "absorption capacity" ongoing in the German public. It would be hard to convince voters—especially from the conservative camp—how the integration of a poor and widely unknown country into the EU would bring them any benefits.

Notes

1. In his study of German-Moldovan relations for the period between 1991 and 1998, Vladislav Froltsov comes to similar conclusions about the Chancellor Helmut Kohl administration. See Vladislav Froltsov, "Politika FRG v otnoshenii Respubliki Moldovy (1991–1998 gg.)," *Zhurnal mezhdunarodnogo prava i mezhdunarodnykh otnosheniy*, no. 2 (2007), http://www.evolutio.info/index.php?option=com_content&task=view&id=1171 &Itemid=188 (accessed June 30, 2011).

2. German Federal Statistical Office, *Foreign trade 2009: Ranking of Germany's trading partners in foreign trade (with turnover and foreign trade balance)* (Wiesbaden: Federal Statistical Office, 2010), 3–4. Due to discrepancies between the Moldovan and German statistics, the figures will not be converted into USD for illustrative purposes.

3. Moldovan Ministry of Economy, "The Republic of Moldova: New Path of Development, Investment Opportunities," http://www.ost-ausschuss.de/sites/default/files/pm _pdf/Vizepremier%20Lazar.pdf (accessed May 15, 2011). The higher figure for the Netherlands of 17.1 percent is mainly due to tax optimization purposes of Moldovan investors using the legal umbrella of holding companies registered in the Netherlands and can therefore not be considered as FDI in the classical sense. The same is valid for Cyprus which makes up 9.6 percent of the FDI.

4. Figures December 31, 2008, according to Deutscher Bundestag 17. Wahlperiode, *Unterrichtung durch die Bundesregierung. Migrationsbericht 2008*, Drucksache 17/650, February 8, 2010, 185. This figure is, however, slightly misleading, as the Moldovans holding Romanian passports are not included in this category.

5. Ibid., 42.

6. For example, one of Germany's main newspapers, the *Sueddeutsche Zeitung* (SZ) published 48 articles between 1991 and 2011 in which the key words "poverty" and "Moldova" are mentioned in the article (for example: SZ, July 14, 1992, 3; SZ, December 14, 1994, 56; SZ, November 14, 1996, 11; SZ, July 13, 1997; SZ, October 15, 2010, 44–45 etc.). The words "prostitution" and "Moldova" appear in 17 articles on Moldova, whereas the words "crime" and "Moldova" appear together in 25 articles (for example: SZ, November 29, 1993, 10; SZ, July 9, 1998, 2; SZ, July 23, 2002, 6; SZ, November 26, 2002, 5; SZ, April 15, 2009, 3 etc.).

7. See for example SZ, November 22, 1994, 3; SZ January 11, 2000, 4; SZ, September 19, 2006, 9; September 7, 2010, 4; SZ, October 26, 2010, 8 etc.).

8. For a detailed discussion see Hanns W. Maull, introduction to *Germany's Uncertain Power. Foreign Policy of the Berlin Republic*, ed. Hanns W. Maull (Basingstoke: Palgrave Macmillan, 2006), 1–12 and Ulrich Roos, *Deutsche Außenpolitik: Eine Rekonstruktion der grundlegenden Handlungsregeln* (Wiesbaden: VS Verlag für Sozialwissenschaften / GWV Fachverlage GmbH Wiesbaden, 2010), 159–68 and 191–96.

9. A methodological caveat remains: while parliamentary debates reflect the communicative political discourse on a given subject, equally important undocumented and inaccessible co-coordinative discourses that occur behind closed doors cannot be

taken into account in the analysis. This might result in an overstatement of what is "said" in relation to what is really "meant." A motion prepared by a certain party on a given subject might therefore create the impression of disagreement, while on a working level divergences are in fact marginal.

10. Bundespresseamt, "Thema: Unterzeichnung einer gemeinsamen Erklärung. Sprecher: Bundeskanzler Dr. Helmut Kohl und Ministerpräsident Dr. Mircea Ion Snegur: Doknr: 95102a," October 11, 1995. The reference to Mircea Snegur as Prime Minister instead of President in the title of the document shows clearly the lack of information on Moldova.

11. Egon Jüttner, "Frage 65," in *Fragen für die Fragestunden der Sitzungen Deutschen Bundestages Mittwoch, dem 20 April 1994 Donnerstag dem 21 April 1994*, Drucksache 12/7295, 1994, 14 and Egon Jüttner, "Frage 24," in *Fragen für die Fragestunden der Sitzungen Deutschen Bundestages Mittwoch, dem 26. Februar 1997*, Drucksache 13/7013, 1997, 8.

12. Ursula Seiler-Albring, "Antwort der Staatsministerin Ursula Seiler-Albring auf die Fragen des Abgeordneten Dr. Egon Jüttner (CDU/CSU) (Drucksache 12/7295 Fragen 54 und 65)," in *222. Sitzung des Deutschen Bundestages. Bonn, den 21 April 1994*, 1994, 19272 and Deutscher Bundestag 13. Wahlperiode, *159. Sitzung: Bonn, Mittwoch, den 26. Februar 1997*, 1997, 14285.

13. Paul D. Quinlan, "Back to the Future: An Overview of Moldova Under Voronin," *Demokratizatsiya* 12, no. 4 (2004): 485–504.

14. Hermann Gröhe, "Frage 5," in *Schriftliche Fragen mit den in der Woche vom 31. März 2003 eingegangenen Antworten der Bundesregierung*, Drucksache 15/791, 2003, 3 and Hermann Gröhe, "Frage 6," in *Schriftliche Fragen mit den in der Woche vom 31. März*, 4.

15. Kerstin Müller, "Antwort der Staatsministerin Kerstin Müller vom 3. April 2003," in *Schriftliche Fragen mit den in der Woche vom 31. März*, 3–4.

16. Deutscher Bundestag 15. Wahlperiode, *Kleine Anfrage der Abgeordneten Claudia Nolte [...] CDU/CSU. Aktuelle Situation in der Republik Moldau*, Drucksache 15/1377, July 1, 2003, 1.

17. Deutscher Bundestag 15. Wahlperiode, *Antwort der Bundesregierung auf die Kleine Anfrage der Abgeordneten Claudia Nolte [...] CDU/CSU – Drucksache 15/1377 – Aktuelle Situation in der Republik Moldau*, Drucksache 15/1456, July 25, 2003, 7.

18. Deutscher Bundestag 15. Wahlperiode, *Antrag der Abgeordneten Claudia Nolte [...] CDU/CSU. Den Weg zur Einheit und Demokratisierung in Moldau unterstützen*, Drucksache 15/1987, November 11, 2003, 1.

19. Deutscher Bundestag 15. Wahlperiode, *Antrag der Abgeordneten Dr. Rainer [...] FDP. Grundsätzliche Neuausrichtung der EU-Hilfsmaßnahmen für Südosteuropa*, Drucksache 15/2424, January 28, 2004, 4.

20. Deutscher Bundestag 15. Wahlperiode, *Deutscher Bundestag. Stenografischer Bericht: 114. Sitzung*, Plenarprotokoll 15/114, June 17, 2004, 10467.

21. Deutscher Bundestag 15. Wahlperiode, *Deutscher Bundestag. Stenografischer Bericht: 88. Sitzung*, Plenarprotokoll 15/88, January 29, 2004, 7834–37.

22. Deutscher Bundestag 15. Wahlperiode, *Drucksache 15/1987*, November 11, 2003, 1.

23. Deutscher Bundestag 15. Wahlperiode, *Antrag der Fraktionen der SPD, CDU/CSU, Bündnis 90/die Grünen und FDP. Den Weg zur Einheit und Demokratisierung in Moldau unterstützen*, Drucksache 15/3052, May 5, 2004.

24. Deutscher Bundestag 15. Wahlperiode, *Deutscher Bundestag. Stenografischer Bericht: 108. Sitzung*, Plenarprotokoll 15/108, May 6, 2004, 9861.

25. Claudia Nolte, "Frage 6," in *Schriftliche Fragen mit den in der Woche vom 22. November 2004 eingegangenen Antworten der Bundesregierung*, Drucksache 15/4295, 2004, 3.

26. Klaus Scharioth, "Antwort des Staatssekretärs Dr. Klaus Scharioth vom 19. November 2004," in *Schriftliche Fragen mit den in der Woche vom 22. November*, 3.

27. Deutscher Bundestag 15. Wahlperiode, *Unterrichtung durch die Bundesregierung. Bericht über die Entwicklungen und Ergebnisse der Bemühungen um eine stärkere Anbindung Moldaus an Europa*, Drucksache 15/4887, February 14, 2005.

28. Bundespresseamt, "Pressebegegnung der Bundeskanzlerin Dr. Angela Merkel und dem Präsidenten der Republik Moldau, Vladimir Voronin: Doknr: 2006-054a," May 15, 2006.

29. Deutscher Bundestag 16. Wahlperiode, *Kleine Anfrage der Abgeordneten Markus Löning [...] FDP. Zur Situation in Transnistrien (Republik Moldau)*, Drucksache 16/2133, June 29, 2006.

30. Deutscher Bundestag 16. Wahlperiode, *Antwort der Bundesregierung auf die Kleine Anfrage der Abgeordneten Markus Löning [...] FDP – Drucksache 16/2133 – Zur Situation in Transnistrien (Republik Moldau)*, Drucksache 16/2289, June 20, 2006.

31. Deutscher Bundestag 16. Wahlperiode, *Große Anfrage der Abgeordneten Marieluise Beck [...] BÜNDNIS 90/DIE GRÜNEN*, Drucksache 16/4932, March 29, 2007, 7.

32. Deutscher Bundestag 16. Wahlperiode, *Deutscher Bundestag. Stenografischer Bericht: 118. Sitzung*, Plenarprotokoll 16/118, October 11, 2007, 12318–19.

33. Deutscher Bundestag 16. Wahlperiode, *Kleine Anfrage der Abgeordneten Dr. Hakki Keskin [...] DIE LINKE. EU-Nachbarschaftspolitik und die wirtschaftliche und soziale Entwicklung Moldaus*, Drucksache 16/8672, March 17, 2008.

34. Deutscher Bundestag 16. Wahlperiode, *Antwort der Bundesregierung auf die Kleine Anfrage der Abgeordneten Dr. Hakki Keskin [...] DIE LINKE. – Drucksache 16/8672 – EU-Nachbarschaftspolitik und die wirtschaftliche und soziale Entwicklung Moldaus*, Drucksache 16/8848, April 17, 2008, 2.

35. Deutscher Bundestag 16. Wahlperiode, *Antrag der Abgeordneten Rainder Steenblock [...] BÜNDNIS 90/DIE GRÜNEN. Die europäische Integration der Republik Moldova unterstützen*, Drucksache 16/9358, May 28, 2008.

36. Instead of providing a perspective to join the EU, the German government was asked in the second point "to plead for the reception of a mandate as soon as possible, in order to conduct talks on the subsequent agreement [i.e., of the Partnership and Cooperation Agreement that was signed in 1998 and would have expired in 2008] which is to be negotiated." Deutscher Bundestag 16. Wahlperiode, *Antrag der Fraktionen CDU/CSU, SPD, FDP und BÜNDNIS 90/DIE GRÜNEN. Die europäische Integration der Republik Moldova unterstützen*: Drucksache 16/9755, June 25, 2008, 3.

37. Deutscher Bundestag 16. Wahlperiode, *Deutscher Bundestag. Stenografischer Bericht: 172. Sitzung*, Plenarprotokoll 16/172, June 26, 2008, 18381–82.

38. Martin Sieg (expert on German-Moldovan relations and board member of the German-Moldovan Forum), in an interview with the author, February 22, 2011.

39. Angela Merkel and Vladimir Filat, "Pressestatements von Bundeskanzlerin Dr. Angela Merkel und dem Ministerpräsidenten der Republik Moldau, Vladimir Filat," Berlin, May 12, 2010, http://www.bundesregierung.de/nn_1516/Content/DE/Mitschrift /Pressekonferenzen/2010/05/2010-05-12-filat-merkel.html (accessed June 30, 2011).

40. Angela Merkel and Dmitry Medvedev "Pressestatements von Bundeskanzlerin Angela Merkel und dem Präsidenten der Russischen Föderation, Dmitri Medwedew," Meseberg, June 5, 2010, http://www.bundesregierung.de/nn_1516/Content/DE/Mitschrift /Pressekonferenzen/2010/06/2010-06-05-merkel-medwedew.html (accessed June 30, 2011).

41. Angela Merkel and Vladimir Filat, "Pressestatements von Bundeskanzlerin Dr. Angela Merkel und dem Ministerpräsidenten der Republik Moldau, Vladimir Filat," Berlin, May 19, 2011, http://www.bundesregierung.de/nn_1516/Content/DE/Mitschrift /Pressekonferenzen/2011/05/2011-05-19-statment-bk-filat.html (accessed June 30, 2011).

42. Exports increased by 59 percent in 2003, 11 percent in 2004 and 27 percent in 2005 (table 7.2).

Chapter Eight

Hungary: A Supporter of Moldova's Independence*

András Rácz and Andrea Ambrus

Hungary, a country of 10 million people in the heart of Central Europe, has always had a foreign policy that prioritizes relations with its geographic neighbors, for several reasons. One of these reasons was an obvious need to settle and institutionalize relations with neighbor states, since this was a requirement for NATO and EU accession. Another was a sense of responsibility felt toward the approximately 2.5 million ethnic Hungarians living in neighboring countries. Hence the question arises: Why has Hungary had such an intensive relationship with Moldova since its independence, although Moldova neither directly neighbors Hungary, nor is home to any substantial population of ethnic Hungarians?

This chapter seeks to describe the aims and motivations behind Hungary's special attention to its relationship with Moldova. Academics argue this question needs to be considered separately in the periods before and after EU accession. The reason for this is the fundamental change induced in Hungarian foreign policy by EU accession. After 2004, in addition to its already-existing bilateral relations with neighboring countries, Budapest also had to find its place in the newly born European Neighbourhood Policy.

Therefore, this chapter is divided into three main parts. The first, introductory section, surveys the role of the Hungarian minority question in the wider context of Hungarian foreign policy, and examines how it is connected to Hungarian-Moldovan relations. In the second part, Hungarian foreign policy toward Moldova is placed in the wider context of Hungary's external relations and neighborhood policy in the 1990s and early 2000s. This era lasts until the 2004 EU accession of Hungary. The third part deals with the role of Moldova in Hungarian foreign policy following EU accession. It provides an outlook on Hungarian-Moldovan development aid cooperation as a practical area of foreign policy implementation.

The authors intend to use a high number of primary sources in order to support their arguments. Therefore, various government documents concerning Hun-

---

* The views expressed here are of the authors' own, and they do not represent the official positions of the institutions they are affiliated to.

garian foreign policy over the last two decades receive particular attention. In addition to these documents, several official declarations and interviews of policy makers were also used.

The Wider Context: The Role of the Minority Question in Hungarian Foreign Policy

Responsibility felt toward Hungarian minorities abroad has been a decisive factor in Hungarian foreign policy following the 1989 democratic transition. The reason for this long-lasting commitment is historical: After WWI, the Kingdom of Hungary lost approximately two-thirds of its territory and one-third of its population according to the Treaty of Trianon, signed in 1920. As a result, approximately 2.5 million ethnic Hungarians became citizens of foreign countries, namely Romania, the newly established Czechoslovakia, and the also new-born Kingdom of Serbs, Croats and Slovenes. From Trianon onward, a new dimension emerged in Hungarian foreign policy: commitment to the national minorities living abroad. This dimension has always been present in Hungarian foreign policy thinking and identity ever since, though with varying intensity.[1] In the two decades between the world wars, the primary objective of Hungarian foreign policy was the revision of Trianon, i.e., to get back as much of the lost territories and population as possible. Although before and during WWII some minor revisions were indeed made, after the war the post-Trianon borders were re-established with only a few minor changes. In the Communist era, Hungarian foreign policy intentionally did not pay much attention to the issue of Hungarian minorities abroad. The Hungarian minorities living in neighboring countries (in the modern Slovakia, Ukraine, Romania, Serbia, Croatia, Slovenia and Austria) were perceived only as ordinary citizens of the neighboring countries, toward which Hungary did not feel any special responsibility or commitment.

This official attitude has radically changed with the democratic transition in 1989. Independent Hungary defined its foreign policy with three main pillars. These were: 1. Euro-Atlantic integration; 2. good relations with neighboring countries; 3. a responsibility to Hungarian minorities living abroad.[2] Some experts argue that this first government, although it took important steps toward the Euro-Atlantic integration of the country, failed to realize how strongly these three priorities were interconnected. Thus, minority policy became an absolute priority between 1990 and 1993.[3] The question of national minorities has played a key role in Hungarian foreign policy since 1989, which continues even today. In the early 1990s, however, the issue was an absolute priority in relations with neighboring countries.

"The Neighbor of Your Neighbor": Hungarian-Moldovan relations in the 1990s and early 2000s

Hungarian-Moldovan relations in the early 1990s

By far the largest community of Hungarians abroad has lived in Romania. They numbered over 1.5 million in the early 1990s. During this period, nationalist governments were in power, both in Hungary and Romania. For Budapest the issue of ethnic Hungarians living in Romania was a priority; the Hungarian government intended not only to ensure their human rights and minority status, but was also in favor of winning some sort of territorial autonomy for them. On the other hand, the Romanian authorities perceived these Hungarian intentions as a threat to the very territorial integrity of the country. However, it is important to note that neither territorial revision, nor the possibility of forcibly changing borders was ever raised by any Hungarian government since 1989. Budapest has been striving for the rights of Hungarian minorities abroad, which are guaranteed only by means of diplomacy and international law.

At the same time, Romania also had a minority-related problem with the Republic of Moldova. The core difference from the Hungarian-Romanian case was that changing the borders through a re-unification of Moldova and Romania was high on the agenda in both of those countries at least until 1994. In this period Hungary was an active supporter of pro-independence forces in Moldova. Budapest interpreted the term "independence" to mean that Moldova should preserve its independence both from Romania and the Soviet Union/Russian Federation. The latter was in line with the strong anti-Soviet attitude[4] of the József Antall government (1990–1993). Hungary was among the very first countries to recognize the independence of Moldova, as early as December 26, 1991. Diplomatic relations were established between the two countries in January 1992, when Hungarian Foreign Minister Géza Jeszenszky visited Chisinau.[5]

Besides supporting independence, Budapest was also in favor of preserving the territorial integrity of Moldova. Though in official declarations this was applied only to the Transnistrian conflict, in reality it also implied that Budapest was strongly against any scenario of Moldova joining Romania without the Transnistrian territories.[6]

In addition to this, and due to the high priority given to minority-related issues, Budapest observed the situation of the Gagauz minority and the function of the Gagauz autonomy in Moldova with particular interest. Since Hungary wanted to achieve territorial autonomy for Hungarians living in Romania, it was obvious that Budapest would strongly support the territorial autonomy of the Gagauz people on ethnic grounds. Generally speaking, from 1990 to 1994, Hungary fostered and promoted the same sort of minority-related initiatives and tendencies in Moldova that Budapest also would have welcomed in Romania. These initiatives supported not only territorial autonomy, but also the right to use minority languages in education, etc.

Of course in many cases this resulted in harsh responses from Bucharest. At a conference held in London in May 1992, for example, Hungarian Foreign Minister Jeszenszky mentioned a possible solution to the Transnistrian and Gagauzian problems in Moldova based on the Swiss canton system. Romanian Foreign Ministry Spokesman Traian Chebeleu reacted with harsh criticism against "Hungarian intervention" in the conflict—although Minister Jeszenszky had made a proposal only about a third sovereign country (Moldova), and it was hard to understand why Romania felt it necessary to protest.[7]

Hungary's motivation to build intense relations with Moldova was explained by the Hungarian analyst and politician Iván Bába in a book written in 1994.[8] According to Bába, Hungary was interested in fostering relations with Moldova in order to counterbalance tensions with Romania. In Bába's opinion, Budapest intended to demonstrate that problems with Romania were not based on any historical aversions about Romanians in general, but were related to concrete questions about the situation of the Hungarian minorities living there. Thus, good relations with Romanian-speaking Moldova were, in a way, the consequence of Hungarian-Romanian tensions. In other words, Budapest used relations with Chisinau as a tool in its debates with Bucharest. As a retired Hungarian diplomat put it: "You know, you are usually good friends with the neighbor of your neighbor."[9]

Hungarian-Moldovan relations from the mid-1990s until 2004

This situation changed decisively after 1994. In Hungary a new, leftist-liberal government came to power, headed by Prime Minister Gyula Horn. The Horn government (1994–1998) dedicated much less attention to the issue of Hungarian minorities abroad than the earlier the Antall and Péter Boross governments. Besides, Hungary needed to sign basic treaties with both Slovakia and Romania necessary for the process of NATO, and later EU accession. This reality also pushed Hungary toward a less confrontational, more cooperative neighborhood policy. The Treaty on Good-Neighborly Relations and Friendly Cooperation was signed with Slovakia in 1995, and with Romania in 1996. Of course, as ties with Romania started to improve, relations with Moldova received less attention from the Hungarian side.

Moldovan domestic politics also changed in 1994. The new Democratic Agrarian Party government of Moldova that came to power in 1994 broke with the pro-unionist policy of the Popular Front of Moldova. Instead, it started to promote a pro-independence course. A majority of the population reacted positively, as it was shown in a March 1994 referendum. With a voter turnout of approximately 75 percent, more than 90 percent of voters supported the idea of Moldova developing as an independent country. Thus, the possibility of unification with Romania was removed from the mainstream Moldovan domestic political agenda. This change meant a transformation of Moldovan-Hungarian relations as well.

Hungarian-Moldovan relations shifted to a more practical course. In order to broaden political relations, Moldovan President Mircea Snegur visited Hungary in April 1995 at the invitation of Hungarian President Árpád Göncz. During the visit, Hungary praised the freshly established Gagauz autonomy, and the parties agreed on the importance of managing minority issues in a democratic way. Oddly enough, in the end Hungarian Prime Minister Gyula Horn did not meet President Snegur, even though such a meeting was indeed planned to take place. The official explanation mentioned only "technical reasons."[10] However, this did not hamper the parties from signing the Hungarian-Moldovan Basic Treaty on April 19, 1995. The document was ratified by both parliaments in 1996.[11]

Former Foreign Minister Jeszenszky (1990–1994) criticized the Horn government in an article because the Recommendation of the Council of Europe no. 1201 was not included in the Basic Treaty.[12] This recommendation concerned the political and administrative measures necessary for guaranteeing the rights of national minorities.[13] Jeszenszky also criticized the cancellation of the Horn-Snegur meeting; according to him, such a mistake might have endangered Hungarian business interests, namely the export of two hundred Ikarus buses to Moldova.[14] Regardless, in the second half of the 1990s, Hungarian-Moldovan relations continued to develop. In June 1997, Moldovan Prime Minister Ion Ciubuc visited Budapest and met Prime Minister Horn. Hungary welcomed Moldova's intention to continue a pro-independence course in domestic and foreign policy. Intergovernmental agreements were signed on re-admission, cooperation against illegal drugs and terrorism, and also on the international inland transport of passengers and goods. A phytosanitary and plant-protection cooperation agreement was also signed.[15] Agriculture is one of the main fields of cooperation between Hungary and Moldova even today. The two prime ministers agreed that bilateral trade needed to be improved. In 1996, the total trade turnover was only $24.5 million, more than 80 percent of which was composed of Hungarian exports to Moldova.[16]

In October of the same year, Hungarian President Göncz visited Chisinau and met Moldovan President Petru Lucinschi. In his speech Göncz expressed Hungary's intentions to support Moldova on its path to Europe by transferring the knowledge and transformation experience Hungary gained during its EU approximation process.[17]

All in all, in the second half of the 1990s, Hungarian-Moldovan relations were focused more on technical cooperation and trade. The basic treaty between the two countries set up a general framework, and from then on political questions received much less attention in comparison to the early years of the decade.

However, the minor importance of Eastern Europe overall for Hungarian foreign policy was documented in a parliamentary Resolution on the Principles of Hungarian Security and Defence Policy issued in 1998. The document stated,

"Besides Euro-Atlantic integration, Hungarian foreign policy focuses on neighborhood policy and the well-being of Hungarian minorities abroad."[18] This meant that out of the six countries of post-Soviet Eastern Europe, only Ukraine was present on the radar of Hungarian foreign policy; the others received no mention. In the case of Ukraine, however, a certain element of solidarity was present, due to the well-being of Hungarian minorities there.

The new National Security Strategy adopted in 2004—after Hungary's NATO and EU accession—did not change this situation significantly. Regarding Eastern Europe, the document declared that Hungary "considers the situation of Russia and Ukraine of crucial importance, from the point of view of security in the region, and therefore is particularly interested in the stability of these two states, and the advancement of their democratic reforms, as well as in the success of their economic and social modernization processes."[19] On Ukraine the strategy specifically stated, "Hungary has an interest in the successful socioeconomic transformation of an independent and democratic Ukraine."[20] However, neither Moldova nor Belarus was mentioned at all. The South Caucasus was addressed only in a very general way, essentially with a list of the security-related problems of the region, without mentioning any countries concretely. Generally speaking, the National Security Strategy took a security-based, rather functional approach toward Eastern Europe.

Hungarian Foreign Policy in the EU Context

Compared to the pre-2004 period and since its EU accession, Hungary has significantly intensified its presence and activities in Eastern Europe. The EU accession offered Hungary the chance to become "a policy shaper" from the pre-accession position of "a policy taker." This change applied also to the European neighborhood policy dimension. However, the priorities of the European Neighbourhood Policy and of Hungarian neighborhood policy only partially overlapped. While the EU promoted its relationship with both the wider eastern and southern neighborhood, Hungarian neighborhood policy focused on the integration of Romania and Croatia, and in the Eastern neighborhood it paid attention only to reforms conducted in Ukraine and Moldova.[21] The previously mentioned National Security Strategy from 2004 specifically mentioned the opportunity to use the European Neighbourhood Policy to support Hungarian objectives in Eastern Europe.[22]

In reaction to the changed environment, the first Ferenc Gyurcsány government, in office from 2004 to 2006, reshaped the three main pillars of Hungarian foreign policy. In an interview given to the *Népszabadság* daily, then-Foreign Minister Ferenc Somogyi declared that EU accession had transformed the neighborhood policy of Hungary. As a result, the three traditional pillars of Hungarian foreign policy also needed to be modified. The new priorities were listed as: 1. active participation in the policy making of the Euro-Atlantic organizations; 2. strengthening regional cooperation formats, primarily the Visegrad Group; 3. development of bilateral relations. Of course, a focus on minority issues still prevailed. As Minister Somogyi put it, "the well-planned implementation of these three foreign policy tools may provide opportunities for pursuing our political interests, economic goals, and also for realizing our efforts aimed at improving the situation of Hungarian minority communities."[23]

Somogyi also declared that the geographical focus area of Hungarian development policy should be Eastern and South-Eastern Europe. Besides this, he stated that Hungary should influence European Neighbourhood Policy, including the enlargement and also the engagement of the EU in the Western Balkans in such a way as to include a more effective protection of minority rights, and to focus infrastructural development projects on territories populated by Hungarian minorities.[24] However, in the Eastern European region, this approach included only Ukraine and Moldova.

Hungarian interests in Ukraine have been obvious, taking into account the geographic proximity and the Hungarian minorities living there. However, Moldova was rather a deliberate choice from Budapest: Based on the already existing good political ties, Budapest decided that Moldova should be the Hungarian niche in the eastern dimension of the ENP.[25]

Moldova: Hungary's Niche in the ENP?

The External Relations Strategy, drafted in 2007 and adopted in 2008, prescribed that Budapest needed to "reinforce its presence in the Eastern partner countries of European Neighbourhood Policy." Moldova and Ukraine were concretely mentioned as two countries whose integration efforts should be supported by Hungary.[26] The three main pillars were again reshaped. As the External Relations Strategy states, the three priorities of current Hungarian foreign policy became: 1. a competitive Hungary in the European Union, which means realizing the political, economic and social interests of Hungary in the framework of the EU. (To this point, the Hungarian Foreign Ministry declared: "We regard strengthening the eastern dimension of European Neighbourhood Policy as an important objective, and we regard Ukraine and Moldova as special partners in doing so." Besides this, the ministry states that the Euro-Atlantic integration of neighboring states, namely Croatia, Serbia and Ukraine, are key Hungarian interests.[27]) 2. the success of Hungarians living abroad in the region, the protection of their rights and interests in order to ensure their welfare and well-being in their home countries. 3. a responsible Hungary in the world, enumerating the international commitments of Hungary.[28] The strategy used clear wording regarding the role of the EU in Hungarian foreign policy: "The European Union is the most important framework for Hungarian foreign policy and action."[29]

Regarding Moldova, the External Relations Strategy mentioned concretely the need to support the country's EU accession:

> Hungary encourages an effective European Neighbourhood Policy, which builds balanced relations based on cooperation and risk-handling in the eastern and southern directions, and leaves open the opportunity for EU accession for East European countries, Ukraine and Moldova among them, by helping their preparation through political and practical means.[30]

Concerning political support, Hungarian diplomats and experts were remarkably successful in acquiring EU positions related to Moldova since 2004. Hungarian General Ferenc Bánfi was the first commander of the European Union Border Assistance Mission to Moldova and Ukraine, launched in 2005. He performed his duties with highly satisfactory results. In addition to him, the second (and final) EU Special Representative to Moldova was a Hungarian ambassador, Kálmán Mizsei. He was appointed in 2007, and replaced Dutch Ambassador Adriaan Jacobovits de Szeged.

Additionally, the first-ever EU Common Visa Application Centre has operated in the Hungarian embassy in Chisinau since 2007. Here one may apply for short-term (type A and C) Schengen visas to fifteen EU countries[31] that have either no diplomatic representation in Chisinau or very limited personnel.

This evidence demonstrates that Budapest has been quite successful in realizing its plans to make Moldova a "Hungarian niche," at least in the early years that followed EU accession. This, of course, was made easier by the fact that at this point Romania was not yet a member of the EU.

Since the Romanian EU accession, Bucharest has clearly been the most important supporter of Moldova in the European Union. However, although Hungarian contributions and engagement is marginal compared to Romanian efforts, they seem to have one unique advantage for Moldovan leadership: They are much more neutral concerning Moldovan domestic politics. According to an active Hungarian diplomat, "Moldovans learned that if Romanians offer something, there is always something else in the background. Our ties are weaker in this regard, we are simply too far away—thus if Moldovans have problems either with the EU or with Romania, they very often come to Budapest."[32]

High-ranking Moldovan officials frequently visit Hungary, especially since the pro-Western turn in Moldovan domestic politics in 2009. Since then, Moldovan Foreign Minister Iurie Leancă has already visited Budapest *six times*, alongside several lower-level delegations exchanged between Budapest and Chisinau. Besides these political ties, Hungary also plays an active role in supporting the administrative and judicial reforms in Moldova.

Hungarian Development Assistance in Moldova

Outlines of the Hungarian development policy were adopted by the government in 2003, in a document titled *Hungarian International Development Cooperation Policy*. This strategy prescribed that sharing transition experiences should be one of the main focal points of Hungarian development cooperation, besides assistance in education, knowledge transfer, agriculture, healthcare, water management, and infrastructure planning. The strategy openly declared that Hungarian development assistance should be planned in accordance with the coming EU accession, and by taking into account the EU and OECD development principles.[33]

The geographical focus of international development cooperation and democracy assistance conducted by the Hungarian government is oriented mostly toward the Balkans. Moldova and Ukraine are the main partners from eastern Europe. Until 2008, both were declared strategic partners, but funding was cut due to the financial crisis. Thus, now the status of Ukraine is degraded to a project-based partner country.

Bilateral development cooperation with Moldova is regulated by a bilateral agreement that was signed in 2007 for three years, which was further extended recently. The strategic objective is to support the approximation of Moldova to EU norms, and to help Moldova develop in terms of economy and social affairs.[34] From 2009 to 2010, the most important success of Hungarian development policy in Moldova was assistance in creation of the Dniester Euroregion, in which Transnistria is also included. Hungarian diplomats and experts of the International Centre for Democratic Transition managed to establish good working relations with the separatist leadership of Transnistria; Hungarian Ambassador to Moldova György Varga even had a personal bilateral meeting with Igor Smirnov. In addition to this, several smaller projects were conducted: training, a contribution to the Second World Congress of Gagauzians, and others. Besides this, the Hungarian embassy in Chisinau also conducted some micro-projects.[35] They could do so because, from 2006 onward, Budapest decided to extend the authorities of the Hungarian Embassy in Chisinau to give it more influence in deciding micro-level development projects, based on their local experience and knowledge. Since then, allocation of some of the international development cooperation funds dedicated to Moldova has been decided directly by the embassy.[36] For the amounts of Hungarian assistance to Moldova, see table 8.1.

As one may see in table 8.1, even though Moldova is declared a strategic partner in development cooperation, if compared to the overall Hungarian spending, Moldova's share is very limited. It has never exceeded 5 percent, and in some cases it has even been below 1 percent. However, the diversity of the Hungarian development assistance project is remarkable: from supporting agricultural projects to providing assistance to police and army personnel. Hungary has also been engaged in humanitarian assistance, democracy assistance, and infrastructural projects.

Table 8.1. The Moldovan share in Hungarian bilateral international development cooperation from 2003–2010

Year	All Hungarian bilateral international development cooperation (in thousand USD)	Funds spent on Moldova (in thousand USD)	Moldovan share in Hungarian international development assistance (in %)
2003	6,148.6	74.3	1.21
2004	4,108.5	133.3	3.24
2005	3,904.6	n.a.	n.a.
2006	1,843.1	n.a.	n.a.
2007	8,186.9	402.1	4.91
2008	15,194.4	444.9	2.93
2009	29,345.8	162.5	0.55
2010	8,699.6	67.9	0.78

Source: The pre-2011 webpage of the Hungarian Foreign Ministry, http://www .mfa.gov.hu (accessed June 5, 2011).

Notes: Amount of funds spent on Moldova in 2003 and 2004 was calculated by authors due to the lack of accessible, comprehensive official information. Generally the authors feel it necessary to express their dissatisfaction with the transparency and accessibility of Hungarian official documents related to international development assistance activities.

Conclusion

Since Hungarian independence in 1989, relations with Moldova received special attention from Budapest. Yet concerning the question raised at the beginning of this chapter, the authors argue that the relatively intense level of Hungarian engagement was not caused by the general importance of Moldova per se, but rather motivated by external factors. In the early 1990s, Budapest's main motivation was tension between Hungary and Romania connected with the situation of Hungarian minorities living in Romania. The first two democratic governments of Hungary paid particularly strong attention to the issue of Hungarians living in neighboring countries, and thus relations with Moldova were also relatively important, because of their potential to be used as leverage against Romania. In other words, Budapest used intensive relations with Chisinau to put pressure on Bucharest by supporting pro-independence forces in Moldova.

However, since the mid-1990s, this "derivative" importance of Moldova has decreased. First, in Budapest a more leftist-liberal government came to power in

1994, for which the question of Hungarian minorities abroad held considerably lower importance. As a consequence, the level of commitment toward Moldova also decreased. Second, Moldovan politics also changed: the second Andrei Sangheli government that came to power in 1994 kept much more distance from Romania than did the Moldovan Popular Front. An act emblematic of this era was the Moldovan Referendum of 1994, which closed the way to Moldovan-Romanian unification. The Moldovan constitution adopted in 1994 was also in favor of preserving the country's independence. Consequently, the activities of Budapest also shifted to areas of more technical cooperation, such as trade, knowledge transfer, etc.

Hungarian foreign policy toward Moldova was further intensified following the EU accession of Hungary. When the European Neighbourhood Policy was launched, Budapest needed to find its niche. Ukraine and Moldova were chosen as two priority countries in the eastern neighborhood. The new External Relations Strategy, adopted in 2008, clearly reflects this choice. In the ENP context, Hungary managed to reach some important and spectacular successes: The first-ever EU Common Visa Application Centre was opened in the Hungarian embassy in Chisinau, the first commander of the EUBAM mission was a Hungarian, and so was the second (and final) EU Special Representative, etc.

However, this relative importance of Moldova for Hungary applies only in the narrow context of Hungary's contribution to the eastern dimension of the ENP. With a wider perspective, it becomes clear that in the East, Russia is still Hungary's key partner, and it will remain so for the foreseeable future. This is reflected in the amount of Hungarian development assistance funds spent on Moldova. Among the Eastern European target countries, Moldova is clearly prioritized. However, in the wider context, its share is marginal.

All in all, the level and nature of political and technical cooperation between Hungary and Moldova is not likely to change in the near future. Hungarian experiences transferred to Moldova seem valuable to Chisinau; technical, non-politicized development projects are important contributions. Concerning Moldova in the wider framework of the ENP, Budapest is an important, committed player, if not a dominant one. The success of the pro-European and pro-independence foreign policy pursued by the current Moldovan leadership is in the best interests of Hungary, and therefore a relatively high level of Hungarian engagement will likely prevail in the future.

Notes

1. László J. Kiss, *Magyarország szomszédsági kapcsolatainak jövője* [The future of Hungary's neighborly relations] (Budapest: Magyar Külügyminisztérium, 2007), http://www.mfa.gov.hu/NR/rdonlyres/0B215186-028A-4C5E-A871-FEF9C68A5DB8/0/Magyarorszag_szomszedsagi_kapcs070508.pdf (accessed June 20, 2011).

2. For more information see the program of the József Antall government, *A nemzeti megújhodás programja. A Köztársaság első három éve* [Program of national rebirth.

116   *András Rácz and Andrea Ambrus*

The first three years of the Republic] (Budapest, 1990), 177–84.

3. Pál Dunay, "Az átmenet magyar külpolitikája" [Foreign policy of the Hungarian transition], in *Magyar külpolitika a 20. században* [Hungarian foreign policy in the twentieth century], ed. Ferenc Gazdag and László J. Kiss (Budapest: Zrínyi Kiadó, 2004), 227.

4. László Lengyel, "Külpolitika vagy nemzetpolika" [Foreign policy or national policy], in *Kormány a mérlegen* [Government on the scales], ed. Csaba Gombár et al. (Budapest: Korridor, 1994), 353–54.

5. Hungarian Embassy to Moldova, "Fontosabb egyezmények" [Main agreements], http://www.mfa.gov.hu/kulkepviselet/ML/hu/Bilateralis/politikai_kapcsolatok.htm (accessed July 2, 2011).

6. A Hungarian diplomat in an interview with the authors, July 20, 2011.

7. "A Külügyminisztérium tájékoztatója (szóvivője útján) a magyar-román viszony megítéléséről" [Communiqué of the Ministry of Foreign Affairs (through the spokesperson) on the Hungarian-Romanian relations], in *Magyar Külpolitikai Évkönyv 1992* [Yearbook of Hungarian foreign policy 1992], (Budapest: Magyar Külügyminisztérium, 1993), 211–13.

8. Iván Bába, *Irányváltás a magyar külpolitikában 1990–1994* [Direction change in Hungarian foreign policy 1990–1994] (Budapest: Windsor Klub Füzetek 2, 1994), 23.

9. A Hungarian diplomat in an interview with the authors, Budapest, March 2011.

10. "Snegur Gönczel találkozott, Hornnal nem" [Snegur met only Göncz, not Horn], *Magyar Hírlap*, April 21, 1995.

11. Hungarian Embassy to Moldova, "Fontosabb."

12. Géza Jeszenszky, "A magyar-moldovai szerződésről. Elfelejthető-e az 1201-es?" [The Hungarian-Moldovan treaty. May one forget the 1201?], *Magyar Hírlap*, May 20, 1995.

13. Parliamentary Assembly of the Council of Europe, Recommendation 1201 (1993), "On an additional protocol on the rights of national minorities to the European Convention on Human Rights," February 1, 1993, http://assembly.coe.int/Main.asp?link=/Documents/AdoptedText/ta93/EREC1201.htm (accessed July 2, 2011).

14. Géza Jeszenszky, "A magyar-moldovai."

15. Hungarian Embassy to Moldova, "Fontosabb."

16. "Moldova kitart a semlegesség mellett" [Moldova persists in neutrality], *Népszabadság*, June 5, 1997.

17. "Moldova számít tapasztalatainkra" [Moldova counts on our experiences], *Népszabadság*, October 28, 1997.

18. 94/1998 (XII. 29.) OGY határozata a Magyar Köztársaság biztonság- és védelempolitikájának alapelveiről [Parliamentary Resolution No. 94/1998 (XII. 29.) on the Principles of the Security and Defence Policy of the Republic of Hungary], pt. 11.

19. The National Security Strategy of the Republic of Hungary, 2004, ¶ III.2.3, http://www.mfa.gov.hu/NR/rdonlyres/61FB6933-AE67-47F8-BDD3-ECB1D9ADA7A1/0/national_security_strategy.pdf (accessed June 20, 2011).

20. Ibid.

21. László J. Kiss, *Magyarország szomszédsági*, 6–8.

22. National Security Strategy, ¶ III.2.3.

23. Ferenc Somogyi, "Magyar érdekek, uniós értékek. Az euroatlanti bővítés új helyzetbe hozta Magyarország szomszédságpolitikáját" [Hungarian interests, EU values. Euro-Atlantic accession put Hungarian neighborhood policy in a new context], *Népszabadság*, April 2, 2005, http://www.nol.hu/archivum/archiv-357249 (accessed June 23, 2011).

24. Ibid.

25. Hungarian diplomat, July 20, 2011.

26. Hungary's External Relations Strategy, 2008, http://www.mfa.gov.hu/kum/en/bal/foreign_policy/external_relations_strategy/ (accessed July 2, 2011).

27. Hungarian Foreign Ministry, "Hungary in the world," http://www.kulugyminiszterium.hu/kum/en/bal/foreign_policy/hungary_in_the_world/ (accessed December 9, 2009).

28. Hungary's External Relations.

29. Ibid.

30. Ibid.

31. Common Visa Application Centre, http://www.cac.md/about_en.html (accessed July 2, 2011).

32. Hungarian diplomat, March 2011.

33. The document describing the policy priorities was made in 2006, but it is still valid: *A Brief Summary of Hungary's International Development Co-operation Activities* (Budapest, 2006) http://www.mfa.gov.hu/NR/rdonlyres/6C909959-3C4A-4881-9096-9C8F368B4748/0/061206_ODA_HU.pdf (accessed December 20, 2009).

34. *Beszámoló a magyar nemzetközi fejlesztési együttműködés és humanitárius segítségnyújtás 2009-ben megvalósított tevékenységéről* [Report on the Hungarian international development cooperation and humanitarian aid activities conducted in 2009] (Budapest, 2010), 9.

35. Ibid., 29–30.

36. *Beszámoló a magyar nemzetközi fejlesztési együttműködés és humanitárius segítségnyújtás 2006-ban megvalósított tevékenységéről* [Report on the Hungarian international development cooperation and humanitarian aid activities conducted in 2006] (Budapest, 2007), 14.

Chapter Nine

Italy: A Missing Actor on the Moldovan Regional Stage?

Davide Zaffi

As Moldova emerged as an independent state, Italy was engaged in a tentative policy aimed at defining its role in Central Europe. The "kidnapped" countries of this region, as the parlance of the era called them, had only recently been released, one after another, into freedom. Their return to history raised apprehensions, but it also opened the way to new opportunities.

For decades, Italy had lacked a policy on its own toward the East. Comfortably embedded in Western international organizations, it found itself subjected to what was known, and accepted willingly, as the "foreign constraint" of the post-war bipolar world.[1] This constraint was not unpleasant, because it created a situation in which all of the former European great powers, with the exception of Russia in the guise of the Soviet Union, were placed in parity. Parity with Germany and France, "this eternally and almost pathetically pursued condition,"[2] was now realized, admittedly in a status of dependency, but the dependency was general, and imposed by a superpower so mighty that there was no room for even insincere recriminations. In other words, it was parity without effort: An ideal situation for those who, under normal circumstances, had had no chance to reach it.

When dealing with international problems, Italy acted as a member of Western organizations, content to identify with their actions and not really interested in increasing or diminishing its share in them. Italian foreign policy during this period has been judged by some as "passive, lifeless," and at certain moments even "prone to choices made by others."[3] Stern judgments like these reveal less an intention to place blame, perhaps, than a recognition that Italy could have developed a slightly more self-conscious policy while keeping perfect observance of its international obligations. Although it is true that Italy seldom raised its voice to influence the course of Western organizations, it is easy to see, on the other hand, that this attitude did not prevent the fomenting of concrete national interests, albeit not openly formulated nor even deliberately assumed. As a matter of fact, in the Cold War decades Italy recorded, for many concurrent reasons, noteworthy social and economic advances, both in respect to its own history and in comparison to other states.

Almost unable to say how it had been possible, in the second half of the 1980s Italy had got the sixth place among the great economies of the capitalist world, and the newspapers often indulged in picturing the *sorpasso* of England as if it were within reach.[4]

Toward the end of the Cold War, the Italian government instinctively realized that some additional activity in the international arena or, as the diplomatic jargon puts it, some additional assumption of responsibility would well suit a G7 member in full ascent. Italian public opinion, usually apathetic when issues of foreign policy are at stake, indicated in many ways its satisfaction at this new inclination of the government. Single decisions of the latter, which seemed to suggest a desire to matter more in Europe and the world, met with broad support—even though they were taken, as a rule, more to please a vein of rhapsodic patriotism, than to implement a comprehensive strategy.[5] The disintegration of the Communist bloc, and even more still the fall of the Berlin Wall, which paved the way for the German reunification, lent a note of urgency to the search for a new definition of the Italian foreign policy.

By the mid-1980s, however, some fundamental questions had not yet been answered. Italy was, in all appearances, ready to play a bigger role, but to the service of what cause? With what goals in mind? And, last but not least, in what direction?

Quite unexpectedly a new stage, before almost entirely inaccessible, was now opening. It was not far from home, in an area that was once familiar, and where the hierarchy of power (or influence) was still to be determined: Central Europe.

In the glorious days of Risorgimento, hatred of the Habsburgs and the principle of nationality had brought forth in the Italian lands a loud, but not superficial solidarity with Poles and Hungarians, coupled with a belief that any serious plan aimed at reshaping politically this part of the continent directly affected Italian interests. For both Giuseppe Mazzini and Count Cavour, each in his own way, Central Europe was a region of great relevance to the Italian future. But after unification, it rapidly disappeared from the Italian horizon. Liberal Italy was hunched over internal questions—perhaps not as categorically as some authors pretend,[6] but internationalist ideologies and inventive foreign policy, which had thus far proven so useful to Italian goals, ceased to inspire the government, once it came to establish itself in Rome.

In the interwar period, Italy under fascist rule made a comeback in Central Europe. It was not prompted by regained confidence or newly acquired resources, but rather by an overstretched effort, encouraged by the countries of the region themselves, to establish a system of alliances, and later, in the early days of war, of military forces, centered on Italy and strong enough to limit, at least in South-Eastern Europe, expanding German power.

After the end of the unnatural Cold War division of the continent, a second Italian comeback, naturally in pursuit of different values, seemed possible.

The Danube and Beyond

Although not directly connected to Moldova, it was important to stress some of the elements marking the start of a new Italian policy toward the East in 1989. For the same reason, it seems appropriate to briefly discuss the so-called Quadrangolare, the most promising Italian initiative in Central Europe since WWII. Free from the "foreign constraint" imposed on it by the Cold War, Italy eventually felt able to demonstrate its potential and to offer political leadership, whatever this word may imply, to a group of neighboring countries.

Responding to a *ballon d'essai* coming from Budapest, where the prospect of German reunification aroused (anti-Soviet) hopes, but also some concerns,[7] the Italian government acceded in the first half of 1989 to the idea of a new regional configuration, albeit not an original one,[8] in which Italy would function as a pole of attraction for Central European countries prepared to leave the Warsaw Pact, or to soften their neutrality and approach the West. Italy would accompany or, rather, guide them during the possibly problematic time of transition.

Besides Italy and Hungary, neutral Austria and non-aligned Yugoslavia adhered to the organization, which was thus named Quadrangolare. In some Western capitals it was immediately perceived, with non-benevolent exaggeration, foremost as an instrument to serve Italian ambitions.[9] The overexposure of Italian Foreign Minister Gianni De Michelis in the media, and his inclination to vibrant statements at press conferences, may have contributed to this sentiment.

He took a more academic tone, however, for an article published in early 1990 in the influential American magazine *Foreign Policy*, in which he explained the mission of the organization.[10] It is perhaps noteworthy that he started with a reference to Germany. He quoted Benjamin Disraeli, who had labeled German reunification of his time the "real revolutionary event of the century," a definition De Michelis found not inappropriate for the unconditional merger of the DDR into the BRD. This epochal change suggested the opportunity to build "other groupings" which, of course, ought not to be viewed as a "counterweight" to Germany, destined to grow strong even against its will, but as "a means of ensuring a balanced process of integration in every part of Europe." According to the Italian foreign minister, the Quadrangolare was meant to be "temporary," a "bridging solution" toward the full accession of certain countries into the European Community. If there was an Italian ambition, then it lay in the will to better serve the Community itself. It was to be hoped, therefore, that some unspoken misgivings might be quickly dispelled, and the European Community support both politically and economically groupings of regional collaboration like the one created in the area defined by De Michelis as "South Central Europe."

This geopolitical definition was, by the way, unusual for Italian scholarship. Was it meant to be a cautious suggestion that Italy would not have objected to German hegemony in Northern Central Europe, provided Germany accepted Italian leadership, however soft, in the South? Recurrent statements of De Michelis on the existence of two Central Europes, one gravitating on the Baltic and the other on the Adriatic,[11] seem to confirm this interpretation.

Besides the political aspect, but not entirely independent from it, Italy via the Quadrangolare sought to prepare for an "Italian economic penetration"[12] of the Danube basin. De Michelis, himself born in Venice, understood more rapidly than others that in the so-called North-East of the country, especially in the Veneto region, a figurative army of mostly small-sized entrepreneurs was ready to march eastward to occupy several sectors in the opening Central European economies.[13] Italian foreign and economic policy, strengthening one another, would create a coordinated system with promising perspectives for both.

A diplomatic initiative, as anything else, is never good or bad in itself. It receives qualification from its context. In the case of the Italian-sponsored Quadrangolare, the context soon proved unfriendly. The European Community met the initiative with coldness, despite the fact that the documents of the organization, renamed in March 1992 the Central European Initiative, painstakingly declared to serve the communitarian aim of eastwards integration. It may be assumed that some European Community countries, especially among the big ones, were not enthusiastic at unilateral Italian activism in Central Europe. On the other hand, it is uncertain whether the Italian government had at least tried to undertake in Brussels and the major European capitals the necessary lobbying to gain a previous European Community's support for its enterprise.

De Michelis's internal critics, on the other side, feared that Italy was overreaching itself, engaging in an ill-prepared action, whose concrete aims, in spite of lofty declarations, remained unclear, the only visible one being a hedge against rising German influence. In political and diplomatic circles, many saw the Mediterranean, not Central Europe, as the natural place for Italian engagement.[14] There was moreover a certain reluctance to seek alternatives to the multilateralism that had ensured for decades many advantages to Italy at a convenient price.[15]

All of these critics stressing that Italy lacked the ability to play a role in Central Europe, coalesced into a kind of self-fulfilling prophecy.

In fact, state institutions, like the parliament and the public administration, did not react as a coherent foreign policy would have required. Since autumn 1989, it was clear that engagement in Central Europe would involve a considerable amount of money, but the law making funds available for public investment in the countries of the Quadrangolare, the only international organization with Italian leadership, came only three years later. Moreover, they were made dependent on such terrific bureaucratic procedures that their impact, though not at all irrelevant, failed to shape the political environment.[16]

Against this background, a readjustment of Italian foreign policy was inevitable. In April 1993 a new minister, Beniamino Andreatta, took office at the Farnesina.[17] In a programmatic article written some weeks later for *Il Mulino*, he announced indirectly that things would change with regard to Central Europe. He stressed that Italy would increase its contribution in ideas and resources to the international organizations instead of starting, or continuing, unilateral action.

Since, however, an era had come in which it was no longer sufficient for Italy "to belong" but imperative for it "to act," Andreatta went on indicating what Italy, also in pursuit of its own interests, was willing to offer to each organization one by one, and what expectations it held. In his long listing (ranging from the United Nations to NATO, European Community, CSCE, G7, GATT) he eloquently omitted the CEI, thus making it clear that this Italian experiment had been for all practical purposes closed down.[18]

The initiative that had begun with the aim of asserting Italy's international role ended by displaying the limits of its possibilities.[19] The fate of the CEI discouraged further action in the region and it perhaps too rapidly convinced Italian think tanks that their country's autonomous initiatives were doomed for the future to suffer from the chronic malady known in Italy as *velleitarismo*.[20] It is a peculiar kind of feeble volition, i.e., a sincere and sometimes even generous desire to act, which, unfortunately, at any time can awaken to its own limits and get volatile.

This pessimistic mood, clothed in objective terms by some analysts, rendered a lasting imprint on Italian foreign policy toward the East in the years to come. It was not balanced by the recognition that with the aim of avoiding the risk of *velleitarismo*, Italian foreign policy had often fallen into the opposite evil and "remained beneath the line of what was just and possible."[21] The character of post-1989 Italian-Moldovan relations is very much determined by this structural and mental background.

Does Culture Matter?

In the last Soviet years, many Moldovans came to realize that they spoke a Romance language, not a Slavic one. What unbiased philologists had always held, and the ruling Communist party always openly or surreptitiously denied, was growing evident to all. The question of language assumed a huge importance in Moldova and fueled the centripetal forces from the Soviet Union no less than the prospect of a free market or the enactment of political rights.[22]

Italy, like many countries in the West, was more inclined to deal with a Soviet Union more or less reformed,[23] than with a number of new states, whose viability was not certain and whose frontiers were in many cases the result of whimsical decisions made by Communist leaders in Moscow. When, however, it became apparent that precisely this latter option was to pass, official Italy assigned no particular meaning to the fact that among the post-Soviet states, there was one whose official language "draws itself from Rome,"[24] and where the majority of the people felt they were a community sharing most important things with ancient Italy.

Right after the creation of the Moldovan Foreign Ministry in September 1991, which came as a consequence of the declaration of independence, Chisinau, following the example of other republican capitals, requested from Moscow that its own diplomats be appointed as personnel of certain Soviet Embassies. In particular it asked for Moldovan representation among the diplomatic staff in Germany, Italy and Spain. This choice was dictated in part by a predictable engagement of these countries in South-Eastern Europe, and in part by the desire to revive alleged ties of origin and language. Italy was the only country important under both headings.[25]

It was, of course, in the interest of Moldova to stress the existence of cultural ties with the West, and to have them play a role in the realm of international policy. Precisely this Moldovan interest, if not the cultural ties themselves, might have called Italy's attention to the new state. Yet, in the first years of Moldovan independence it is difficult to detect any sign of Italian encouragement or solidarity given on the ground of special cultural bonds.

The first piece of official Italian-Moldovan correspondence after the collapse of the Soviet Union was a letter written by the Italian head of state, Francesco Cossiga, to his Moldovan colleague Mircea Snegur, dated January 3, 1992. In it no mention was made of any special connection existing between the two countries nor, it may be added, to any particular Italian concern with reference to the independence and prosperity of the Moldovan state. As a matter of fact, Cossiga dwelled comparatively long on the Commonwealth of Independent States, of which Moldova happened to be a member, and seemed to hint that the CIS, rather than Moldova itself, had a contribution to make to the stability of the region. The letter further contains an invitation to Moldova to stay in line with the international obligations falling upon it and ends with the dry statement that "since Moldova has now become a subject of international law . . . Italy is ready to establish diplomatic relations with your country."[26]

In a way, this letter of Cossiga, sticking to the strictest formalities of wording and content, anticipated how Italian policy and diplomacy would handle contact with Moldova in the years to come.

Official relations between the two countries were established on February 21, 1992. For a transitional period it was agreed, according to an Italian suggestion, that they would be entrusted to the competence of the two countries' respective embassies in Moscow. It could, however, hardly pass unnoticed that Rome sent ambassadors to the three Baltic capitals as early as March 1992. Only a couple of months later, Minsk and Kiev followed. By June 1992, all post-Soviet states on European soil hosted an Italian Embassy, except for Moldova.

The reasons for this peculiar dislocation of the diplomatic corps are not clear. Even well-informed insiders admit that "it is difficult to understand if this happened due to political considerations or just out of economic constraint."[27]

It may be that Rome did not consider it advisable to open an embassy in a country where, precisely in early 1992, an armed conflict had arisen, in which Russia was involved, albeit with unclear status. On the other hand, it remains true that Germany, for example, did open an embassy in Chisinau in spring 1992.

Either a row of weighty but undeclared considerations or, rather, protracted neglect, came to bear on the Italian position in the following years. Only in November 2008 was the time judged ripe for the opening of an embassy in Chisinau. Italian-Moldovan relations had been assigned, after Moscow, to the Italian Embassy in Budapest (from 1996 to 2004) and then to the one in Bucharest, before finally arriving at its natural location.[28]

The discomfort provoked on the Moldovan side by what was felt to be a persistent lack of understanding of Moldovan interests, soon manifested itself and with time it became a constant element in diplomatic talks between Chisinau and Rome. In April 1995, for instance, at a meeting between deputy ministers for foreign affairs, the Moldovans stressed "the difficulties we meet in trying to contact the Italian Embassy [then in Moscow]. It is evident that even the most engaged ambassador cannot follow step-by-step the development of bilateral relations, if he is accredited to nine states." The Moldovans begged the Italian government for "other arrangements, which can permit our relations to get to a qualitatively higher level."[29]

The situation was indeed unsatisfactory if credit is to be given to an internal note of the Moldovan Foreign Ministry, from which we learn that until the end of 1995, in the first four years of independence, the Italian ambassador accredited to Moldova never once visited the small republic. Not even "a representative of the Italian Embassy" had at that point been dispatched there.[30]

The question of diplomatic representation, with its great practical and moral impact, epitomizes, for a rather long period, the general picture of political relations between Italy and Moldova, to which the two nations' asserted kinship made a modest contribution, if any.

Fluctuations

From the very beginning, the Moldovan side showed a keen interest in signing bilateral documents, with the twin goals of regulating collaboration with a first-rate EU country and of improving the international standing of the apparently fragile Moldovan state.[31]

First of all Chisinau aspired to a Treaty of Friendship, the wording of which would have been, in a sense, less important than its mere existence. But specific issues, like the bilateral regulation of public and private economic activities, were also waiting for official agreements. These issues might have, at first glance, only a technical character, but they were nevertheless occasions, in Moldovan eyes, for strengthening the overall collaboration between the two states.

Italy too might have found it opportune to substantiate its relations with Moldova. No major obstacles seemed to prompt the rejection of the requests coming from Chisinau for a somehow intensified political recognition. But progress along this path, which hardly entailed more than the fulfillment of standard procedures, proved lengthy and troublesome. From February 1992 to March 1997, not a single bilateral document was signed by the two countries.

Interesting in this context is the report that the Moldovan ambassador in Vienna, Valentin Ciumac, sent to Chisinau on February 22, 1996. Ciumac had been shortly before appointed cumulatively ambassador also to Italy and he had made his first trip to Rome in this capacity in order to present his letters of accreditation to the local authorities.[32]

On February 7, 1996, he had a meeting with Italian President Oscar Luigi Scalfaro. On that occasion, among courteous expressions, he drew attention to the fact that while assisting "a growing activity on the part of the economic agents of both countries, no interstate agreement exists, determining at least the principles of development in bilateral relations." To this remark Scalfaro, according to the Moldovan delegation's report, did not react and only expressed his desire to visit Moldova in the near future, a country in which he claimed to have a keen interest (this desire, by the way, was to remain unfulfilled).

The previous day the Moldovan Ambassador had been received by representatives of the Italian foreign ministry (neither the minister himself nor a vice-minister was available). To them he handed a draft of the Treaty on Friendship and Cooperation prepared by Chisinau. In doing so he loyally executed his government's instructions, but he could have hardly believed in the opportunity of such a step. Moldovan diplomacy knew full well that the Italian government was not ready to go that far.

The note of the Moldovan Foreign Ministry quoted above, dealing with Italian issues, read as following: "As to the State Treaty, the Italian side made clear to us its position, which consists of this: We should not begin by signing so broad and 'ambitious' [quotation marks in the original] a Treaty but rather a political Common Declaration, the text of which will be prepared by the Italians."[33] The talks of the new Moldovan ambassador in Rome did not change the attitude of the counterpart.

Finally Ciumac informed Chisinau that "I reiterated the wish . . . to take up again the process of bilateral negotiations aimed at coming to an agreement on the reciprocal protection of investments." Dialogue on this point had been apparently broken off or at least de facto suspended, and the prospects for its resumption were gloomy.

The general tone of the report shows that at no moment did Ciumac have the impression that he was speaking to people really interested in doing business.[34]

When the first bilateral document since Moldova's independence was eventually finalized, on March 20, 1997, it was not the treaty the Moldovan side thought was needed, but a low-profile common declaration. It deals with the "Principles of the Relations between the Republic of Moldova and the Italian Republic." The text stresses, obviously for the first time, "the common Latin origin . . . and the cultural and linguistic affinities between the two peoples." It mentions further, in general terms, the values shared by the parties (peace, democracy, human rights, protection of the environment, etc.), and contains one article with political implications, which states that the parties support "a quick, unconditional and total withdrawal of the military Russian formations from the territory of the Moldovan republic."[35]

Did the declaration mark a change in the attitude of Italy toward Moldova? Was it signaling the emergence of a concrete Italian interest for the region, as the allusion to the Russian military presence might have suggested? The impression that something had changed was strengthened only a few months later, October 21, 1997, when in Rome the Agreement on the Mutual Protection of Investments was signed, which had taken so much work, or simply so much time, to be completed.

As a matter of fact, in May 1996, a new government had taken office, led by Romano Prodi. Convinced that in the near future some Central and even Eastern European countries would gain accession to the EU, he felt that Italy had to quickly improve its standing in the region. Deputy Minister Piero Fassino, much more than the titular Foreign Minister Lamberto Dini, who had been appointed mainly for reasons of party balancing, was the inspired executor of this new or, more precisely, renewed eastward orientation. He found his way to Chisinau, the highest ranking officer at the time ever to make the trip, in order to sign the '97 declaration.

Fassino himself had shortly before published an interesting article in the quasi-official review *Affari Esteri* under the title "La Ost-Politik dell'Italia."[36] In this article, for the first time since the distant De Michelis days, Italy was anew presented as a "bridge between Central-Europe and the European Union;" once again a member of the Italian government happened to honestly believe in "the possibility to become a privileged partner for many Central-European countries."[37] Once again the idea was evoked that Italy enjoyed much credit in the region as the only "great power" which "does not have and does not want to have hegemonic intentions." It was only natural that Fassino came to speak also of the opportunity to "revitalize" the CEI. And in a genuine CEI spirit he wrote: "To the simplistic remark: 'Germany is already there' . . . [we answer] that we do not accept the idea of *domaines reservés*. It would be stupid if, after we succeeded in overcoming the logic of hostile blocs, we would replace it with a policy of "spheres of influence."

Words, in this particular case, were followed by deeds. The vice minister traveled much, and signed many bilateral documents. In most of the Eastern capitals, where the interest for an active political collaboration with Italy was still high, he left a good impression. At home he had an excellent relationship with his prime minister. Unlike De Michelis, he did not need to fear the mistrust of his colleagues in the government, although they offered him more an uncommitted acquiescence than an active support.

Sustainable *Ostpolitik*, however, cannot rely merely on the goodwill or the desire of a few politicians to improve their personal stance. It has to be, or must strive to be, the common enterprise of several leading circles of the country, involving diplomacy, finance, economy and the media. It must try to win, at least in broad terms, a degree of popularity or conscious acceptance in public opinion. At the moment Fassino was writing his bold article, these elements were, unfortunately, still lacking. With his activity, bordering on activism, he tried to create the conditions of which his activity should have been the expression. Chancing to jump without solid ground under the feet, the phantom of *velleitarismo* once again loomed inescapably.

No later than the end of 1997 the center-left Prodi government entered a deep political crisis, and in April 1998 it finally fell. Prodi left the scene for a while,[38] and in the following D'Alema government, Fassino smoothly moved to another ministry. The political color of the cabinet had not changed, but Italian *Ostpolitik*, in the way it had been conducted for a year and a half, ceased to be a priority. Its disappearance from the agenda was rapid and, in general, unwept.[39]

This development of domestic policy was mirrored by the fate of the Agreement on the Mutual Protection of Investments mentioned above. Four years elapsed from the day it was signed until it could get parliamentary ratification in Rome. It entered into force only in June 2001. In the beginning, with the Quadrangolare, a vision was entertained of an Italian bicycle driving to Central and Eastern Europe on two wheels. Ten years later, the political wheel was still not spinning at the pace of the economic one.

By 2001, exchanges between Italy and Moldova had strongly increased and, on the aggregate, had brilliantly pushed Italy to the top of the list of Western economic partners in the post-Soviet republic.[40] This record has not changed to the present date. According to official sources, in 2010 Italy received 9.56 percent of total Moldovan exports and delivered 7.02 percent of all imports (the same figures for Germany were 4.89 percent and 7.64 percent respectively; for France 1.51 percent and 1.77 percent).[41]

To trade is to be added a less conventional, but no less important economic tie. Since the final years of the past century, Italy has become an essential point of reference for Moldova, because of the many emigrants working temporarily in the peninsula. Considering the total amount of remittances, which constitutes in its entirety a quarter of the Moldovan GNP, emigration to Italy is both socially and economically a key issue. After Russia, which for Moldovans is a visa-free country with, for obvious reasons, a familiar mentality, Italy hosts the largest number of Moldovan workers. Italy alone accounts for almost half of all Moldovans legally residing in the EU.[42]

Mention of these figures is made not just in view to give a more complete picture of Italian-Moldovan relations, but in line with the basic intention of this paper, to highlight additional elements, which theoretically would allow Italy to exert its political influence in and around Moldova, helping ensure the positive development of local affairs.

Perhaps against the intentions of the successive actors in bilateral relations, but in accordance with the available documents and facts, it can be stated that up until the current day, Italy has barely made use of the objective *atouts* it possesses in this most eastern part of South Central Europe.

Conclusion

Italian policy in the Moldovan region is conducted entirely within and through international organizations, primarily the European Union. This attitude corresponds not only to the existing obligations of Italy, but reflects also the country's loyal commitment to these institutions. It remains true, however, that in this context the Italian input, insofar as there is actually one, goes almost unnoticed and does not increase the value that other countries attach to Italian collaboration.

States with more weight in international organizations, irrespective of the fact that here their expectations and interests are regularly taken into account,[43] let on the contrary their voice be heard also individually, if they believe it may serve the general welfare.

On her visit to Bucharest on October 12, 2010, German Chancellor Merkel, for instance, felt able to kindly advise the Romanian and the Moldovan governments to regulate once and for all the delineation of their common border.[44] Leaving aside the fact that a border agreement was indeed signed on November 8, Merkel's readiness to touch in public upon a subject concerning third-party countries and on which EU Commission President José Manuel Barroso had already devoted several declarations, shows and increases a remarkable German self-confidence, which by the way may prove beneficial also to the stability of that part of Europe. The insertion of the highly sensitive issue of the Transnistrian-Moldovan conflict settlement into the so-called Meseberg Memorandum, agreed on by Germany and Russia in June 2010, seems to go along the same lines. The agreement, still awaiting implementation, clearly originates in the framework of unilateral German foreign policy and has only weak connections, if any, to decision making in the EU.[45] Future developments of course remain uncertain, but after the memorandum, it is clear that no solution in Transnistria will be reached without the involvement of Germany. This perception alone enhances Germany's image and the desire of foreign policy actors to come to terms with Berlin.

There is no need to challenge Germany, whose initiatives do not harm, in principle, the credibility of the EU or its allies. But, likewise, Germany would not feel disturbed by initiatives of others, if they were conducive to the common goals of stability and prosperity.

Moldova is an important test of the seriousness of Italy's claim to count as a first-rate European power, which it is, to its own trouble.

With a frozen conflict on one side, requiring political solutions at the international level, and, on the other side, with an interesting economic potential that clearly includes the Ukrainian province of Odessa and the Romanian Black Sea coast, the Moldovan region, placed at the crossroads between East and (South)West, manifests a peculiar openness toward a possibly increasing Italian attention. Linguistic affinity, which makes the trouble of reciprocal understanding easier, or at least, lets people believe so, contributes to it as much as more concrete, material considerations.

Exerting influence nowadays does not mean that a state try to impose conditions of unilateral advantage on its partners. Rather it means contributing more than others to orderly international relations, also there, if required, where no direct political self-interest is at stake, or, rather, just a long-term one, like the winning of moral capital is.

Notes

1. Franco Frattini, "The Fundamental Directions of Italy's Foreign Policy," *International Spectator* 39, no. 1 (2004): 95–100.
2. Fausto Bacchetti, "Considerazioni sulla politica estera italiana," *Affari Esteri* 25, no. 100 (1993): 749.
3. Carlo Santoro, *La politica estera di una media potenza. L'Italia dall'Unità ad oggi* (Bologna: Il Mulino, 1991). See in particular 187–207.
4. Ennio Di Nolfo, ed., *La politica estera italiana negli anni Ottanta* (Bari: Mandria, 2003). For the purposes of this paper see in particular Giorgio Petracchi, "L'Italia e la Ostpolitik," 293–318.
5. Antonio Varsori, *L'Italia nelle relazioni internazionali dal 1943 al 1992* (Bari: Laterza, 1998), 219–23.
6. See for instance the classical Federico Chabod, *Storia della politica estera italiana. 1870–1898* (Bari: Laterza, 1971), 1:540.
7. According to Péter Medgyessy, *Polgár a palyán* [Travelling citizen] (Budapest: Kossuth Kiadó, 2006), 167.
8. Italy and Hungary, alongside Austria, had already given life to an alliance, based on the so-called Protocolli di Roma (March 1934). Also in that case the original suggestion had come from Hungary and was meant not to contrast but to contain Germany.
9. On the organization's birth and early life, see Giovanni Baiocchi, "Origini ed evoluzione istituzionale dell'Iniziativa Centro Europea (INCE)," *Rivista di studi politici internazionali* 67, no. 2 (2000): 239–60.
10. Gianni De Michelis, "Reaching out to the East," *Foreign Policy*, Summer 1990, 44–55.
11. De Michelis elaborated on this also recently in an interview with *Rivista di Studi Ungheresi*, no. 10 (2011): 159–68. Right after the German reunification the idea that Central Europe could possibly admit a North-South divide, was not only De Michelis's. See, for instance, Flora Lewis, "Bringing in the East," *Foreign Affairs* 69, no. 4 (1990): 15–26, especially 19–20.
12. Baiocchi, "Origini ed evoluzione," 243.
13. "The original impulse to establish strong relations in the region came on the pressing of the businessmen of North-Eastern Italy. It was therefore a spontaneous thrust, with an economic rather than a political character." De Michelis, interview, 159.
14. As an authoritative voice had it "the glamour of Mitteleuropa, blurred by the passing of time, is in essence alien to the Italian character, except for Trieste . . . Italy wanted to enter a Central-European dimension which was not its own." Luigi Ferraris, "Dal Tevere al Danubio. L'Italia scopre la geopolitica da tavolino," *Limes* 1, nos. 1–2 (1993): 213–25.
15. This line of thought considers that "Italy's greatest successes have been achieved when it was able to influence important multilateral choices . . . attained within well-defined multilateral frameworks." Ettore Greco et al., "Fifteen proposals for a bipartisan European policy in Italy," *International Spectator* 41, no. 1 (2006): 7–32, here 20.
16. Law 212 of February 26, 1992, *Gazzetta Ufficiale*, no. 55, March 6, 1992. For 1992 were earmarked around $280 million, distributed on an area covering Yugoslavia (quickly split into "new" members Slovenia, Croatia and Bosnia-Herzegovina), Czechoslovakia, Poland, Hungary. The amount was not negligible, but remained modest if the goal was the consistent "Italian economic penetration" in Central-Eastern Europe.

17. After two post De Michelis interludes: Vincenzo Scotti (June/July 1992) and Emilio Colombo (August 1992–April 1993).

18. "Unilateral answers are insufficient and since the EU is the clearest expression of the tendency [to integration] we support, it is in it that Italy is called to define its role." Beniamino Andreatta, "Una politica estera per l'Italia," *Il Mulino* 42, no. 5 (1993): 881–91, here 883–84 and 889.

19. Since then the CEI survives bare of political meaning. Moldova joined the organization in 1996, possibly out of the anemic consideration that membership in it can bring no harm.

20. Due to its cultural connotation, the word can hardly be translated. In any case, it can be argued that no book on Italian foreign policy written in Italian omits it.

21. Santoro, *La politica estera*, 85. At the same time when Andreatta was announcing the quoted principal change in the Italian policy, Hungarian prime minister József Antall stated in an interview: "In the decades after the Second World War the influence of Italy in Central Europe decreased . . . But in the '80s Italy became stronger, also economically. Then the Italians came out of their isolation and rediscovered Central Europe, to which in part Italy too belongs. It would now prove very useful if Italy could further ensure its leading role in the CEI and remain active in our region." József Antall, "A Közép Európai Kezdeményezés és Magyarország" [The Central European Initiative and Hungary], interview with *Európai Utás* 4, no. 2 (1993): 2–3.

22. Gheorghe Cojocaru, *1989 la Est de Prut* (Chisinau: Prut Internaţional, 2001), especially 128–32.

23. Gorbachev was tremendously popular in Italy. His visits to Rome in 1989 and 1991 stirred up enthusiasm in the media and in the public opinion. Roberto Gaja, *L'Italia nel mondo bipolare* (Bologna: Il Mulino, 1995), 244–47. Only in Germany was he more cherished, but there *pour cause.*

24. According to the words of the first Moldovan historian Grigore Ureche, *Letopiseţul Ţării Moldovei* [Chronicle of the Moldovan country] (ca. 1645, repr., Bucharest: Minerva, 1978), 11.

25. Nicolae Ţâu, *Diplomaţie în culise: Suveranitate, independenţă, război & pace. 1990–1998* (Bucharest: Editura Enciclopedică, 2002), 87.

26. Cossiga to Snegur, January 3, 1992, Arhiva Diplomatică a Ministerului Afacelor Externe şi Integrării Europene a Republicii Moldova (AMAE), Fond 2, inv. 3-B, d. 178.

27. Luigi Vittorio Ferraris, *Manuale della politica estera italiana. 1947–1993* (Bari: Laterza, 1996), 434–35. Despite its unassuming title, the book offers lots of valuable insights.

28. Until then, Moldovan citizens had to buy a visa to buy a visa. There was no Italian consulate either in Chisinau.

29. "Intilnirile la MAE," AMAE, Fond 2, inv. 3-B, d. 176.

30. "Nota informativă," AMAE, Fond 2, inv. 3-B, d. 134. The statement is accompanied on the quoted document by five exclamation marks.

31. To which should be added the legitimate desire of single dignitaries to enhance their public image at home through public ceremonies in Western capitals or with Western politicians. See the media coverage of the visit Petru Lucinschi paid to Rome in 1997. For instance *Moldova Suverană*, September 27, 1997.

32. V. Ciumac to M. Popov, "Nota informativă," AMAE, Fond 2, inv. 3-B, d. 168.

33. See note 29.

34. During his mission to Rome he did however meet a person who "proved to be well informed about our country." It was the papal nuncio to Italy. With him he discussed

also political questions, like the release of the members of the Ilaşcu group, at that time unlawfully imprisoned by the separatist Transnistrian authorities in Tiraspol. See note 32.

35. Full text at http://itra.esteri.it/trattati/MOLDO002.pdf (accessed July 1, 2011).

36. Piero Fassino, "La Ost-Politik dell'Italia," *Affari Esteri* 116, no. 29 (1997): 677–700.

37. Fassino offered a list stretching from Albania and Macedonia in the West to Romania and the Ukraine in the East, mentioning all the countries of the area, except Moldova. The omission was certainly unintentional.

38. He moved to Brussels, where, during his term as President of the European Commission (1999–2004), he proved very much committed to the EU enlargement to the East.

39. Events in Yugoslavia both in 1991 (breakdown of the federal state) and 1999 (NATO war against Serbia) were of course a tremendous blow to the Italian Ostpolitik, for which Belgrade was an important partner. It would, however, be an overstatement to declare them the cause of its vanishing.

40. Italy had reached a leading position in the foreign trade of several countries of the so-called new Europe. See Giorgia Giovannetti and Francesca Lucchetti, "Dinamica dell'interscambio commerciale e degli investimenti diretti tra l'Italia e i paesi della Nuova Europa," in *L'Europa allargata, l'Est, l'Italia*, ed. Marco Fortis and Alberto Quadrio Curzio (Bologna: Il Mulino, 2007), 123–42, in particular 128–32.

41. *Anuarul statistic al Republicii Moldova: 2010* [Statistical Yearbook of the Republic of Moldova: 2010] (Chisinau: Statistica, 2010), 423–25, http://www.statistica.md /pageview.php?l=ro&idc=263&id=2193 (accessed July 1, 2011).

42. In 2008 61.4 percent of Moldovan emigrants worked in Russia, 18.3 percent in Italy (38.8 percent in the EU as a whole). National Bureau of Statistics of the Republic of Moldova, "Labour force migration in the Republic of Moldova," 2008, http://www .statistica.md/public/files/publicatii_electronice/migratia/Migratia_FM.pdf (accessed July 1, 2011). The number of Moldovan citizens in Italy, officially 106,000, is likely to be higher due to illegal immigration. Valeriu Moşneaga et al., *Faţetele unui proces. Migraţia forţei de muncă din Republica Moldova în Italia* [Aspects of a process. Workers' emigration from the Republic of Moldova to Italy] (Chisinau: Editerra Prim, 2011), 10. The Latin roots of the language played apparently a role in directing the workers. Asked why they chose Italy as their destination, many of them answered "because it is easy to learn the language." Moşneaga et al., *Faţetele unui*, 7.

43. To a journalist asking him to comment on the fact that "within the EU nothing can happen without Germany's assent and most debates end up being settled along the lines Germany is comfortable with" former German chancellor Schmidt succinctly answered: "I dislike the impression, but I am afraid you are right." Helmut Schmidt, "The opposite of calculability," interview with *International Politics* 12, no. 4 (2011): 52.

44. See "In Schengen nu este spaţiu pentru corupţie" [No room for corruption in Schengen], *Evenimentul Zilei*, October 13, 2011, 1.

45. Somehow biased against the Russian leadership, but accurate in the information: Vladimir Socor, "Meseberg Process: Germany Testing EU-Russia Security Cooperation Potential," *Eurasian Daily Monitor*, October 22, 2010, http://www.jamestown.org /single/?no_cache=1&tx_ttnews[tt_news]=37065 (accessed July 1, 2011).

Chapter Ten

Lithuania: Restoration of Old Links with Moldova for New Goals

Laura Kirvelytė

Lithuania's cooperation with Moldova could be described as a perfect example of collaboration between two small states on the path toward their strategic goals. This kind of partnership confirms that small states, despite their relatively small resources, can play an important role in the international arena. At the same time, in the light of the Lithuanian-Moldovan partnership, the notion that small states can benefit only from cooperation with big powers might be challenged.

Although the contemporary history of Lithuania's relations with Moldova is a moderately short story—about two decades—the development of mutual cooperation has gone through a vibrant evolution. During this period, Moldova's status within Lithuania's foreign policy agenda managed to shift from a quiet ex-counterpart to an active beneficiary of Lithuania's experience in the field of successful post-Soviet transition and EU-integration.

In retrospect, the development of Lithuania's relations with Moldova can be divided into three stages.

The first stage of bilateral relations began in the early 1990s, when both countries regained their independence. This phase of bilateral cooperation could be described as the establishment of bilateral relations. In this period, most of the important bilateral agreements constituting the legal basis of mutual relations were signed. Still, relations between the two countries did not exceed the level of politeness and quiet co-existence. Moldova was viewed by Lithuania's politicians as a remote country, linked to Lithuania only by the Soviet experience. On one hand, attempts to elaborate more intensive collaboration between ex-Soviet states could have been considered as a kind of nostalgia for the Soviet Union, which was highly undesirable at this time in both Lithuania and Moldova. On the other hand, newly independent Moldova faced numerous social and economic hardships, as well as a threat to its territorial integrity. Due to these factors, Chisinau concentrated on its domestic affairs.

A new phase of Lithuania's cooperation with Moldova began after Lithuania joined the EU in 2004. The second stage, which lasted for several years, could be described as an "outbreak of cooperation." The shift in the quality of mutual relations was inspirited by political and geopolitical changes on both sides. First, Lithuania joined the EU in May 2004, creating new demand and new opportunities in the field of foreign policy. Lithuania felt it had appropriate constructive "input" to contribute a role as a bridge between the EU and the new EU's Eastern neighbors. Experience of successful transformation and EU integration, combined with Lithuania's willingness to share this experience with its ex-counterparts, now EU neighbors, was a powerful "toolbox" for intensifying cooperation with countries like Moldova. Second, Moldova's Communist party was re-elected as the ruling party for a second term in parliament, but, this time with a brand-new political agenda, putting the country's EU integration at the top of political priorities. In this light, Lithuania obtained a potential "client" in the area of EU integration. Finally, after the biggest wave of expansion in 2004 and 2007, the EU "re-discovered" its Eastern neighbors, paying much more attention to cooperation with them.

The third stage of bilateral relations, which is still ongoing, could be described as a consolidation of partnership. From about 2008, the "declarative" phase of the enhanced partnership between Lithuania and Moldova transformed into a more silent, but more productive one. The decrease in the level of declarations does not mean that the cooperation itself has loosened. Rather it indicates that a more qualitative level of bilateral cooperation has been reached.

One of the factors turning Lithuania's engagement toward Moldova to a success story was the "inherited" social capital in the sphere of mutual relations with Moldova, which seemed to persist through the period of independence, and became applicable to the achievement of new goals.

In this chapter the development of Lithuania's policy toward Moldova, the main driving forces and obstacles for bilateral cooperation, as well as the prospects for further collaboration of the two countries in the international arena will be analyzed.

The First Stage of Bilateral Relations: Formation of the Fundamentals for Further Cooperation

At the beginning of the 1990s, Lithuania and Moldova traveled parallel paths toward independence—both countries, in the context of growing national movements, decided to restore their independence. In the light of an outbreak of renascent national self-identification and rising efforts to strive for independence, both countries demonstrated mutual support for each other's aspirations. For example, representatives of the Lithuanian national-intellectual movement Sąjūdis[1] took part in the Great National Assembly in Chisinau in late August 1989,[2] during which a mass demonstration occurred, demanding the Romanian language be proclaimed the state language in Moldova. Later on, the Great National Assembly became the first step on the path toward Moldova's independence.

After both countries regained their independence, various internal and external problems arose on both sides and distracted attention from possible cooperation. Huge social and economic hardships in the early stage of the transition to a market economy, followed by political instability, left neither the motivation nor the material base for deeper engagement between Lithuania and Moldova. Moreover, at the very beginning of its independence, Moldova faced a problem of territorial integrity, which still has not been resolved. The main efforts of Chisinau were directed toward managing the situation with the breakaway region of Transnistria and searching for a *modus vivendi* with Moscow.

The priorities of Moldovan foreign policy did not support deeper cooperation with Lithuania. Just after the proclamation of independence, Moldova's foreign policy became purely pro-Romanian. Many believed that the independence of Moldova might be an intermediary step toward merging with Romania. Several years later, after an unsuccessful confrontation with breakaway Transnistria, the vector of Chisinau's foreign policy was forcefully turned back toward Moscow. Neither the primary nor the secondary vector of Moldova's foreign policy left room for Lithuania's deeper involvement. Moreover, in 1994 Lithuania declared its foreign policy priorities would be EU and NATO integration. Lithuania and Moldova were still far away from common denominators in their foreign policies during this period.

Despite the differences in the sphere of foreign policy, in the last decade of the twentieth century, the two countries signed a main bilateral agreement establishing the proper legal basis for bilateral cooperation. In 1995, the Agreement on Friendship and Cooperation was signed, followed by the Agreement for the Avoidance of Double Taxation and the Prevention of Fiscal Evasion with Respect to Taxes on Income and on Capital in 1998, and the Agreement on the Promotion and Reciprocal Protection of Investments, signed in 1999.[3]

Relations between Lithuania and Moldova in the last decade of the twentieth century could be described as "polite co-existence" without excess. All the bilateral agreements necessary for smooth cooperation were signed, the two countries had no major disagreements or mutual issues, but they also failed to find any "common denominator" on which to base bilateral cooperation, since Lithuania was looking westwards, and Moldova still was forced to face Russia.

The Second Stage of Bilateral Relations: Lithuania— Moldova's Advocate Inside the EU

The "calm" bilateral relations between Lithuania and Moldova gained some impetus in 2004, when Moldova finally appeared to become one of the priorities of Lithuania's foreign policy. This move was prompted by several factors.

First, in 2004 Lithuania became a full member of the EU and NATO. Consequently, the main goal of Lithuania's foreign and security policy since the 1990s had been successfully realized. As far as Vilnius was neither ready nor willing to give up an active foreign policy, Lithuania started to search for a new niche of action. A "new window" of opportunity for Lithuania's active foreign policy appeared in the formerly "forgotten" Eastern neighbors. The focal point of Lithuania's Eastern foreign policy[4] has been the idea that all former Soviet countries in the early 1990s were at a similar starting point, but that by 2004 their position in the international arena—also their domestic situations—seriously differed. Lithuania, as well as the other Baltic countries, aimed to share their know-how and their experience gained through implementing a successful transition to democracy and a market economy in order to help Eastern European countries implement the reforms necessary on their way to achieving strategic goals. Lithuania had more than valuable knowledge to share, but also a comprehensive understanding of the challenges the Eastern neighbors had been facing, coupled with the political will necessary to actively assist those countries.

A second factor influencing Moldova's appearance on the Lithuanian foreign policy agenda was a shift in Chisinau's foreign policy priorities. In 2001, the Moldovan Communist party won parliamentary elections with a purely pro-Russian program.[5] Four years later, in 2005, the same Moldovan Communist party once again won elections to the country's legislative authority, but this time it did so by completely changing its political priorities and turning from Moscow to Brussels. The implementation of an EU-integration policy by the Communists was full of shortcomings;[6] nevertheless, the idea of Moldova's EU integration itself created favorable conditions for Lithuania to actively engage in Moldova, as well as to play the role of Moldova's advocate in Brussels.

Third, after the largest expansion of the EU in 2004 and 2007, post-Soviet countries, including Moldova, approximated significantly toward the borders of the EU. Brussels clearly had an interest in expanding the zone of democracy, peace, stability and prosperity in the neighborhood. Consequently, Eastern European countries, including Moldova, received increased interest from Brussels.

Lithuania's Eastern policy was directed toward all six Eastern European countries (Belarus, Ukraine, Moldova, Georgia, Armenia, and Azerbaijan). Nevertheless, in political practice several countries, namely Georgia, Moldova and Ukraine, were prioritized by Vilnius. The logic behind this was that more assistance should be provided for those countries actually willing and demonstrating efforts to follow the path of EU integration. For Lithuania, a small country with limited financial and human resources, the visibility of its policy results in the international arena has been a key priority.

At this point, several important documents aiming at assisting Moldova to reach its EU integration goals were signed, such as the Agreement Regarding Cooperation and Mutual Assistance in Customs Matters in 2005, and the Memorandum on Partnership for European Integration in 2007.[7]

The practical steps taken by Lithuania to assist Moldova's EU integration aspirations were also sound. The main threat to Moldova's security, as well as a main stumbling block toward the country's successful EU integration, has been the unresolved territorial conflict with the separatist Transnistria region. In order to enhance Moldovan border control, in 2005 the EU initiated the European

Union Border Assistance Mission to Moldova and Ukraine. Lithuania also joined the EUBAM, sending border control and customs officers to the mission.

Academic interest in Moldova also grew significantly during this period. Starting from 2004, several think tanks and studies centers focusing on Eastern Europe, including Moldova, were established, namely the Centre for Strategic Studies and the Eastern Europe Studies Centre. From 2004, the European Integration Studies Centre began successful expansion of its activities—in 2007 a branch in Chisinau was opened, aiming at facilitating the implementation of bilateral and multilateral projects, as well as people-to-people contacts.

The Third Stage of Bilateral Relations: Consolidating the Partnership

The nucleus of bilateral cooperation between Lithuania and Moldova is concentrated on the EU agenda. In 2008, the EU–Moldova Partnership and Cooperation Agreement expired. Negotiations on a new bilateral cooperation document were expected to start mid-2009, after parliamentary elections, but this deadline was prolonged since the elections were followed by widespread unrest that resulted in fresh parliamentary elections in late July 2009, after which the ongoing institutional crisis[8] in Moldova began. For now, the negotiations between Chisinau and Brussels on the new cooperation document—the Association Agreement— are still ongoing.

Lithuania, as before, remained a strong supporter and advocate of Moldova's EU-integration aspiration. In 2010, the Joint Declaration on Cooperation in the Field of European Integration was signed.

Thus, it can be said that from late 2008, the declarative period in Lithuania's policy toward Moldova came to the end, leaving room for a more intensive period of cooperation—filling out the declared framework of support and aspirations with concrete material.

Lithuania has not lost its interest nor decreased its activity in Moldova. In 2011, Lithuania chaired the Organization for Security and Cooperation in Europe. One of the key priorities of Lithuania's chairmanship became the peaceful resolution of the frozen conflicts of South Ossetia and Abkhazia in Georgia, Transnistria in Moldova, as well as Nagorno-Karabakh between Armenia and Azerbaijan.[9]

The main difference between this stage of cooperation and previous ones was a stricter assessment of Moldova's progress. Lithuania's President Dalia Grybauskaitė, during a working visit to Chisinau in July 2011, stressed that Moldova's progress with its "homework" had significantly slowed.[10]

The paradox is that, on the one hand, an enduring institutional crisis in Moldova and its uncertain future act as a brake in Moldova's relations with the EU; the two sides have not yet negotiated a cooperation agreement. But, on the other hand, the Alliance for European Integration,[11] which has had a majority in

Moldova's parliament since late July 2009, intends to push Moldova on its way to EU integration more than its predecessor, the Communist party. So, with the demand for EU integration-related assistance now at a peak, the lack of a clear framework interrupts these processes. In practice, from mid-2009 increased activity from the Moldovan side to receive Lithuanian experience in EU-related fields could be observed. Moreover, keeping in mind that the new foreign policy of Moldova is directed much more toward the goal of EU integration and involves much less balancing between Russia and the West, enhanced partnerships with countries like Lithuania is important both politically (from the ideological point of view) and practically.

Keeping in mind Moldova's prolonged institutional crisis and the murky prospects for its fast resolution, the intensiveness of this current stage of Lithuania–Moldova cooperation depends on Moldova's preparation to continue with reforms and Chisinau's relations with Brussels.

Why Moldova Matters? Driving Forces and Perspectives of Lithuania's Policy toward Moldova

Lithuania's active engagement in Moldova has benefited both sides. For Moldova, Lithuania's support and assistance has been a helpful source of useful advice and valuable support in the international arena, especially within the EU structures. For Lithuania, active cooperation with Moldova has been a source for strengthening the country's influence and prestige in the international arena. One of the most promising ways "out of the shadow" of the international community for a small country like Lithuania is to gain the status of expert in some specific knowledge-based niche. For Lithuania, that niche was its transition experience and the rising demand for consulting and assistance from Eastern European countries.

There were several driving forces that prompted Lithuania's active engagement in Moldova, facilitating cooperation between the two countries, and giving Vilnius a relative advantage. First of all, Lithuania and Moldova previously never had any problematic bilateral issues. Lithuania's help to Moldova was not seen as a self-interested attempt. Lithuania's assistance to Moldova has successfully avoided the risk of politicization, unlike Romanian or Ukrainian assistance. Moreover, in this perspective, Lithuania's cooperation with Moldova should be less volatile and much less dependent on the rotation of the political elite than either Romanian or Ukrainian cooperation.

Second, the Moldovan perception of Lithuania has been supportive of the intensive development of partnership. Benefiting from Lithuania's knowledge and position as a full member of the EU and NATO, Moldova viewed Lithuania more as an elder friend than a teacher. This perception has facilitated the process of cooperation since Moldova's politicians and experts feel themselves more free and open-minded when working with Lithuanian experts.

Third, when the period of intensive bilateral cooperation started, decades-old people-to-people contacts managed to be restored. Most Moldovans still remember personal contacts with Lithuanians during the period of the Soviet Union. Moreover, both sides still know the Russian language quite well. So, this convenient tool of communication for both sides also stands as a factor, facilitating cooperation.

Nevertheless, Lithuania's policy toward Moldova also has several shortcomings, which, under the negative circumstances, could become risks to the continuity of cooperation. First, Lithuania's cooperation with Moldova is too dependent on the EU agenda, and at the same time, much too sensitive to the Russian factor. The EU agenda was a good starting point for the development and consolidation of a bilateral partnership, but the relationship, which has reached a mature stage, could develop further independently, finding common fields for cooperation not directly related to the EU. The Russian factor has also consistently been exerting leverage on both sides. Lithuania's Eastern policy and its active engagement in "Russia's sphere of privileged interests" are primarily interpreted by Russia as direct threats to Moscow. On the other hand, EU integration efforts by the Eastern European countries themselves have been viewed by Russia as a "zero sum game" and a challenge to Moscow.

Second, unless bilateral cooperation is quite highly developed, there is a lack of bilateral approaches to cooperation at the political level. Moldova has often been grouped with the six Eastern Partnership countries, or together with Ukraine. Since all of these countries are quite different in terms of their current situation, the progress they have made, and the intensity of their aspirations, there is a need to develop individual approaches to each partner in order to advance the quality of cooperation.

Conclusion

Lithuania's cooperation with Moldova has developed gradually from the early 1990s, although the most intensive period of bilateral relations started in 2004, when both countries managed to find a common denominator for partnership—European integration. The linkage of the EU between Lithuania and Moldova ensures cooperation between the two states be a long-term project, not a short-term attempt. At the same time, there is a risk that concentration solely on the EU agenda, over topics of inter-state cooperation (for example trade, entrepreneurship, tourism), may turn the collaboration into a one-sided and limited tool.

It is important to point out that the success of this most recent stage of cooperation and the prospects of further partnership depend on Moldova's practical progress in implementing necessary reforms, and also on Moldova's ability to resolve its institutional crisis, and on Lithuania's activity and its ability to propose new incentives, programs, or tools for cooperation.

Notes

1. Sąjūdis (full name: the Reform Movement of Lithuania) was a political-intellectual movement established at the end of the 1980s, which in general supported Gorbachev's *perestroika*, but sought national goals, first and foremost regaining Lithuania's independence. It is important to note that Lithuania's Sąjūdis was a wide national movement that involved both Communist and non-Communist intellectuals. In February 1990, Sąjūdis won an absolute majority in the Supreme Council of the Lithuanian SSR. As a result in March 1990, the restoration of Lithuanian independence was declared.

2. Vicu Bucătaru, *Clopotul reînvierii* [The Bell of Renaissance], documentary film, http://www.jurnaltv.md/ro/news/11230/#clopotul-reinvierii-11230 (accessed May 30, 2011).

3. Lithuanian Foreign Ministry, "Moldova," February 17, 2010, http://www.urm.lt /index.php?1006176699 (accessed May 25, 2011).

4. Artūras Paulauskas, "Naujoji Lietuvos užsienio politika" [Lithuania's New Foreign Policy] (speech by the Lithuania's Acting President, Vilnius University, May 24, 2004), http://www.paulauskas.lt/index.asp?DL=L&TopicID=113&ArticleID=773&Page=4 &SearchTXT=&iDay=&iMonth=&iYear= (accessed September 12, 2011).

5. Trevor Waters, *The "Moldovan Syndrome" and Re-Russification of Moldova: Forward into the Past!* (Conflict Studies Research Centre, 2002), http://www.da.mod.uk /colleges/arag/document-listings/cee/G105 (accessed September 10, 2011).

6. Diana Molodilo, "The Republic of Moldova within the European security system: Partners, challenges, perspectives" (paper presented at the training seminar, "European and NATO Neighbouring policies—new dimensions for regional cooperation," Chisinau, November 28–29, 2007).

7. Lithuanian Foreign Ministry, "Moldova."

8. In early April 2009, after falsified parliamentary elections, the citizens organized against the falsified victory of the ruling Moldovan Communist party, demanding a new election. Nevertheless, the ruling Communist party, which held a simple majority in parliament, but not enough to elect a president, ignored the citizens' demand, and early elections were triggered only when opposition parties, using an institutional mechanism, twice successively refused to support the Communists' candidate for president of Moldova. After early elections were held in July 2009, again no political camp—neither the Alliance for European Integration, a formation of four parties, nor the Communist party—held a qualified majority, enough to elect a president. Then the Communists used the same mechanism of not electing the president. The second round of early elections were held in late 2010 have not changed the situation—both political camps received approximately equal support from the voters. Until now, rival political camps failed to reach a compromise. As a result, Moldova has an acting president only, and lives in permanent anticipation of new early elections.

9. "Lithuania Outlines OSCE Priorities, Prods Belarus," *Radio Free Europe/Radio Liberty*, January 13, 2011, http://www.rferl.org/content/lithuania_osce_priorities/2275056 .html (accessed January 15, 2011).

10. Mindaugas Jackevičius, "D.Grybauskaitė apie Moldovą" [D. Grybauskaitė about Moldova], *Delfi News Agency*, July 13, 2011, http://www.delfi.lt/news/daily/lithuania/dgrybauskaite-apie-moldova-es-ne-ta-organizacija-kuri-priims-tik-del-to-kad-priimtu.d?id=475 49409 (accessed July 20, 2011).

11. The Alliance for European Integration is a political formation of several parties united by common goals and visions: The Liberal Democratic Party, the Liberal Party, the Democratic Party and the Our Moldova Alliance (after the early election of 2010, the Our Moldova Alliance failed to enter parliament). However, the Alliance for European Integration is only political, not an electoral block.

Chapter Eleven

Poland: Rediscovering Moldova[*]

Marcin Kosienkowski

Despite the fact that Moldova is situated in Eastern Europe—an area in which Poland has always been interested—the country has been pushed into the background of Polish foreign policy. This results from the fact that Moldova is not Poland's immediate neighbor and has quite limited political, economic, military and demographic capabilities.

However, it should be noted that Polish policy toward Moldova is gradually developing over the course of time. There are three main catalyzing events. The first was Poland's accession to the European Union in 2004. This has considerably improved Poland's ability to act in international relations, and has allowed it to focus on raising its prestige and improving its standing internationally. The eastern direction of Polish engagement has been a natural fit, the more so because Warsaw wants to become the leading voice of expertise on Eastern Europe within the EU. It should be mentioned that since 2003, Moldova, including its breakaway region of Transnistria, has started to appear annually in several consecutive addresses on Poland's foreign policy made by foreign affairs ministers.[1]

A second catalytic event occurred when Poland and Sweden announced the Eastern Partnership initiative in 2008, which the EU accepted as a project in 2009. In short, the program aims to assist six states from Eastern Europe and the Caucasus, including Moldova, with nearing and integrating into the EU.

Last but not least, the coalition known as the Alliance for European Integration in Moldova came to power in mid-2009, and had a significant influence on the intensification of Poland's policy towards the state. The first-ever visit of a Polish prime minister (Donald Tusk)—the key figure in the Polish political system—to Moldova in March 2011 offered meaningful proof of this. Warsaw believes that Moldova under the rule of the pro-European parties can become "a success story" in the Eastern Partnership and in Polish eastern policy. Importantly, Moldova's advancements in nearing and integrating with the EU could encourage other states—such as Ukraine, which is a far more important partner for Poland—to follow the Moldovan path.

---

* This article is partially based on field research conducted in Warsaw and Chisinau between 2006 and 2011. The author would like to thank all persons interviewed.

143

The objectives of Poland's policy toward Moldova have been static since the beginning of the 1990s. They are as follows: a) the development of good-neighborly relations; b) support for the political and economic transition of Moldova, as well as its European aspirations; c) the endorsement of Moldova's territorial integrity; d) enhancement of economic cooperation and e) support for the Polish diaspora. These objectives are generally in harmony with Polish eastern policy.[2]

The Development of Good-Neighborly Relations

Poland recognized Moldova, along with nine other former Soviet republics on December 27, 1991, exactly four months after it declared its independence.[3] Bilateral diplomatic relations were established on July 14, 1992. The Polish embassy was opened in Chisinau in 1994, while the Moldovan diplomatic mission started operations in Warsaw in 1997.

Polish-Moldovan relations are based mainly on the Treaty on Friendship and Cooperation. It was signed on November 15, 1994, during a visit of Moldovan President Mircea Snegur to Poland, the first visit of such a high level. The treaty came into effect on March 2, 1996.[4] In the document, the two states commit themselves to shaping their relations according to the basic principles of international law. They express their will to facilitate and maintain cooperation in diverse matters, including political, trade and economic, military, environmental, cultural, scientific and technical, transport, social and humanitarian matters. In order to enhance their collaboration, Poland and Moldova have concluded about thirty agreements and other bilateral documents so far.[5] Warsaw and Chisinau also agreed in the Treaty on Friendship and Cooperation to expand their political dialogue at various levels. Over the course of time they have managed to establish regular contact, which has intensified since 2008 and 2009.[6] Importantly, official meetings usually occur in a positive, sometimes even downright cordial atmosphere.[7]

The development of good-neighborly relations between Poland and Moldova depends on at least three factors. First, the two states are linked by various historical ties. Contacts between Poland and the Moldavian Principality, from which modern Moldova traces its origin, were established as early as the fourteenth century. Political relations were broken when Poland ceased to exist at the end of the eighteenth century. It is worth mentioning that the Moldavian Principality was a loosely controlled, periodically fading fiefdom of Poland between 1387 and 1497, and the Polish-Turkish condominium in the first half of the seventeenth century. Although these historical bilateral relations were not free from conflict, Poland and Moldova refer to them nowadays almost exclusively as traditions of cooperation and friendship. In addition, the fact that Poles contributed to the development of the Moldovan territories, while they were a part of the Russian Empire in the nineteenth and early twentieth century, also bears some significance.[8]

Second, there is no major friction between Warsaw and Chisinau. Probably the most publicized and, indeed, serious problem was related to the activity of the Mint of Poland, which had been producing Transnistrian commemorative and change coins for a few years at the turn of the twenty-first century. Moldova strongly opposed this practice, perceiving it as support for the separatists, and it eventually succeeded in stopping it.[9]

Third, Warsaw and Chisinau have common interests in the advancement of the European integration process. Since the fall of the Soviet Union, Poland has been "vigorously support[ing] the process linking East and West into a single whole."[10] Moldova in turn has been seeking, at least in rhetoric, to enhance its cooperation with the EU since gaining independence with its first European aspirations officially expressed in 1996.

However, it should be noted that despite the fact that Poland and Moldova are constantly developing good-neighborly and friendly relations, cooperation commitments made through bilateral documents, and declarations during diplomatic meetings do not always translate into action. Moreover, both Warsaw and Chisinau seem to lack a strategic approach toward their relations.

Support for the Transition of Moldova and Its European Aspirations

Poland permanently supports the political and economic transition of Moldova, as well as its European aspirations.[11] There are at least two main reasons for this support. First, Warsaw strongly believes that the more democratic and prosperous Moldova is, and the more integrated with the EU it is, the more safe and stable adjacent Eastern Europe will become. This position in turn enhances Polish and European security. Moldova's accession to the EU is considered the best guarantee of this course. Second, having successfully gone through its own transition, and finally joining the EU, Poland feels morally obliged to show solidarity with Moldova, a state willing to follow the same path.[12]

For many years, support for Moldova's democratic and free market reforms, and its European aspirations, has been expressed by Warsaw almost exclusively verbally, and mostly during bilateral meetings. Poland has been encouraging Moldova to maintain its European direction and to continue democratic and free market reforms. Delays have been noted in this process.

Poland's accession to the European Union added some substance to this policy and strengthened its position. First, Warsaw has started to act in favor of Moldova within the EU. Poland has called on the EU to offer membership prospects to Moldova, without setting a specific date, since Poland recognizes that membership can only happen after Moldova meets the necessary conditions. Warsaw would also like the EU to include Moldova in the Western Balkans region, where states already have a clear European prospective. It thinks that, without membership prospects, Moldova—especially if ruled by a government less committed to the European integration idea—may lose its interest in pursuing profound reforms. Poland also calls for greater involvement of the EU in the political and economic transition of Moldova, as well as for the further enhancement of cooperation. These policies currently are spelled out in the following agreements: Moldova-EU association, deep and comprehensive free trade, and visa liberalization. In addition, Warsaw strongly supports the use of a "more for more" principle, which has been discussed within the EU for some time. This policy rewards neighboring countries of the EU when they achieve progress in domestic political and economic reforms with a higher level of political and financial support. The point is that Moldova, under the rule of the Alliance for European Integration, could be one of the main beneficiaries of such an approach, since it is considered to be above average among the European neighborhood states.[13]

In order to achieve these objectives or to make them more realistic, Poland, first of all, elaborated the previously mentioned Eastern Partnership program in cooperation with Sweden in 2008. It does not offer membership prospects to its six participants, but it may facilitate their full integration with the EU. As Polish Foreign Minister Radosław Sikorski stated, "The success of . . . these steps [taken within the Eastern Partnership] will make the idea of EU membership for Eastern European countries less likely to meet with as much opposition as it faces today. In an optimistic scenario, their rights to membership prospects could become an obvious matter."[14] In other words, Poland and the Eastern Partnership will help those EU members reluctant about Chisinau's European aspirations to learn about Moldova. It should be added that Poland tries to keep a balance between the EU's involvement in the Eastern and Southern neighborhoods. This is a very significant objective, because the early 2011 revolutions in North Africa and the Middle East attracted much attention from many of the EU's members. It should also be mentioned that Poland eagerly joined the Friends of Moldova Group, an informal arrangement of meetings between EU foreign ministers, which was created in 2009 to support Moldova's European aspirations.

Second, Warsaw and Chisinau developed their cooperation in European matters by creating the Moldovan-Polish Forum for European Integration in 2008. The forum, which started operating in 2010, gives Poland a greater chance to share its own experience with Moldova and to stay better informed about Moldova's needs and problems.[15] It should be added that Poland gives its full support to the Alliance for European Integration. Warsaw would like this coalition to stay in power in Moldova—which is not certain because of the serious political crisis affecting this country—considering it to be the best guarantor of the country's pro-European direction.

Third, Poland started providing development assistance to Moldova (and other developing countries) in an organized fashion and on a larger scale in 2004. This was possible to a considerable degree due to Poland's membership in the European Union. Moreover, this practice was required and expected by the organization. The basic forms of Polish aid include assistance in cash, in kind, and in technical expertise. Depending on the manner of aid, bilateral, trilateral, and multilateral assistance can be distinguished. Bilateral aid is implemented by non-governmental organizations, central and local administrations, and also Polish embassies and consulates.[16]

It is significant that Moldova has been among the priority recipients of Polish aid since 2004. The amount of bilateral technical assistance in consecutive years was as follows (in millions, USD): 2004—0.10; 2005—0.35; 2006—1.11; 2007—1.00; 2008—1.45; 2009—0.61; 2010 (allocation)—0.66; 2011 (appropriations)—1.39. Projects implemented in 2010 concerned the support and promotion of good governance, agricultural and rural development, counteracting human trafficking, and implementing European standards. In 2011, Poland will give aid for the following: good governance, migration and border management, rural and agricultural development, and small and medium enterprises.[17] Moreover, Poland granted Moldova a tied aid credit of $15 million in 2007. It should have been spent on the modernization of the drinking water supply and the sewage system, as well as other investments related to environmental protection. However, it was not used, because Moldova was not able to co-finance these projects.[18] The same amount of money was granted by Poland in 2010 as a loan for budgetary support of Moldova.[19] Additionally, Poland provided Moldova with humanitarian aid for combating the consequences of the 2007 draught ($360,000) and 2010 flood (ca $128,000).[20]

The weakness of Poland's endorsement of the political and economic transition of Moldova lies in its lack of support on the ground. This does not fully reflect the declarations made by Warsaw. In addition, despite the existence of different forums and projects, the results are not evident enough. All of this seems to represent a triumph of form over substance.[21] Another problem is that Poland places too much confidence in the Alliance for European Integration. Warsaw did not react when the Moldovan ruling coalition took some less than democratic steps, such as the manipulation of the Moldovan electoral code to resolve the political crisis and stay in power. Moreover, Poland is not, at least officially, critical of the increasingly apparent delays in introducing real reforms in Moldova by the Alliance for European Integration. However, it should be added that this problem has been noted by a Polish think tank financed by the state budget.[22]

Support for the Territorial Integrity of Moldova

Poland has supported the territorial integrity of Moldova since its independence. This was reflected as early as in 1991, in a Polish government resolution concerning the recognition of Moldova, and in 1994 in the Treaty on Friendship and Cooperation. Moreover, Warsaw sympathizes with Moldova rather than Transnistria, since the latter is a region under heavy influence from Russia. It should be emphasized that, in fact, there are no official contacts between Poland and Transnistria, except for economic intermediaries, which are, for the most part, accepted by Moldova (the aforementioned Mint of Poland is an exception). Crucially, Warsaw takes the view that Moldova should be reunited by peaceful means and that negotiations should be conducted within the official format.[23]

Poland is indirectly involved in the settlement of the Transnistrian conflict, in full respect of the territorial integrity and sovereignty of Moldova. First of all, Warsaw supports steps taken by the international community and acts within the international organizations that it belongs to. For many years, Poland had set its hopes of resolving the Transnistrian problem on the Organization for Security and Cooperation in Europe.[24] It is worth noting that the recommendations of a Pole, Adam Daniel Rotfeld—who visited Moldova and Transnistria in September 1992 as the Personal Representative of the Chairperson-in-Office of the CSCE—led to the establishment of its mission to Moldova in early 1993.[25] Poland was particularly active on the Transnistrian issue while holding the OSCE chairmanship in 1998. In addition, Warsaw has respected Russia's leading role in the settlement process.

Since the mid-2000s, when it appeared that the OSCE had failed in helping the conflicting sides resolve their dispute, and when Russia became more assertive, Poland began calling for a greater involvement of the West in the reunification of Moldova. The European Union has been identified by Warsaw as the most important actor capable of settling the Transnistrian problem. Essentially, Poland has started to believe that profound political and economic reforms in Moldova—taken within the European integration process and with the help of the EU—would contribute to a resolution of the Transnistrian conflict, since it would make Moldova more attractive for Transnistrians.

It should also be said that Poland supports the international community's efforts to fully withdraw Russian troops and arms from the Transnistrian region under the Istanbul Commitments made by Russia in 1999. Additionally, for the past few years, Warsaw has been calling for a change in the format of the peacekeeping mission in Transnistria, which is now composed of Transnistrian, Moldovan and Russian troops, into a mission of civil observers operating under an international mandate.[26] It cannot be excluded that Poles might take part in this mission, if it were ever deployed. They are well experienced and, as representatives from a Slavic nation, they could be accepted by Transnistria with relative ease. Warsaw also endorsed the establishment of the European Union Border Assistance Mission to Moldova and Ukraine in November 2005. One of its main goals is to help fight illicit cross-border activity in the Transnistrian section of the Moldovan-Ukrainian border, which has been said to be crucial for Transnistria's survival. Poland actively works within EUBAM; it is sufficient to say that Poles are the most numerous in this structure and hold managerial positions, including the position of the Deputy Head of EUBAM (since October 2010).[27]

The problem of Moldova's territorial integrity is also raised in Poland's bilateral relations with Moldova. The topic is a permanent fixture in Polish-Moldovan diplomatic meetings. Additionally, Poland occasionally brings up this issue during talks with two neighbors of Moldova, Romania and Ukraine. Critically, the later has been acting as both a guarantor and a mediator in the Transnistrian conflict since the mid-1990s. Moreover, due to their common border, Ukraine serves as Transnistria's window to the outside world.

It can be added that for a few years, Poland has been trying to get involved in issues related to the Autonomous Territorial Unit of Gagauzia (Gagauz Yeri), one of Moldova's most undeveloped areas, located in the South. Poland provides Gagauzia with modest development assistance. Moreover, together with the European Union partners, it called on the Moldovan Communist authorities—in power in Moldova from 2001 to 2009—to respect Gagauz autonomy.[28] Warsaw believes that a well-functioning Gagauzia could contribute to the Transnistrian conflict settlement. It could serve as proof that the Moldovan central authorities would respect Transnistria's political, economic, and cultural rights within a unified state.

Enhancement of Economic Cooperation

Poland has been placing much emphasis on the enhancement of economic cooperation with Moldova, including Transnistria, since the beginning of the 1990s. It is sufficient to say that the first bilateral agreement (signed in February 1992) concerned trade and economic cooperation.[29] Moreover, in 1994, the Polish foreign minister said in his address on Poland's foreign policy that relations with Moldova—mentioned for the first time in this annual speech—are "concentrat[ed] above all on creating conditions fostering economic cooperation."[30]

In order to develop their collaboration, Poland and Moldova signed other inter-governmental agreements, among other things, on: the Avoidance of Double Taxation on Income and Property and the Prevention of Fiscal Evasion (1994), the Promotion and Mutual Protection of Investments (1994), Air Transport Services (1995), International Road Transports (1997), Interregional Co-operation (1998), and Cooperation and Mutual Assistance in Customs Matters (2002). Because of Poland's accession to the European Union, the 1992 document was renounced and Polish-Moldovan economic relations have been regulated since by the Partnership and Cooperation Agreement between the EU and Moldova. This has been complemented by the Agreement on Economic Cooperation adopted by Poland and Moldova in 2006. Moreover, bilateral documents on cooperation between ministries, for example of agriculture (2002) and environment (2003), as well as between state agencies, such as departments of standards (1998) and foreign investment agencies (2008), were signed.

Furthermore, Poland and Moldova decided to create joint bodies to enhance their economic cooperation. The first one—the Joint Commission—was established under the provisions of the Agreement on Trade and Economic Cooperation of 1992. It operated between 1998 and 2003, holding four sessions. Then a new body—the Polish-Moldovan Commission for Economic Cooperation—was set up under the 2006 agreement; it started working in 2008. In addition, the Polish-Moldovan Chamber of Commerce was established in Warsaw in 2007. There are also economic forums and other events organized in Poland and Moldova.[31] Similar steps as described above were taken to develop economic cooperation with Transnistria. Poland, for example, would like to conclude an agreement on cooperation between the Lublin Business Club and the so-called Chamber of Commerce and Industry of Transnistria. Most importantly, Polish activity has intensified over the last few years.[32]

Poland's exports to Moldova, including Transnistria, showed a growing trend for the greater part of the 1990s, reaching $61.7 million in 1998. It dropped the next year by more than one-third, as a consequence of the Russian financial crisis. A stable positive tendency in Polish exports reappeared in 2002, soon reaching the pre-crisis level. This was partially possible thanks to export-stimulating measures taken by the Polish government. The export volume was raised from $50.3 million in 2002 to $184.2 million in 2008. Then it was affected by the global financial and economic crisis, collapsing by one-third to $122.0 million in 2009. However, growth in Polish exports was observed in 2010. It should be noted Poland has always enjoyed a considerable positive trade balance with Moldova. Poland's imports from this country, including Transnistria, were low for many years. It started increasing sharply, beginning in 2004. In 2008 the volume of Polish imports from Moldova reached $130.1 million, growing as many as 32.5 times in comparison to 2003, when it was $4.0 million. Then it dropped by more than two-thirds to $37.5 million in 2009 in the aftermath of the global crisis. But in 2010 Poland's imports from Moldova started to grow again. For all details, see the table 11.1.

The commodity structure of Polish exports to Moldova, including Transnistria, is diversified. In the 2000s, Poland delivered chiefly machinery and mechanical appliances, electrical and electrotechnical equipment; plastics and rubber and articles thereof; textiles and textile articles; products of the chemical industry; prepared foodstuffs; base metals and articles thereof; transport equipment; animal and vegetable products; and articles of wood. Polish imports from the whole of Moldova included mainly raw materials and supplies. In the 2000s, the biggest commodity group, which had much influence on the dynamics of Polish imports, were base metals and articles thereof. The next most important groups were beverages and spirits, mainly fruit juices and wines, as well as vegetable products and oils.[33] Poland is the biggest importer of Moldovan wines within the European Union.[34]

Although the trade turnover between Poland and Moldova, including Transnistria, is quite low, this state is a relatively important economic partner for Poland, especially among the Commonwealth of Independent States. The situation is similar for Moldova, the difference being that Poland's percentage share, and consequently its position in Moldovan foreign trade, is higher.[35] Poland is one of the main trading partners of Transnistria, particularly when it comes to its exports.[36] It is sufficient to say that base metals and articles thereof—the biggest product group in Polish imports from all of Moldova—come mainly from the Transnistrian region. It is important to note that Poland and Moldova, including Transnistria, recorded growth in trade volumes. The situation looks much worse in the case of Polish investment in the Moldovan economy. This amounted to $0.5 million in 2009.[37]

Table 11.1. Poland's trade with Moldova in the period of 1997–2010

Year	Export to Moldova		Import from Moldova		Trade turnover		Trade balance
	mil. USD	prev. year = 100	mil. USD	prev. year = 100	mil. USD	prev. year = 100	mil. USD
1997	52.2	154.5	2.1	123.9	54.3	153.0	+50.1
1998	61.7	118.4	2.5	118.9	64.2	118.4	+59.2
1999	39.7	64.2	7.2	284.5	46.9	72.9	+32.5
2000	49.6	124.8	5.5	77.5	55.1	117.5	+44.1
2001	44.6	89.9	4.9	88.2	49.5	89.8	+39.7
2002	50.3	112.9	4.1	83.9	54.4	109.9	+46.2
2003	79.3	157.1	4.0	97.8	83.3	153.1	+75.3
2004	92.5	116.3	23.1	571.0	115.6	138.8	+69.4
2005	111.0	120.0	31.3	135.7	144.3	124.8	+79.7
2006	138.8	125.0	39.9	127.5	178.7	123.8	+98.8
2007	173.6	125.1	121.4	304.3	295.0	165.1	+52.2
2008	184.2	106.1	130.1	107.2	314.3	106.5	+54.1
2009	122.0	66.2	37.5	28.8	159.5	50.7	+84.5
2010	155.1	127.1	50.8	135.5	205.9	129.1	+104.3

Sources: Ministerstwo Gospodarki [Polish Ministry of Economy], "Współpraca gospodarcza Polska–Mołdowa" [Poland-Moldova economic cooperation], May 2006, quoted in Julita Urbanowska, Paweł Gębski, and Henryk Borko, *Mołdowa. Przewodnik dla przedsiębiorców* [Moldova business guide], 4th ed. (Warsaw: United Nations Industrial Development Organization, 2006), 144, http://www .eksporter.gov.pl/Informacja/Zalaczniki_informacje.ashx?Id=13992&Nazwa=01 131_01.pdf (accessed May 5, 2011); Foreign Trade Database (2004–2010) of the Central Statistical Office of Poland, http://hinex.stat.gov.pl/hinex/aspx/index .aspx.

Support for the Polish Diaspora

Support for the Polish diaspora living in Moldova, including Transnistria, is an important task of Poland's policy toward this state. However, there are not many Poles and that is why this group attracts less attention than the far more numerous Polish residents of other post-Soviet republics, such as Belarus, Lithuania, Ukraine, Russia, Kazakhstan and Latvia. According to the 1989 Soviet census there were 4,739 people of Polish origin in the Moldavian Soviet Socialist Republic. This number dropped within the space of the next ten to fifteen years. According to a census taken in 2004, in the territory under control of the Moldovan central authorities there were 2,383 Poles; a small group of people of Polish origin also lives in Transnistria. However, it should be noted that in the opinion of some experts, this number is significantly higher.[38]

Policy toward the Polish diaspora in Moldova, including Transnistria, is an element of Poland's policy toward Poles from post-Soviet republics. Poland strives to build and enhance various ties with people of Polish origin living abroad, secure their rights as a national minority, keep their Polish national identity, and help them cultivate the Polish language, traditions and culture; develop the Polish educational system, media and entrepreneurship in countries of their residence; raise the position of Poles in diverse fields within local societies; develop their organizational structure, etc. Warsaw would also like the Polish diaspora to promote Poland in the post-Soviet states.[39]

Many of the aforementioned tasks have started in Moldova from scratch, and the realization of some has met difficulties. One of the main reasons for this was that the network of the Polish organizations had been destroyed during the Soviet period; Poland could not help the Polish diaspora in this case. As a consequence, only a small percentage of Poles living in Moldova speak the Polish language. One should not forget about the difficult economic situation in this state, which also hampers the development of the Polish diaspora. The position of Poles in Transnistria is even worse. All of this means that Poland's assistance was, and still is, necessary.

Steps taken by Poland to support people of Polish origin living in Moldova are typical of diaspora-support activities. First, the Polish and Moldovan governments adopted appropriate laws and regulations in the Treaty on Friendship and Cooperation. Notably, they agreed to the treaty on Cultural and Scientific Cooperation signed in 1997, and its Executive Program for the years 2006 to 2008. Second, the issue of the Polish diaspora in Moldova is discussed during Polish-Moldovan diplomatic meetings. Critically, Moldovan authorities have always regarded its citizens of Polish origin with favor. Third, Polish state institutions and non-governmental organizations receive money from the state budget, and organize cultural, educational, and other events in Moldova. Fourth, Poland supports the work of Polish diaspora organizations, for example by providing them with equipment and financial assistance. The Polish embassy also tries to consolidate the organizational structure of Poles—in other words, to unite them, since their present organizations compete with each other and are often at odds. Fifth, The Card of the Pole—a document stating adherence to the Polish nation—was introduced in 2007, giving some privileges to its holders, such as education in Poland free of charge. Poland tries to provide similar assistance as described above to Poles living in Transnistria.[40]

Kazimierz Jurczak—an expert on Romania and Moldova—stated in the mid-2000s that the revival of Polishness in Moldova was already a fact, and he called it "a kind of historical miracle," made possible thanks to the determination of the Polish diaspora and effective assistance provided by the Polish state institutions, NGOs and the Catholic Church (but it cannot be said that the Polish government's policy has been so excellent[41]). However, he concluded that programs aimed in favor of Poles living in Moldova should be redefined. They should not be focused so exclusively on teaching the Polish language, and on national patriotic aspects. Otherwise the Polish diaspora could become "an open-air ethnographic museum and then disappear."[42]

Conclusion

Poland is gradually rediscovering Moldova, a country that was linked to it by various ties for a few centuries in the distant past. Bilateral cooperation is strengthening over time, especially during the last few years. Furthermore, in the opinion of Jan Borkowski, a senior official in the Polish Foreign Ministry, due to its activities there, Poland "has discovered Moldova for Europe."[43] Even if this statement is an exaggeration, it should be said that Warsaw has played a role in making the European Union more interested in Moldovan affairs. However, it must be noted further that the quite dynamic development of relations between Poland and Moldova is not guaranteed. A change of authorities, for example, in either of these countries could be enough to influence bilateral cooperation in a negative way.

Notes

1. See "Ministers Annual Address on foreign policy (2002–2011)," http://www.mfa .gov.pl/Ministers,Annual,Address,on,foreign,policy,2156.html (accessed April 19, 2011).

2. See more about Poland's foreign policy and its eastern dimension in Roman Kuźniar, *Poland's Foreign Policy after 1989* (Warsaw: SCHOLAR, 2009); Andrzej Gil and Tomasz Kapuśniak, eds., *Polityka wschodnia Polski. Uwarunkowania – Koncepcje – Realizacja* [Poland's eastern policy. Conditions – Concepts – Realisation] (Lublin–Warsaw: Instytut Europy Środkowo-Wschodniej, 2009).

3. "Council of Ministers of the RP Resolution No. 170/91 (concerning the recognition by the Republic of Poland of the Republic of Armenia, the Republic of Azerbaijan, the Republic of Belarus, the Russian Federation, the Republic of Kazakhstan, the Republic of Kyrgyzstan, the Republic of Moldova, the Republic of Tajikistan, Turkmenistan

and the Republic of Uzbekistan), Warsaw, December 27, 1991," *Zbiór Dokumentów. Recueil de documents*, no. 4 (1991), http://78.133.255.100/1991/4/2.html (accessed April 19, 2011).

4. "Treaty between the Republic of Poland and the Republic of Moldova on Friendship and Cooperation, Warsaw, November 15, 1994," *Zbiór Dokumentów. Recueil de documents*, no. 1 (1996), http://78.133.255.100/1996/1/7.html (accessed April 19, 2011).

5. Inter-governmental agreements are available in at least one of the following languages: Polish, Romanian, English and Russian in the Internet Treaty Base run by the Polish Foreign Ministry, http://www.traktaty.msz.gov.pl/. A detailed analysis of Polish-Moldovan treaty relations can be found in an article by Natalia Cwicinskaja, "Stosunki traktatowe między Rzeczpospolitą Polską a Republiką Mołdowy" [Treaty relations between the Republic of Poland and the Republic of Moldova], in *Spotkania polsko-mołdawskie* [Polish-Moldovan encounters], ed. Janusz Solak (Toruń: Wydawnictwo Adam Marszałek, forthcoming).

6. A list of Polish-Moldovan diplomatic meetings can be found on the website of the Moldovan Embassy to Poland, "Political-Diplomatic relations," http://www.polonia .mfa.md/poliltical-diplomatic/ (accessed April 21, 2011).

7. See, e.g., The Chancellery of the Prime Minister of Poland, "Meeting of Prime Ministers of Poland and Moldova," February 18, 2010, http://www.premier.gov.pl/en /press_centre/news/meeting_of_prime_ministers_of_,4439/ (accessed April 21, 2011).

8. See more on the historical Polish-Moldovan relations in Edward Walewander, ed., *Polacy w Mołdawii* [Poles in Moldova] (Lublin: "Wspólnota Polska," 1995).

9. "Poland Refuses to Mint Coins for Transnistria," *Infotag*, April 19, 2005, http://old.azi.md/news?ID=33899 (accessed April 21, 2011).

10. Andrzej Olechowski, "Presentation of Polish Foreign Policy in 1994 – Statement by Minister of Foreign Affairs of the Republic of Poland Andrzej Olechowski in Sejm, Warsaw, May 12, 1994," *Zbiór Dokumentów. Recueil de documents*, no. 2 (1994), http://78.133.255.100/1994/2/5.html (accessed April 21, 2011). See also Sławomir Dębski, "Ewolucja doktryny polityki wschodniej Polski" [The evolution of Poland's eastern policy doctrine], in Gil and Kapuśniak, *Polityka Wschodnia Polski*, 187–200.

11. See, e.g., Kancelaria Prezydenta RP [The Chancellery of the President of Poland], "Wizyta Prezydenta RP w Republice Mołdowy – dzień pierwszy" [Visit of the Polish President in the Republic of Moldova – day first], December 9, 1997, http://www .prezydent.pl/archiwum/archiwum-aktualnosci/rok-2000-i-starsze/art,158,199,wizyta-prezydenta-rp-w-republice-moldowy-dzien-pierwszy.html (accessed April 23, 2011).

12. Dębski, "Ewolucja doktryny," 187–200; Radosław Sikorski, "Polish FM Tells Moldova That European Integration 'Worth It In The End,' " interview with *Radio Free Europe/Radio Liberty*, July 11, 2008, http://www.rferl.org/content/Polish_FM_Tells _Moldova_That_European_Integration_Worth_It_In_The_End/1183157.html (accessed April 27, 2011). Cf. Kazimierz Wóycicki and Adam Balcer, "Orientacje polskiej polityki zagranicznej. Punkty regionalnego odniesienia" [Orientations of the Polish foreign policy. Points of regional reference], *Debata*, no. 3 (2010): 29.

13. Andrzej Cieszkowski, "Policy of the Enlarged European Union toward Eastern Neighbours: Poland's Contribution," *Yearbook of Polish Foreign Policy*, 2004, 103–14, http://www.msz.gov.pl/publications/2004/content/Publications_and_analyses/yearbook .pdf (accessed April 27, 2011); Veaceslav Berbeca, "Poland's presidency – an opportunity to gain recognition of Moldova's European prospects," *Moldova's Foreign Policy Statewatch*, no. 18 (March 2011), www.viitorul.org/public/3236/en/Policy_Statewatch19_en .pdf (accessed April 27, 2011); Kerry Longhurst and Marcin Zaborowski, "Keeping an Eye on the East: The Foreign Policy Priorities of the Central European Presidencies of

the European Union," *Issue Brief of the Center for European Policy Analysis*, no. 118 (March 2011), http://www.cepa.org/file_manager/pdfstorage/streamfile.aspx?name=Issue +Brief+No.+118%2c+Keeping+an+Eye+on+the+East.pdf (accessed April 27, 2011); The Chancellery of the Prime Minister of Poland, "Prime Minister: Moldova belongs to Europe, even though it is outside the EU yet," March 11, 2011, http://www.premier.gov .pl/en/press_centre/news/prime_minister_moldova_belong,6330/ (accessed April 27, 2011).

14. Radosław Sikorski, "Co Unia i Polska robią na Wschodzie?" [What do the European Union and Poland do in East?], interview with *Polska The Times*, November 16, 2010, http://www.polskatimes.pl/fakty/kraj/333260,co-unia-i-polska-robia-na-wschodzie ,id,t.html (accessed April 27, 2011).

15. "Poland strong supporter of Moldova in rapprochement with EU – Polish official," *Moldpres*, March 5, 2010, http://www.moldpres.md (accessed April 26, 2011).

16. Polish Foreign Ministry, "Development Assistance," September 19, 2006, http://www.polskapomoc.gov.pl/Development,Assistance,200.html (accessed April 27, 2011); Polish Foreign Ministry, "Why We Provide Assistance," September 21, 2006, http://www.polskapomoc.gov.pl/Why,We,Provide,Assistance,204.html (accessed April 27, 2011).

17. Polish Foreign Ministry, "Partner Countries. Moldova," February 4, 2011, http://www.polskapomoc.gov.pl/Moldova,187.html (accessed April 27, 2011); Polish Foreign Ministry, *Poland's Development Co-operation Programme Implemented Through the Ministry of Foreign Affairs of the Republic of Poland in 2011* (Warsaw, 2010), 7–8, http://www.polskapomoc.gov.pl/files/inne%20dokumenty%20PDF/Pomoc%20zagraniczna %202011/Programme2011_PL.pdf (accessed April 27, 2011).

18. Ministerstwo Gospodarki [Polish Ministry of Economy], "Mołdowa" [Moldova], September 15, 2010, http://www.mg.gov.pl/Wspolpraca+z+zagranica/Wspolpraca+ gospodarcza+Polski+z+krajami+wschodnimi+i+pozaeuropejskimi/Moldowa.htm# (accessed April 28, 2011).

19. "Poland lends US $15m to Moldova to support budget," *Moldova Azi*, February 22, 2010, http://www.azi.md/en/story/9546 (accessed April 28, 2011).

20. Polish Foreign Ministry, "Humanitarian Aid," March 9, 2011, http://www .polskapomoc.gov.pl/Humanitarian,aid,251.html (accessed April 28, 2011).

21. Cf. Maksim Kuzovlev, "Respublika Moldova – kak 'istoriya uspekha' dlya Pol'shi?," *Kommersant PLUS*, April 15, 2011, http://km.press.md/index.php/politica/345 3----q-q---.html (accessed April 29, 2011).

22. Witold Rodkiewicz, "Moldova's pro-European course: progress in negotiations, but no real reforms," *Eastweak* (Centre for Eastern Studies), April 20, 2011, http://www .osw.waw.pl/en/publikacje/eastweek/2011-04-20/moldova-s-proeuropean-course-progress -negotiations-no-real-reforms (accessed April 28, 2011).

23. Since 2005, the negotiation format is called 5+2. Along with the two opposing claimants—Moldova and Transnistria—it includes Russia, Ukraine, the Organization for Security and Co-operation in Europe, as well as the European Union and the United States of America as observers.

24. See Marek Menkiszak and Marcin Andrzej Piotrowski, "Polska polityka wschodnia" [Polish Eastern policy], in *Polityka zagraniczna RP 1989–2002* [Foreign policy of the Republic of Poland, 1989–2002], ed. Roman Kuźniar and Krzysztof Szczepanik (Warsaw: SCHOLAR, 2002), 252.

25. Maria Raquel Freire, *Conflict and Security in the Former Soviet Union. The Role of the OSCE* (Aldershot: Ashgate 2003), 203–4.

26. Krzysztof Suprowicz, "Moldova should become Eastern Europe's Switzerland, Polish ambassador to Moldova says," interview with *Moldpres*, July 24, 2006, http://www.moldpres.md (accessed April 26, 2011).

27. For more information see a website of EUBAM http://www.eubam.org/.

28. "Joint statement on Bashkan elections in the autonomous territorial unit of Gagauzia within the Republic of Moldova, Chisinau, November 28, 2006," http://www.osce.org/moldova/47970 (accessed April 26, 2011); "Pol'skaya delegatsiya posetila Komrat," *Kommersant PLUS*, no. 10 (2007).

29. "Agreement between the Government of the Republic of Poland and the Government of the Republic of Moldova on Trade and Economic Cooperation, Warsaw, February 10, 1992," *Zbiór Dokumentów. Recueil de documents*, no. 2 (1994), http://78.133.255.100/1992/2/4.html (accessed April 29, 2011).

30. Andrzej Olechowski, "Presentation of Polish Foreign Policy."

31. Moldovan Embassy to Poland, "Commercial economic relations," http://www.polonia.mfa.md/commercial-economic/ (accessed April 30, 2011).

32. "Pol'sha namerena razvivat' torgovyye otnosheniya s Pridnestrov'yem," *RIA «Novyy Region» 2*, June 26, 2008, http://www.nr2.ru/economy/184241.html (accessed March 27, 2011); "Pridnestrov'ye i Pol'sha planiruyut razvivat' ekonomicheskoye sotrudnichestvo," *RIA «Novyy Region» 2*, October 8, 2009, http://www.nr2.ru/pmr/252043.html (accessed March 27, 2011).

33. See Foreign Trade Database (2004–2010) of the Central Statistical Office of Poland, http://hinex.stat.gov.pl/hinex/aspx/index.aspx.

34. Angelina Taran, "Iskusstvo vinodeliya. Podvodim itogi goda," *Ekonomicheskoye obozreniye LOGOS-PRESS* 884, no. 4 (2011), http://logos.press.md/Weekly/Main.asp?IssueNum=884&IssueDate=04.02.2011&YearNum=4&Theme=10&Topic=28 808 (accessed May 4, 2011).

35. See a website of the National Bureau of Statistics of the Republic of Moldova http://www.statistica.md/.

36. See *Statisticheskiy yezhegodnik Pridnestrovskoy Moldavskoy Respubliki. 2006* (Tiraspol: Ministerstvo ekonomiki Pridnestrov'ya, 2006), 164–68, and a website of the so-called Ministry of Economy of Transnistria http://www.mepmr.org/.

37. Ministerstwo Gospodarki, "Mołdowa."

38. See Piotr Marciniak, "Polacy w Mołdawii" [Poles in Moldova], *Wspólnota Polska* 141, no. 2 (2007), http://www.wspolnota-polska.org.pl/index.php?id=kw7_2_20 (accessed May 3, 2011).

39. See more about Poland's policy toward the Polish diaspora in the post-Soviet republics in Mirosław Habowski, "Polityka Polski wobec Polaków – obywateli państw poradzieckich" [Poland's policy towards the Poles – citizens of the post-Soviet Union states], in Gil and Kapuśniak, *Polityka Wschodnia Polski*, 309–25.

40. See more about the Polish state institutions and NGOs (receiving money from the state budget), and activities in favor of the Polish diaspora in Moldova at the following websites: the Polish Foreign Ministry—http://www.msz.gov.pl/; the Polish Embassy to Moldova—http://www.kiszyniow.polemb.net/; the Senate of Poland—http://www.senat.gov.pl; The Foundation Aid to Poles in the East—http://www.pol.org.pl/; the Association "Polish Community"—http://www.wspolnota-polska.org.pl/; the Semper Polonia Foundation—http://www.semperpolonia.pl/.

41. See Międzyresortowy Zespół ds. Polonii i Polaków za Granicą [Inter-Ministerial Group for *Polonia* and Poles Abroad], *Raport. Polityka państwa polskiego wobec Polonii i Polaków za granicą 1989–2005* [Report. Poland's policy towards *Polonia* and Poles abroad 1989–2005] (Warsaw, 2007).

42. Kazimierz Jurczak, introduction to *Polacy w Mołdawii. Wybór dokumentów prawnych dotyczących mniejszości narodowych* [Poles in Moldova. A selection of legal documents about national minorities] (Warsaw: "Wspólnota Polska," 2004), http://www.wspolnota-polska.org.pl/index.php?id=mold00 (accessed May 4, 2011).

43. Jan Borkowski, "Prezydencja Polski w UE – polityka wschodnia UE" [Polish presidency in the EU – the EU Eastern policy] (lecture, University of Warsaw, February 21, 2011), quoted in Kinga Kalinowska, "Prezydencja Polski w Radzie UE a relacje wschodnie Unii" [Polish presidency of the EU Council and the EU's Eastern relations], March 3, 2011, Portal Spraw Zagranicznych, http://www.psz.pl/tekst-36697/Kinga-Kalinowska-Prezydencja-Polski-w-Radzie-UE-a-relacje-wschodnie-Unii (accessed May 7, 2011).

Chapter Twelve

Romania: From Brotherly Affection with Moldova to Disillusionment and Pragmatism

Octavian Milevschi

The Republic of Moldova appeared on the political map as a de jure subject of international relations two decades ago. The larger context in which Moldova's recognition took place is telling: The collapse of a bipolar system, the retreat and partial dismantlement of an empire and, consequently, a parade of nationalities that thereto had formed its peripheries. Thus, August 27, 1991, on Romania's eastern border, a new and, in many respects, kindred state emerged, bearing the name of the Republic of Moldova. The first international anointment of its independence came from no other state than Romania, which immediately recognized Moldova and established diplomatic relations.[1]

For obvious reasons of geography and politics on a disputed borderland between empires, this new state had been a frankensteinian geopolitical patchwork for almost two centuries of repeated imperial advance and retreat, as well as revolutionary events resulting from the world wars of the twentieth century, both "hot" and "cold." Hypothetically, its morphology could have led to a repetition of the 1918 scenario, when the then-Bessarabian region decided to unify with the Kingdom of Romania. In spite of all that, and in spite of many outside voices coming especially from the former metropolitan center, pointing to covert designs of Romanian infringement on Moldova's sovereignty and territorial integrity, for the last two decades Romania has been a consistent and convinced follower of the Republic of Moldova's fulfillment as a full-fledged state. In fact, few official positions during the two decades have been formulated in a way that would raise any doubts about its firm support for Moldova's independence.

In the political imagination of Romanian political and cultural elites, Moldova's exclusive kindred character has been a leitmotif or a background in their understanding of the new Moldovan state. Whether this "identity kinship" has developed into a sustained strategy toward Moldova is a totally different question, but the acceptance of an independent Moldova has always been, from an identity viewpoint, a challenging if obligatory task. The social substance (history, language, geography, and demography) of Moldova that informed Romanian, and at least some Moldovan, elites about this kindred character, include common ethnic, social, and cultural traits shared by both populations. On the other hand, it has been obvious that the treatment of Moldova's grave post-Soviet setbacks never could have risen to the top of Romania's foreign policy agenda given the latter's own structural debilitation after more than four decades of communism. Although Moldova's autonomy was assured, the new post-1989 Romania had from the very beginning made no priority of Moldova's return to the West and modernization. The idyllic relationship between Romania and Moldova started even prior to the latter's declaration of independence in the spring of 1990. The two Romanian-speaking states, or soon-to-be states, seemingly were headed toward a repetition of the 1918 events, i.e., unification, through short openings of the borders (which before then had been practically sealed by the Soviet state), as well as by ecstatic declarations by some public figures on both sides and a gradual increase in people-to-people communication. In the revolutionary context of German unification, the demise of communism and the collapse of the USSR, the two countries seemed to many observers perfect candidates for such a reunion. In retrospect, it was a somewhat inept exaggeration. Compared to the only existing precedent of unification, in 1918, the international environment and internal Moldovan dynamics highly differed from the situation post-WWI. Moreover, compared to other analogous cases—in Germany and South Korea—the Romanian constitution had no provision for unification with the Republic of Moldova. Thus, this special relationship started with high expectations, which in the tumultuous years of both countries' post-Communist transition, reached many nadirs and many fewer zeniths.

Yet, after two decades, the romanticism of the early nineties has been considered as no more than an exaltation of national feelings in a revolutionary era, so much so that by the end of the second decade the Romanian-Moldovan or Romanian-*Romanian* relationship took a pragmatic turn, although the relationship was still not devoid of mutual appreciation. The relationship between the two countries has undoubtedly been a multi-layered one, from time to time acquiring a rhetorically pronounced commitment from both sides to develop an ambitious number of projects together involving not only the political and economic spheres, but also social-cultural and human dimensions. That is why, although the lion's share of this analysis will be devoted to the first two dimensions, the core of this relationship at present, some space will also be allocated to other relational concerns in order to give a comprehensive depiction of a bond that has consistently shaped this complex relationship. Therefore, first and foremost, any analysis of Romanian-Moldovan relations should start with a historical context. This will provide the reader with insight on the hidden and path-dependant historicizing aspects of this relationship. The reason is simple and evident, for nothing but history can better explain the words of the Romanian president on the start of WWII and Romania's role on the Axis side: "We had an ally and *a territory to recover* [emphasis added]. If I had faced the same conditions, I would have probably done the same."[2] Next, we will proceed to a short description of the founding pillars of Romanian foreign policy in the last decades, in order to explain the failure of the "Bessarabian issue" to reach a higher position on Romania's foreign policy agenda. The subsequent sections will be devoted to the political, economic, and social-cultural dimensions of this relationship.

The Historical Dimension: The Story of a Pact and an Identity

It is next to impossible to select one single historical reason for Romania's poor record in this relationship. However, the geopolitical ideal of the Romanian state has always been identified politically, geographically, socially and demographically with the *belle-époque* of the interwar period, when the whole territory of modern Moldova without Transnistria was part of the then-Romanian Kingdom, along with the lands of Northern Bukovina and the other parts of historical Bessarabia. The conditions for a remaking of that idealized state in the aftermath of the fall of the USSR and the events of 1989 in Romania were impossible to replicate, although according to the then-Romanian Prime Minister Petre Roman "there was a chance for unification with the Republic of Moldova."[3] Moreover, in retrospect, seeking such reunification might have pushed Romania into a geopolitical adventure of epic consequence, such as occurred in Yugoslavia.

Thus, Romanian-Moldovan relations have always borne the brunt of history. The creation of the modern Romanian state (1859–1878) itself was the product of the two principalities of Wallachia and Moldavia, i.e., the latter principality's western part, the one area that had escaped annexation to the Russian Empire in 1812. Starting with this unification, the two Romanian territories have been developing—with a short interlude during the 1918–1940 interwar period and from 1941–1943 during Romania's alliance with Nazi Germany—under different political systems, political constructions and, consequently, with different politically constructed mythologies. The fact that the imperially objectified Bessarabian lands have almost never comprised the Romanian state and society up until 1918, left a nearly indelible mark on the collective conscience or identity of the majority of the Bessarabians. This, of course, was reflected in how Moldovans regarded the Romanian state in the subsequent decades. To the detriment of both conventional Romanian territories, during the interwar period Bessarabia, the then-eastern Romanian territory, was unsuccessfully managed by Bucharest in almost every social dimension—economic, human, and military. Suffice it to say, perhaps the biggest failure of the interwar Romanian state was the incapacity to instill among the great majority of the Bessarabians a vivid Romanian national conscience. It merely took for granted the Bessarabians' Romanian identity, which had been a nationalizing-unifying concept constructed during the second part of the eighteenth and the first part of the nineteenth century by Transylvanian scholars. Whatever the truth of that construct, the two decades of the Romanian Kingdom's administration were not sufficient to forge a modern Romanian identity among the rural and localist Bessarabian population.

Moreover, after the re-establishment of the Bessarabian polity in the aftermath of the Molotov-Ribbentrop Pact and WWII—only a truncated two-thirds of what it had been before and with the perfidious addition of Transnistria—the legitimization of the new structure has added a new (non-)value to the construction of this identity in the psyche of the nascent Moldavian Soviet Socialist Republic. Thus the social engineering of *homo sovieticus* ensued for the next two or three generations, one of the results of which has been the low self-esteem vis-à-vis one's own [Romanian\Moldovan] culture and a sense of surrogate proto-imperial arrogance by many present day Moldovans toward the Romanian state. On the level of mutual knowledge, this has fostered a "self-ist" vision of the other, to a degree that there have been few debates, if any, in the last seven decades on the implications of WWII and the Yalta system for the two Romanian states' strategic identities. Nor has there been any discussion on the absence of the Bessarabian Moldovan component from the nation-building projects of the modern Romanian state. Thus, nowadays even those academics and intellectuals who really understand the implications do not devote too much effort to understanding their role in the formation of Moldovan perceptions.

To top it all, in the eyes of certain segments of both countries' elites, the mistake of surrendering Bessarabia without "a single bullet" to the USSR in June 1940 left a psychological scar that still haunts both sides. Hastily surrendering Bessarabia in June 1940 (unlike Finland's reaction to the 1939 German-Soviet pact's previsions, which resulted in the tragic 1939–1940 Winter War), abandoning two million of its "citizens unprotected and helpless,"[4] and then committing the "geopolitically motivated error"[5] of entering an alliance with Hitler's Germany, which led to Romania's defeat, are nowadays considered to be "erroneous" and to "still cost us"[6] on moral ground.

Therefore, the historical dimension has had an impact on Romania's position toward Moldova, not least because it puts redoubled importance on the rightness of every political act toward this neighbor state. Seemingly, in the conscience of many Romanian political elites, it would be better not to do anything than to err again and consequently alienate even further the "Romanians on the other side of the Prut river."

Romania's Post-1989 Foreign Policy

Before delving into a more detailed evaluation and analysis of bilateral Romanian-Moldovan relations proper, a very succinct introduction to Romania's overall foreign policy trajectory after 1989 is necessary in order to better explain both its successes and achievements as well as its failures and misunderstandings.

In spite of all appearances, especially to some countries regionally (e.g. Russia or Ukraine), in the last two decades Moldova has never been a true strategic objective of Romania's foreign policy. Although it is most certainly true that Moldova has a special place in the Romanian psyche, the primary task of Romania's foreign policy in the aftermath of the 1989 regime change and the end of Cold War was a "return to the West." In practice, that meant joining NATO, integrating into the European Union, and everything this presupposed in terms of establishing political and economic structures, and modernizing Romanian society. In sum, those steps have been synonymous with Romania's bid for westernization and Europeanization.

At the same time, also as a precondition of entering the Western structures, Romania redefined its relations with all its neighbors based on cooperation and non-interference in internal affairs, closely abiding by the norms and principles of the organizations it was part of or intended to join. While mainly successful in the consolidation of bilateral relations, it, firstly, could not officially endow Moldova with a favored position as it might have wanted, and, secondly, the post-Soviet environment dominated by Russia's multi-level and assertive presence, especially in the case of Moldova, put additional pressure on Romania's choice of policies and actions toward its neighbor.

Romania's overall foreign policy during the past two decades can be divided into two stages. The 1990–2004 period of reintegration into the Western and European family and the stage from 2005 to the present that is characterized by a consolidation of the previous achievements and the search for a new continental and regional role. One of the distinctive characteristics of this last stage is the inclination to selectively bandwagon with the United States in the latter's regional and continental projects, while trying to define for itself an indispensable role as "active bridge between EU and the new democracies of the Eastern neighborhood."[7]

During the period of Romania's return to the West, there were two principles that guided its foreign policy. The first, dictated by the international operational environment, set foreign policy objectives compatible with the international system. The second, conditioned by the internal structure of the state, sought to follow the democratic norm of consensus. Therefore, Romania's policies toward Moldova had to take into consideration on the international level the normative aspects of the European and international order, wherein the sovereignty of a state is to be strictly respected. At the same time, it had to find internal consensus so that between public opinion and the policy of the state, any given policy would not contradict society at large. Thus, on one hand, Romania had to face the reality of another Romanian state on its eastern border and to treat it as an equal; on the other hand, it had to take into account the democratic principle of accountability for its actions in the face of a society that sanctioned concrete policies through elections. Moldova was quite low on the agenda of the everyday life of Romanians.

By 2004–2007, Romania's joining the Euro-Atlantic family ended a grand chapter in its foreign policy. Later on, Romanian foreign policy entered a new stage in search of vital interests.[8] Practically since 2007, Romania has pursued a policy of consolidation in the Western organizations and security structures, also promoting regional cooperation projects. At the same time, with the change in power and the advent of Romanian President Traian Băsescu (December 2004), new nuances were added to the role Romania could play on the Black Sea regional scale with the help of the two Western regional stakeholders, the US and the EU. In this greater post-integrative context, the Republic of Moldova has indeed become a subject of higher concern for Romania.

The Political Dimension: One Nation, Two States?

A Moldova "Non-strategy"

In the National Security Strategy (2007), there is only one paragraph specially dedicated to the Republic of Moldova. Compared with the previous document (issued in 2001), this is already a notable progress. The Moldovan problematique takes up space in section V, in which Romania prescribes for itself the role of "regional vector of security and prosperity in the Black Sea Region." The text states in bold type that Romania "will give a distinct attention to cooperation with Republic of Moldova." The guiding pillars are based on a "special relationship" and "natural responsibilities" from the principle of "single nation—two states." The document also states that Romania has the "political and moral responsibility" to do "all possible politically, economically and diplomatically" to back Moldova's "sovereignty and territorial integrity."[9] A similar document, the National Defense Strategy of Romania, echoes the previous strategy but also takes into account the qualitative shifts in the EU's perspective. It affirms that "through Republic of Moldova's joining the common European space, the last barriers that separated a nation will be removed."[10]

Compared to the true strategic course developed during the period of joining the West (1991–2007), a different periodization is possible to discern in bilateral relations with Moldova, a rather reactive approach to the relationship, i.e., based on Chisinau's stance toward Bucharest and the latter's response. Such a periodization is fairly compelling, especially until the middle of the last decade, since the secondary position of Moldova on the foreign policy agenda did not favor a coherent set of policies. In this framework, the first stage was a short romantic opening toward the "brethren on the other side of river Prut" (1991–1994); then, a period of gradual pragmatism and critical reflection between states(1994–2001); then came a period of overall disillusionment (2001–2009), although during this period there have also been ups and downs; and, finally, (2009 to present) a constructive and warm pragmatism.

Taking action and not official rhetoric as a guiding principle, Romania's Moldova policy has not until the present developed into a full-fledged strategy, the two main reasons being Romania's internal modernization priorities and its democratic consolidation. Concurrently, Moldova's internal political and social regime has itself been quite an undertaking for Romania as well. It would be more appropriate to designate Romania's policy as a multi-pronged tactic, at times reactive and hectic, at times prudent and well-balanced. Nonetheless, the unique place Moldova has played in Romania's foreign policy cannot be denied.

Thus, the last two decades of both countries' post-Communist and post-Soviet existence have registered many ups and downs. Simply put, Romanian foreign policy discourse on Moldova has zigzagged from unification in the start of the 1990s, to a quick acknowledgment of the secondary character of the "Bessarabian issue" on the foreign policy agenda starting with the year of 1993 until the end of the decade.[11] It then passed through the harshest period, wherein Bucharest had to tackle a neo-Communist and Romania-phobic administration in Chisinau from 2001–2009. Finally, after 2007, Romania, through President Traian Băsescu, has for the first time *officially* voiced the "same people, two countries" interpretation of Moldova which in fact reinforced the sad truth and widespread opinion that Romania's policy toward Moldova never met the high rhetorical expectations, since it came to officially acknowledge this truism only after one entire generation.

Against a background of purported designs of unification in the romantic aftermath of the USSR's collapse, Ion Iliescu, the first president of Romania and the main foreign policy actor according to the constitution and the institutional arrangement of the state, never made a clear statement on the desirability of unification. For Iliescu there were at least two impediments to that. First, the presence of Soviet/Russian troops in Moldova under the context of the Transnistrian conflict, were a major deterrent together with the "passivity" of the East;[12] secondly, the existence of international treaties on the inviolability of borders in Europe, namely the Helsinki Accords (1975), and the Paris Peace Treaty (1947), and also the Soviet-Romanian Treaty on Friendship, Collaboration and Mutual Assistance (April 1991).

By invoking the first two treaties, Iliescu was declaring his resolution to abide by the legitimacy of the treaties that created and then guaranteed Romania's actual borders, ignoring the banal evidence of the appearance on the map of fifteen new states as a result of the collapse of USSR, five new states as a result of the dissolution of Yugoslavia (in its immediate aftermath), and of course the "absorption" of Eastern Germany by Western Germany and its "automatic integration" into the EU (at that moment still in the form of the European Community) and NATO. Moreover, to the historical contempt of his peers in then-revolutionary Europe, Iliescu was the only head of a former Warsaw Treaty state to sign a treaty with the Soviet Union.[13] There is hardly any more telling proof of the spirit in the corridors of power in Bucharest—as embodied by Iliescu—vis-à-vis the nascent Moldovan state: willingness to concede the independence of Moldova for fear of alienating a possibly recalcitrant USSR/Russia.

Therefore, in the aftermath of Romania's post-Communist era, a state of transitioning confusion due to the yet uncertain direction of the greater European and world orders were one of the period's main characteristics. The dilemma of balancing between the former patron—the USSR—and the constant desire to be part of the West left a confusing imprint on Romania's foreign policy during the first years of post-Communism. In this context, Romania's Moldova policy could not but convey indecisiveness to its "brethren across the Prut." Few official foreign policy statements or actions by Romanian foreign policy makers have envisaged Moldova as an issue of strategic concern. Moreover, few political projects for and with the Republic of Moldova could be labeled as successful, for it would have been premature to have any bilateral breakthrough in an environment so ripe with events and uncertainties for both countries as the beginning of the 1990s.

Moldova's International Advocate

The second stage, the one that gradually led to a more pragmatic stance, can be seen between 1994–2001. On one hand, the political instability related to the two so-called miners' revolts (*mineriade*) and the fallout of the governments of Petre Roman—who was a much more explicit Moldova backer than Iliescu—put cracks in the latter's highly pro-Moldovan positions. On the other hand, Moldova's Transnistrian conflict and the advent of "moldovenist" and anti-Romanian forces on the Moldovan political scene gradually changed the atmosphere between the two countries. The adoption of the Moldovan constitution (1994) whereby the syntagm "Romanian language" was replaced with "state language" or the change of the history curriculum from "history of Romanians" to "*Moldovan* history" (1996), were indicative examples of the changes in the shifting structure of the Moldovan political class. Thus, Romania's until-then robust soft attraction for Moldova came to a halt. By the end of 1994, at the high political level, Romania came to play a much less visible political role for Moldova, while on the internal scene the "Moldovan cause" also lost steam. Suffice it to say that Romania ceased to be a part of the proposal for the Transnistrian conflict's negotiation format by the end of 1993, or that during the presidential campaign of 1992 the only candidate that built his electoral platform on the Moldovan issue was the former prime minister of Moldova (1990–1991), Mircea Druc, who received 2.75 percent of the votes.

Nonetheless, the dialogue has never stopped. Moldova, while becoming secondary on the foreign policy agenda during the tenure of the first two Romanian presidents, was a matter of concern primarily in three directions: continuing the processes of economic integration, consolidation of common cultural and spiritual spaces, and the "evaluation of the implication of various events in Chisinau on the national security of Romania."[14]

In the context of growing mutual difficulties, Romania began playing its cards in Moldova somewhat independently of Moldova's inward or eastern-looking establishment. Romanian foreign policy decision makers set the bilateral political mode on a more declarative and expectant note, while trying to diversify their network of interlocutors on the social and economic level.[15] In this period, the two states started a long dialogue on a series of issues of mutual, but also regional, concern that lingered during the 1990s and well into the 2000s, such as the basic treaty between the two countries, and the treaty on the borders.

Negotiations of the two treaties would see many reversals of fortunes, despite numerous diplomatic meetings and declarations on the impending signing and ratification. The truth behind the lingering consisted, on one hand, of Romania's fear of legitimizing the sort of geopolitical regime that resulted from the Molotov-Ribbentrop Pact. For the Moldovan side, on the other hand, the delay was an instrument of promoting its *moldovanness*, an act that Romania would never agree with. Therefore, the impossibility of reaching a common denominator with successive Moldovan governments on the formulation of the text of a treaty, which by itself would legitimize the loss of a territory, worsened the bilateral record during the 1990s and well into the 2000s. In the context of Romania's joining NATO, Moldova became the only country with which Romania did not sign a basic treaty, which would not bode well in the eyes of some international institutions for both countries.

Nonetheless, Romania never ceased playing the smart card on Moldova at the level of international institutions. Romania became Moldova's most committed advocate, a policy that has remained steady ever since. Indifferent to the tones coming from Chisinau, Romania started permanently backing Moldova's bid for membership and positions in the major European, (sub-)regional and global organizations and policy projects, such as the United Nations, the Council of Europe, and the Organization for Security and Cooperation in Europe. It subsequently advocated for Moldova's interests in the World Trade Organization, the European Neighbourhood Policy and the Danube Strategy. Moreover, Romania has been a constant advocate of Moldova's inclusion in the Western Balkans "package" for an Association Agreement with the EU. As an enhancement, Romania actively backed Moldova's admission in the Central European Initiative, the Stability Pact for South Eastern Europe, the Process for Political Cooperation in South-East Europe and the Central European Free Trade Agreement.

During the presidential tenure of Emil Constantinescu (1996–2000), the relationship did not evolve significantly in real economic terms, albeit the political and social-cultural connectivity of the two Romanian states continued to grow. Contrary to the initial expectations, the pragmaticism of the then-Moldovan president Petru Lucinschi met fruitful ground in his Romanian counterpart, who was born in the interwar Bessarabia. In the first two years of the Constantinescu administration, five bilateral summits would take place. Starting in 1998, the two executives would have more than yearly summits. Both presidents were active in the Romania-Moldova-Ukraine Trilateral, which started enthusiastically in 1998 and led to the creation of two Euroregions: the Lower Danube (1998) and the Upper Prut (2000).

This period *was* indeed characterized by intense dialogue at the level of parliamentary commissions and governments. The usual range of topics was on the agenda: the Treaty on Partnership and Collaboration (April 2000), which was finally initialed after seven years of difficult negotiations whereby the Republic of Moldova finally agreed with the stipulation of the commonality of history, culture and language; the border status agreement; the creation of free economic zones (Iași-Ungheni and Galați-Giurgiulești-Reni), energy cooperation and rescheduling of the debts on energy (starting from 1998, Moldova was connected to the Romanian power grid, after refusing in 1994 on political grounds to cosponsor the building of one of the reactors at Cernavodă nuclear plant), customs regulations and movement of people, participation of Romanian capital in the privatization process, and the negotiation of education and science protocols. These were the usual issues in the bilateral relations. The fact that many of them remained on paper or without a solution until the end of the next decade suggests that there has never been enough political will or perhaps resources to up the ante in bilateral Romanian-Moldovan relations. Given what would be in store over the greater part of the next decade, this period could be called a period of lost chances since the internal political instability of the two countries precluded the advance of many projects.[16]

Growing Disillusionment

With the change of the political guard in Bucharest (November 2000) and then in Chisinau (February 2001), Romania gradually entered a period of real disillusionment with Moldova. The not very enthusiastically Moldova-minded Ion Iliescu was back in power. Romania's strategic concerns about Euro-Atlantic integration were proving well-founded. Stimulated by integrative concerns and being on the verge of becoming the external EU and NATO border, Romania had to implement a series of policies in order to secure border areas, affecting hundreds of thousands of Moldovans. At the same time, Moldova was opening a political chapter where Romania would have the strange role of "significant other" in the ideology of "moldovenism" (the idea of a primordial Moldovan ethnicity established in the historic Principality of Moldavia) then fervently promoted by the ruling party of Moldovan Communists. Lastly, Moldovan foreign policy displayed a subservient attitude toward Russian interests in Moldova, which by its design is an automatic zero-sum prescription for Romania.

After a period of exploring Chisinau's willingness to deepen dialogue, during which Iliescu and Moldovan President Vladimir Voronin met in Bucharest (May 2001) and avoided as much as possible any reference to the delicate issues of identity, language and compatibility of strategic vectors of both countries, economic issues seemed the only hope for pragmatic cooperation. The chancelleries of the countries ostentatiously avoided any discussions on the thorny issues of the Basic Treaty (partly negotiated during the Constantinescu administration) or the Border Agreement.[17]

Thus, aware of not having a sincere counterpart in Chisinau, Romania started focusing on practical issues affecting its record for Euro-Atlantic integration. It negotiated granting $2 million for passports for Moldovan citizens, especially

for Bessarabians living in the border area with Romania as a preemptive measure against the subsequent change of a facilitated regime for entering Romania,
until then based only on an identity card. It signed an Agreement on Readmission for persons illegally crossing the border from the Republic of Moldova and
it achieved sectoral agreements on small border traffic and the opening of common customs checkpoints.

Yet, starting in July 2001, the Moldovan Party of Communist's adoption of
a number of laws providing for equal status to the Russian language and the
promotion of the "theory of moldovenism" at the state level, provoked the first
public spat between the countries. According to Iliescu, this was an attempt at
"denationalizing"[18] Moldova, while for the state-sanctioned "luminaries" of this
ideology, led by the speaker of the Moldovan Parliament Victor Stepaniuc,
Romania had no right to an opinion since "Romanians were a minority"[19] in
Bessarabia.

Hence, by the end of 2001, the relations between the two capitals took a
nosedive. In the autumn of 2001, the Romanian prime minister openly criticized
the duplicity of the Moldovan government for inconsistency between official
economic agreements and their implementation, while the Moldovan side retali-
ated by lashing out at Romania at the European Court for Human Rights with
the delicate dossier of the Bessarabian Metropolitan Church that until then had
been kept under wraps by Bucharest. The issue had been smoldering for many
years, because the Moldovan government refused to register the canonical rights
of the BMC, which covers approximately one-fifth of the Bessarabian territory.

For the next few years, Romanian-Moldovan relations were politically frozen. Romania preferred to act on its own, avoiding as much as possible the political center in Chisinau. It resorted to its tested approach of advocating and promoting its interests in Moldova by means of international institutions and the
low-level policies of people-to-people contact, education and culture. Romania
backed Moldova's candidacy for the Cooperation Process in South-Eastern
Europe, it lined up on the EU Council decision banning the free movement of
Transnistrian secessionist leaders, and it postponed the introduction of visas for
Moldovan citizens as long as possible, until the autumn of 2006.

The next breakthrough in Romania's relationship with Moldova came,
again, following a reactive pattern. In the aftermath of the Russian Kozak Memorandum failure (November 2003), in which Moldova would have been transformed into an asymmetric federation with its sovereignty diluted between Chisinau and Tiraspol (read Moscow) under the "unprejudiced" guarantee of a Russian military presence, Chisinau mellowed its attitude toward Bucharest. At the
same time, Băsescu's advent to power (December 2004) and his self-proclaimed
Bucharest-London-Washington axis, seemed to Voronin a temporary refuge in
which to isolate Chisinau from Moscow. In the context of another political
change in Bucharest, the "player-president," as Băsescu called himself, who
planned to finish two five-year terms as president, did not have much leisure
time for new political explorations in Moldova. Immediately after his investi-
ture, Băsescu visited his Moldovan colleague on the latter's campaign trail,

showing a wide openness to cooperation. This time Bucharest adeptly tried to play the European card in attracting Moldova to the Western capitals' agendas, a policy it had not used optimally before. The most eloquent example of this came in the repeated promotion of Moldova at all the summit meetings Romania attended during the following year in Washington, London and even Kiev. It also established a permanent phone line with Voronin. Moreover, Bucharest tried to circulate its own plan for a solution to the Transnistrian conflict and advocated for a rapid inclusion of Moldova in the "Western Balkan package" for an Association Agreement with the EU.

These tactics bore fruit only in the near to mid-term, as long as Voronin needed to balance against his temporary loss of fortune in Moscow. By 2006, having in mind a "putinist" scenario for his political future, Voronin began playing the same game he had played at the beginning of the decade. Time and again, Romania raised the same contentious scenario. This time, however, he had to grapple with a regime in Chisinau intent on selective openings only so long as Bucharest would approach Chisinau as a "partner and not advocate."[20] This stance meant that Bucharest had to deal again with the same useless negotiations over issues like the Basic Treaty or the Treaty on Border Delimitation, before it could gain significant breakthroughs in more substantial collaborative projects. The beginning of a new cycle of political spats came quickly, when Băsescu declared at a meeting with Moldovan students that "Romania offered Moldova the possibility to enter the EU together, but the decision depended on Chisinau and the people of Republic of Moldova" and that Romanian-Moldovan unification would take place "within the EU, in a not very distant future."[21] In a case of déjà vu, the retaliation from Chisinau was, of course, recourse to the bashing of "imperialistic Romania."

In October 2006, three months before Romania's integration in the European Union, an article in a major Romanian newspaper titled, "How much would unification with Republic of Moldova cost?" presented the sum of $20 billion as a likely cost of a unification with Moldova.[22] That such an article appeared in a major newspaper in itself represented a reflection of the search for new foreign policy paradigms and the fact that, after fifteen years, even if a discussion of unification seemed indeed quixotic in the public space, Moldova was in the deep Romanian psyche a "*self* subject." Thus in this period, against the background of the "color revolutions," but also new openings of Băsescu toward Moldova, even if dominated by the same Romania-phobic neo-Communists, the Moldovan problematique began to leave behind the marginal position it had occupied on the political agenda. Although the ups and downs of the relationship persisted, the discourse coming from Bucharest gave signs of greater wishes for engagement.

By the end of Voronin's term at the helm of the Moldovan state, Romania's interest in Moldova became officially blasé. It officially avoided as much as possible any direct engagement in dialogue with the Moldovan establishment, and it began unofficially working with the alternative and potential future avenues of political power in Moldova—civil society and low-political actors. Although still modest and seldom exceptional, this policy indirectly contributed to the tipping point seen in the April 7–8 riots in Chisinau, which led to the delegitimization and fall of the proto-Communist rule.

A New Pragmatic Beginning

With the advent of a new, pro-European, and much more Romania-friendly coalition in Chisinau (August–September 2009), new political opportunities became visible. Romania had been waiting for this for many years. Although it has been a daunting task, no less because of Moldova's own internal political instability, Romania brought more visibility to Moldovan pro-integration circles and made itself a vehicle for promoting the "Moldovan cause" on the path to a European course. One of the most successful pro-Moldova lobbying efforts by Romania was launched in January 2010, an initiative called the Friends of Moldova Group,[23] in partnership with France. Within this framework, Romania succeeded in attracting nine EU foreign ministers in September 2010 and investing both itself and its Moldovan partners with "credibility within the EU."[24] Also, although overall Romania has been to a degree less active in the Eastern Partnership—Poland encouraged Romanian politicians from both Bucharest and Brussels to visit the Moldovan streets at every possible occasion. Moreover, at the level of the EU, Romanian MEPs are assiduous advocates of the Moldovan cause. This is most visible primarily through the visits paid almost monthly to Moldova by Romanian MEPs as constituents of different EU delegations as well as by their public positions in the European parliament on Moldova.

A further breakthrough in the bilateral relations occurred with the signing of the—what de facto is considered in Romanian political circles—*political* bilateral treaty regarding the borders between Romania and Moldova in November 2010. The saga of its signing has finally ended after seventeen years of wrangling and as a result of intense negotiations, not least under the influence of Brussels and Berlin. As mentioned, Romania initially had opposed such a treaty on the grounds that it did not want to historically legitimize the Molotov-Ribbentrop Pact. In order to compromise between the mutually necessitated technical aspects of the border-line (also related to Romania's bid for entering the Schengen zone) and the politically loaded issue of both countries' reading of themselves, a more technical treaty was signed, called Treaty on the State Border Regime, Collaboration and Mutual Assistance in Border Issues.[25] It should also be mentioned that the treaty came as a response (to a degree European driven) to Russia's recurrent use of this issue against the supposedly hidden agenda of Romania on the Republic of Moldova. It was hoped that its signing would represent an added value to the larger context of the so-called "Meseberg process" on Transnistria.

The thorny issue of the basic treaty met an unusual solution. The situation seemed propitious for Romania because it had a suitable political interlocutor for a compromising solution in the person of the acting President Mihai Ghimpu. Instead of a basic treaty, the countries signed a political document called The Common Declaration on the Setting of a Strategic Partnership between Romania and Republic of Moldova for the European Integration of Republic of Moldova."[26] According to Traian Băsescu, the declaration establishes a "three dimensional framework—political, economic and cultural—for extending and deepening cooperation" and for its implementation there will be an "action plan to be agreed and signed by the prime-ministers."[27] Hitherto, the basic treaty between the countries has not been signed and according to Romanian Foreign Minister Teodor Baconschi "Romania will never sign a basic treaty with Republic of Moldova," because such treaties "are obsolete documents."[28] It has been considered that the Intergovernmental Action Plan (a set of six technical agreements) and the EU Partnership for Integration (the political vehicle of the whole series of agreements signed by the two presidents) represent an "ambitious and realistic" bilateral juridical foundation.[29]

Finally, a series of new bilateral instruments have been further developed, such as the implementation of the Small-Scale Border Traffic Agreement (March 2010), the opening of new Romanian consulates in Cahul and Bălţi (July 2010) and a consular office in Ungheni (January 2011), and, symbolically very important, a new branch of the Romanian Cultural Institute in Chisinau (September 2010).[30] Thus a new pragmatic, "well structured and more targeted"[31] rhythm between the capitals has been sounded since 2010, indicating how much Romania's performance in Moldova has depended on the existence of a willing partner in Chisinau, and how it learned to distance itself as much as possible from the internal Moldovan political struggle.

The Economic Dimension: Incremental Involvement

The overall economic relationship between the two countries has been quite dynamic, although somewhat undervalued by the political class in both countries. It has been falsely given a secondary importance and subordinated role at the level of political discourse. By the end of the two decades, both countries still labor under the uneasy feeling that economic potential never reached expectations. A number of factors contributed to this: the political tensions, especially under the two neo-Communist governments in Chisinau; the rent-seeking and corrupt practices of the business environment, especially in Moldova; derelict infrastructure and incompatible railway systems; and low governance quality in general. In addition, the structural economic problems with which Romania itself was confronted in the beginning of the 1990s severely conditioned deeper implications in the Moldovan economy.

In the 1990s, and even later, Moldova provided a series of advantages to Romanian investors. It has always had low-cost workforce and industrial construction sites; it represented a bridge and opportunity for access to the post-

Soviet markets, Romania had practical (including linguistic) knowledge of the Eastern markets and societies; it later offered fiscal facilities under the form of tax-exemption for the reinvested revenue. Some Romanian companies have indeed entered the Moldovan market and have left a mark there, such as Petrom and Rompetrol in oil products, Romstal for heating installations, Arabesque in construction materials, European Drinks in refreshments and services, MediaPro, Jurnal Trust Media and Realitatatea in media, or BCR (Romanian Commercial Bank) in banking and finance.[32] In foreign direct investments, Romania's position has been slowly improving. Generally, the Romanian FDI has never been in the top five of Moldova. In 2008 Romania was at the tenth position, representing 3.5 percent of the total FDI, with $68 million.[33] An evolution of the last 3–4 years has been the "migration" of a number of Romanian light industry companies to the Republic of Moldova. Usually, these are companies in textiles and leather, which specialize in loan regime operations, and choose this strategy because of cheap labor costs.

Trade between Romania and Moldova has followed an incremental increase with a few exceptions, while Romania has been the main destination for Moldovan exports. Thus, from 1997 to 2007, when Romania integrated in the EU, the bilateral exchange grew from $160.0 million to $882.0 million. Of this $632.4 million were exports and $246.4 million were imports. Moreover, Moldovan exports continued to grow on the Romanian market, placing it in 2008 at first place for Moldovan exports,[34] ahead of the Russian market, which until then tended to dominate. Although free trade agreement provisions ended once Romania became an EU full-fledged member, the bilateral trade did not suffer too much, due to the higher quality of the Romanian products (e.g. refrigerators, construction materials, household products), itself a result of complying with higher European standards.

Moreover, tens of thousands of Moldovans benefited from the small border trade with Romania over the 1990s and until 2007. Agricultural products, dairy and tobacco (though not always on a legal basis) have been at the top of these traded goods. Romania's integration in the EU, which entailed visa regulations and high import taxes on certain goods, as well as the lack of a border trade agreement have dealt a severe blow to petty trade. The entry into force of the Agreement on the Small-Scale Border Traffic (spring 2010) has, to a certain degree, re-invigorated the presence of Moldovans in the border cities of Iași, Galați, Botoșani and Vaslui.

For the reasons explained above, and mainly related to its own weaknesses and problems of transition, the Romanian state's substantial economic commitment to Moldova's development came only after almost two decades of bilateral relations. Practically, on March 28, 2011, an agreement between the governments of Romania and Moldova on the implementation of a program for technical and financial assistance worth €100 million entered into force. The program is scheduled for the next four years. The sum is slated first and foremost for the development of the Iași-Ungheni interconnecting gas pipeline, at an estimated cost of $19–20 million, which will be designed for both imports and exports of gas. Two-thirds of the financing for the pipeline will be supported by Romania. Although the idea of its construction was included in Romania's Energy Development Strategy in 2007, its implementation became possible only with the advent of a true interlocutor from the Moldovan side. Both parties are set to gain equally from the pipeline. For Moldova it will increase its energy security, diversify the sources of gas supply, and boost the Moldovan government's program for connecting some areas to gas, which were never before part of a gas network. Moreover, the gas to be imported from Romania by Moldova will be significantly cheaper, as currently Moldova's only supplier—Russia's Gazprom—sells the gas at a price of $320 pcm, while the Romanian gas currently costs $165 pcm.[35]

In line with the re-energized interest after the European integration, Romania included Moldova on its list for direct economic assistance (along with Georgia, Serbia and Afghanistan). During 2007–2009, it assisted Moldova through UNDP projects with a total sum of €1.64 million in projects dedicated to infrastructure, local development, social protection and human rights. For the period 2010–2013, Romania began the bilateral financing of six projects (total worth €1.30 million) in areas like agriculture, infrastructure, health, good governance, education and media. Thus, although a beginner in economic assistance, Romania has developed more gravitational pull through such projects. In this respect, it also tried to join other more experienced bodies like the UN Food Agency, UNDP, US Millennium Challenge Corporation and Swedish Aid Agency in common projects on infrastructure, transportation and environment for the near future.[36]

Also in 2010, Romania successfully restored and opened a new bridge over the Prut River at Lipcani. The bridge was destroyed during WWII and has been closed since. Although it is not a major traffic artery between the two countries, it has been more than a sign of goodwill and it gave impetus to the further planning of similar projects in the next years. On the same note, Romania hopes to bring to a conclusion two projects connecting the Moldovan and Romanian electric grids, in Suceava-Bălți and Fălciu-Gotești. It will bear the biggest cost of the construction. Finally, a feasibility project on changing the railway segment Iași-Chisinau to European gauge standards has been on the economic agenda of both countries, but so far the eventual returns of such a project have put a major brake on its start.

The Social-Cultural Dimension: Inevitable Attraction

The so-called soft means of attracting Moldova have always been a success in bilateral relations. This has been one of the main factors contributing to the positive improvement in Romania's image after generations of Soviet Romania-bashing and social engineering of "ethnic Moldovans." It had also been the driving force for the improvement of the quality of the language, which was altered under the imperial conditions of russification. Moreover, the cultural dimension has been a platform for circumventing the political controversies Romania occasionally had to face in Moldova. Finally, Romania has become a major object of attraction as an EU member, and controversially has given Moldovans hope for better economic prospects on the EU labor market and the possibility for free movement by exercising their right to Romanian citizenship.

Education and Culture

As moral compensation for the "brunt of history," Romania has had consistent educational-cultural and social-human concerns for the Republic of Moldova. This concern has manifested since the very beginning of the 1990s, when Moldova, while still part of the USSR, was allocated 1,150 scholarships at the graduate, 1,200 on the undergraduate and 200 on the post-graduate levels from the Romanian state budget.[37] Ever since, the average number of Bessarabians with state-sponsored scholarships graduating from Romanian educational institutions has been maintained at the level of approximately 2,500 per year, while starting in 2009 the number has doubled. The fruits of this Romanian investment in human resources may have become symbolically ripe when in 2009 a quarter of the ministers in the Moldovan government proved to be graduates of Romanian educational institutions led, of course, by Moldovan Prime Minister Vlad Filat, a graduate in law from the Alexandru Ioan Cuza University of Iaşi. Moreover, in Moldovan universities, the civil society and public sphere Moldovan graduates of Romanian universities have become a norm of the day.

Thus, one of the most successful Romanian policies for Moldova has been the education of tens of thousands of Bessarabians in institutions all over the country in the last two decades at the undergraduate, graduate and postgraduate levels. In this area, too, there have been ups and downs, but on the whole, Romania has registered a sizable success in progressively winning the hearts and minds of younger generations of Moldovans. The success was also due to the fact that, overall, Romania did not necessarily need an official accord from Chisinau to attract young and educated segments of Moldovans. This attraction has been natural, considering the commonality of language and culture, but also because Romania was able to provide Moldovans with, generally speaking, higher standards of education and life opportunities.

Strictly in the cultural sphere, Romania has been an all-time donor through two state institutions: the Romanian Cultural Institute and the Department for Romanians Abroad. The Chisinau branch of the RCI (finally opened in September 2010) is involved in financing activities for organizing cultural, humanities and fine arts events, book translation, publication and distribution, as well as awarding scholarships for outstanding personae. The DRA has been focused on financing Romanian print media, NGOs and supporting schools and public libraries with books in the Romanian language. It is also involved in organizing summer camps for youth and forums for academics. On the whole, in spite of their relatively low-profile character and not so generous budgets, these institutions were among the most consistent Romanian instruments for promoting a good image of Romania in Moldova and succeeded to avoid politization of sensitive issues. They also helped alleviate a sense of political introversion that Romania used to display from time to time before 2009.

Granting Citizenship

One of the most discernible policies to take root in the historical dimension of bilateral Romanian-*Romanian* relations is the right to regain Romanian citizenship. The process of regaining citizenship has been quite controversial over the last two decades. Officially, the justification of the Romanian legislation on regaining citizenship is moral and reparatory, not least for having left their former citizens at the mercy of the Soviet annexation in 1940–1941 and 1944.

During the 1990s, the majority of the Bessarabians did not consider Romanian citizenship a very attractive asset. Virtually only pro-union intellectuals and those who really made their living in Romania proper, who had a strong personal and professional bond with the country applied for citizenship, or those who visited Romania on an almost daily basis. No more than 100,000 regained their citizenship from Moldova's independence to the end of 2001.[38] With the advance of Romania toward the Euro-Atlantic community and its repositioning at the external frontier of NATO and the EU, a dilemma unfolded. On one hand, the attractiveness of Romania grew exponentially for Bessarabians, and on the other hand, Romania had to implement certain standards regarding the security of the frontiers and the freedom of movement, visa regulations, and the passage of people.

Starting from 2001, the Romanian government, under formal and informal pressures from Brussels and other EU capitals, has significantly toughened its citizenship policy. Basically, until 2003 it either temporarily suspended the citizenship regaining procedures process or it added new legal provisions which toughened and virtually discouraged any application for citizenship by Moldovans. In this period no more than several thousand Moldovans regained Romanian citizenship. With integration proper into NATO (2004) and then the EU (2007), the process of regaining citizenship was practically stalled. All in all, approximately 3,000 Moldovans regained citizenship in this period. On the other hand, 800,000 official demands to regain Romanian citizenship (an intentional act) had been sent to the address of the Romanian Consulate Office in Chisinau by the end of 2007, which constitutes no less than a quarter of the mature population of the Republic of Moldova.[39]

In the context of the Traian Băsescu administration's search for a new foreign policy paradigm, the relationship with the historic diaspora, and especially of Moldova, was granted a new value. Moreover, as a result of the Moldovan neo-Communist government's rhetorical lashings against Romania's new policies, Bucharest tended to retaliate with a stronger commitment to the citizenship issue. Thus, after a number of legal modifications to the law on citizenship in 2007 and 2008, and the creation of a specialized institution—the National Administration for Citizenship—under the aegis of the Ministry of Justice, the new citizenship policy brought a gradual growth in the number of Moldovans who regained citizenship. In 2008 approximately 5000 Moldovans regained citizenship; in 2009 the number grew to slightly over 12,000. In 2010 with the opening of the new consulates in Cahul and Bălţi, and of five new branch offices of the NAC on the territory of Romania, the pressure that was building on the Romanian authorities from the historical diaspora on this issue began to gradually alleviate. In 2010 the total number of Moldovans to regain citizenship was close to 15,000. At the moment of writing, end of October 2011, almost 45,000 Bessarabians have regained their citizenship, which is an absolute record and a policy success by Romania paralleled only by the policies in education. At present, around 200,000 Moldovans have double Moldovan and Romanian citizenship.

Conclusion

For the sheer evidence of history, language, culture, ethnical-social demography and what could be called inductively and with a historically laden connotation of "common regional-cultural space," Romania has always had a special vision of Moldova. Everything boils down to deep identity resemblance, plain and simple. Romania and the present state of Moldova—whether or not they have existed within actual borders, whether or not they have had state autonomy or independence during the last two centuries, and, finally, whether or not they have been called their actual name—have always had an intimately close relationship. The last twenty years of bilateral relations proved this truism innumerable times. Yet, the Republic of Moldova's lack of historic DNA also meant that Romania would have to grapple with a geopolitically and identity-challenged state, often excessively mindful of its lack of historic legitimacy. This reality has repeatedly mired many of the grand political projects Romania intended to implement with Moldova.

For these reasons, in the past two decades, Romania's vision of Moldova has never managed to overcome a certain degree of contemplativeness and passive waiting for a Moldovan "awakening." Romania's Moldova policy could be divided mainly into two grand baskets of "theoretical" facts and achievements. The former is replete with rhetorical commitments; the latter is the real outcomes basket. On the rhetorical side, Romania had no equals until 2009. Romania has sincerely championed Moldova's cause in all international platforms, often to its own detriment, but it did not have convincing political returns from all of these efforts, not least so because it had an interlocutor that it wanted to take for granted as an "identical *self*." Most often, it took time and patience until a workable partner would appear in Chisinau. On the outcomes side, though starting with a slim record in the 1990s, it began to recover the lost ground due to the rise of a new generation of politicians in Moldova with a much more friendly view of Romania. Romania's EU membership did have a say in this new attractiveness. Romania started acting with considerably more pragmatism and it began building on a discourse generally devoid of pompous declarations and confirmed by few actions. This incremental reversal has been visible in the economic sphere, where Romania became Moldova's main EU commercial partner and an increasing, though still wanting, source of FDI. In social terms, Romania achieved a much more weighty presence through its educational policies among the hearts and minds of younger generations of Moldovans, those who will likely be the political stakeholders of tomorrow. On the humanitarian level there seems to be an incremental and steady cultural-linguistic "re-Romanianization" of Moldova. The main mechanism that has contributed to this is, again, the constant education of tens of thousands of Bessarabians in Romanian schools and universities, the increasing interest of the Romanian private sector in Moldova and a more competitive Romanian-speaking media resulting from Romanian private investments.

As of today, Moldova has come to obtain a priority position in Romania's foreign policy, not only as a result of its geographic position along Romania and EU's eastern border, but also a priority which results from the capacity and know-how to build new European foreign policy projects in the Black Sea Region. Starting from this reality, officially, "the fundamental references of this relationship are, firstly, assistance to the European trajectory for Republic of Moldova, and secondly, intensified bilateral cooperation."[40] Moreover, an impressive number of Romanians—72 percent according to a 2011 survey—identify Moldova on their mental map as a country belonging to the same European space as Romania,[41] which serves as a popular stimulus for Bucharest's bid to anchor Moldova in the EU in the long term. Thus, the prospect of a special relationship may in the future consist of deepening privileged interests with Moldova based on the practical application—both political and economic—of a European-oriented partnership. Such a partnership could indeed become visible through committed economic assistance for development, but as the two decades of Romanian-*Romanian* relations have proved, it will primarily depend on a willing interlocutor in Chisinau, cogent political elite in Bucharest and a potent Romanian economy.

Notes

1. Romania was the first state to open an embassy in Chisinau in 1992.
2. Romanian president Traian Băsescu declared this on the B1 channel in an interview on June 22, 2011.

3. Petre Roman, "A existat o legătură cauzală între puciul de la Moscova şi mine-riada din spetembrie" [There was a causal relationship between the putsch in Moscow and the miners' revolt in September], interview with *Historia* 11, no. 116 (2011): 23.

4. Igor Boţan, "România, Republica Moldova şi grşelile trecutului" [Romania, Republic of Moldova and mistakes of the past], interview with *Radio Europa Liberă*, May 5, 2011, http://www.europalibera.org/content/article/24318714.html (accessed June 7, 2011).

5. Adrian Cioroianu, "O eroare motivată geopolitic" [A geopolitically motivated error], *Historia* 11, no. 114, (2011): 26–28. Cioroianu has also served as Romanian Foreign Minister from April 2007 till April 2008.

6. A Romanian high official in an interview with the author, August 12, 2011.

7. Strategia de Securitate a României [National Security Strategy of Romania], 2007, 30, http://presidency.ro/static/ordine/SSNR/SSNRepublicpdf (accessed August 10, 2011).

8. Ruxandra Ivan, *La politique étrangère roumaine (1990–2006)* (Bruxelles: Editions de l'Université de Bruxelles, 2009), 28.

9. Strategia de Securitate, 36.

10. Strategia Naţională de Apărare a României [National Defense Strategy of Romania], 16.

11. Charles King, *Molodvenii. România, Rusia şi politica culturală* [The Moldovans: Romania, Russia, and politics of culture] (Chisinau: Arc, 2005), 169–171.

12. Ion Iliescu, *Transnistria "a împiedicat unirea Basarabiei cu România"* [Transnistria "has prevented the unification of Bessarabia and Romania"], interview with *Radio România Actualităţi*, October 18, 2011, http://www.romania-actualitati.ro/transnistria_a_impiedicat_unirea_basarabiei_cu_romania-34277 (accessed October 20, 2011). Two decades after the events, Iliescu declared: "The unification of Germany was done on an impulse from East to West. It was not up to Bucharest to be the active factor in determining such a thing, on the contrary."

13. Gheorghe Cojocaru, *Colapsul URSS şi dilema relaţiilor Româno-Române* [The Collapse of the USSR and the dilemma of the Romanian-Romanian relations] (Bucharest: Editura Omega, 2001), 88–110.

14. Marian Enache and Dorin Cimpoeşu, *Misiune diplomatică în Republica Moldova, 1993–1997* [Diplomatic mission in the Republic of Moldova, 1993–1997] (Iaşi: Polirom, 2000), 167.

15. Ibid., 169.

16. Victor Chirilă, "Relaţiile Republicii Moldva cu România" [The Relations of the Republic of Moldova with Romania], in *Evoluţia Politicii Externe a Republicii Moldova 1998–2008* [The evolution of the external policy of the Republic of Moldova] (Chisinau: CARTDIDACT, 2009), 13–15.

17. Ibid., 15–16.

18. "Preşedintele României consideră că teoria moldovenismului urmăreşte deznaţionalizarea românilor" [Romanian president considers that the theory of moldovenism is intended at denationalizing Romanians], *Basa-press*, July 9, 2001.

19. "Liderul grupului parlamentar al comuniştilor afirmă că în Republica Moldova românii constituie o minoritate etnică" [The leader of the Communist parliamentary group says that in the Republic of Moldova Romanians are a minority], *Basa-press*, July 7, 2001.

20. "Moldova are nevoie de parteneri, nu de avocaţi" [Moldova needs partners not advocates], *BBC*, May 11, 2006, http://www.bbc.co.uk/romanian/news/story/2006/05/060 511_moldova_romania_relatie.shtml (accessed September 3, 2011).

21. The original version said: "România a oferit Republicii Moldova varianta de a intra împreună în Uniunea Europeană, dar decizia le aparține autorităților de la Chișinău și poporului Republicii Moldova," and ". . . unificarea se va face in interiorul Uniunii Europene, si nu altfel, intr-un viitor nu foarte indepartat." "Traian Basescu afirma ca Romania a oferit Republicii Moldova sansa de a intra impreuna in UE" [Traian Basescu declares that it offered R. of Moldova the chance to enter EU together], *Moldova.org*, July 6, 2006, http://politicom.moldova.org/news/traian-basescu-afirma-ca-romania-a-oferit -rmoldova-sansa-de-a-intra-impreuna-in-ue-13798-rom.html (accessed September 3, 2011).

22. Vlad Macovei et al., "Câți bani ne-ar costa unirea cu Basarabia?" [How much would unification with Bessarabia cost?], *Cotidianul*, October 2, 2006. The sum of $20 billion came from an interview with Daniel Dăianu, a reputed Romanian economist, presently an MEP with the Alliance of Liberals and Democrats for Europe (ALDE).

23. The Romanian Foreign Ministry informed then that "the initiative is open to all member states which are interested to support the Republic of Moldova on its democratic and European pathway." The initiative was backed by EU ministers, state secretaries and ambassadors from Austria, the Czech Republic, Estonia, Germany, Latvia, Lithuania, Italy, Poland, Slovakia, Slovenia, Sweden, United Kingdom and Hungary, who attended the event. Anne-Marie Blajan, "Romanian Foreign Affairs minister launched 'Moldova friends group' in Brussels," *HotNews.ro*, January 25, 2010, http://english.hotnews.ro/stiri -top_news-6844085-romanian-foreign-affairs-minister-launched-moldova-friends-group -brussels.htm (accessed August 15, 2011).

24. Teodor Baconschi, "Teodor Baconschi explică misterul votului-minune de la alegerile prezidențiale din 2009" [Teodor Baconschi explains the mystery of the wonder-votes during the 2009 presidential elections], interview with *Evenimentul Zilei*, October 31, 2011, http://www.evz.ro/detalii/stiri/baconschi-ion-iliescu-m-a-pedepsit-pentru-ca-l -am-adus-pe-papa-ioan-paul-al-ii-lea-in-rom-951875-1.html (accessed October 14, 2011).

25. Romanian Foreign Ministry, "România și Republica Moldova au semnat Tratatul privind regimul frontierei de stat, colaborarea și asistența mutuala în probleme de frontiere" [Romania and the Republic of Moldova signed Treaty on the State Border Regime, Collaboration and Mutual Assistance in Border Issues], November 8, 2010, http://mae.ro/node/5893 (accessed, September 25, 2011)

26. Traian Băsescu and Mihai Ghimpu, "Joint press declaration," April 27, 2010, http://presidency.ro/?_RID=det&tb=date&id=12060&_PRID=search (accessed, September 27, 2011).

27. Ibid.

28. "Baconschi la Chișinău: România nu mai încheie tratate de bază, sunt documente învechite" [Baconschi in Chisinau: Romania does not sign basic treaties anymore, these are obsolete documents], *Gândul*, May 27, 2011, http://www.gandul.info/internatio-nal/baconschi-la-chisinau-romania-nu-mai-incheie-tratate-de-baza-sunt-documente-inve-chite-8290729 (accessed October 27, 2011).

29. "Baconschi: România nu va mai semna tratate de bază cu nici un stat" [Baconshi: Romania will not sign basic treaties anymore with any states], *Evenimentul Zilei*, May 27, 2011, http://www.evz.ro/detalii/stiri/romania-nu-va-mai-semna-tratate-de-baza-cu-niciun-stat-931740.html (accessed October 27, 2011)

30. Romanian Foreign Ministry, "Vecinătatea de interes a României ca stat. Republica Moldova" [Romania's interests in the neighborhood. Republic of Moldova], April 2011, http://mae.ro/node/1421 (accessed September 15, 2011).

31. Romanian Foreign Ministry, "Participarea vice-prim ministrului, ministru al Afacerilor Externe și Integrării Europene al Republicii Moldova, la Reuniunea Anuală a Diplomației Române" [Participation of vice-prime-minister and minister of External

Affairs and European Integration of Republic of Moldova to the Yearly Reunion of the Romanian Diplomatic Corps], September 1, 2011, http://mae.ro/node/10044 (accessed September 15, 2011).

32. Ministry of Economy, Trade and Business Environment of Romania, *Îndrumar de afaceri pe relaţia cu Republica Moldova* [Business Guide on the Republic of Moldova] (Bucharest, 2009), http://www.dce.gov.ro/Materiale%20site/Indrumar_afaceri /Indrumar_afaceri_Moldova.pdf (accessed September 15, 2011).

33. Ana Popa et al., *România – Republic Moldova. O analiză a relaţiilor economice bilaterale* [Romania-Republic of Moldova. Analysis of bilateral economic relations] (Chisinau, 2009), 48–49.

34. Ibid., 9.

35. Claudia Pârvoiu, "Vicepremierul moldovean: Proiectul gazoductului Ungheni-Iasi este sustinut atat de UE cat si de Rusia/ Prin conducta se vor face si importuri si exporturi de gaze" [Moldovan vice-premier: The project of the gas-pipeline Ungheni-Iasi is backed both by the EU and Russia/ The pipeline will be suitable for imports and exports of gas], *HotNews.ro*, May 2, 2011, http://economie.hotnews.ro/stiri-energie-875 8814-vicepremierul-moldovean-proiectul-gazoductului-ungheni-iasi-este-sustinut-atat-cat -rusia.htm (accessed September 20, 2011).

36. Valentin Lozovanu, "România – Republica Moldova: accelerarea unei cooperări întârziate" [Romania Republic of Moldova: acceleration of a belated cooperation], *Centrul Român pentru Politici Europene Policy Brief*, no. 8, May 2011.

37. Cojocaru, *Colapsul URSS*, 129.

38. "Calvarul cetăţeniei române pentru moldoveni" [The nightmare of Romanian citizenship for Moldovans], *Ziua*, March 21, 2007.

39. Valentina Dimulescu and Andrei Avram, "Banali în UE. Politica românească de redobândire a cetăţeniei în comparaţie cu alte state din UE" [Ordinary in Europe: Romanian policy of regaining citizenship in comparison with other EU states], *Centrul Român de Politici Europene Policy Memo*, no. 22, July 2011, 6–8.

40. Romanian Foreign Ministry, "Vecinătatea de interes."

41. Cristian Ghinea, "Agenda politică a României faţă de Republica Moldova" [Romania's political agenda toward Moldova], in Cristian Ghinea et al., *Republica Moldova în conştiinţa publică românească* [The Republic of Moldova in the Romanian public consciousness] (Bucharest: Fundaţia Soros România, 2011), 103, 202.

Chapter Thirteen

Russia: Relations with Moldova under a Paradigm of Ambiguity[*]

Andrey Devyatkov

Relations with the newly independent states remain a high priority on the Russian Federation's foreign policy agenda. These relations are like a litmus test for the normalization of post-Soviet Russia's foreign policy identity, the core feature measuring the political transition of the country.

Moldova is located between the enlarged European Union and Russia, not only geographically, but politically and economically. For Moscow, it is a challenge to build balanced relations with this country, and it is particularly difficult because of the context in which Moldova is embedded for Russian foreign policy.

This chapter is based on the idea that Russian-Moldovan relations can be best analyzed not by a thesis about Russian geopolitical interests, nor hard and soft power abuses, but by a paradigm of ambiguity. Vadim Kononenko made an important contribution to the understanding of EU-Russian relations with this paradigm. "As far as Russia-EU interaction is concerned, it is often understood in the dichotomous and allegedly incompatible terms of cooperation or conflict, interaction or integration, interdependence or self-exclusion. In practice, these dichotomous pairs are rarely the case."[1]

The first section of the chapter refers to practices and critical indicators in bilateral interactions, which are evidence of their growing normalization. In the second part, the focus will be placed on the connection of Russian national security preferences, i.e., to the Transnistrian settlement. This aspect is the main source of the aforementioned state of ambiguity and, to a certain degree, an expression of failure of Russia's integration into Europe politically and institutionally. How Russia formulates and pursues its interests in the Transnistrian settlement (with or without honoring Moldovan sovereignty, a sufficient degree of internationalization of conflict settlement, etc.) predetermines not only the relations of Russia with Moldova but also with the international community in general.

---

[*] The author would like to stress that this article was written during his research stay at the Chair InBev-Baillet Latour EU-Russia (Institute for International and European Policy of K.U. Leuven, Belgium) in May–June 2011. In the article the materials of interviews, conducted in Brussels with the support of the Chair, were used.

Moving toward Pragmatism?

Moscow and Chisinau have been developing their partnership in various spheres with an ever-extending intergovernmental rationalism. One of the main factors contributing to this was Moscow's lack of any exclusive structural or discursive (normative) powers over Chisinau.

The Degree of Integration

In the 1990s, Moldova did not take part in any of the illusory projects within the Commonwealth of Independent States (like the Economic Union), and it was neither politicized nor securitized by Moscow, just acknowledged as a reality. In order to further the withdrawal of Russian forces from its territory, Chisinau declared constitutional neutrality as the basic principle of its national security identity. Like Azerbaijan, Moldova abstained from any substantial military cooperation with Moscow.[2]

Moldova also rejected any participation in Russian-led political integration. In this area, Chisinau has been more loyal to the GU(U)AM project, which is an expression of the ideological orientation of its member countries (Georgia, Ukraine, Azerbaijan, Moldova, and Uzbekistan, which participated in the organization until 2005) toward European and Euro-Atlantic integration. When the Concept on Further Development of the CIS was worked out in 2007, Moldova made its reservations clear, stating that the country would not participate in political cooperation among member states. Political cooperation was planned only at the level of exchanging views on major issues of world politics and co-operation in monitoring elections, without any further ambitions.[3] Conversations about eventual Moldovan participation in institutions like the Union of Russia and Belarus were held in the context of the domestic pre-election agendas of certain politicians including Vladimir Voronin, who was elected to the Moldovan presidency in 2001 with pro-Russian slogans, and they did not lead to any serious changes in the Moldovan stance towards Russia.

All of these circumstances contributed to changes in how Moldova has been perceived by Moscow. Unlike Belarus or Ukraine, Moldova began to outgrow the status of the "Russian near abroad" early.

Regimes of a common free trade area and visa liberalization let Moldova take great advantage of economic cooperation with Moscow during its own ongoing economic instability—without any substantial political concessions. The transfer of migrant workers provided an existential ground for the Moldovan society. Russia still remains one of the top markets for Moldovan exports.

On the other hand, this interconnectedness means a situation of asymmetrical dependence cannot be identified. Trade with Russia in the past few years amounted only to 14–16 percent of total Moldovan foreign trade.[4] The visible politicization of bilateral trade relations began only after the deterioration of bilateral relations in 2005. In 2006, Russia banned the import of alcohol produced in Moldova, mainly in response to a change of the border regime for Transnistrian exports, which was perceived by Moscow as "political action" aimed at "bringing the entirety of Transnistrian external economic activity under the control of Chisinau, undermining the regional budget, and causing social unrest there."[5] In 2010, Russia restricted the import of vegetables and fruits from Moldova, supposedly because Moscow could no longer tolerate the explicitly anti-Russian rhetoric of the interim Moldovan President Mihai Ghimpu.[6] But in all of these cases, both sides were interested in normalization of the situation as soon as possible (price stability in the Russian market also depends on relatively cheap imports from Moldova). From a strategic perspective, the situation even brought some advantages for Chisinau: Despite short-term economic damage, Chisinau was motivated to improve the quality of its exported goods and abandon any kind of "special treatment" from the Russian side. This special treatment existed where Moldova was provided with unfettered access to the Russian market in exchange for the symbolic demonstration of a strategic partnership with Moscow. The purely commercial logic of "just doing business" is one of the main results of all the trade sanctions and restrictions.

One of the main external instruments used to influence Moldovan policy is the allocation of credit. The country needs foreign loans because of its integration into the world economy—the dissolution of the Soviet Union brought many extreme challenges to its economy and social sphere. This instrument is fully controlled by Western institutions like the International Monetary Fund and the World Bank. During 2009–2012 the country will receive $588 million from the IMF, according to the agreement signed on October 28, 2009.[7] Financial assistance of €273.1 million will be transferred to Moldova from 2011–2013 by the EU.[8]

In 2009, Russia tried to negotiate the allocation of a $500 million loan to Moldova. It was even reported that the Russian President Dmitry Medvedev signed a federal law regulating this operation.[9] But the agreement was not consummated and in the end the Moldovan authorities managed to receive funding from the IMF.

Moldova's almost complete dependence on gas deliveries from Russia is a sensitive issue for both Moscow and Chisinau. Some criticize Russia for using gas prices to influence the political process in Moldova.[10] This sort of analysis is without solid empirical evidence, yet nevertheless it attempts to calculate what Russia might have gained politically by increasing gas prices at any given moment. For example, it is an exaggeration to say that Gazprom increased prices for Moldova from 1998–2000 in order to influence the destabilized political situation. Gazprom policy was based instead on fiscal logic—the Russian government was seeking to fill out the budget in order to overcome the critical socio-economic situation in Russia, and the government dramatically toughened its tax policy toward the gas giant, putting Gazprom under the threat of non-profitability.[11]

It can be said, however, that the Russian government later used the energy dependence of Moldova as a political carrot, and as a means to acquire energy transmission networks. For example, in the period of "strategic partnership" from 2001–2003, gas prices were frozen for Chisinau, and Moldova was even given the right to delay payments. This carrot policy better illustrates the additional motivation on the Moldovan side to deepen relations—and it is as legitimate as EU policy in the sphere of integration. Derek Averre speaks in this regard about the logic of structural power, according to which Russia should be involved with the events happening in its neighborhood and try to influence them in order to have "friendly" relations with neighboring countries.[12]

The gradual increase of gas prices can be better understood in the Moldovan case through commercial logic. In contrast with Ukraine, the issue in Moldova looks more economic than political. In the case of Ukraine, Russian President Vladimir Putin officially acknowledged the political motivation of Russian foreign policy behind the gas crisis in 2006:

> Our European and American partners decided to support the "Orange Revolution" even to the point of breaking the constitution. They supported this. First, the political result is problematic enough, and we see how the situation developed there. Second, if you supported this political outcome and want it supported further, you pay for it. You want to have the political dividends, but we should pay for it. This cannot be tolerated.[13]

That is why Moscow insisted on such a tremendous increase of gas prices for Ukraine and showed for such a long time no readiness to find a compromise in giving Kiev enough time to get accustomed to high energy costs. Moldova did not face this kind of treatment.

Sources of Political Misunderstandings

In the political sphere, relations between the two countries are burdened with some tensions on both sides, but these tensions are more of a rhetorical and ideological character than any kind of practical conflicts.

The ideological conflicts are caused by the Russian method of conducting foreign policy. Russian foreign policy is in general too state-centric, not transparent enough, problematic in terms of working with civil society in partner countries, and filled with rhetoric unacceptable to foreign audiences (like theses about Russia's prevailing position of sovereignty, or a common historical heritage which keeps the post-Soviet states together, etc.).[14]

A lack of the instruments generally regarded as soft power options makes it very difficult for Russia to be effective in the struggle for Moldova's geopolitical orientation. Every action undertaken or supported by Russia is symbolized in Moldova as a reminder of Russian realpolitik, even in cases where the cumulative effect is quite the opposite, or does not influence the situation at all. The first normalization step of Russian foreign policy, namely commercialization, is also perceived as a threat. Nevertheless, it should be stressed that this is a positive way forward that must be followed with the decentralization and democratization of policy practices and transparency of policy actions.

One of the most scandalous situations concerning "Russian interference into internal affairs of Moldova" took place during the Moldovan parliamentarian elections in 2005. A majority of experts shared the opinion that Russia sent a hundred "election observers" to Moldova to lead a propaganda campaign for the opposition, and Moscow tried to overthrow or simply punish the Moldovan leader Voronin for his rejection of a document for the resolution of the Transnistrian conflict proposed by Russia unilaterally in November 2003 (the so-called Kozak Memorandum), and his general turn to the West. That's why Voronin became, in the eyes of the West, "better for democracy than the opposition," despite his formerly close relations with Moscow.[15] But it is doubtful that Russia would dare to assist the center-right and right-wing opposition, which was hardly perceived as "pro-Russian," because the competition between Moldovan political parties consisted at that time of who could better monopolize the rhetoric of the "Orange Revolution."[16] In reality, the original aim of Russian authorities was to prevent an "Orange Revolution" in Moldova by keeping Voronin, the leader of the Moldovan Party of Communists, in power. The deputy head of the Russian Presidential Administration from 2005–2007, Modest Kolerov, described this in an interview about the so-called color revolutions. He stated that the revolutions were absurd and that Russian policy should be directed at the further absurdization of them.[17] Could the activity of Russian "observers," who were declared non-grata by Voronin, really be an instrument to assist the Moldovan president indirectly by tripping up the opposition with this sort of "help"? If so, it would have been an ambiguous, but not necessarily anti-democratic contribution to Moldovan politics. Nevertheless, the instruments Russia used during these events are unacceptable within soft power logic.

Besides, it is hard to understand whether Russia benefited much anyway from the presidency of Voronin, who remained in power after 2005. It is possible that the illusory cooperation with Russia, which was initiated again in the second half of 2006 (after some declaratory rapprochement between Moldova and the EU), brought much more advantages personally to Voronin than it did to Moscow. It seems that for Moscow, the formal "pro-Russianness" of the Party of Communists has been more important than even the practical content of Moldovan geopolitical orientation. Psychologically, it is very hard for Russia to be comfortable with any government in its immediate neighborhood that it perceives as primarily against Russia. The symbolism of "strategic partnership" is very important in the context of supporting a "ring of friends" around Russia, which claim to be excluded from the processes of European integration. A more "friendly" government was also needed within the context of the Transnistrian settlement (more in the second part of this chapter).

Also, after the Alliance for European Integration (a governing coalition of four, and later three parties united around the idea of European integration) came into power in 2009, Moscow demonstrated that the Party of Communists was its preferred partner among Moldovan political forces. This support has been irrational to most observers. After the last parliamentary election campaign in November 2010, when the Liberal Democratic Party of Prime Minister Vlad Filat gained the support of almost 30 percent of the electorate, the Russian authorities sent Head of the Presidential Administration Sergey Naryshkin, who demonstratively ignored Moldovan Prime Minister Filat, and instead had meetings with Marian Lupu (Democratic Party), Voronin (Party of Communists) and even Ghimpu (Liberal Party), in order to further the coalition between the Democratic and Communist parties, with an eye to the dissolution of the AEI. The growing support of Filat in Moldovan society, and thereby the true Europeanization of the country, is obvious (in parliamentary elections in July 2009 the PLDM gained only 17 percent of votes[18] and then doubled its count in 2010), but Sergey Naryshkin described his mission in opposite terms upon his arrival in Chisinau:

> Discussions are being held in today's Moldova concerning issues of statehood, sovereignty, and the search for a geopolitical orientation. We understand that only a truly strong government of Moldova is able to solve these problems, and we would like these problems solved in the context of a strategic partnership between Russia and Moldova. The elections have shown that those forces which favored an antagonistic Russian-Moldovan agenda have received an adequate evaluation.[19]

The notorious period of Moldovan politics, when Voronin was president from 2001–2009, is still a consolidating factor for the cooperation of other parties, and the leader of the Democratic Party, Lupu, did not decide to break relations with his AEI partners, despite some political contradictions already appearing among them. The result was damaged relations with the Moldovan prime minister, who expressed his disappointment in the following way: "You will see a difference between Russian and European officials coming to Moldova in the next days. I can already say that the Europeans will have consultations with all parties without distinctions, and without giving us orders."[20]

Nevertheless, Russian misperceptions are also fueled by ultra-political tendencies in Moldova itself, where the Soviet history is politicized in domestic Moldovan political struggles. Because relationships with the legacy of WWII and to today's Russian peacekeeping presence in Moldova are the main indicators measuring pro-Russianness or anti-Russianness, Russian officials (Naryshkin, or Russian Ambassador Valeriy Kuz'min) have referred to the "adherents of right-liberal parties" as "antagonistic" to Russia.[21] They obviously meant two parties—the Liberal Democratic and the Liberal parties.

The representatives of both parties have been constantly appealing to Russia to withdraw its forces, including the peacekeepers. Prime Minister Filat, who is perceived as a more pragmatic politician compared to the explicitly pro-Romanian ex-Acting President Ghimpu, even stated that Russia was a participant in the Moldovan-Transnistrian conflict.[22] The logical consequence of this statement is that Russia cannot be a neutral mediator and should give this right to the international community.

The Liberal Party describes the Russian presence as an "occupation" and groups it with the Soviet "annexation" of Bessarabia in 1940, which divided the Romanian nation.[23] The attempt of Ghimpu during his presidency to make June 28 the Day of Soviet Occupation caused a very critical reaction from the Russian foreign ministry.[24] On June 28, 1940, Soviet troops regained control over Bessarabia (Moldova)—a region which had been incorporated into Romania during the dissolution of the Russian Empire in 1918—under the conditions of the infamous Molotov-Ribbentrop Pact. Ghimpu claimed, in fact, that one occupation (namely the Romanian one) was better than the Russian one because it meant the re-unification of the Romanian nation.

In May 2011, during the preparation of celebrations devoted to May 9 (in Russia this is the official day celebrating the victorious end of WWII), the deputy head of the Liberal Democratic Party, Liliana Palihovici, made a statement that contributed to the polarization of Moldovan society concerning the interpretation of recent history. Commenting on the St. George's band (an armband worn as a Russian heraldic symbol of military victories), she said that by wearing this band many people in Moldova demonstrated they do not know what it really means, and they have adopted foreign traditions. To her mind, the Moldovan government should actively implement a strategy aimed at supporting Moldovan national traditions.[25] The Party of Communists actively participated in the discussion with the slogan "Moldova! Victory!"[26] Prime Minister Filat tried to maintain the fragile balance: On May 9, 2011, he met with the veterans of both the Soviet and Romanian armies,[27] who had struggled on various sides of the front, but it hardly calmed the heated atmosphere in the country. This turmoil is caused by ideological and ultra-political positions within Moldovan society, which is deeply split on the issues of identity and history.

In conclusion, it can be said that a pragmatic line is developing in bilateral relations, first of all because Moldova has already outgrown the status of the Russian near abroad in an economic, political and normative sense. But the so-called Europeanization agenda in Moldova is accompanied with political incidents that cause fears and suspicion in Moscow. The discourses of both parties are emotional and "irrational" towards each other, which prove that the learning process in mutual understanding is still underway.

Transnistria: The Odd Man Out?

The most ambiguous issue in Moldovan-Russian relations is the participation of Moscow in the Transnistrian conflict settlement. Transnistria is a small territory officially belonging to Moldova, with no more than 500,000 inhabitants. But since 1992, Tiraspol (the administrative center of Transnistria) managed to build a de facto state, so Moldova does not control a part of its territory. And this occurs with some involvement from Moscow.

Firstly, the Russian Federation has still not withdrawn the military presence it left in Transnistria after the dissolution of the Soviet Union. Official Russian policy seeks a "synchronization" of the withdrawal of military depots, which belonged to the former Soviet Fourteenth Army, and the 800 soldiers, who claim to observe the security of these depots. Russian statements that Tiraspol has been opposing the withdrawal because Moldova rejected the Kozak Memorandum and destroyed relations with the left bank are not persuasive to the Moldovan and European public. De jure, Russia has been damaging the principle of state sovereignty in an independent country, a principle which it defends strongly in the international arena.

A second aspect of why Russian policy in Moldova is legitimately criticized is Russian assistance to the Transnistrian side. Transnistrian debt for Russian gas, which is de facto an instrument of indirect support, has reached a tremendous amount, over \$2.5 billion.[28] Transnistrian citizens and firms make their payments, but in recent years the money is transferred to the Transnistrian budget and not to Gazprom.[29] According to official information, the deficit of the budget in 2011 is 50 percent[30] and the discrepancy between incomes and spending should be covered. Russian direct assistance is not very significant: From 2007–2010 it amounted to \$55.5 million and was spent on increasing pensions and improving the work of some institutions in the social sphere.[31]

The Transnistrian Settlement and Russian National Security Preferences

What motivation is behind this stance toward Transnistria? Can the Russian factor be perceived as a constant detriment to the conflict settlement?

When considering Russian policy toward Transnistria in the historic retrospective, its partiality in favor of one party can be seen, but also its sincere attempts to arrange the conflict resolution in 1994, 1997, 2001–2002 and 2009—although activation of the negotiations process happened in many cases in close cooperation with the Organization for Security and Cooperation in Europe and other actors. But in the last eight years, the problem of Russian policy's lack of transparency with regards to Moldova has increased tremendously: EU representatives characterize the lack of Russian policy's visibility and the absence of day-to-day depoliticized interaction with the European Union on many issues of mutual interest as the main problem in relations with Moscow.[32] Former Head of the OSCE Mission to Moldova William Hill shares the opinion that Russia apparently considers primacy in the region more important than cooperation, and favors a myopic, unilateralist path.[33]

It is not possible here to analyze all the periods of Russian political involvement in the conflict resolution process. Rather this analysis will try to find relatively stable elements in Russian motivation toward the Transnistrian conflict and will concentrate its attention more on today's realities of the settlement, which can bring it either a substantial breakthrough or a recurrent disappointment.

Russian involvement in the Transnistrian issue began in March–April 1992, predominantly under the influence of local events. The conflict between Chisinau and Tiraspol reached the level of direct clashes between police and military forces. The former Soviet Fourteenth Army was stationed in the region, and because of withdrawal of Soviet troops from Eastern Europe and a redistribution of military personnel, the forces in Transnistria were to a large degree composed of local inhabitants.[34] Until June, the army commander, General Yuriy Netkachev tried, according to orders from Moscow, to withhold the officers and soldiers from interference in the conflict, but lost the main levers of control over the situation.[35] The appointment of General Alexander Lebed in June 1992 and his smart military operation against Moldovan forces on July 2–3, 1992, were aimed at preventing civil war with the participation of Russian forces on the territory of the sovereign state and, secondly, at neutralizing the nationalistic opposition in the Russian Supreme Council which accused President Boris Yeltsin of giving up on the Russian national minority in Transnistria. Russian foreign policy was not motivated substantially by any geopolitical calculations (like the prevention of Moldovan-Romanian unification, etc.). In the agreement of 1994 with Moldova Russia acknowledged the obligation of the withdrawal of the Fourteenth Army but with the reservation of "synchronization." At that time it was motivated by calculations which have shown that the withdrawal of such a huge amount of weapons would face many technical and financial obstacles that would last for years and not months, and an understanding that rapid withdrawal could destabilize the security situation on the Dniester.

But in 1994–1995 the geopolitical rationale for stationing the Fourteenth Army in Transnistria became obvious. The official statements of representatives of the Russian Defense Ministry and General Lebed, who remained in command of the Fourteenth Army till 1995, clearly showed how the Fourteenth Army began to be perceived as a response to NATO enlargement eastwards and (by some groups of the governing elite) as an instrument for Russia to keep its influence within the CIS.[36]

For those in Russia who preferred to think in neo-realist terms, NATO enlargement meant a tremendous increase of Western structural and military power in the Russian neighborhood. The Russian Foreign Minister Yevgeniy Primakov (1996–1998) stated in response to claims that NATO was no longer a threat for democratic post-Soviet Russia: it is not intentions that are important but potentials.[37] This problem only grew when the administrations of George W. Bush and then Barack Obama announced plans for building an anti-missile defense system in the Central and Eastern European countries. The Russian Ambassador in Moldova Valeriy Kuz'min stressed many times that the Transnistrian settlement is seen by Moscow within the context of the whole European security system and its main trends, like NATO enlargement and the deployment of an American anti-missile system.[38]

For those who tend to think in identity terms, NATO enlargement and the extension of such an exclusive regime as the Schengen area are evidence of the exclusion of Russia from Europe and its marginalization. With this logic, the movement of Western institutions and regimes near Russian borders are perceived as an important if intangible challenge which touches upon the existential grounds of Russian identity.

As a result, the securitization of these trends in the European security system has led to the formation of a fundamental principle in the Transnistrian settlement, which Russia strictly adheres to. It is formulated as a "constitutional neutrality of the Republic of Moldova" which should be kept even after the reunification of the country. This principle was repeated in almost every speech and document issued by the Russian Federation on the topic of the Transnistrian settlement. Russian Foreign Minister Sergey Lavrov said in March 2011 that Moscow perceives this principle as an important contribution to the creation of European security architecture.[39] Besides this, he stated that Transnistria should have the right to secession if Moldova decides to join any military block.[40]

Moscow has wanted to implement this principle at whatever costs it may bring in terms of international image. That's why the symbolic presence of the Fourteenth Army's remnants is not yet eliminated, and Russia even dares to "freeze" the political commitments it made at the 1999 Istanbul OSCE summit. Because of the consolidated position of NATO member states regarding these commitments, the Treaty on Conventional Forces in Europe is still not ratified. Russia deprives itself of an international regime, which Moscow itself strongly admires, because it would eliminate all fears related to the deployment of NATO's military infrastructure near Russian territory. Obviously this calculation is being made not only because of possible Moldovan accession to NATO: Ukraine is the chief factor. This position expresses the deep mistrust Russia has towards the West, which "promised to the Soviet Union in 1990 not to enlarge NATO, but has done so after its dissolution." Some analysts in Europe confirm the rectitude of this opinion.[41] But the main problem related to the Transnistrian settlement has always been that Tiraspol used the presence of Russian forces as a basic resource for its de facto independence, despite the fact that Russia made considerable attempts to bring Chisinau and Tiraspol to a compromise.

Originally, the neutrality of Moldova could have been called the main "Russian interest" in the Transnistrian settlement. But when relations between Russia and the West deteriorated the most, for example because of the "color revolutions," the policy of Moscow gained some features of a containment strategy. The deputy Head of the Presidential Administration, Modest Kolerov, openly wrote around that time about "sovereignization" of the Pridnestrovian Moldavian Republic.[42] Moscow and Tiraspol even signed a protocol in 2006 where areas of bilateral cooperation were described and Smirnov was called "President of Transnistria."[43] In 2003–2007 Russia preferred a status quo in the settlement process, and fully tolerated Smirnov as a leader who provided predictability in geopolitics.

The Return of Multilateral Diplomacy

The shift again toward a more pragmatic stance took place in 2008–2009. President Obama initiated a "reset" in relations with Russia, and his first contribution to this process of rapprochement was an acknowledgment that the accession of Ukraine and Georgia to NATO is "politicized" and "not an urgent" issue.[44] In this atmosphere, Russia was determined to smooth over the negativity which resulted from the proclamation of independence of Abkhazia and South Ossetia. Moscow's active diplomacy in the settlement process of Transnistria and Nagorno-Karabakh in 2008–2009 was aimed at demonstrating that Russia is committed to solving internal conflicts (in this case conflicts around de facto states in the post-Soviet space) without damaging international norms. But negotiations were held in the same style as before and in the 2+1 format (Transnistria and Moldova as conflict parties and Russia), and consequently they brought no substantial results.

But in 2010–2011 some positive factors appeared which could mean a breakthrough in the negotiation process. The possibility of such an outcome was already announced by Ukrainian officials.[45]

First, the "reset" in the American-Russian relations seemed to find a way of spilling over into the Russian-EU relations. The Transnistrian case is now being perceived as a test case for EU-Russian relations, first of all by the European Union.[46] In the past, Brussels tried to communicate with Russia on the Transnistrian issue rarely and incoherently from the strategic point of view. The EU position contained ideas formulated like demands to Russia: the immediate withdrawal of Russian troops; replacement of Russian peacekeepers that do not have an international mandate and whose effectiveness is questionable; principle non-recognition of Transnistria as an independent state. That's why the first EU Special Representative for Moldova, Adriaan Jacobovits de Szeged, got only one answer from the EU High Representative Javier Solana on his question about EU strategy towards Transnistria: "Your nomination is our strategy." Besides this exchange, Jacobovits de Szeged asserted that the EU should raise the Transnistrian issue to a head of government of one of its larger members who can speak directly to Dmitry Medvedev or Vladimir Putin.[47] The relative success of French president Nicolas Sarkozy during talks with Russia on war in Georgia in August 2008 clearly shows the usefulness of this instrument in dialogue with Moscow.

This mission was taken over by Germany. A German official in an interview with the author confirms the importance Berlin attaches to bringing Russia closer to the community of European values and interests—a policy particularly relevant against the background of the intensive partnership Germany enjoys with Russia. The Transnistrian issue could be a natural focus area for a common approach to conflict resolution in a strategic EU-Russia partnership. The political rather than ethnic nature of the conflict improves the prospects for a political solution. Finally, the fact that Moldova is located in the common neighborhood suggests even more a common Euro-Russian approach to the solution of the conflict. These circumstances result in the consideration that Transnistria might play the role of a test case for European-Russian conflict resolution and a model for deepened political and security dialogue.[48]

The practical result of the German diplomacy was the Meseberg Memorandum (June 5, 2010). This document proposed to explore the establishment of an EU-Russia Political and Security Committee on the ministerial level (EU High Representative Catherine Ashton and Russian Foreign Minister Lavrov). The committee was meant to work on EU-Russian cooperation in the Transnistrian issue, including "a joint EU-Russian engagement, which would guarantee a smooth transition of the present situation to a final stage."[49] However, prior to establishing new institutions, practical progress in cooperation should be obvious.[50] Reference to many experts who discussed the problem of institutions in EU-Russian relations can be made here: Russia prefers to have a very institutionalized network of interaction but this network is not fueled with any concrete initiatives.[51] This EU condition demands concrete steps, not just declarations from Russia. As German Foreign Minister Guido Westerwelle put it: "We await that the Russian government will push the Transnistrian leadership to flexibility and more serious negotiability and it would be an evidence of the Russian readiness to confirm its good will with practical measures."[52]

The German initiative seems to be coordinated with other EU states. The Transnistrian issue was discussed among other problems in Deauville (October 2010) with the participation of Sarkozy, Angela Merkel and Medvedev,[53] and during German-Polish-Russian consultations of state secretaries on July 9, 2010.[54] In September 2010 the German State Minister even undertook a common visit to Bucharest and Chisinau, together with his British colleague. One of the main purposes of the visit was to work on the Transnistrian issue in the framework of the German-British partnership on the EU foreign policy agenda.[55]

Berlin initiated also consultations in Bucharest, Chisinau and Tiraspol on topics related to the Transnistrian settlement. During her visit to Bucharest in October 2010, Merkel appealed to Romania to make further progress in signing a border treaty with Moldova[56] which is very important in order to tackle the issue of the eventual unification of the two states and send a signal respectively to Russia and Ukraine. In 2010–2011, the German delegations visited Transnistria several times and, in reaction, large Transnistrian delegations of businessmen and officials visited Germany in April 2011 in order to get acquainted with the German experience of federalism and discuss prospects for economic cooperation with the EU.[57]

Incentives for Russia to cooperate closer with the EU include a liberalization of the visa regime and the establishment of a common free trade area. Looking at today's Russian foreign policy discourse, it is obvious that both issues have great importance for Russian decision makers. The liberalization of the EU visa regime is even on the election agenda of the Russian authorities as is clear from the last press conference of President Medvedev.[58] The Russian Foreign Ministry has already reported on June 1, 2011, that within a 1–3-year period the agreement with the EU on five-year visas for the Russian citizens could be reached.[59] But the reservation about the "1–3-year period" makes clear that this is not yet a finalized issue and Brussels brings in a political conditionality when further progress in the dialogue on visas depends on Russian behavior in other areas. In trade relations, the Russian accession to the WTO is also interpreted as one of the main incentives for building a closer partnership with the EU.

The second aspect of change in the motivational background of Russian policy toward Transnistria is the interests of Russian companies and the Russian budget. The gas debts of Transnistria have already crossed all normal bounds. Gazprom already tried to negotiate with Moldova that the company Moldova-gaz, which is the distributor of Russian gas in Moldova and is possessed jointly by Russia, Moldova and Transnistria, would be divided and all the debts for gas delivered to Transnistria would be ascribed to the Transnistrian administration.[60] Smirnov insists that in calculations of payment structure, the withdrawal of the military depots of the former Soviet Fourteenth Army should be considered.[61] This means that Transnistria is not going to pay anything because Tiraspol has announced in the past that it should get its own payout from the military proper-ty of the Fourteenth Army. Within the trend of the so-called "economization" of Russian foreign policy, this position of Smirnov is unconstructive.

A further group of business interests is connected to the Moldova Steel Works—a big factory producing export steel and owned by the Russian holding, Metalloinvest, of a very influential businessman, Alisher Usmanov.[62] In recent months Transnistria was shocked by the information that the so-called Transnis-trian Customs Committee had for a long period stopped the import operations of the steel works (predominantly raw materials) in response to the absence of some customs documents. This put the activity of the factory, which did not operate anymore because of the financial crisis, under a great threat.[63] The Cus-toms Service is headed by one of the sons of Smirnov, so there were obviously political reasons behind the prohibition. It is remarkable that the influential Russian newspaper *Kommersant*, also owned by Usmanov, has regularly pub-lished articles on Transnistria since the company Metalloinvest had come into Moldova. These articles have been very critical toward Smirnov.

The Russian budget has already directly and indirectly financed social pro-grams in Transnistria, but it is becoming clear that Transnistria is not functional any more as an autonomous economic system. In an open report published in May 2011, Vladimir Antyufeev, so-called Transnistrian Minister of State Secu-rity, described Transnistria as being besieged by the West, which only wants to pull Russia out of the post-Soviet space and destroy the Pridnestrovian Molda-vian Republic as a supporter of a "great" Russia. Antyufeev stressed the im-portance of increasing assistance into the Transnistrian social sphere, hinting that the West is suggesting to Transnistria it should participate in various lucra-tive programs and that Russia should be more generous toward Tiraspol.[64]

This is hardly tolerable for the Russian authorities. In an evident response, the Russian side initiated discussions on a strategy of Transnistrian development until 2025.[65] The document will be prepared by Russian expert institutions with the general responsibility at the Center for Strategic Research which is a key analytical institution for Russian Prime Minister Vladimir Putin. It shows how Moscow tries to work out a more complex approach to Transnistria, whose de facto statehood costs more and more money.

But a more important shift in Russian policy toward Transnistria is that Moscow furthers political changes in Tiraspol. The Transnistrian leader is almost 70 years old, but in December 2011 he is going to be reelected. There were, however, some signals from Moscow that Smirnov should leave the presidency. A clear message was broadcast by Russian TV presenter Mikhail Leontiev who is well known for his propagandistic programs on state TV Channel One. He visited Transnistria on June 2, 2011, and during a dialogue with a broad Transnistrian audience announced that Smirnov should be treated as a historical monument but kept far away from power. Official Moscow, on whose behalf Leontiev claimed to speak, could not further support the current political regime in Transnistria, which caused political stagnation in the republic.[66] The leading Russian party, United Russia, stated that it would support a candidate for the presidency presented by the Transnistrian party Obnovleniye (Renewal).[67] This party has been strongly opposing the centralization of power practiced by Smirnov. The executive branch of the Russian authorities demonstrates that Obnovleniye is one of the leading political forces in Transnistria today: Anatoliy Kaminskiy, chairman of the Transnistrian parliament and head of the party Obnovleniye, has appointments on the same institutional level as Smirnov does (Russian Security Council, Presidential Administration, State Duma, etc.).[68] The representatives of the Russian State Duma also welcomed changes into the so-called Transnistrian Constitution initiated by the party Obnovleniye and aimed at restricting the power of the president.[69]

The leader of Transnistria is also an obstacle for Russian diplomacy, which is determined to further a compromise between Tiraspol and Chisinau. He has already made it clear that he would not favor any reunification with Moldova. One leading, semi-official Transnistrian expert even called the Russian authorities who sympathize with the Western and Moldovan plans aimed at the elimination of the Pridnestrovian Moldavian Republic as the "dreamers in the Kremlin."[70]

At the practical level, the Transnistrian leader adheres to a strategy of obstructing any conflict resolution. In August 2010, a meeting took place between Prime Minister Vlad Filat and Smirnov, arranged at the football stadium in Tiraspol (hence "football diplomacy"). One of the most important agreements reached at this meeting was the decision to restart the train connection going through both banks and to improve the conditions for the export of Transnistrian goods[71] (since March 2006 the Transnistrian companies have had to be registered in Chisinau and its export goods cleared in Moldovan customs, which has brought new transaction costs). The latter issue was one of the most negative in bilateral relations. But the political arrangement should have been further negotiated by technical specialists from Transnistrian and Moldovan customs services in order to be implemented. In any case, the Transnistrian side did not attend these negotiations.[72] Filat and Smirnov only exchanged some rhetorical statements, which indicated the failure of "football diplomacy."

This motivational background has already stimulated Russian officials to make some unexpected statements and initiate active diplomatic consultations, primarily with Tiraspol and Kiev. A new representative of the Russian Foreign Ministry in the Transnistrian settlement, Sergey Gubarev, rejected the idea of Transnistrian independence in a very expressive manner: "Transnistria can live independently from Moldova only if it flies to the Moon." In 2006, the Russian authorities expressed sentiments in support of the Transnistrian referendum on independence, so the rhetorical change of position is clear. Additionally Gubarev stated that "if we want to take away the tension in this part of Europe we should bring the situation faster to the solution."[73]

Concerning the peace-keeping mission, the Russian Foreign Minister Lavrov announced that it should be "reformed" in accordance with needs of the conflict resolution process.[74] But more important evidence of progress in Russia's position is a number of statements made by Ambassador Kuz'min, who said that after reaching a comprehensive agreement on conflict resolution, the international presence should consist of police forces.[75] This position is close to the position of Moldova and the EU, and it means that in principle Russia is ready for a demilitarization of conflict management in the region. To station 2,000 Russian soldiers until 2020 was one of the main reasons why the Kozak Memorandum failed in November 2003. From the statements of 2001–2002 and 2009, it is known that Russia seeks an OSCE mandate for these forces.[76]

Obstacles in the Way Ahead

In thinking over the possibilities for a "breakthrough" in the Transnistrian settlement in the near future, some factors which could play against a positive outcome should be noted.

1. The structure of the EU-Russian dialogue is based on principles of bargaining, including in the Transnistrian issue. Both parties have been playing this game, possessing their own stakes and interests in it (Russia—WTO accession and liberalization of visa regime; the EU—liberalization of the energy market, resolution of frozen conflicts, human rights, produce trade, etc.). Both Russia and the EU have already fallen into the trap of this bargaining, where they do not know who could make the first step toward compromise and how this concession can be evaluated regarding the "stakes" in other fields. The last EU-Russia summit in June 2011 has clearly shown this stalemate.[77]

2. There is no fundamental consensus in Russia on its relations with the West. As a consequence the Russian foreign policy oscillates by looking historically at how Moscow treated various issues of world politics. External factors (primarily the behavior of Western countries) predetermine the development of Russian foreign policy. That is why a decision such as the stationing of the US

Anti-Missile Defense system in Romania can undermine the fragile consensus in Moscow and give opportunities to the groups of elite against any experiments in foreign policy. The Russian military has already shared its opinion that the American plans in Romania would directly threaten Russian security after 2015.[78] The presence of a strong pro-Transnistrian line in such leading Russian mass media as *Regnum* and *Nezavisimaya Gazeta* proves that some elements of the sovereignization strategy facilitated by powerful groups could return if the "reset" completely fails. Russia will support the political change in Transnistria, but it can play back all the rhetoric Moscow demonstrated last year.

The response of Russia via the Transnistrian issue would be a bureaucratization of the negotiation process, where everything would be ascribed as the responsibility of the conflict parties. In this case, a stalemate is unavoidable. For example, Russia ignored the meeting which should have taken place in 5+2 format on May 18, 2011, and has already evidenced a failure of communication with Western partners.[79] The remark of the Russian Foreign Ministry on the issue of local elections in Chisinau in June 2011, which hinted that the results were manipulated against the candidate from the Moldovan Party of Communists,[80] is also evidence of a general negativity in relations between the Alliance for European Integration and Moscow, which does not bode well for the progress of 5+2 negotiations at all.

3. Both conflict parties by themselves do not favor the compromise now, because for them any deal reached by Russia and the European Union is more a problem than a solution and a win-win game. For Moldova, the main problem is rooted in any equality which Tiraspol would claim as a main principle of reunification. Chisinau fears conversations about federation because it would then have to share its sovereignty. The Moldovan Foreign Minister is ready to accept reintegration but not the federalization of the country.[81] The diplomatic demarche of the Moldovan delegation, which left the reception at the Russian Embassy in Chisinau on June 10, 2011, because Russian Ambassador Kuz'min called Vladimir Yastrebchak "head of the Transnistrian diplomacy,"[82] shows that Moldova is ready to obstruct the dialogue if it seems needed. The Moldovan officials see in the Europeanization strategy the means to make Chisinau stronger and to reach a better solution in terms of power-sharing in the future.[83]

Conclusion

The paradigm of ambiguity well describes relations between Russia and Moldova, particularly what is happening now around the Transnistrian issue. On one side, we have a trend of pragmatism in mutual relations based on economic and political realities, the diplomatic wave of "reset" in dialogue between influential European countries and Russia on Transnistria. But on the other side, the relations are disturbed by the politicization of history and identity, by Russian intentions to have a symbolic reality of "strategic partnership" with Moldova by reference to common history, values and geopolitics.

Unfortunately skepticism is more appropriate to describe the prospects of not only negotiations within the 5+2 format, but also of the common atmosphere in bilateral relations, at least in the foreseeable future. The positive factors which were accumulated up to this moment create a good basis for substantial progress but they seem to be more a coincidence than a prelude for any stable political constellation. The times of great political deals like the peace treaty between Egypt and Israel in the 1970s are over. The postmodern political conjuncture does not allow any revolutionary political act. The legitimate and international-ized resolution of the Transnistrian conflict could be such an act.

Notes

1. Vadim Kononenko, "Boundaries of Sovereignty, Frontiers of Integration: Re-thinking 'conflict' between Russia and the EU," in *Russia's European choice*, ed. Ted Hopf (Basingstoke: Palgrave Macmillan, 2008), 210.

2. John Wollerton and Mikhail Beznosov, "Russia's Pursuit of its Eurasian Secu-rity Interests: Weighing the CIS and Alternative Bilateral-Multilateral Arrangements," in *The CIS, the EU and Russia*, ed. Katlijn Malfliet, Lien Verpoest, and Evgeny Vinokurov (Basingstoke: Palgrave Macmillan, 2007), 59–60.

3. "Kontseptsiya dal'neyshego razvitiya Sodruzhestva Nezavisimykh Gosu-darstv," October 5, 2007, http://cis.minsk.by/page.php?id=18763 (accessed May 29, 2011).

4. Natsional'noye byuro statistiki Respubliki Moldova, *Moldova v tsifrakh. Statis-ticheskiy spravochnik*, 6 vols. (Chisinau: Statistica, 2005–10), http://www.statistica.md/pageview.php?l=ru&idc=263&id=2195 (accessed May 28, 2011).

5. Ministerstvo inostrannykh del Rossiyskoy Federatsii, "Kommentariy Departa-menta informatsii i pechati MID Rossii v svyazi s situatsiyey vokrug Pridnestrov'ya, vyzvannoy vvedeniyem Moldaviyey i Ukrainoy novogo tamozhennogo rezhima vnesh-neekonomicheskoy deyatel'nosti regiona," March 17, 2006, http://www.mid.ru/bdomp/ns-rkonfl.nsf/90be9cb5e6f07180432569e00049b5fb/432569e00034005fc3257134005 8ac4a!OpenDocument (accessed December 25, 2007).

6. Vladimir Solov'yev, "Raskvitalis' yabloni i grushi," *Kommersant*, August 26, 2010.

7. Ibid.

8. European Commission, "Republic of Moldova. National Indicative Program 2011–2013," http://ec.europa.eu/world/enp/pdf/.../2011_enp_nip_moldova_en.pdf (accessed June 1, 2011).

9. "Prezident RF podpisal zakon, predusmatrivayushchiy vydeleniye Moldove kredita v 500 mln. doll.," *Moldova.ru*, July 21, 2009, http://www.moldova.ru/index.php?tabName=articles&owner=19&id=5043 (accessed May 10, 2011).

10. Chloe Bruce, "Power resources. The political agenda in Russo-Moldovan Gas relations," *Problems of Post-Communism*, May/June 2007, 29–47.

11. Boris Nemtsov and Vladimir Milov, *Nezavisimyy ekspertnyy doklad «Putin i Gazprom»* (Moscow: RID «Novaya gazeta», 2008), 3.

200 Andrey Devyatkov

12. Derek Averre, "Competing Rationalities: Russia, the EU and the 'shared neighbourhood,' " *Europe-Asia Studies* 61, no. 10 (2009): 1703.

13. Vladimir Putin, "Stenogramma vstrechi Vladimira Putina s uchastnikami tret'yego zasedaniya Mezhdunarodnogo diskussionnogo kluba 'Valday,' " September 14, 2006, http://gtmarket.ru/laboratory/publicdoc/2006/424 (accessed May 20, 2011).

14. Andrey Makarychev, "Russia's Moldova Policy: Soft Power at the Service of Realpolitik?," *PONARS Eurasia Policy Memo*, no. 94, March 2010, http://www.gwu.edu /~ieresgwu/assets/docs/pepm_094.pdf (accessed May 20, 2010).

15. "V Moldove vse proshlo bez revolyutsiy, kommunisty snova v bol'shinstve," *Regnum*, March 8, 2005, http://www.regnum.ru/news/polit/417615.html (accessed May 20, 2011).

16. Stefan Wagstyl and Tom Warner, "Moldova polls take on 'orange and yellow' hue," *Financial Times*, March 4, 2005.

17. Modest Kolerov, "Yesli vasha revolyutsiya vol'no ili nevol'no obsluzhivayet interesy vneshney storony, to ona v lyubom sluchaye obsluzhivayet eti interesy za vash schet," *Ekspert*, May 16, 2005.

18. Democracy.md, "Dosrochnyye parlamentskiye vybory v Moldove 29 iyulya 2009 goda," http://www.e-democracy.md/ru/elections/parliamentary/20092/ (accessed May 20, 2011).

19. "Rukovoditel' Administratsii Prezidenta Rossii Sergey Naryshkin pribyl v Moldovu," *IA Novosti – Moldova*, December 5, 2010, http://www.newsmoldova.ru /multimedia/20101205/188537558.html (accessed May 10, 2011).

20. "Vlad Filat: Vizit Naryshkina – vmeshatel'stvo vo vnutrenniye dela strany," *Point*, December 8, 2010, http://point.md/News/Read.aspx?NEWSID=123848 (accessed May 20, 2011).

21. Valeriy I. Kuz'min, "Uroki Nyurnberga i sovremennaya Moldaviya. Tezisy doklada Posla Rossii v Moldavii V.I.Kuz'mina na konferentsii, posvyashchennoy 65-letiyu nachala Nyurnbergskogo protsessa," Tiraspol, November 24, 2010, http://www .moldova.mid.ru/press-slujba/pr_10_51.htm (accessed May 10, 2011).

22. "Vladimir Filat zayavil o prichastnosti Rossii k moldavsko-pridnestrovskomu konfliktu," *RIA «Novyy Region» 2*, July 22, 2010, http://nr2.com.ua/kishinev/293258 .html (accessed May 10, 2011).

23. Mihai Ghimpu, interview with *Radio Svobodnaya Evropa*, May 31, 2010, http://www.president.md/press.php?p=1&s=7706&lang=rus (accessed May 10, 2011).

24. Ministerstvo inostrannykh del Rossiyskoy Federatsii, "Kommentariy MID Rossii v svyazi s ukazom i.o. prezidenta Moldavii M.F.Gimpu," June 25, 2010, http://www .mid.ru/bdomp/ns-rsng.nsf/6bc38aceada6e44b432569e700419ef5/c325749c004f2933c325 774d003284ea!OpenDocument (accessed May 10, 2011).

25. Irina Krasil'nikova, "Diskriminatsiya po istoricheskomu priznaku," *Moldavskiye vedomosti*, May 4, 2011.

26. Partiya Kommunistov Respubliki Moldova, "Marsh Pobedy v Kishineve (VIDEO)," May 9, 2011, http://www.pcrm.md/main/index.php?action=news&id=6253 (accessed May 20, 2011).

27. "Pobeda 'veteranov vtoroy mirovoy' i georgiyevskaya lenta na grudi Kirtoake: v Moldavii otprazdnovali 9 maya," *Regnum*, May 10, 2011, http://www.regnum.ru/news /polit/1402962.html (accessed May 10, 2011).

28. "Obshchiy dolg PMR za rossiyskiy gaz prevyshayet $2,5 mlrd," *Kommersant.md*, February 4, 2011, http://www.kommersant.md/Obschii_dolg_PMR_za_rossiiskii _gaz_previshaet_$25_mlrd843 (accessed May 10, 2011).

29. "Spiker parlamenta Pridnestrov'ya rasskazal, na chto idut den'gi za rossiyskiy gaz," *Regnum*, January 15, 2010, http://www.regnum.ru/news/1243066.html (accessed May 10, 2011).

30. "Byudzhet Pridnestrov'ya na 2011 god prinyat s defitsitom $190,8 millionov," *Alltiras*, November 25, 2010, http://alltiras.com/economy/4641----2011-----1908--.html (accessed May 10, 2011).

31. Klimova Ol'ga, "Rossiya brosayet Pridnestrov'yu 'spasatel'nyy krug,' " *Kommersant.md*, March 24, 2011, http://www.kommersant.md/node/1960 (accessed May 10, 2011).

32. An EU official in an interview with the author, Brussels, May 16, 2011.

33. William Hill, "Who's Next? Russia's Cat and Mouse Game with Moldova," openDemocracy, October 24, 2008, http://www.opendemocracy.net/article/russia-theme/who-s-next-russia-s-cat-and-mouse-game-with-moldova (accessed May 10, 2011).

34. Alexander Lebed', "V den', kogda mirotvorcheskiye sily uydut iz Pridnestrov'ya, ya nachnu ser'yezno gotovit'sya k voyne," *Izvestiya*, no. 37 (1993).

35. Yuriy Netkachev, "Pridnestrovskiy konflikt: khod, prichiny, posledstviya. Byvshiy komanduyushchiy 14-y armiyey general-leytenant Yuriy Netkachev vspominayet 1992 god," *Voyenno-promyshlennyy kur'yer*, no. 33 (2005).

36. "V 'planovuyu boyevuyu podgotovku' vyvod armii ne vkhodit," *Kommersant*, November 30, 1994.

37. Yevgeniy Primakov, "Mezhdunarodnyye otnosheniya nakanune XXI veka: problemy, perspektivy. Na gorizonte – mnogopolyusnyy mir," *Mezhdunarodnaya zhizn'*, no. 10 (1996): 3–13.

38. Posol'stvo Rossiyskoy Federatsii v Respublike Moldova, "Posol Rossii v RM: na venskoy vstreche uchastnikov peregovorov po Pridnestrov'yu budet rassmotren vopros 'ofitsializatsii' formata 5+2," February 8, 2011, http://www.moldova.mid.ru/press-slujba/pr_10_65.htm (accessed May 10, 2011).

39. "Lavrov: RF vystupayet za osobyy status Pridnestrov'ya v yedinoy Moldavii," *RIA Novosti*, March 29, 2011, http://www.rian.ru/politics/20110329/358925975.html (accessed May 10, 2011).

40. Sergey Lavrov, interview with *Radio Ekho Moskvy*, June 5, 2011, http://www.echo.msk.ru/programs/beseda/781605-echo/ (accessed June 12, 2011).

41. Uwe Klussmann, Matthias Schepp, and Klaus Wiegrefe, "NATO's Eastward Expansion," *SPIEGEL*, November 26, 2009, http://www.spiegel.de/international/world/0,1518,663315,00.html (accessed May 10, 2011).

42. Modest Kolerov, "Nepriznannaya zhizn'," *Apologiya. Novyy gumanitarnyy zhurnal*, no. 5 (2005).

43. "Protokol po itogam rabochey vstrechi Zamestitelya Predsedatelya Pravitel'stva Rossiyskoy Federatsii A.D. Zhukova s Prezidentom Pridnestrov'ya I.N. Smirnovym," Moscow, May 23, 2006, http://point.md/News/Read.aspx?NEWSID=22188 (accessed May 10, 2011).

44. Vladimir Solov'yev, "Ukraina opozdala v NATO. Eye vstupleniye v al'yans priznano neaktual'nym," *Kommersant*, November 26, 2008.

45. "Ukraina rasschityvayet na skoryy 'proryv' v pridnestrovskom uregulirovanii," *Regnum*, May 27, 2011, http://www.regnum.ru/news/1409375.html (accessed May 29, 2011).

46. European Parliament, "EU-Russia summit (debate)," Strasbourg, June 8, 2011, http://www.europarl.europa.eu/sides/getDoc.do?type=CRE&reference=20110608&secondRef=ITEM-013&language=EN&ring=P7-RC-2011-0347 (accessed June 14, 2011).

47. Bart Scheffers, "Tempering expectations: EU involvement with the Transdniestrian conflict," *Security and Human Rights*, no. 4 (2010): 293–301.

48. A German official in an interview with the author, by phone, May 27, 2011.

49. "Memorandum (Meeting of Chancellor Angela Merkel and President Dmitry Medvedev on 4–5 June in Meseberg)," http://www.bundesregierung.de/.../2010-06-05 -meseberg-memorandum.html (accessed May 10, 2011).

50. German official.

51. Christer Pursiainen, "Theories of Integration and the Limits of EU-Russian Relations," in Hopf, *Russia's*, 166.

52. Guido Westerwelle, interview with *Süddeutschen Zeitung*, October 30, 2010, http://www.auswaertiges-amt.de/DE/Infoservice/Presse/Interviews/2010/101030-BM-SZ -Russlandreise.html (accessed May 10, 2011).

53. Administratsiya prezidenta Rossii, "Zayavleniye franko-germano-rossiyskogo sammita v Dovile," October 19, 2010, http://www.kremlin.ru/ref_notes/742 (accessed May 10, 2011).

54. Auswaertiges Amt, "Deutsch-Polnisch-Russisches Dreieck," July 9, 2010, http:// www.auswaertiges-amt.de/DE/Europa/DeutschlandInEuropa/BilateraleBeziehungen/Polen /Aktuelles/100709-D-POL-RUS-Konsultationen.html (accessed May 10, 2011).

55. David Lidington, "Moldova and Romania," *UK Minister for Europe blog*, September 23, 2010, http://blogs.fco.gov.uk/roller/lidington/entry/moldova_and_romania (accessed May 10, 2011).

56. Angela Merkel and Emil Boc, "Pressestatements von Bundeskanzlerin Angela Merkel und dem Premierminister von Rumänien, Emil Boc," October 12, 2010, http://www.bundesregierung.de/Content/DE/Mitschrift/ Pressekonferenzen/2010/10/2010 -10-12-pk-bk-bukarest.html (accessed May 10, 2011).

57. Ministerstvo inostrannykh del Pridnestrov'ya, "Ob uchastii delegatsii Pridnestrovskoy Moldavskoy Respubliki v rabochey vstreche v Vostochnom komitete nemetskoy ekonomiki i drugikh meropriyatiyakh v Germanii," April 9, 2011, http://mfapmr.org/index.php?newsid=1006 (accessed May 10, 2011); Verkhovnyy Sovet Pridnestrov'ya, "Vizit delegatsii Pridnestrovskoy Moldavskoy Respubliki v Federativnuyu Respubliku Germaniya," April 19, 2011, http://vspmr.org/News/?ID=4955 (accessed May 10, 2011).

58. Dmitry Medvedev, "Press-konferentsiya Prezidenta Rossii," Moscow, May 18, 2011, http://www.kremlin.ru/video/824?page=4 (accessed June 5, 2011).

59. "MID: cherez dva-tri goda rossiyane smogut poluchat' pyatiletniye shengenskiye vizy," *Gazeta.ru*, June 1, 2011, http://www.gazeta.ru/news/lenta/2011/06/01/n_18 65385.shtml (accessed June 5, 2011).

60. "MVF i Vsemirnyy bank khotyat, chtoby gazovyy dolg Pridnestrov'ya oplatila Moldaviya," *Regnum*, May 12, 2011, http://www.regnum.ru/news/polit/1403975.html (accessed May 2, 2011).

61. "Smirnov: Pri raschetakh Pridnestrov'ya za gaz budet uchten vyvoz iz PMR voyennogo imushchestva," *Regnum*, May 30, 2011, http://www.regnum.ru/news/polit /1410395.html (accessed June 1, 2011).

62. Mariya Simonova, "Alisher Usmanov svedet aktivy k yedinolichnomu upravleniyu," *Kommersant*, July 7, 2006.

63. "Pridnestrovskaya tamozhnya blokiruyet rabotu MMZ," *Lenta PMR*, April 27, 2011, http://www.tiras.ru/tema-dnja/23979-pridnestrovskaya-tamozhnya-blokiruet-rabotu -mmz.html (accessed May 10, 2011).

64. "MGB Pridnestrov'ya: Plan Zapada – likvidatsiya PMR, 'evroadaptatsiya' Moldavii i transformatsiya Ukrainy," *Regnum*, May 17, 2011, http://www.regnum.ru /news/polit/1405527.html (accessed May 20, 2011).

65. Dmitriy Matveyev, "Anatoliy Kaminskiy: kachestvennaya razrabotka strategii razvitiya opredelit budushcheye Pridnestrov'ya," *RIA «Novyy Region» 2*, March 14, 2011, http://www.nr2.ru/pmr/324170.html (accessed May 10, 2011).

66. "Mikhail Leont'yev: 'Smirnov – eto pamyatnik, a Rossii nuzhen novyy prezident Pridnestrov'ya,' " *Lenta PMR*, June 3, 2011, http://tiras.ru/tema-dnja/24411-mihail -leontev-smirnov-eto-pamyatnik-a-rossii-nuzhen-novyy-prezident-pridnestrovya.html (accessed June 10, 2011).

67. " 'Yedinaya Rossiya' poboleyet radi 'Obnovleniya,' " *Kommersant.md*, May 16, 2011, http://www.kommersant.md/node/2899/mobile (accessed June 6, 2011).

68. Verkhovnyy Sovet Pridnestrov'ya, " 'Itogi vizita v Moskvu' – tema press-konferentsii, kotoraya proshla segodnya v Verkhovnom Sovete respubliki," http://vspmr .org/newvideo/showvideo.php?id=892 (accessed June 10, 2011).

69. Partiya Yedinaya Rossiya, "Kosachev: Parlament Pridnestrov'ya smozhet usovershenstvovat' Konstitutsiyu," July 16, 2009, http://www.edinros.ru/text.shtml?8/9267 (accessed May 10, 2011).

70. "Ekspert: 'Kremlevskiye mechtateli' slishkom otkrovenno simpatiziruyut planam po unichtozheniyu Pridnestrov'ya," *Regnum*, May 31, 2011, http://www.regnum.ru /news/polit/1410863.html (accessed June 10, 2011).

71. "OBSYe, YeS i RF privetstvovali neformal'nyye kontakty prem'yera Moldavii i prezidenta Pridnestrov'ya," *Regnum*, September 21, 2010, http://www.regnum.ru/news /polit/1327694.html (accessed May 20, 2011).

72. EU official.

73. Vladimir Solov'yev, "Konflikt na Dnestre poprobuyut razmorozit," *Kommersant*, April 29, 2011.

74. "MID RF vystupil za 'pereformatirovaniye' mirotvorchestva v Pridnestrov'ye," *RIA Novosti*, March 29, 2011, http://www.rian.ru/politics/20110329/358935791.html (accessed May 10, 2011).

75. Valeriy I. Kuz'min, interview with the Internet portal *AllMoldova.com*, December 9, 2010, http://www.moldova.mid.ru/press-slujba/pr_10_53.htm (accessed May 10, 2011).

76. "Sovmestnoye zayavleniye, prinyatoye po itogam peregovorov Prezidenta Rossiyskoy Federatsii D.A.Medvedeva s Prezidentom Respubliki Moldova V.N.Voroninym i glavoy Pridnestrov'ya I.N.Smirnovym," Barvikha, March 18, 2009," http://www.mid.ru /ns-rkonfl.nsf/90be9cb5e6f07180432569e00049b5fb/432569e00034005fc325757d0056c04 e?OpenDocument (accessed May 10, 2011).

77. Administratsiya prezidenta Rossii, "Sammit Rossiya – Yevropeyskiy Soyuz," Nizhniy Novgorod, June 10, 2011, http://kremlin.ru/news/11531 (accessed June 12, 2011).

78. "Amerikanskaya PRO budet ugrozhat' Rossii posle 2015 goda," *Lenta.ru*, May 20, 2011, http://www.lenta.ru/news/2011/05/20/pro/ (accessed May 29, 2011).

79. German official.

80. Ministerstvo inostrannykh del Rossiyskoy Federatsii, "Kommentariy Departamenta informatsii i pechati MID Rossii otnositel'no predvaritel'nykh itogov proshedshikh v Moldavii 5 iyunya vseobshchikh munitsipal'nykh vyborov," June 6, 2011, http:// www.mid.ru/bdomp/ns-rsng.nsf/6bc38aceada6e44b432569e700419ef5/c32577ca001744b6 c32578a900550ab3!OpenDocument (accessed June 12, 2011).

81. "Lyanke: V khode vstrechi s Lavrovym obsuzhdalos' 'ob"yedineniye' Moldavii i Pridnestrov'ya, a ne federatsiya," *Regnum*, June 9, 2011, http://www.regnum.ru/news /1414226.html (accessed June 10, 2011).

82. "V posol'stve RF v Moldove proizoshel diplomaticheskiy skandal mezhdu rossiyskimi, moldavskimi i zapadnymi diplomatami," *Interlic*, http://ru.interlic.md/2011 -06-10/v-posolstve-rf-v-moldove-proizoshel-diplomaticheskij-skandal-mezhdu-rossijskimi -moldavskimi-i-zapadn-21393.html (accessed June 12, 2011).

83. Bruno Coppieters in an interview with the author, Brussels, June 7, 2011.

Chapter Fourteen

Turkey: Politics of Balance and Caution toward Moldova

Özgehan Şenyuva

Turkey and the Republic of Moldova have long historical ties, stretching back to the sixteenth century. Moldova was a tributary state of the Ottoman Empire for three hundred years, until the 1812 Treaty of Bucharest, when the region was ceded to the Russian Empire.[1] Despite three centuries of Ottoman presence in the region, Moldova was not considered part of the inner circle, like the Balkan or Middle Eastern territories. Thus, not much Ottoman heritage was left in the territory, except for a significant number of references within Moldovan national history and several Turkish words in the Moldovan language (Romanian).[2] The biggest national hero of Moldova, Stephen the Great, is remembered and revered for his victories against the Ottoman armies in the fifteenth century. Relations between Turkey and Moldova were revived following the independence of Moldova from the Soviet Union in the 1990s.

Relations between Turkey and the Republic of Moldova can be viewed in three dimensions: political, economic and humanitarian. Turkish foreign policy toward Moldova is constructed and conducted within the framework of these three aspects, albeit with differing degrees of involvement and importance.

This chapter argues that Turkish policy toward Moldova has clear characteristics. First of all, it is stable. Since the independence of Moldova in 1991, Turkey has been careful to retain close relations with the Moldovan state, despite changes in Moldovan government. Second, it has been pragmatic and balanced. Turkey has been cautious to follow policies that would not put Turkish interests at risk. Turkey maintains close relations with the Gagauz, the Orthodox Christian Turk[3] minority of Moldova, without damaging relations with the Moldovans; it also maintains close relations with Moldova, without risking Turkey's close relationship with the Russian Federation. Turkey has been careful to protect the interests of the Gagauz people while simultaneously remaining close to the Moldovan state—and this imperative constructs the backbone of Turkish policy toward Moldova. Third, Turkey keeps an eye on its economic interests in Moldova. Fourth, and finally, Turkey contends with negative public perceptions between the two countries stemming from irregular migrant movements and the sex trade. In this analysis, each of these issues will be elaborated.

The Political Dimension of Turkish-Moldovan Relations

Turkey was among the first countries to recognize the independence of Moldova on December 16, 1991, only three months after its declaration. The Treaty on Friendship and Cooperation between the Republic of Moldova and the Republic of Turkey, which is the founding document of relations between the two countries, was signed on June 3, 1994. Officially, the Turkish Foreign Ministry states that Turkey's approach to Moldova is "based on the principles of cooperation and mutual understanding, of supporting this country's contribution to peace and stability in the region as an independent and sovereign state, and of improving the atmosphere of friendship and cooperation at a bilateral, multilateral and regional level that serves mutual interests of both countries."[4]

This approach has several implications, especially in the Gagauz and Transnistria regions, and in Turkey's reaction to the political uprisings in Moldova in 2009.

In the political uprisings following the April 5, 2009, elections and the political turmoil that followed, Turkey kept its balanced and stable approach.[5] When the Communist authorities, previously in power for almost a decade, lost power in favor of a coalition of pro-Western parties, Turkey followed a "wait and see" approach, careful not to get involved in the domestic affairs of Moldova. The only consistent concern was the protection of the rights of the Gagauz people, and since the political change did not jeopardize them, Turkey kept a very low profile.

The Gagauz, Transnistria and Turkish Policy

Turkey's policy position toward the Gagauz and Transnistria issues has been steady and clear from the very beginning: Turkey does not support the independence of breakaway regions and calls for the territorial integrity of Moldova. Over the years, the actions and discourse of successive Turkish governments have been in line with this position.

If the origin of Turkey's foreign policy toward the Gagauz and Moldova following independence from the Soviets is analyzed, it is observed that Turkey has held one clear position: Respecting the territorial integrity of Moldova, as long as this was possible. This approach is true for both the Gagauz region and Transnistria: "Turkey also supports the solution of the Transnistrian problem through dialogue, while preserving the territorial integrity, political unity and sovereignty of Moldova."[6] Turkey is not involved in the Transnistrian negotiations, but follows the 1999 Istanbul Summit decision of the Organization for Security and Cooperation in Europe, and calls for the departure of Russian troops and military equipment out of region.

The Gagauz issue is the most important element within Turkish foreign policy toward Moldova. Following the dissolution of the Soviet Union, Turkey had the opportunity to re-establish links with other Turkic states, mainly in Central Asia, that used to be a part of the Soviet Union and shared ethnic, linguistic and religious ties. Turkey, taking the political climate and its limited capabilities into consideration, aimed to establish bilateral relations with these Turkic states without making Russia uncomfortable, and without making the newly independent states feel patronized. An example of such sensitivity can be observed in Turkish-Azeri relations. Turkey's relations with Azerbaijan were the closest because of their shared Turkic nationality, and a very popular motto for relations with Azerbaijan, which still prevails today, was "one nation, two states." The Gagauz, because of their Turkish roots and language were also of particular interest to Turkey. Direct relations with the Gagauz population were complicated for two main reasons. First, they are too small and confined within another state, Moldova. The Gagauz population in Moldova is estimated around 147,500, forming 4.4 percent of the Moldovan population.[7] Second, although linguistic proximity with the Gagauz is very strong (especially compared with other Turkic people of Central Asia, e.g., Turkmenistan), the Gagauz are predominantly Orthodox Christians. Therefore, speaking of religious solidarity or using religious institutions as a policy tool (which Turkey did frequently in those years, particularly in Central Asian countries) was out of question. On the contrary, Turkey had to adapt to the religious sensitivities of the Gagauz in formulating mutual relations. However, one may argue that Turkey has been following a stable and consistent policy toward the Gagauz, by addressing the needs of both the Gagauz and the Moldovans. Turkey also played an influential role in distancing the Gagauz from Russian influence, at least in cultural terms. Turkey strongly encourages the use of the Gagauz language instead of Russian, and has been supporting the use of the Latin alphabet in written Gagauz instead of Cyrillic.[8]

The Gagauz issue followed a different path than the Transnistrian problem in the aftermath of Moldovan independence. Turkey played a decisive role in the development of these events. The Gagauz, in fear of a possible unification of Moldova with Romania, traditionally followed a pro-Soviet policy, which later transformed into closer ties with Russia. Their concerns were intensified with the change of official language from Russian to Moldovan (Romanian) in 1989.[9] This was perceived by the Gagauz as another step on the path to the unification of Moldova with Romania, and it fed their nationalist concerns. The first separatist initiative came on November 12, 1989, when the Gagauz Autonomous Soviet Socialist Republic was proclaimed by an assembly in Comrat. This step was regarded as unlawful by the Moldavian Supreme Soviet.[10] On August 19, 1990, the Gagauz declared a separate Gagauz Soviet Socialist Republic in the south of the then-Moldavian Soviet Socialist Republic, independent from Moldova, but part of the Soviet Union, even earlier than the proclamation of the Pridnestrovian Moldavian Republic in Transnistria on September 2, 1990.[11] Both were declared null by the Supreme Soviet of the Moldavian SSR.[12]

With the escalating possibility of a civil war and the call of the Popular
Front of Moldova for a volunteer armed militia to prevent the breaking away of
Gagauzia and Transnistria, Turkey started to act in the role of an intermediary.
Politically moderate Gagauz received support from Turkey, which urged the
leadership of the Gagauz Republic to negotiate with the Moldovan government
rather than resort to violence, as in the case in Transnistria.[13] Then-Turkish
President Süleyman Demirel played a decisive role in the resolution of the
Gagauz issue. He constantly urged the Gagauz to accept regional autonomy and
remain citizens of the Republic of Moldova, making pledges of economic and
structural investments in the Gagauz region via Chisinau. In his visit of June
1994, President Demirel visited both Comrat, the capital of Gagauzia, and Chisinau, urging parties to reach an agreement. A few days before President Demirel's visit to Moldova, in a goodwill gesture to Turkey, Moldovan President
Mircea Snegur declared that the Gagauz would be given regional autonomy.[14]
During this visit, President Demirel had repeatedly stressed that the Turkish role
in Moldova and Gagauzia was by no means confrontational to Russia.[15]

On December 23, 1994, the Moldovan parliament produced a peaceful resolution to the dispute by passing the Law on the Special Legal Status of Gagauzia
(Gagauz Yeri). Gagauzia became a "national-territorial autonomous unit" with
three official languages—Russian, Gagauz and Moldovan (Romanian)—and that
date is now a Gagauzian holiday. In case of changes to the status of the Republic
of Moldova as an independent state, the people of Gagauzia have the right to
external self-determination.[16] This was a clear reference to a possible unification
of Moldova with Romania, in which case the Gagauz would be entitled to decide
whether or not to remain a part of the new state by means of a self-determination
referendum.

President Demirel's role in the peaceful resolution of the Gagauz issue is
not forgotten. He remains an "honorary citizen" of Gagauzia, and is often referred to as one of the "founding fathers" of Gagauzia. In 2009, a statue of President Demirel was erected in Comrat, during the tenth anniversary of Gagauzia's
autonomy, with the approval of the Moldovan authorities.[17] One of the two
Turkish high schools in the region is also named after Demirel.

Turkish Policy Tools in Moldova: The Role of State and Non-state Agencies

Turkey's careful political approach to Moldova, a balance of relations with
Moldova, Russia and the Gagauz people, forces Turkey to use a mix of policy
tools when dealing with Moldovan issues. Turkey is very active in Moldova
through its embassy, but other state and non-state agencies also play a role.
Among these, four pillars stand out as particularly active and influential.

First is the Turkish Agency for International Development and Cooperation
(TIKA) in Moldova. TIKA was established in 1992 as part of the Turkish For-

eign Ministry, with the aim of supporting development projects within the Turkic sphere. In 1999, TIKA was directly linked to the Prime Minister's office. TIKA became active in Moldova in 1994, following the signing of the Treaty of Friendship and Cooperation. The principal activity of TIKA in Moldova was to support infrastructure investments in the Gagauz region. Other activities financed by TIKA range from internship programs for Gagauz teachers in Turkey to the construction of water and sewage systems in the Gagauz region. More than a hundred projects dealing with capacity-building programs, health and safety programs, internships, infrastructure construction, employment and vocational training have been implemented in Moldova by TIKA. In 2009 Gagauzia was the region with the highest expenditure per capita in terms of Turkish aid abroad.[18] The administration of all kinds of technical aid (e.g. technological equipment for schools, medical equipment for hospitals) is performed by TIKA, but the Turkish embassy remains in the oversight of all large-scale projects, and deals with matching the demands and offers between the Gagauz and Turkish authorities and institutions.

The second state agency that covers Moldova in general, and Gagauzia in particular, is the Prime Ministry Presidency for Turks Abroad and Related Communities, which has been established as recently as March 2010. Although still in the early years of its establishment, it is foreseen that this institution will actively administrate relations with the Gagauz people, especially on scholarships and mobility of people.[19]

Thirdly, Turkey continues direct relations with Moldova within the frame of the Black Sea Economic Cooperation Organization. BSEC was established in 1992, in Istanbul, with strong Turkish initiative. It promotes multilateral political and economic cooperation among its twelve member states. The Republic of Moldova was a founding member, although it does not have a Black Sea coast. BSEC has offered an opportunity for the Republic of Moldova to improve its relations with other countries in the region, as well as benefit from economic and structural funds, as well as other programs in the organization.

Finally, there are the Turkish schools that operate in Moldova, mainly in Gagauzia. There is Kongaz Süleyman Demirel Turkish Moldovan High School. It was established by the Turkish Ministry of Education in 1999, and it educates in English, Gagauz, Turkish, Moldovan and Russian. The salaries of eleven permanent Turkish teachers and the building and facility expenses are covered by the Turkish state. The other Turkish schools are owned by a Turkish foundation, Orizont (Horizon). They operate a private high school and a primary school in Chisinau, as well as a high school and two language schools in Gagauzia. All these schools teach Turkish and serve to improve the image of Turkey and to strengthen Turkish soft power.

Although the Gagauz are the main reason that elevates Moldova high on the Turkish foreign policy agenda, economic relations between the two countries and Turkish investments in Moldova are also important.

Economic Relations and Turkey's Economic Interests

Turkey is one of the most active countries operating economically in Moldova. There were 757 Turkish enterprises registered with the Moldovan Chamber of Commerce in 2008, and 84 of them were established that same year.[20] However, Moldova forms a very tiny part of Turkey's trade volume. If we take into consideration the fact that Turkey's trade volume in 2010 was around $300 billion; the trade volume with Moldova, $259 million, is only a fraction. Despite their size, active economic relations constitute a very important dimension of Turkish-Moldovan relations. The economic investments and activities of Turkish business circles in Moldova play an especially important role in keeping Moldova on the radar for Turkey. Following the establishment of political and diplomatic relations after Moldovan independence, a series of economic treaties and agreements were signed between these two countries (table 14.1).

Table 14.1. Trade and Economic Agreements between Turkey and Moldova

Name of agreement	Date of signature
Trade and Economic Cooperation Treaty	February 14, 1994
Treaty on Mutual Encouragement and Protection of Investments	February 14, 1994
Agreement on Prevention of Double Taxing	June 25, 1998
Joint Economic Commission 1st period Protocol	October 9, 1998
Joint Economic Commission 2nd period Protocol	March 31, 2004
Joint Economic Commission 3rd period Protocol	October 14, 2005

Source: Turkish Undersecretariat for Foreign Trade, *Moldova Country Profile 2009* (Ankara: DTM, 2010), 3.

Starting in 1997, Turkey enjoyed a positive trade balance with Moldova. In 2008, Turkish exports to Moldova were around $198.0 million, but due to the global crisis it decreased to $117.0 million, while Turkish imports from Moldova increased from $69.5 million to $86.5 million (table 14.2).[21] Turkey mainly imports fruits, unfinished leather and fur products, grains and wine, while exporting finished industrial and pharmaceutical products as well as textiles, automobiles and construction materials to Moldova. In 2009, Turkey was ninth among the top ten countries for Moldovan exports and seventh among imports to Moldova, representing 5 percent of all imports.[22]

Table 14.2. Turkey's trade relations with Moldova (mil. USD)

Year	Exports	Imports	Balance	Volume
1992	0.2	1.7	-1.6	1.9
1993	0.4	28.9	-28.5	29.3
1994	3.6	20.4	-16.8	24.0
1995	7.3	15.6	-8.3	22.9
1996	14.3	14.4	-0.1	28.7
1997	21.3	15.1	6.2	36.4
1998	27.6	11.8	15.8	39.4
1999	20.6	10.9	9.7	31.5
2000	26.2	7.1	19.2	33.3
2001	27.8	2.6	25.2	30.4
2002	39.1	4.7	34.4	43.8
2003	46.8	10.6	36.2	57.4
2004	65.7	26.6	39.1	92.2
2005	80.4	31.4	49.0	111.8
2006	104.8	31.3	73.5	136.1
2007	145.7	53.0	92.7	198.7
2008	197.2	69.5	127.7	266.7
2009	117.6	86.5	31.1	204.1
2010	148.3	110.7	37.6	259.0

Source: Turkish Statistical Institute, "Foreign trade and investment Meta data," http://www.turkstat.gov.tr/VeriBilgi.do?tb_id=12&ust_id=4 (accessed April 23, 2011).

In addition to the positive trade balance with Moldova, Turkey's main economic interests lie in Turkish investments. Turkey is one of the leading investors in the Republic of Moldova. The Turkish Foreign Ministry estimated the amount of Turkish investment was around $260 million, excluding Turkish partnerships with third country enterprises.[23] Turkish enterprises have been increasingly active in making further investments in a variety of fields ranging from hotels to tile factories. Some of the most significant Turkish investments are worth mentioning. The main mobile provider of Moldova, Moldcell, started operating in 2000 with 77 percent of its shares belonging to Turkcell of Turkey. Now, 66 percent of its shares are owned by Fintur, a partnership of Turkcell and Sorena from Finland.

On December 2002, Efes Pilsen Brewery of Turkey purchased Vitanta Intravest S.A., a major beverage producer in Moldova. Vitanta controls 70 percent of the beer market in Moldova. In addition to Moldcell and Efes-Vitanta, another source of major Turkish investment is the hotel business. Hotel Dede-man Grand Chisinau, part of a Turkish hotel chain, opened with a $12 million investment in 2002 and served as the only five-star hotel in Chisinau for the greater part of the 2000s. There are also other factories owned completely or partially in different parts of Moldova, such as Nefis, producing biscuits; Infini-ty, textiles and Sanitex, tiles.[24] Turkish construction companies took contract work in the value of approximately $130 million from 2002–2008, including the renovation of Chisinau International Airport.[25] In 2009, the construction of the biggest shopping center in Chisinau, Malldova, was also undertaken by Turkish construction companies.

Turkey may play an active role in the economic and political aspects of bi-lateral relations. However, there is another important dimension of Turkish-Mol-dovan relations over which Turkey has very little control: It is the destination of a large number of Moldovan migrants. The situation of these migrants in Turkey is another factor that affects Turkey's relations with Moldova and must be taken into consideration.

Moldovan Migrants in Turkey and Turkish State Policies toward Them

Although traditionally Turkey has been considered a "sending" country, since the end of the Cold War, Turkey has also been a "destination" country for the flow of immigrants from certain parts of the world. Migrants come from Moldo-va to find better living standards and work.

The initial wave of Moldovans, along with others from the post-Soviet area was through what is popularly known as the "suitcase trade." Suitcase trade refers to people operating with small capital and carrying goods to sell between countries.[26] The suitcase trade started to decline in the mid-1990s due to the normalization of export-import relations between Turkey and the post-Soviet countries, and the number of Turkish business people investing in these coun-tries to sell products directly. But the migrant flow from Moldova continued.

A strict visa regime applied to Moldovan citizens from EU member states, and the geographical proximity of Turkey as well as Turkey's loose border and relaxed visa regimes allowed Moldovans to obtain visas in airports upon arrival with only passports, and some cultural and linguistic proximity (mainly for the Gagauz people) are the main reasons Moldovan citizens preferred immigrating to Turkey.[27] Moldovans coming to work and live in Turkey are categorized as "circular migrants." As typical for circular migrants, these migrants cross the Turkish borders legally and do not try to use Turkey as a jumping board for migrating to another country. They either move in circles, back and forth con-tinuously between Turkey and Moldova, or, after having stayed and worked for long periods, they move back to Moldova. However, they are more often than not illegal in Turkey as they overstay tourist visas, or enter the work force without a work permit. These characteristics distinguish these migrants from asylum seekers, refugees, or clandestine migrants.[28] Many of these migrants are employed by Turkish farmers, construction companies, and by private families as domestic workers.[29]

It is very difficult to estimate the number of Moldovans living in Turkey as irregular migrants. One common method for such estimation is to look at the number of deportations to Moldova. The findings of studies focusing on the issue paint a very dim picture. Moldova appears to be one of the main source countries for the irregular migrants in Turkey. Among the approximately 400,000 migrants apprehended by police in Turkey between 1995 and 2001, one-fourth were from the post-Soviet area, with Moldovan citizens forming the largest group, followed by Russian and Ukrainian nationals.[30] Gathering all available data on the issue, Görkem Dağdelen concludes that a total of 568,000 Moldovans arrived in Turkey between 1997 and 2005, and 458,000 Moldovans left Turkey in the same period. According to his calculations 15,456 Moldovan migrants were deported, and 51,415 Moldovans were apprehended between these years. At the end, he estimates that nearly 40,000–45,000 Moldovan irregular migrants live in Turkey.[31]

There is also a darker side to this picture. Along with Moldovans working in the informal sector, Turkey also appeared as a destination country for trafficking of Moldovan women as sex workers. According to the records of General Directorate for Foreigners, Ministry of Interior, 94.9 percent (21,582 migrants) of all foreigners' deportations between 1996 to 2001 because of "illegal prostitution" (22,752) were citizens of post-Soviet countries.[32] The coercion and deception of women from the post-Soviet area into the sex trade, and the related legal issues, emerge as an important factor affecting mutual public perceptions between Turkey and Moldova. In Turkish public opinion, female migrants in the sex industry from the entire post-Soviet area were labeled with the nickname "Natasha," which holds very pejorative connotations. This negative factor remains strong even today, and Moldova is considered to be a destination for sex tourism. There are also cases of Moldovan and other Eastern European women being subjected to occasional harassment with "Natasha" slurs in Turkey.

The Turkish state sees the high influx of Moldovan immigrants as a domestic problem, and tries to keep it separate from its relations with the Moldovan state. However, the policies of the Turkish state towards these Moldovan migrants are also subject to criticism. Mine Eder's study analyzing Turkish state policies toward irregular Moldovan migrants offers some insights. Eder analyzes the "relations" between Moldovan migrants and the Turkish state in terms of three dimensions of state power: the enabling state, the coercive state, and the corrupt/informal state.[33] The liberal visa regime of Turkey toward Moldovan citizens is a major factor that enables migrants to enter Turkey. This aspect should be taken as the first dimension of migration policies of the Turkish state. By means of the durations of visa exemptions, the extent of "openness" in terms of borders can be modified. Secondly, the coercive state shows itself by means of the explicit or subtle violence of police toward irregular migrants in everyday life and increasing fines for overstayers.[34] Thirdly, Eder explains how the state becomes a part of "criminal" and "illegal" activities by means of bribery mechanisms at borders or in everyday life.[35] The Turkish state, as many states in the neo-liberal age, tries both to control the population movements and to behave as if it has control on the influx of people.[36]

Conclusion

If one considers the economic and political size and activities of Turkey, the Republic of Moldova is not an important component of Turkish foreign policy. However, the Gagauz people, with whom Turkish public opinion has a strong ethnic attachment, makes relations with Moldova an important issue for Turkey. Turkey has been very careful in constructing its foreign policy toward the Gagauz over the years. Their main approach has been not to alienate the Moldovans when dealing with the Gagauz, and in general Turkey has strived for a reconciliatory tone. Turkey's role in the peaceful settlement of Gagauz calls for independence, in contrast to the ongoing conflict of Transnistria, was an important factor in shaping the future of Moldovan-Turkish relations. Turkey follows a pro-Moldovan policy on the Transnistrian conflict as well, in line with the recommendations of OSCE and the Council of Europe, in calling for the removal of Russian troops and military equipment from the region. However, Turkey also keeps a rather low profile on the issue and would not let it influence its close economic and political relations with the Russian Federation. In other words, Turkish foreign policy is careful not to harm relations with the Republic of Moldova because of the Gagauz, and not to harm relations with the Russian Federation because of Moldova.

Turkey pursues an active policy toward Gagauzia and is a major source for the reconstruction and renovation of the region's infrastructure, economy and human capital. However, Turkey does not ignore the rest of Moldova. The Turkish business community is very active, and Turkey is one of the most important trade partners of Moldova.

Yet, there is a major challenge for both countries in future bilateral relations: mutual negative public perceptions. Irregular migration and the sex trade are the sources of these negative opinions. Although it has decreased over the years, the deception and coercion of Moldovan women into the sex trade in Turkey has created a general sense of mistrust in Moldova. On top of that, Moldova's emergence as a destination for sex tourism also diminished and harmed the image of Turkey over the years in the eyes of the Moldovan public. In Turkish public opinion as well, Moldova and Moldovan people are often associated with sex workers and sex tourism. Irregular migrants from Moldova are also subjected to exploitative working conditions in Turkey and this also creates negative repercussions in Moldovan public opinion on Turkey.

Over the years, Turkey has been trying to improve its image in Moldova. Turkish state and non-state agencies have been playing an important role by encouraging exchanges, education and scholarship programs. Turkey has also became a popular tourist destination for the Moldovan upper and upper-middle classes, and the number of Moldovans visiting Turkey as tourists is on the rise. However, the image of a country in public opinion is built over years and can only be altered in the long run with careful and detailed work. This should be Turkey's approach to augment its balanced and cautious approach to Moldova.

Notes

1. For detailed information on Moldovan history and nationalism see Jonathan Eyal, "Moldovans," in *The Nationalities Question in the Soviet Union*, ed. Graham Smith (New York: Longman, 1990), 123–41.

2. The language of Moldova is officially named "Moldovan" in the constitution. Yet, in reality it is not any different than Romanian. As the issue is linked with the Moldovan identity, calling it Romanian is disputed by some Moldovan nationalists. In this text any reference to the language will be used in the form of "Moldovan (Romanian)."

3. The ethnical origin of Gagauz is subject to different theories. However, in Turkish public opinion and official position they are considered to be ethnically Turkic. For other theories and discussion on the ethnic origins of Gagauz see Claus Neukirch, "Autonomy and Conflict Transformation: The Case of the Gagauz Territorial Autonomy in the Republic of Moldova," in *Minority Governance in Europe*, ed. Kinga Gal (Budapest: Open Society Institute, 2002), 105–23.

4. Turkish Foreign Ministry, "Turkey's Political Relations with Moldova," http://www.mfa.gov.tr/turkey_s-political-relations-with-moldova.en.mfa (accessed April 23, 2011).

5. For detailed information on the 2009 Moldovan elections and the political change, see Ozgehan Senyuva, "Parliamentary Elections in Moldova, April and July 2009," *Electoral Studies* 29, no. 1 (2010): 190–95.

6. Turkish Foreign Ministry, "Relations with Moldova."

7. National Bureau of Statistics of the Republic of Moldova, "Population Census 2004," http://www.statistica.md/pageview.php?l=ro&idc=295 (accessed May 12, 2009). However, it should be noted that the 2004 Population Census covers only the territories controlled by Moldovan authorities in Chisinau, excluding the left bank of Moldova.

8. "Gagavuzlarin Ana Sozu" [The Mother's Voice of Gagauz], *Milliyet daily*, March 29, 1993. The language issue between Gagauz and Moldovan authorities continues to be a source for tension and despite Ankara's extended efforts, Russian remains as the dominant language. In 2011, about 10 percent of the graduating students in the Autonomous Territorial Unit of Gagauzia failed their final exams in Romanian language and literature. For a detailed account of the language issue between Gagauzia and Moldova see Valentina Ursu and Robert Coalson, "Moldova's Gagauz region struggles to find common language with Chisinau," *Radio Free Europe/Radio Liberty*, August 3, 2011.

9. Legea cu privire la functionarea limbilor vorbite pe teritoriul RSS Moldovenesti [Law regarding the usage of languages spoken on the territory of the Moldavian Soviet Socialist Republic], no. 3465-XI, September 1, 1989.

10. Neukirch, "Autonomy and Conflict," 107.

11. William E. Crowther and Helen Fedor, "Moldova," in *Belarus and Moldova: country studies*, ed. Helen Fedor (Washington, DC: Library of Congress, 1995), 165.

12. For a detailed account of the events on Gagauz-Moldovan relations between 1991–1994 see Neukirch, "Autonomy and Conflict," 105–7.

13. Crowther and Fedor, "Moldova," 185.

14. "Moldova'dan Demirel'e Jest" [Goodwill gesture to Demirel from Moldova], *Milliyet daily*, May 30, 1994.

15. "Rusya Tehdit Degil" [Russia is not a threat], *Milliyet daily*, June 4, 1994.

16. Law on special legal status of Gagauzia (Gagauz-Yeri), no. 344-XIII, December 23, 1994, art. 1, pt. 4.

17. "Süleyman Demirel Bustunun acilisi icin Moldova'ya geliyor" [Süleyman Demirel is coming to Moldova for the inauguration of his statue], *Cihan News Agency*, December 22, 2009.

18. Turkish Agency for International Development and Cooperation-TIKA, *Country Report, Moldova 2010* (Ankara: TIKA, 2010), http:// www.tika.gov.tr (April 23, 2011).

19. For more information see the website of the Prime Ministry Presidency for Turks Abroad and Related Communities at http://www.ytb.gov.tr/.

20. Turkish Foreign Ministry, "Turkey's Commercial and Economic Relations With Moldova," http://www.mfa.gov.tr/turkey_s-commercial-and-economic-relations-with -moldova.en.mfa (April 23, 2011).

21. All data related to trade and investment are taken from Turkish Statistical Institute, "Foreign trade and investment Meta data," http://www.turkstat.gov.tr/VeriBilgi.do ?tb_id=12&ust_id=4 (accessed April 23, 2011).

22. Turkish Undersecretariat for Foreign Trade, *Moldova Country Profile 2009* (Ankara: DTM, 2010), 2.

23. Turkish Foreign Ministry, "Turkey's Commercial and Economic."

24. Eduard Baidaus, "Moldova si Turcia – Realitati Ale Unei Colaborari (1992–2002)" [Moldova and Turkey, realities of cooperation], 2004, http://www.iatp.md/articles /baidaus_eduard.htm (accessed April 20, 2011).

25. DEIK-Foreign Economic Relations Board, *Turkey-Moldova Relations Report 2008* (Ankara, 2009), http://www.deik.org.tr/Pages/TR/IK_TicariIliskilerDetay.aspx?tiDetId= 106&IKID=33 (accessed May 5, 2011).

26. Most of these suitcase traders were women from middle-income groups. These women were making two- or three-day visits to Istanbul four or five times in a year. They bought goods such as leather, shoes and cloths, and then transported them to their home country by bus or by plane. For an extensive analysis of the initial trade relations, see, H. Deniz Yükseker, *Laleli-Moskova Mekigi: Kayıtdısı Ticaret ve Cinsiyet Iiskileri* [Laleli–Moscow shuttle: Informal trade and gender relations] (Istanbul: Ietisim Yayınları, 2003).

27. Ahmet Içduygu, *Irregular Migration in Turkey*, Migration Research Series of the International Organization for Migration 12 (Geneva: International Organization for Migration, 2003).

28. Görkem Dağdelen, "Changing labor market positions and workplace interactions of irregular Moldovan migrants: the case of the textile/clothing sector in Istanbul, Turkey" (master's thesis, Middle East Technical University, 2008), 123.

29. International Organization for Migration, *Migration in Turkey: A Country Profile* (Geneva: International Organization for Migration, 2008), 31.

30. Sema Erder and Selmin Kaska, *Irregular Migration and Trafficking in Women: The Case of Turkey* (Geneva: International Organization for Migration, 2003).

31. Dağdelen, "Changing labor market," 127.

32. Erder and Kaska, *Irregular Migration and Trafficking*, 20.
33. Mine Eder, "Moldovyalı Yeni Göçmenler Üzerinden Türkiye'deki Neoliberal devleti Yeniden Düsünmek" [Reconsidering the NeoLiberal State in Turkey through the New Migrants from Moldova], *Toplum ve Bilim*, no. 108 (2007): 136.
34. Ibid., 138.
35. Ibid., 141.
36. Dağdelen, "Changing labor market," 122.

Chapter Fifteen

Ukraine: Inconsistent Policy toward Moldova

Vladimir Korobov and Georgiy Byanov

Ukraine underestimates the significance of its policy toward Moldova. The post-Soviet diplomacy of Ukraine has been affected by the same stereotypes of its past. Diplomats of the Soviet school, by force of inertia, consider relations with the United States, China, the European Union and Russia as the most important area of their activities. In the yearbook *External policy of Ukraine: Strategic estimates, forecasts and priorities* there is not a single mention of Ukraine's relations with Moldova.[1] At the same time, it is impossible to overestimate the significance of Moldova for Ukraine, as it is a natural ally in preventing latent Romanian threats to Ukraine's territorial integrity. Ukraine's policy toward Moldova is distinguished by its inconsistency on Moldova's split. On the one hand, Ukraine supports the sovereignty and independence of the Republic of Moldova; on the other hand, it has a special relationship with Transnistria, which territory historically belonged to Ukraine. More than 160,000 Ukrainians live in Transnistria, which makes up 28.8 percent of the population of this non-recognized republic.[2] By different estimates, from 70,000 to 100,000 Transnistrian inhabitants have Ukrainian citizenship and Ukrainian passports. Ukraine is party to the negotiations settlement of the Transnistrian conflict.

Incomplete, Emerging Policy

Ukraine's policy toward Moldova is marked by incompleteness and dynamism. After the Soviet Union's collapse, the newly independent states virtually had to shape their relations "from scratch." In the past, under the Soviet Union, there used to be relations between the Soviet republics that had a somewhat superficial, cultural and educational nature. During the Friendship Days of the Republics, exchanges of delegations took place, and agreements of a declaratory nature were signed. These economic and political activities were defined by the Kremlin in a non-federal but unitary state style, the basis of which was the Communist Party—a "state within the state."

After obtaining independence, Ukraine encountered the challenging goal of shaping its own foreign policy and its own diplomacy. Yet for a rather long time, Kiev would "go astray," falling back into Soviet stereotypes in the course of its relations with the neighboring former Soviet republics. The basis of foreign policy toward Moldova was nominally formed in the 1990s; but even nowadays, this policy is incomplete and conceptually insufficient.

Four stages can be outlined in foreign policy relations between Ukraine and Moldova, each of which is characterized by a different level of formation, comprehensiveness and other particular features. The first stage, from 1992–1996, was the birth of Ukraine's foreign policy toward Moldova. The second stage, from 1997–2004, was a period of shaping Moldovan policy and intensifying Ukraine's engagement in the area. The third stage, from 2005–2008, was a time of sustained effort to solve issues of conflict with Moldova. The fourth stage, from 2009–2011, has been a period of "reset" in Ukrainian-Moldovan relations.

The Genesis of Moldovan Policy in Ukraine

Independent Ukraine needed to shape the basic principles of its foreign policy at the beginning of the 1990s. This task emerged at the center of Ukraine's policy toward Moldova in 1992–1996. The period was characterized by inertia of Soviet politics, as well as elements of spontaneous reaction and chaotic motion in foreign policy.

A number of accomplishments were achieved during this time: In March 1992, the newly independent Ukraine and Republic of Moldova set up diplomatic relations; in October 1992 in Chisinau, the two nations signed the Treaty on Good-Neighborhood, Friendship and Cooperation, based on the principles of sovereign equality, territorial integrity, and the inviolability of borders. In 1993, Ukraine and Moldova signed the Agreement on International Road Transports (ratified only in 1999 in Moldova, and in 2000 in Ukraine). The Agreement on Mutual Recognition and Regulation of Relations on Property was also signed in 1994. The distinctive feature of these agreements was the fact that contracts were signed but not ratified and, actually, not executed by both parties.

By the end of the first stage, in January 1995 an agreement was achieved establishing a Joint Commission on Economic and Commercial Cooperation. The result of this commission's work was the Agreement of August 1995 on Free Trade.

The first period of relations between the nations was hampered by the 1992 war and the split of Moldova into two states—the sovereign Republic of Moldova and the unrecognized Pridnestrovian Moldavian Republic. Ukraine responded to those events ambiguously. On one hand, it was thought that Ukrainian citizens were involved in the armed struggle on the Transnistrian side. They were mostly supporters of the radical party Ukrainian National Assembly–Ukrainian

National Self-Defence (UNA-UNSO) aimed at the protection of national interests and use of nationalist ideology. On the other hand, the Ukrainian President Leonid Kravchuk and the government of Ukraine came up with a demand to stop the fighting, which led to a mass influx of refugees into Ukrainian territory. The Ukrainian government's statement read, "We call on the conflicting parties to create the right conditions for refugees to return to their homes; and reserve our right to claim expenses related to the refugees' stay."[3] Moreover, Ukraine had to take emergency measures to prevent the spread of hostilities and armed persons from Transnistria and Moldova into the territory of Ukraine. The borders that used to be transparent were blocked on the Ukrainian side by border and security forces.

The "Transnistrian factor" affected the nature and development of Ukrainian-Moldovan relations from their very beginning. As early as 1991, Ukraine pursued inconsistent policies toward Moldova.

On one hand, Kiev secretly negotiated with representatives of Transnistria, including on the possibility of Transnistria merging into Ukraine in light of historical circumstances. This was confirmed by the analyst and former Ukrainian presidential administration worker Dmytro Vydrin.[4] Those talks were possible due to a negative attitude between Chisinau and Kiev elite resulting from the 1939 Molotov-Ribbentrop Pact. Under its provisions, Bessarabia was detached from Romania and incorporated into the Soviet Union in 1940. The core of Bessarabia was merged with a part of the Moldavian Autonomous Soviet Socialist Republic, which up to then had belonged to the Ukrainian SSR, into the Moldavian SSR. The remaining northern part (known as Northern Bukovina) and the southern parts of Bessarabia were incorporated into the Ukrainian SSR. In 1991, the Moldavian Parliament denounced the Molotov-Ribbentrop Pact. It created international legal precedents for returning to the status quo of 1939: Moldova's entry into Romania, and Transnistria's return to Ukraine. Also, some unverified sources report that even the option of exchanging Transnistria for Southern Bessarabia was considered.

However, the aforementioned negotiations did not result in any actual geopolitical changes. Kiev leaders did not have the determination to take such a bold step that might cause unpredictable consequences. Vydrin writes the following about those negotiations:

> In 1992, I worked at Administration of Ukrainian President Leonid Kravchuk and met head of Transnistria [Igor] Smirnov. He asked me to hand over a letter to Kravchuk, where he suggested Kiev start the procedure of Transnistria joining Ukraine, using a parliamentary mechanism. The Transnistrian parliament was at that time, and it is still, one of most civilized parliaments: All debates and documents are available in three languages—Russian, Ukrainian, and Moldavian. Smirnov's idea did not seem too practical to me: but the political lava was still hot in 1992, borders might be changed. Of course, there were some illusions that Transnistria might be reverted to the past, but if Kravchuk had supported the idea and the parliament had followed him, finding a joining procedure, we would have such a headache. From my point of view, Kravchuk was

so frightened of the letter; it has been quietly lying somewhere ever since. The Ukrainian president did not respond to Smirnov's initiative. Perhaps it is time to return to it? No. The hot lava has already hardened. And there are no hammerers to destroy it. There was such a chance in 1992.[5]

On the other hand, on August 29, 1991, Smirnov was arrested during his visit to Kiev by the Moldovan police, who brought him to Chisinau, where he was imprisoned.[6]

The duality of Ukrainian policy remained up to 2010. It manifests itself in a controversial foreign policy position: Ukraine would like to collaborate with Moldova—Ukraine's geopolitical resources have been repeatedly employed to place economic pressure on Transnistria; at the same time, Kiev continuously offers certain support to Transnistrians and the Ukrainian citizens residing in Transnistria. In the past decade, this has mostly taken the form of humanitarian and educational assistance. As for the economy, Ukraine and Transnistria's cooperation has been developing in an inter-regional context. In particular, some agreements on socio-economic, educational and cultural cooperation were made between Transnistria and a number of regions (Odessa, Kherson, Vinnytsya, Ternopil'). The contacts have been based on traditional economic as well as centuries-old historical and cultural ties, since for more than a hundred years, from 1806 to 1920, the left bank of the Dniester River with its center in Tiraspol was an uyezd of the Kherson Guberniya.

In the Soviet period, many members of the Transnistrian economic elite, for example, Igor Smirnov (town Hola Prystan, city Kakhovka of the Kherson region) were biographically tied to the southern regions of Ukraine.

In the second half of the 1990s and at the beginning of the 2000s, when the "iron curtain" at the Transnistrian sector of the Ukrainian-Moldovan frontier had not descended very low, and the mythology of black PR had not reached its devastating centrifugal effect, there was a frequent exchange of official delegations. An agreement between the Kherson region and Transnistria was signed in September 2000 as a result of the Kherson region state administration's visit to Tiraspol. That visit was not covered much by the press, apparently due to political reasons. Today a similar political underground seems impossible.

From 2001 to 2010, when the relations between Moldova and Transnistria fluctuated from escalation to stagnation, these kinds of contacts were rendered null. Ukraine collaborated with Transnistria turning constantly back to Moldova and it tried to cooperate with Moldova following its own interests in Transnistria and European integration.

Two opposite poles of political tension affected and continue to shape the dual nature of Ukraine's foreign policy toward Moldova: historically and mentally close Transnistrian, on the one hand, and pro-European Moldova on the other.

Laying the Foundation of Ukraine's Moldovan Policy

The second stage of Ukraine's foreign policy toward Moldova refers to 1997–2004. During this period, the basis for the policy was actually formed, and Ukraine increased its activities in Moldova.

In January 1997, the previously mentioned Treaty on Good-Neighborhood, Friendship and Cooperation between Ukraine and the Republic of Moldova came into force. That agreement contributed to the solution of the border argument and settlement of property issues, and it intensified foreign economic relations.[7]

On October 10, 1997, in Strasbourg, at the summit of the Council of Europe, a new international organization, GUAM, was founded, consisting of four countries: Georgia, Ukraine, Azerbaijan and Moldova.[8] The aim of this newly founded structure was its members' cooperation in strengthening stability and security in Europe, based on principles of respect for sovereignty, territorial integrity, inviolability of state borders, democracy, superiority of law and respect for human rights.[9] Unfortunately, the effort of setting up bilateral relations between Ukraine and Moldova within that structure turned out to be unsuccessful from its very start and has not yet led to positive results.

In 1998, with the assistance of the European Union, the European regions Upper Prut and Lower Danube were set up. Creation of those European regions was aimed at substantial improvement of relations between the countries in the region and intensifying cross-border collaboration. Unfortunately, the effect of the European regions failed to become as strong as had been expected.

In 1999 Moldova and Ukraine signed the Treaty on the State Border that was ratified by Moldova only in the year 2001, while Ukraine ratified it immediately in the same year, 1999. But actually, this agreement with regard to controversial issues got executed only in the year 2011.

Regarding the Transnistrian issue, Ukraine obtained a full mediator status in the Transnistria conflict settlement of 1997. This was followed by the signing of the Moscow (or Primakov) Memorandum, which is one of the fundamental documents of the negotiation process. This became possible due to strengthening of Ukrainian-Russian relations (in 1997 a friendship treaty with Russia was signed, and the deployment issues of the Russian Black Sea Fleet were settled).

In the Moscow Memorandum, Ukraine guaranteed it would ensure freedom in foreign economic activities to the regional actors, and support the principle of settling the arguments between Moldova and Transnistria through negotiations.

But again Ukraine revealed contradiction and duality in its policy. In 2001 at Moldova's request, Ukraine did not let Transnistrian merchandise across its borders that was not certified by the Chamber of Commerce and Industry of the Republic of Moldova and cleared by Moldovan Customs. Transnistria qualified those actions as sanctions aimed against Transnistria ("economic blockade").

And yet, Ukraine resumed passing some goods without being certified and cleared in Moldova. Those goods did not have certificates of their country of origin, which led to an increase in their cost.

Unsuccessful Attempts

The third stage of Ukraine's foreign policy toward Moldova covered 2005–2008. This period is characterized by Ukraine's attempts to prove itself as a regional leader by enhancing the mechanisms of GUAM to contribute to the solution of the Transnistrian conflict on the basis of a plan proposed by Ukraine to settle contentious issues of property and borders.

In 2005 Ukraine initiated the GUAM summit in Chisinau aimed at giving a new impetus to the international organization. The headquarters of the organization were moved to Kiev; at the summit "Yushchenko's plan–7 steps" was presented to settle the Transnistrian conflict by running free, democratic elections to the Transnistrian Supreme Soviet under international community monitoring (a full version was presented during a negotiation meeting in Vinnytsya in May 2005). Moldova actually terminated the prospect of implementing that initiative by passing the Law on Basic Principles of the Special Legal Status of the Settlements on the Left Bank of the Dniester (Transnistria). Moldova showed reluctance to make use of the mediators' assistance in the conflict settlement, leaving it completely up to the Moldovan authorities to solve it; however, under the law, elections to the Transnistrian Supreme Soviet should be organized and monitored by the international community. In fact, it was a negative response to Ukrainian initiatives. Up to the end of the year 2005, the inertia of implementing the "Yushchenko plan" and the GUAM mechanisms continued.

On December 2, 2005, a "Community of Democratic Choice," was created in Kiev in the framework of GUAM; the organization included the commonwealth of democracies of the Baltic–Black Sea–Caspian region. The initiators of the new organization creation were Ukraine and Georgia, the countries that had experienced colorful revolutions. It was an attempt to form an alternative to the Commonwealth of Independent States with its center located in Kiev. Except for the proclamation, no further actions came of the initiative. But an important factor in Ukrainian-Moldovan relations was that the declaration adopted at the founding forum of the Community stated the member countries seek to join Europe without any "frozen conflicts."[10]

In 2005, elections to the Transnistrian parliament took place and were won by the Obnovleniye party. In addition to the hope for the prospect of democratization of the Transnistrian regime, the new parliament and elite happened to be more "pro-Ukrainian" than its predecessors.[11] This factor contributed to the improvement of the Ukrainian-Transnistrian relations and to the complication of the Ukrainian-Moldovan ties.

A characteristic feature of the third stage was the strengthening of European influence on Ukrainian-Moldovan relations. On November 30, 2005, the European Union Border Assistance Mission to Moldova and Ukraine was established; it started to operate also on the Transnistrian part of the Ukrainian-Moldovan border. The aim of the mission is the monitoring of borders to detect possible smuggling, drug and arms trafficking, and to identify "gray patterns" of illegal trade. The results of the mission work were positively evaluated both by Ukraine and Moldova. Even Transnistria reacted positively to the fact that the mission had assisted in ending the "black hole" stereotype with regard to Transnistria, which stayed outside the current international legislation. In the opinion of the Ukrainian ambassador in Moldova, Serhiy Pyrozhkov:

> Due to EUBAM, two major problems have been solved. First, EUBAM confirmed that there was no so-called "black hole" on the border between our countries, which had negatively affected the image of our countries in the EU. Second, an active dialogue was launched between border and customs services of Moldova and Ukraine. Also, thanks to EUBAM, efforts in the process of demarcation of the borders was restored.[12]

In March 2006, Ukraine, in accordance with an agreement with Moldova, introduced a new procedure letting goods across the border of Ukraine and Moldova (Transnistrian section). The nature of the decision was to have Transnistrian ventures register in Chisinau for receiving a document package required for foreign economic activities. Transnistrian enterprises had to get a permit for export from Moldovan customs. That agreement was the foreign policy equivalent of an advance from Ukraine based on expected returns of concessions from Moldova in the solution of border issues.

"Reset" of Ukraine and Moldova Relations

The fourth and final stage was from 2008–2011. It was a phase of "reset" of Ukrainian-Moldovan relations. A favorable internal political situation developed both in Moldova and Ukraine that facilitated this "reset."

As a result of the victory in the early-2010 presidential elections, the head of the Party of Regions, Viktor Yanukovych, came to power. Both President Yanukovych and representatives of the governing party repeatedly stated their firm desire to radically improve Ukrainian-Moldovan relations. In Moldova, the Alliance for European Integration came to power in mid-2009, also declaring guidelines for improving the relations of the two countries.

By the time of Yanukovych's presidency, the expert community of Ukraine had developed the idea of an urgent need for immediate changes in policy toward Moldova. In 2009, a round-table conference was held in Kiev under the distinctive title "What do we have to do with Moldova?" A participant of the event, Kiev analyst Yuriy Romanenko rather definitively articulated the common attitude:

> Ukraine has already reached the point at which it has to identify priorities in foreign policy, as there appears a range of new and a range of old, but sharpened challenges that cannot be ignored any longer. In particular, Ukraine ought to determine a fresh approach in its interaction with Moldova. As it is obvious, that southern-western direction is the most critical part of Ukraine's foreign policy in regards to vulnerability of national interests.[13]

The fast-changing situation inside Moldova, in particular the events on April 7, 2009, in Chisinau (disorder in the streets of Chisinau; the crowd was protesting against the ruling regime and accusing it of election fraud) proved that "a new political reality" had started to develop in Moldova, and it just confirmed the urge in Kiev to update policy toward Moldova.

In the opinion of well-known Ukrainian analyst Vitaliy Kulyk, Ukrainian-Moldovan relations by 2009 were in "inertial and critical condition." Those relations were characterized by an abundance of unsolved problems and diverse "areas of pain."[14]

Experts and diplomats consider Ukraine made unilateral concessions to Moldova without obtaining anything in response. Those concessions, primarily, related to the Transnistrian issue. Ukraine agreed to limit the activities of Transnistrian economic agents; introduced restrictions on food supplies from Transnistria; and undertook other measures that negatively affected Transnistria's livelihood and economy. That policy of Ukraine was defined not so much by Ukrainian-Moldovan relations, as by "assistance of the European Union policy toward the Transnistria settlement and relations with Moldova."[15]

Moldova considered relations with Ukraine since 1992 mostly within the context of the Transnistrian problem. Indeed, the Transnistrian problem is the major issue, the main "area of pain" of Ukrainian-Moldovan relations. One of the most significant sources of Transnistria's sustainability is its multilateral relations with Ukraine and its southern regions; especially the Odessa Sea Port. The common Transnistrian section of the Ukrainian-Moldovan border has become a crucial factor of survival for the non-recognized Pridnestrovian Moldavian Republic. But this interpretation of the situation is avoided in Ukraine. The Transnistrian issue seems to be considered outside Ukrainian-Moldovan relations, within a geopolitical context of relations with the US, EU, Russia and other participants of the Transnistrian settlement.

In 2009, the major problems of the Ukrainian-Moldovan relations were enumerated: 1) the "Palanca problem"—for more than 10 years, Ukraine did not receive an allotment near the village Palanca in exchange for a plot of land near the village Giurgiuleşti on the Danube. The matter has vexed Ukraine since; against its economic interests, it had assisted Moldova in becoming a sea power by extending it a coast plot of land to set up Giurgiuleşti Sea Port; 2) the issue of ownership concerning the Dniester Pumped Storage Power Station; 3) Moldova's refusal to execute demarcation of the borders, which has caused the disagreement of Ukraine on a number of territorial issues.[16]

A specific matter in the policy of Ukraine towards Moldova and Transnistria is consideration of population residing in this area. As of the data of the year 2004, 159,000 Ukrainians[17] live in Transnistria; more than 282,000 Ukrainians live in Moldova.[18] By the estimates of experts, up to 100,000 citizens of Ukraine reside in Transnistria. Moreover, this population has never left Ukraine for Moldova, but is factually the indigenous population. The people appeared in Transnistria due to a number of geopolitical, territorial and administrative changes; at first, the Moldavian Socialist Republic was created in 1924 as an autonomy within the Soviet Ukraine and included Ukrainian territories along with the local population dwelling there. In its foreign policy Ukraine takes into account the need to protect the rights of Ukrainian diaspora in Moldova and requires the same from Moldova and Transnistria. Also, in the opinion of Kulyk, the status of the Ukrainian minority in Moldova might have been increased; following Transnistria's experience, Moldova could have accepted the use of three languages, approving Moldovan as an official language along with the Ukrainian and Russian languages as well.[19]

The new Ukrainian administration has demonstrated determination to intensify trade and economic relations with Moldova. The customs boards of the two countries signed a Declaration on Transportation Priority in June 2011 for fruit and vegetable products across customs borders of Ukraine and Moldova. It should be noted that export of fruit and vegetable products is vital for both countries; in Moldova as well as in the south of Ukraine this merchandise is the major export within traditional economic households, common for the entire southern historic Novorossiysk region.[20]

According to information compiled by the Ukrainian embassy to Moldova, Ukrainian investments in Moldova constitute $15 million. Due to the global financial crisis and the unstable political situation in Moldova, Ukrainian business people have not invested recently in Moldova. By now, 623 enterprises with Ukrainian capital operate in Moldova, including 190 that are 100 percent financed by Ukrainian capital. They are typically small and medium-sized enterprises. Ukrainian business people are interested in setting up joint ventures, as since March 1, 2008, Moldova has had EU trade preferences. Ukrainian investments in Moldova are promising in the economic development of relations for both countries.[21]

Trade and economic relations of Ukraine and Moldova are characterized by stable, positive and dynamic merchandise turnover. Ukraine keeps a leading position in the external trade of Moldova. According to the data of the Moldovan National Bureau of Statistics, as seen in table 15.1, volumes of export to Ukraine and import from Ukraine keep intensively growing. In Ukrainian exports to Moldova, fuel and grocery products are dominating groups.

One positive note that may favorably affect further development of bilateral dialogue on economic issues is the agreement on renewal of the operation of the intergovernmental Ukrainian-Moldovan Commission on Economic and Commercial Cooperation, which acts as a coordinating mechanism for the development of bilateral economic relations.

Table 15.1. Moldova's trade with Ukraine in 1997–2010 (in mil. USD)

Year	Export to Ukraine	Import from Ukraine
1997	49.4	211.2
1998	48.7	151.5
1999	32.6	71.9
2000	35.5	104.6
2001	57.2	152.6
2002	61.4	203.6
2003	56.1	309.2
2004	64.8	436.3
2005	99.9	479.7
2006	128.8	516.5
2007	167.9	687.0
2008	142.8	839.0
2009	81.3	458.8
2010	91.6	528.5

Source: National Bureau of Statistics of the Republic of Moldova, "External trade," http://www.statistica.md/category.php?l=en&idc=336 (accessed August 10, 2011).

Ukrainian contribution into the development of Ukrainian-Moldovan relations and in the settlement of the Transnistrian conflict may appear successful if the priority is given to efficient trade and economic relations between the countries. Experts have promoted the idea of establishing the Odessa Macroeconomic Region. The speech is about establishing a new quantity: a macro-region, naturally including practical cross-border cooperation: Moldova, Transnistria, Gagauzia and the Ukrainian Black Sea area. Interest in the formation of a single market, common communications, and a common style and way of life, to merge interests and cultures has long been going on here; the time has come to realize and recognize this process.[22]

The "Palanca" Case

Further development of Ukrainian-Moldovan relations is impossible without resolving the issue of the borders. The peculiarity of Moldova, in the author's opinion, is that this state, "recognized de jure by the international community, is de facto a state with limited internal sovereignty. This internal sovereignty is not recognized in a substantial part of its territory. This syndrome of non-recognition affects the condition of its external borders."[23]

A part of the motorway between two Ukrainian towns, Odessa and Reni, close to the Moldovan village of Palanca of 7.7 km length, in accordance with the Protocol to the Treaty between Ukraine and Moldova on the State Border of August 18, 1999, should have been transferred under the jurisdiction and operation of Ukraine. But this was not done in 1999, and the issue remained unsettled for 12 years, until 2011.

Ukraine increasingly demonstrated its impatience in the contentious matter of the motorway to Palanca. In the evening on November 15, 2010, Ukrainian authorities unilaterally dismantled and removed boundary markers no. 0608 and no. 0609, 120 meters inside Moldova. The Ukrainian Foreign Ministry declared that "the guards have corrected the mistake made during the demarcation of the border with Moldova."[24]

The Moldovan authorities demanded on November 17, 2010, that Ukraine explain the unilateral actions of the Ukrainian side. They referred to the treaty between the countries, which stated that "the road section is the property of Ukraine on the territory of the Republic of Moldova." The Moldovan Ministry of Foreign Affairs and European Integration declared "that approach will not favor further pragmatic and constructive dialogue on the demarcation of Moldovan-Ukrainian state border, launched between the countries this year."[25]

As always in similar cases, the European Union acted as an arbitrator. European Commissioner for Enlargement and European Neighbourhood Policy Štefan Füle stated that "the issue of the border between Ukraine and Moldova should be solved through negotiations, rather than unilateral actions on the border." He also said that the European Union is ready "to offer expert assistance for determination of the border between Ukraine and Moldova."[26]

Odessa Regional Council considered a relevant statement of the deputy Vyacheslav Strashylin and approved an appeal to President Viktor Yanukovych with the request to dissolve the treaty on transfer to Moldova of the land where Giurgiuleşti is located. That decision was voted for by 114 deputies of the Regional Council, while previously only 25 deputies were in favor.[27]

In April 2011, Ukraine actually brought to Moldova an ultimatum—the demand to solve urgently the issue on "returning to Ukraine its land in the area of Palanca." The Ukrainian Foreign Minister Kostyantyn Hryshchenko stated at the plenary session of the Verkhovna Rada of Ukraine, "No arguments from Moldova will be accepted by Ukraine any longer." He demanded to run an intergovernmental discussion on the matter right after Moldovan local elections were conducted on June 5, 2011. The minister threatened to end trade and economic relations between the countries.[28]

Ukraine has previously demonstrated signs of its impatience and placed pressure on Moldova. In 2009, Moldova was included in the list of migration risk countries. In accordance with this document, citizens of Moldova, when crossing the border of Ukraine, had to submit documentary proof confirming their solvency. It was a hard blow against the interests of working migrants, who mattered much to the economy of Moldova. Other methods of pressure on the partner of the negotiations were also expected, but they happened to be unnecessary.

Those measures of influence on Moldova turned out to be effective. Moldova became more amenable, and the Moldovan elite became more manageable at negotiations. It is worth mentioning the contribution of Prime Minister Vlad Filat, whose name is associated with the breakthrough in the relations of the two countries. There appeared reports in the Ukrainian media that the Ukrainian determination could be partially explained by confidential agreements made between Moldovan Prime Minister Filat and Ukrainian Prime Minister Yuliya Tymoshenko during Filat's visit to Kiev on February 1, 2010.[29] There was much ambiguity about that visit. It was surprising, since the visit was paid on the last days of Tymoshenko's term as prime minister. During the visit, they signed a Protocol on Changes in Intergovernmental Agreement on Property drafted in 1994. That Protocol recognized the property rights of Ukraine for the Dniester hydroelectric power station. During that visit, Filat promised to solve the "Palanca problem."[30]

In accordance with Article 10 of the Ukrainian-Moldovan Treaty on the State Border, "Negotiating parties will sign an additional protocol to that Treaty, which is its integral part and regulates the transfer of a section of the motorway Odessa-Reni near Palanca of the Republic of Moldova, as well as the plot of land it runs through to the ownership and operation of Ukraine."[31] However, the protocol to the treaty on the transfer of the road near Palanca includes a contradictory provision: "1.2 The land transferred is the property of Ukraine on the territory of the Republic of Moldova," but further states: "6.1 As the land is transferred, jurisdiction of Ukraine is enacted."[32]

On July 9, 2011, there was a meeting of Ukrainian President Yanukovych and Acting Moldovan President Marian Lupu. That meeting was timed to the birthday of President Yanukovych. The joint statement declared a solution to the Palanca case. The Ukrainian party "noted with satisfaction the final solution of the issue of recognition of Ukraine's property rights for the section of the motorway Odessa-Reni near Palanca, that was confirmed by the corresponding Act of June 30 the same year and by the transfer of the Cadastre statement."[33]

The solution of the problem caused a storm of criticism in Moldova. In the area of the contentious road there were mass demonstrations by local residents of Moldovan villages against the transfer of land to Ukraine and the change of crossing the contentious road section.

The Moldovan media forwarded the following ideas: 1) there is no agreement about the exchange of land in the corresponding agreement between the countries; 2) Ukraine was transferred the section of the road located on the territory of Moldova and being the ownership of Ukraine on the territory of Moldova; 3) the jurisdiction of Moldova ought to be enacted on this territory rather than Ukraine; 4) local residents will cross the road to get to their land plots and excesses will occur. The conclusion is the following: "The Palanca case is set-tled, but its issues remain unsolved."[34]

The ten-year long solution of the "Palanca problem" demonstrated the fol-lowing characteristic traits of Ukraine's policy toward Moldova: Ukraine does not pay enough attention to clarifying its foreign policy toward Moldova and Transnistria inside the country, to its own citizens. But it also neglects the ne-cessity of external public information in Moldova, explanation of its policy in the Moldovan public arena. This leads to the lack of a legitimate Ukrainian policy toward Moldova, it significantly narrows the chance of positive and con-structive interpretations of its policy, and it leads to the preservation of a high level of conflict around contentious issues. It hampers Ukraine in achieving its foreign policy goals.

There is no civil society dialogue between the two countries on contentious issues, and in particular on the Palanca case. Professionalization and securitiza-tion of the problem significantly narrows the maneuvering room for Ukraine, it complicates the solution of existing problems, it lowers the level of trust be-tween the countries, and it makes foreign policy toward Moldova both ineffec-tive and inefficient.

Besides this, mechanisms for trans-boundary cooperation are not employed at full capacity. Despite the measures undertaken by both countries, the Ukraini-an-Moldovan border is still far from being an ideal "Smart Border" designed to promote the free flow of verified goods and travelers. It is not a space of open and transparent cooperation, but a barrier in the way of such cooperation.[35]

Conclusion

Two friendly states, Ukraine and Moldova, have yet to overcome the obstacles facing the development of their relations after the collapse of the Soviet Union. In an interview timed to the twentieth anniversary of the establishment of dip-lomatic relations between Ukraine and Moldova, the Ukrainian ambassador to Moldova, Serhiy Pyrozhkov, characterized Ukrainian-Moldovan relations and their major problems:

> Ukraine is a neighbor to the Republic of Moldova and therefore it is necessary to develop mutually beneficial relations. We do not have political or ethnic dif-ferences; what unites us is a common strategy of European integration. The on-ly issues within our relations are the completion of border demarcation and the recognition of property rights for installations built at the time of the Soviet Union. Unfortunately, these issues hinder the development of mutual relations and redirect us to the past.[36]

Unfortunately, it may be concluded, relations between Ukraine and Moldo-va still do not make use of the potential the two countries share. These relations (political, economic and cultural) do not meet the challenges of the time, the needs of the countries nor the expectations of the people. One of the major problems of Ukraine's policy toward Moldova is duality and inconsistency.

Relations with Moldova are considered in Ukraine in a broader context—in the context of relations with Romania and the European Union. The policy toward relations with Moldova is linked with the problem of Ukraine's border security in the south-west direction. Also, a complication of the issue is caused by latent territorial claims of Romania for Northern Bukovina and Southern Bessarabia. Taking this context into account, Ukraine develops its policy toward the Republic of Moldova, and defines its position in the challenging issue of the Transnistrian conflict settlement. Independent and sovereign Moldova is a natural barrier for Romanian expansionism. Strengthening this obstacle corresponds to the national interests of an independent Ukraine. In Vitaliy Kulyk's opinion, "a strong, independent state of Moldova is needed as a constraint against Romania."[37] Romania today is a full member of the European Union. The policy of Ukraine towards Romania and Moldova can be effective in the case of correct coordination of any important decisions and actions in the south-west direction with such a powerful neighbor as the European Union.

The positions of the Moldovan and Transnistrian parties at the negotiations on the Transnistrian conflict settlement are neither flexible nor effective. Those positions hamper the final settlement and the development of a relationship with Ukraine. Moldova, along with the European Union, is trying to exert pressure on Russia and force Transnistria to unconditionally accept the terms proposed by Moldova.

The apparently positive changes in the relationship between the two countries ought to be strengthened. These positive changes are related to the pragmatism of the new foreign policy of Ukraine pursued under the presidency of Viktor Yanukovych. At the recent stage of relationship between the two states, Ukraine tends to exert pressure on Moldova. This tactic works, and it brings serious, positive results.

There are no significant differences in the Ukrainian establishment regarding the prospective development of Ukrainian-Moldovan dialogue and collaboration. Ukraine is interested in the existence of a strong and sovereign Moldova and the quickest settlement of the Transnistrian conflict based on the principles of territorial integrity and sovereignty of Moldova. Solution of this issue, in the context of the border problems, is considered as a favorable factor promoting Ukraine to European integration.

In the near future the policy of Kiev in the Moldovan direction will not undergo global changes. The foreign policy of Ukraine regarding probable external and internal changes will develop following pragmatism and strategic interests of the leadership in the region. The previous passive nature of Ukrainian policy in the Moldovan direction will obtain more reactive features to meet current political challenges.

A positive factor that will to a large extent define the future of the Ukrainian-Moldovan relationship is the accumulated fatigue of the Moldovan elite for the destructive consequences of confrontational politics. For two years Moldovan deputies have not been able to elect the president of the country. In this regard, Chisinau is losing motivation to run uncompromising conflict politics and is trying to adopt a more pragmatic approach in establishing bilateral relations.

In the short term, undoubtedly, the duality and inconsistency toward the Transnistrian matter that is typical for Kiev will remain strung between the gravity of historical links to Transnistria and the urgent political requirement of supporting the sovereignty and territorial integrity of the Republic of Moldova. In the next years, Ukraine will balance between these two poles with a more pronounced emphasis on achieving a reasonable resolution to the conflict within a sovereign Moldova.

However, given some of the negative aspects of the negotiation's political heritage, particularly from 2001–2006, possible future attempts by Moldova to persuade Ukraine to accept exclusively Chisinau's vision of the Transnistrian settlement will from now on likely be rebuffed by Ukrainian diplomacy.

Notes

1. Hryhoriy Perepelytsya, ed., *Zovnishnya polityka Ukrayiny – 2010: stratehichni otsinky, prohnozy ta priorytety* [Foreign policy of Ukraine – 2010: Strategic estimates, forecasts and priorities] (Kiev: Stylos, 2011).

2. *Pridnestrovskaya Moldavskaya Respublika: Kratkiy spravochnik. Spetsial'nyy vypusk* (Tiraspol: Verkhovnyy Sovet Pridnestrov'ya, 2007), 22.

3. Boris Bomeshko, *Sozdaniye, stanovleniye i zashchita pridnestrovskoy gosudarstvennosti (1990–1992)* (Bendery: Poligrafist, 2010), 415.

4. Dmytro Vydrin, "Ukrainian Foreign Minister is to be held personally accountable for Transdnestr blockade," interview with *Regnum*, May 3, 2006, http://www.regnum.ru/news/632014.html (accessed August 10, 2011).

5. Ibid.

6. Anna Volkova, *Lider* (Tiraspol, 2001), http://president-pmr.org/material/100.html (accessed August 10, 2011).

7. Dohovir pro dobrosusidstvo, druzhbu i spivrobitnytstvo mizh Ukrayinoyu ta Respublikoyu Moldova [Treaty on Good-Neighborhood, Friendship and Cooperation between Ukraine and the Republic of Moldova], Chisinau, October 23, 1992, http://zakon1.rada.gov.ua/cgi-bin/laws/main.cgi?nreg=498_161 (accessed August 7, 2011).

8. This structure was called GUUAM in 1999–2005, when Uzbekistan was its member.

9. GUAM, "Istoriya GUAM," http://guam-organization.org/node/240 (accessed August 11, 2011).

10. "Sodruzhestvo demokraticheskogo vybora," Geopolitika, http://www.geopolitics.ru/common/organisations/usdc.htm (accessed August 11, 2011).

11. Vladimir Korobov and Georgiy Byanov, "The 'Renewal' of Transnistria," *The Journal of Communist Studies and Transition Politics* 22, no. 4 (2006): 526.

12. Serhiy Pyrozhkov, "Posle 20 let dvizhemsya vmeste k ES," interview with *Adevărul*, July 25, 2011, http://www.mfa.gov.ua/moldova/ru/news/detail/63996.htm (accessed August 9, 2011).

13. Yuriy Romanenko, "Chto nam delat' s Moldovoy?," (speech, Glavred, Kiev, April 29, 2009), http://www.ukrrudprom.ua/digest/CHto_nam_delat_s_Moldovoy.html (accessed August 5, 2011).

14. Vitaliy Kulyk, "Chto nam delat' s Moldovoy?," (speech, Glavred, Kiev, April 29, 2009).

15. Yuriy Romanenko et al., "Chto nam delat' s Moldovoy?," (speech, Glavred, Kiev, April 29, 2009).

16. Ibid.

17. *Statisticheskiy yezhegodnik Pridnestrovskoy Moldavskoy Respubliki: 2007 (za 2002–2006 gg.)* (Tiraspol: Ministerstvo ekonomiki Pridnestrov'ya, 2006), 29.

18. Natsional'noye Byuro Statistiki Respubliki Moldova, "Postoyannoye naselenie po osnovnym natsional'nostyam 1959–2004 (po dannym perepisey naseleniya)," http://www.statistica.md/public/files/serii_de_timp/populatie/structura_demografica/2.1.14.xls (accessed August 10, 2011).

19. Kulyk, "Chto nam delat'."

20. "Ukraina i Moldova vveli 'zelenyy koridor' dlya provoza cherez granitsu plodoovoshchnoy produktsii," *Finance.ua*, June 5, 2011, http://news.finance.ua/ru/~/1/0/all /2011/06/05/240844 (accessed August 10, 2011).

21. Pyrozhkov, "Posle 20 let."

22. Vladimir Korobov, "Ukrainskiy vklad v formirovaniye obshchego dnestrovsko-prichernomorskogo ekonomicheskogo makroregiona," in *Moldova–Pridnestrov'ye: Obshchimi usiliyami – k uspeshnomu budushchemu. Ekonomicheskiye aspekty*, ed. Denis Matveev et al. (Chisinau: Cu drag, 2009), 30.

23. Georgiy Byanov, "Pridnestrovskoye uregulirovaniye: Zapadnyy i Vostochnyy vektory kompromissa," in *Moldova–Pridnestrov'ye: Obshchimi usiliyami – k uspeshnomu budushchemu. Peregovornyy protsess*, ed. Denis Matveev et al. (Chisinau: Cu drag, 2009), 36.

24. "Kiyev zayavlyaet, chto nichego ne zabiral u Moldovy," *Zerkalo nedeli*, November 17, 2010, http://news.zn.ua/articles/69373 (accessed August 10, 2011).

25. "Moldova obvinila Ukrainu v popytke peredvinut' granitsu," *Zerkalo nedeli*, November 17, 2010, http://news.zn.ua/articles/69373 (accessed August 10, 2011).

26. "YeS osudil Ukrainu za samoupravstvo na granitse s Moldovoy," *Zerkalo nedeli*, November 25, 2010, http://news.zn.ua/articles/69935 (accessed August 10, 2011).

27. "Ukraina otberet u Moldovy port na Dunaye?," *MIGnews*, December 16, 2010, http://mignews.com.ua/ru/print-articles/55154.html (accessed August 10, 2011).

28. "Ukraina trebuyet ot Moldovy vernut' ey zemlyu," *MIGnews*, April 22, 2011, http://mignews.com.ua/ru/articles/69862.html (accessed August 10, 2011).

29. "Moldova obvinila Ukrainu."

30. "Ukraina postavila ul'timatum Moldove," *MIGnews*, May 7, 2011, http:// mignews.com.ua/ru/articles/70963.html (accessed August 10, 2011).

31. Dohovir mizh Ukrayinoyu i Respublikoyu Moldova pro derzhavnyy kordon [Treaty between Ukraine and the Republic of Moldova on the State Border], Kiev, August 18, 1999, http://zakon1.rada.gov.ua/cgi-bin/laws/main.cgi?nreg=498_046 (accessed August 10, 2011).

32. Ibid.

33. Viktor Yanukovych and Marian Lupu, "Sovmestnoye zayavleniye Prezidenta Ukrainy i i.o. Prezidenta Respubliki Moldova," Kiev, July 9, 2011, http://www.president .gov.ua/news/20721.html (accessed August 10, 2011).

34. Konstantin Minayev, " 'Tochka postavlena...?' Strasti vokrug Palanki," AVA MD. Informatsionno-analiticheskiy portal, July 19, 2011, http://ava.md/analytics-commentary /012153-tochka-postavlena-strasti-vokrug-palanki.html (accessed August 10, 2011).

35. By "Smart Border" it is meant the boundary that promotes a free flow of goods and passengers. A sample of such a border is the present boundary between the United States and Canada. The priorities of such a boundary are stated in the Smart Border Declaration and in the Action Plan For Creating a Secure and Smart Border. It provides the most-favored-nation status for trusted travelers and commercial organizations, transfer of commodity control for these organizations from the border area to loading terminals, modernization of cross-border outlets to eliminate congestions at the boundary. To achieve this aim, the programs, similar to American programs on free and secure trade (FAST), may be enacted, which will require certification of importers and carriers as well as registration of drivers, who afterwards might cross the border in a simplified way along designated lanes; or the program NEXUS, which provides for use of ID for permanent residents to make crossing the border easier.

36. Pyrozhkov, "Posle 20 let."

37. Kulyk, "Chto nam delat'."

Chapter Sixteen

United Kingdom: A Developing Engagement with Moldova*

Ronald J. Hill

Moldova's independence was broadly welcomed by British official opinion. Upon the dissolution of the Soviet Union, the United Kingdom recognized the Republic of Moldova on December 31, 1991, and formally established diplomatic relations within three weeks, on January 17, 1992; the opening of a British embassy in Chisinau took place a decade later, and the first UK ambassador took up his post on July 30, 2002. The first Moldovan ambassador to the United Kingdom was accredited in March 2005.

UK policy toward Moldova has been implemented both bilaterally and through the European Union. The EU's mechanisms include its Common Foreign and Security Policy, and since 2009 the Eastern Partnership Initiative, which covers Moldova and five other countries, trade agreements and, in due course, a more comprehensive Association Agreement. Following the Russo-Georgian conflict in August 2008, the British government, with a specific reference to Moldova, stated that "the UK strongly supports the Eastern Partnership as a tool for deepening the Eastern neighbors' relations with the EU and offering strengthened support for accelerating reforms, approximation and integration"; it expressed the view that "the international community has a common interest in promoting the settlement of these unresolved conflicts," including that in Moldova, and supported the mediation efforts of the EU and the Organization for Security and Cooperation in Europe. As a full member of the European Union, the United Kingdom participates in devising the EU's policy toward Moldova and in negotiating agreements that affect Moldova's relations with all 27 member states. Speaking for the British government in the House of Lords in September 2008, Lord Bach stated that "the UK has played an active role in discussions about the nature of this agreement," adding that a conference would be held at the prestigious, government-backed Wilton Park conference center in the

* I am grateful to Laurence Broyd of the British Foreign and Commonwealth Office for advice in locating materials for this study, and to the former British ambassador to Moldova, John Beyer, for helpful comments on an earlier draft. Neither is responsible for interpretations and opinions expressed here.

following month.[1] That conference, "Moldova: Moving Ahead," was held under the auspices of the Foreign and Commonwealth Office and the Lithuanian Ministry of Foreign Affairs, and was attended by leading figures from both sides of the Dniester, international experts, members of the European Parliament, and others, who presented forthright arguments and positive proposals for establishing Moldova as a united modern state enjoying positive relations with her neighbors, notably the EU. That conference was an occasion for further informal talks in the 5+2 format among the parties in the Moldova-Transnistria conflict resolution process.[2] Policies adopted by the EU and administered through the office of the High Representative of the Union for Foreign Affairs and Security Policy, such as the travel ban on government representatives of Transnistria, are implemented by the United Kingdom authorities, as by those of other EU member states.

Apart from relations mediated through the EU, direct UK-Moldova relations are conducted on several different levels, by government, parliament, and civic organizations.

UK Government and Moldova

The British embassy in Chisinau is the primary channel through which UK policy toward Moldova is implemented, and until March 31, 2011, the governmental agency providing most UK funding for Moldova was the Department for International Development (UKaid). The embassy web site[3] lists many projects funded through DfID since independence, totaling some £35.0 million ($55.0 million or €40.0 million, at 2011 rates) in direct aid. From modest beginnings, aid through this channel stood at about £1.0 million ($1.6 million) in 1999, £4.0 million ($6.3 million) a decade later; the amount in 2010/11 was in the region of £8.0 million ($12.5 million). The main purposes of this aid, coordinated with the Moldovan government's National Development Strategy, are poverty reduction, through projects aimed at sustainable growth, improved governance, including the administration of social welfare provision, and conflict resolution and peace building. Projects that received financial support through UKaid include a joint program with SIDA (the Swedish International Development Cooperation Agency), aimed at improving the efficiency and effectiveness of the social assistance system; this project targeted the Ministry of Health and Social Protection, local authorities, civil society organizations and others; a contribution of £1.4 million ($2.2 million) to a multi-donor trust fund, implemented by the World Bank, supporting reform of public administration in the republic; and about half a million pounds sterling ($780,000) to assist integration of disabled children into the education system, raise awareness of disability and combat prejudice, and in other ways support the needs of those with disabilities; the funding benefited children with disabilities and their parents, professionals working in the area, and local schools and communities.

Smaller sums included £25,000 ($39,000) to the Ministry of Local Public Administration to establish a Regional Development Directorate within the ministry; £20,184 ($31,636) to employ two international consultants to advise the Ministry of the Economy and Trade in designing and managing the planning process and developing the National Development Plan, and giving appropriate training to government administrators in this area; and £11,780 ($18,460) to train farmers to maintain sound financial records and enable them to pay taxes on a fair basis.

The National Bureau of Statistics benefited from a grant of £685,000 (about $1 million) to improve the generation, analysis and use of high-quality statistics, so as to enhance the quality of statistical data and the capacity of administrators to handle statistical materials; follow-up grants supported the Department of Statistics and Sociology in standardizing agricultural statistics through surveys of households' and small farmers' activities, and in integrating the Household Budget Survey and the Labor Force Survey.

In the field of conflict resolution, grants were given to the Belfast-based nongovernmental organization MICOM and its Moldovan partner to bring together local leaders and activists from both sides of the Dniester (see below). Grants totaling £20,000 ($31,000) enabled two Moldovan delegates from the philatelic bureau to attend a seminar in the UK to train managers to promote stamp collecting as a new source of income. Several grants were given to broadcasters, especially for training television and radio journalists and managers.

In all, 70 projects are listed, some incorporating detailed programs. As this selection indicates, the range of UK government-supported activities has been substantial. Significant sums have assisted government projects and individual ministries; others have helped broad categories of organization; and smaller sums have targeted projects for particular groups in Moldovan society.

Following the closure of the DfID's bilateral Moldovan program on March 31, 2011, the UK supports EU and other external agencies in enhancing the country's progress toward EU integration: some 15 percent of the money spent by the EU in Moldova is from the UK.[4]

These activities confirm the normalization of relations between the United Kingdom and Moldova, as do visits by representatives of government and the state, and various bilateral agreements between the two countries. The Republic of Moldova's London embassy web site lists a dozen visits to Moldova between May 1992 and February 2010, including five by Lord Dubs, chairman of the All-Party Parliamentary Group for Moldova (discussed below), one by a member of the British royal family, Prince Michael of Kent (who opened the new embassy building in June 2004), one by a deputy Speaker of the House of Commons, and three by ministerial representatives, including the Minister for Europe in February 2007. Of the 14 senior Moldovan officials who came to the United Kingdom, President Mircea Snegur visited in October 1996, the Foreign Minister on four occasions, the Minister of Defense twice, and the Minister of Finance once; other official visitors included the Chairman of the Moldovan Parliament, the First Deputy Prime Minister and two Deputy Prime Ministers.[5]

Various bilateral agreements have been concluded, some to facilitate the work of DfID, and others to encourage cooperation in defense, counter-trafficking and fraud, including a convention on double taxation—standard measures between friendly states in the modern world.

British representatives have regularly engaged in monitoring elections in Moldova (as in other former Soviet countries), most frequently through the OSCE and its Office of Democratic Institutions and Human Rights, but also through, for example, the Congress of Regional and Local Authorities of the Council of Europe. British observers have occasionally challenged reports of monitoring agencies: the British MEP Baroness Emma Nicholson condemned the 2009 elections as "structurally flawed," even though they had been broadly approved by the ODIHR.[6] In November 2010, the British ambassador himself observed the election in the village of Bursuc, and the FCO posted an interview with him on YouTube.[7] Such activities are, of course, irregular, but they serve to supply feedback to the UK authorities about developments in Moldova—a supplement to the regular reports from the embassy—and they are part of the UK's commitment to supporting democratization.

UK Parliament and Moldova

Apart from formal government-to-government relations, public figures in the United Kingdom have shown a keen interest in Moldovan affairs. On numerous occasions since Moldova's independence, members of the House of Commons have tabled "Early Day Motions" to draw attention to specific issues and problems that have arisen. Although EDMs are rarely debated in parliament, they allow MPs to draw attention to an event or cause. MPs register their support by signing individual motions.

Groups of MPs have repeatedly used this device to raise questions concerning Moldova. A few examples: on September 7, 2004, EDM 1603 sponsored by the Liberal Democrat Mike Hanson, and supported by an additional 23 members from four parties in Parliament, expressed concern at the escalation of tension in the Republic of Moldova and a range of other matters in relations between Moldova, Transnistria and Russia, and called on the British government to condemn actions of the Tiraspol authorities, to assist Russia in fulfilling her commitment to withdraw troops and ammunition, and to be more active in the EU, NATO, and the OSCE "to promote a peaceful solution to the conflict, which would ensure the sovereignty and territorial integrity of the Republic of Moldova."[8] Two months later, on November 23, 2004, EDM 133, sponsored by Mike Hancock and another Liberal Democrat MP, used the establishment of a Moldovan embassy in London as an opportunity to repeat the previous expression of concern and again called on the British government to act.[9] Toward the end of 2008, a more comprehensive motion (316), on the future of Moldova, attracted 56 signatories, principally from the governing Labour Party but also including six

Conservatives, 13 Liberal Democrats, a Scottish Nationalist, representatives of three parties in Northern Ireland, and one independent (non-party) MP. Given its broad support, this motion is worth quoting in full:

> [T]his House reiterates its strong support for the sovereignty and territorial integrity of the Republic of Moldova within internationally recognised borders; supports the European integration perspective of Moldova; strongly encourages early adoption of a new EU-Moldova Agreement to pave the way for Moldova's future EU membership; regrets that significant progress in the Transnistrian settlement process has not been achieved; calls on all parties to resume work towards a sustainable and comprehensive political solution with a special legal status for Transnistria within Moldova; calls for the resumption of the 5+2 negotiation format; recognizes that these negotiations are crucial in achieving a viable settlement respecting the principles of international law and the commitments assumed by the OSCE member states; requests the resumption of Joint Working Group activity on measures to build confidence and security; appreciates the work of the EU Border Assistance Mission in improving security and custom control at the Moldovan-Ukrainian border; welcomes the extension of its mandate after 2009; affirms the necessity of fully implementing the 1999 Istanbul OSCE Summit decision on the withdrawal of Russian forces from the Republic of Moldova's territory; calls for the formation of a multinational mission of civilian observers under an international mandate; and supports the initiative to convene a high level Conference of Donors in 2009 on a post-conflict rehabilitation and development programme for Moldova.[10]

Following the Wilton Park conference, this was a timely reminder of the significance of the "frozen conflict" and an invitation to the UK government to boost its engagement. A motion (560) tabled on January 11, 2010, and signed by 14 MPs, used the retirement of Ambassador Natalia Solcan to note that "since the beginning of her term in office in 2008, the two countries have maintained excellent relations;" it also recognized that she was one of Moldova's youngest ambassadors, and thanked her for "all of her support in tackling human trafficking issues" and extended best wishes for her future.[11]

Early Day Motions focusing on the republic are not the only means by which parliamentarians' awareness of Moldovan affairs is raised. Cases from Moldova arise in the course of the work of parliamentary committees and commissions, and in briefing documents prepared for parliamentary use. For example, on March 15, 2011 the Joint Committee on Human Rights heard evidence from an expert witness, Professor Philip Leach, who referred in passing to the illegal treatment of people in Transnistria;[12] a prominent member of that committee is Lord Dubs, a regular visitor to Moldova. Not infrequently, in the preparation of policy documents comparative information is provided to parliamentarians that brings attention to policy or legislation in Moldova, as one country in the world community. Thus, in 2004 it was reported that the human rights organization Liberty had listed Moldova among the countries in which transsexuals are permitted to amend their birth certificates.[13] In these and other ways, British legislators become aware of Moldova, often in a positive sense. As appropriate, Moldovan authorities address relevant parliamentary committees: the Moldovan embassy in London on June 19, 2009, submitted a document to the Committee on Foreign Affairs, reporting on developments in the South East European Countries Cooperation Process, of which Moldova occupied the chairmanship-in-office.[14]

Since 2006 there has existed the All-Party Parliamentary Group for Moldova, whose purpose is "To develop relationships with parliamentarians in Moldova; to host meetings with ministers and delegations from Moldova; and to inform and brief MPs and peers on the situation in the country." Chaired by Lord Dubs (Labour Party), in the summer of 2011 it had 20 members drawn from the main parliamentary parties and independents in both Houses of Parliament.[15] Members of this Group hold regular meetings with the Moldovan ambassador, and they have naturally been the most prominent in raising parliamentary questions concerning Moldova and its relationship with the UK. These All-Party Groups—there are some 130 devoted to relations with countries and territories—enjoy no official status within parliament, but they do permit interested members from a range of political perspectives to develop expertise, and thereby allow them to raise well-informed and timely questions concerning government policy. They also help to ensure that the countries they engage with can benefit from scholarships to study in the UK, funding for English language lessons, exchanges of specialist groups such as librarians, students and others who in a previous era were subject to bilateral cultural agreements, and similar arrangements. As the Moldova Group's stated purpose indicates, promoting inter-parliamentary links can foster a parliamentary tradition in Moldova and support institutions of civil society.

Such a purpose is also served by the government-sponsored British Council. Although this has no office in Moldova, an employee is attached to the British embassy in Chisinau, which administers various programs that benefit citizens of Moldova. When Alun Michael, MP, a prominent member of the All-Party Group, invited the British government, through the device of a parliamentary question, to improve access for Moldovan citizens to the services of the British Council, the responsible Minister, Jim Murphy, in his reply of July 17, 2008, indicated the range of activities that were being undertaken in Moldova.[16]

The first was the Peacekeeping English Project, a program of English-language teaching for military personnel engaged in international peacekeeping and similar undertakings. According to the PEP officer for Moldova, Ana Anghel, this led to the establishment of a study center associated with the Moldovan Ministry of Defense, where military personnel can follow a special curriculum of English lessons to equip them to function in an international community. It has also entailed the training of specialist English teachers within the Ministry, so that the project can become self-sustaining.[17]

The John Smith Fellowships program offers intensive four-week visits to the UK to the next generation of leaders in politics, local government, and civil society in former Soviet republics, to give direct experience of the functioning of a democratic society and institutions. The John Smith Memorial Trust, which honors the memory of a former leader of the Labour Party, sees the program as "not a short-term scholarship, but a life-changing experience which brings new perspectives, long-term friendships, and a lifetime commitment to good governance." It entails placements, workshops, lectures and events, and meetings with leading figures in British public life, including representatives of Scottish affairs (one week of the program is spent in the Scottish capital, Edinburgh). Toward the end of their visit, fellows present action plans: individual projects that they will pursue on their return to their own country. Since the year 2000, 31 Moldovans have been selected as fellows, and a number have later achieved prominence in Moldova as parliamentarians, ambassadors and governmental officials at both regional and national levels.[18]

Further opportunities include Chevening Scholarships, funded mainly through the FCO, and intended for "talented people who have been identified as potential future leaders across a wide range of fields including politics, business, the media, civil society, religion and academia." Most study for masters' programs in the UK, and benefit from the networking opportunities that such a community offers.[19]

Various further facilities are offered, mainly to extend the teaching of English, either online or through scholarships to the UK.

In addition to governmental and parliamentary involvement, either directly or through EU programs, other agencies have been engaged with Moldova. British-based scholars have included Moldova in their research, either with a specific focus or as part of wider studies of the former Soviet states. These include Luke March (Edinburgh University); Stephen White (Glasgow University) in association with Margot Light (London School of Economics) and the present author; and more recently Elena Korosteleva (Aberystwyth University) and an international team of scholars; Stefan Wolff (University of Birmingham), has focused on the Transnistria conflict, as have John Beyer (St. Antony's College, Oxford), and Andrew Williams (formerly of the University of Kent at Canterbury).

Williams also participated (as did the author) in the work of the NGO, MICOM (Moldovan Initiative Committee of Management), inspired by a Belfast peace activist, Joe Camplisson. On his personal initiative, in the 1990s he made contact with the heads of government of the Republic of Moldova and Transnistria, and was inspired by the positive response to set up the NGO. Assisted by experts and specialists in conflict resolution, over several years in the late 1990s MICOM brought together representatives of public life at all levels in Moldova and Transnistria, using the experience of the Northern Ireland troubles and the complex negotiations of the peace process to help Moldovan participants in analyzing and—it was hoped—resolving their differences. Supported financially by the Michigan-based C. S. Mott Foundation and, for specific purposes, the British government through the DfID, MICOM and its NGO partner on the ground, the Joint Committee for Democratization and Conciliation (JCDC), organized three workshops in the "neutral" Black Sea resort of Albena (Bulgaria), and brought representatives of both sides to Northern Ireland, where they met politicians and activists from all sides of the conflict there. The credibility

of MICOM among visitors from both sides was enhanced by the active involvement as chairman from 1994 of Raymond Jolliffe, Lord Hylton, whose
long interest in Northern Ireland affairs and concern for conflict resolution, peace-
building, and inter-faith relations commended him to all parties. The representatives of Russia, Ukraine and the OSCE supported and repeatedly attended these
gatherings, which enjoyed some success in enabling dialogue—but the fact that
the conflict remains unresolved indicates the limitations of such bottom-up approaches.[20] MICOM also, in 1998, made a submission to the parliamentary Select
Committee on International Development investigation of "Conflict Prevention
and Post-Conflict Reconstruction," outlining the history of the Moldovan conflict and assessing the failure of conventional approaches to its resolution.[21]

More recently, the former UK ambassador to Moldova, John Beyer, undertook a study of opinion on both sides of the Dniester under the auspices of the
"Saferworld" organization, with EU financial support. His report made recommendations for action by all interested parties to overcome the stalemate in
relations between Chisinau and Tiraspol.[22]

There is clear interest in Moldova in certain circles, and a growing body of
experience and expertise on which both British and Moldovan policymakers can
draw in handling the developing relationship.

Trade

Trade between Soviet Moldavia and the UK was invisible, since all foreign trade
was handled by the relevant USSR Ministry in Moscow. The bulk of Moldovan
exports went to other parts of the Soviet Union, mainly wine and cognac, tobacco and tobacco products, clothing, and agricultural products, both fresh and
processed.

Since independence, Moldova has sought new markets: a ban on Moldovan
wine imports imposed by Russia in 2006 and again in 2010—ostensibly over
health concerns—demonstrated the vulnerability of reliance on traditional markets. Suspicion of Russia's intentions, and the continuing stalemate over Transnistria, have led Moldova to diversify both its markets and its sources of foreign
direct investment, with a particular trend toward the European Union, including
the UK. According to a 2009 study of EU-Moldova trade potential, companies
in the EU now comprise some 80.0 percent of the FDI stock in Moldova, of
which 6.8 percent is held by British companies;[23] in October 2009, 108 joint-
stock companies with British social capital operated in Moldova.[24] During
1995–2010, according to official statistics, the value of Moldovan exports to the
UK increased by 64 times.[25] In 2010, Moldova exported goods to the UK to the
value of $82.1 million, against UK-sourced imports of $52.6 million; the UK
was the country's fifth largest market, taking 5.3 percent of Moldova's exports,
mainly clothing.

One of Moldova's main quality products—wine—has also been marketed in the UK, although in relatively small quantities to date. According to a longstanding rumor, Queen Elizabeth II favors Moldovan wine, notably the full-bodied red Negru de Purcari. I heard of this as a graduate student in 1967, and it appears regularly in features about the Moldovan wine industry, although it cannot be verified. Britain's major wine-importing mail-order company has been distributing a small range of Moldovan wines for some years through two outlets;[26] in Spring 2009, a new company was established to import superior Moldovan wines into the UK.[27] There may be scope to expand this trade, particularly following current and future trade liberalization measures for a dozen agricultural products central to the Moldovan economy. A new Association Agreement between Moldova and the EU, under negotiation since January 2010, is expected to replace the Partnership and Cooperation Agreement, in force since 1998; in parallel the EU's Autonomous Trade Preferences will develop into a Deep and Comprehensive Free Trade Area that will fully open up all countries of the European Union to Moldova as a trading partner.[28] On July 1, 2011, a new tariff arrangement increased Moldova's export quotas for barley, maize (corn), and wheat for the years 2013–15, and substantially increased the volume of wine that could be exported to the EU—an additional 6.6 million bottles for 2011 alone, rising substantially in the years to 2015. Opportunities for the export of other products including meat, dairy, and eggs will depend on meeting the EU's health requirements.[29] The steady liberalization of trade, dependent on continuing reforms within Moldova, should lead to greater access to the UK market and bring Moldovan products to British consumers.

Moldova and the British public

The British public knows very little about Moldova: few are able to identify it on a map, or even know its approximate location on the globe. It is less than four hours' flying time from London, but there are few direct flights, and those that do operate are not convenient.[30] This reflects, above all, the poor development of Moldova as a tourist destination. In the Soviet era, few tours from the West included Moldavia, and then for only two or three nights along with, perhaps, Kiev, Lviv, or Odessa, and a Russian city or two. Apart from the occasional student (I believe I was the only one), a musician on an official tour of Soviet cities, an engineer installing equipment, and a few hundred visitors (at most) whose package tours included Chisinau, the few British visitors to Moldova were mostly communists on "pilgrimages" to the Soviet Motherland. Direct access to Moldova is now available and unrestricted for private visitors, opening the prospect of tourism for hikers, or tourism based on the wine industry, for both of which vacation-ready markets exist in the UK. However, that is at best a matter for the future. Mass tourism from Britain is unlikely.

The country features occasionally in the British media. A television series in 2007 and a spin-off book by the popular traveler, Michael Palin, included a segment on Moldova and Transnistria.[31] A more quirky reference to Moldova was the account by the comedian, Tony Hawks, of his attempt—ultimately successful—to fulfill a wager that he could play every member of the Moldovan soccer team at tennis;[32] a film version was due for release in 2011. The author used proceeds from the sale of this book to fund the Hippocrates Children's Centre for disabled children in Chisinau.[33]

Further contact is through volunteer groups, including students working in orphanages and on similar humanitarian projects. One such Christian volunteer had visited Moldova 44 times over the past eight years with teams of adult and youth volunteers from the Isle of Lewis in the Outer Hebrides (Scotland). Working closely with Christian organizations in Moldova to engage with youth organizations, schools, hospitals, children's homes and similar bodies, they supplied clothing, gifts and toiletries, and provided fire tenders and ambulances. Children's summer camps have been supplemented by visits to Lewis and by "twinning" arrangements between schools, and a street in the village of Nisporeni has been named after the main town on Lewis, Stornoway.[34]

Such contacts, however few, can only enhance UK citizens' knowledge and awareness of Moldova, an unknown place for the overwhelming majority, except for mainly negative press reports. The fact that Moldova is poor may be known, and it is presented in popular publications as a source of young women lured into prostitution in Western Europe, including Britain. Some of the lurid aspects of this human trafficking are presented in a book on international crime by the British investigative journalist, Misha Glenny.[35] A British charitable organization, The New Hope Trust, declares that Moldova's "current major export is young women destined for the international sex trade."[36] Although it is not suggested that huge numbers end up in the UK, certainly some do, as highlighted in the story of "Katya," sent back to Moldova from Britain only to be brutally treated and again trafficked into the United Kingdom.[37] Such stories are not uncommon, and they do not entice the British public to think positively of Moldova. Neither do alarmist press reports, supported by virtually xenophobic anti-immigration organizations, that 80,000—or, in one unsupported assertion, a million—Moldovans are poised to flood into the United Kingdom through the simple mechanism of obtaining a Romanian passport.[38] Even the respected *Daily Telegraph* covered this story, under the heading: "Romania opens back door for thousands of Moldovans to claim benefits in Britain."[39]

Given this background of negative public opinion, it is perhaps surprising that relations between the two countries are as good as they are.

Conclusion

United Kingdom-Moldovan relations have followed a positive upward trajectory of engagement, directly and through the EU. For the UK, Moldova is a partner that is struggling to emerge from the shadow of the Soviet Union and its successor, the Russian Federation, to take its independent place in the European community of nations. Much of the UK's attention is directed toward resolving conflict, eliminating poverty, and promoting democratic values and institutions, including civil society organizations, and reforming and retraining state institutions and public servants. There is little positive attraction for British citizens at present: Moldova's public image in Britain is largely negative. An active group of parliamentarians closely monitors Moldovan affairs, and brings problems to the attention of government and opinion leaders, who need not, therefore, rely on scurrilous press accounts. Also, by fostering positive developments in Moldova, British authorities can help to counteract factors that push Moldovan citizens toward emigration, even though the UK will remain attractive to Moldovans.

For Moldova, the UK is an important member of the EU, which Moldova aspires to join eventually, and a potentially large market for certain exports. Members of the elite, particularly from the generation of future leaders, can gain experience of British institutions and way of life through training schemes and other channels supported by the UK government. The experience of the Belfast peace process may be useful in resolving the country's biggest domestic problem—the conflict over the eastern territory of Transnistria, in which the UK is engaged both directly and through multilateral organizations.

Both countries, it seems, see the relationship as developing satisfactorily—perhaps surprisingly, given the lack of engagement in the past.

Notes

1. See http://www.publications.parliament.uk/pa/ld200708/ldhansrd/text/80929w0022.htm (accessed September 3, 2011).

2. The "5+2 format" refers to the two Moldovan parties, Russia, Ukraine, the OSCE, and two observers, the EU and the US.

3. See http://ukinmoldova.fco.gov.uk/en (accessed August 9, 2011).

4. British Embassy to Moldova, "Moldova and the UK: Development through Partnership," April 11, 2011, http://ukinmoldova.fco.gov.uk/en/about-us/working-with-moldova/development1/030DFID-moldova-graduation (accessed August 10, 2011).

5. Moldovan Embassy to the UK, "Bilateral relations between the Republic of Moldova and the United Kingdom of Great Britain and Northern Ireland," May 2010, http://www.britania.mfa.gov.md/bilateral-relations-rm-uk (accessed August 10, 2011); Deputy Prime Minister Iurie Leancă visited London in September 2011.

6. Brian Whitmore, "Moldova Vote Controversy Highlights Doubts Over Monitoring," *Radio Free Europe/Radio Liberty*, April 21, 2009, http://www.rferl.org/content/Moldova_Vote_Controversy_Highlights_Doubts_Over_Monitoring/1613208.html (accessed September 4, 2011).

7. "Election monitoring in Bursuc: Impressions of Keith Shannon," YouTube video, 0:53, posted by "ukforeignoffice," November 29, 2010, http://www.youtube.com/watch?v=5PpgEiNQ7nI&NR=1 (accessed September 4, 2011).

8. http://www.parliament.uk/edm/2003-04/1603 (accessed August 22, 2011).

9. http://www.parliament.uk/edm/2004-05/133 (accessed August 9, 2011).

10. http://www.parliament.uk/edm/2008-09/316 (accessed August 22, 2011).

11. http://www.parliament.uk/edm/2009-10/560 (accessed August 9, 2011).

12. "Minutes of evidence taken before Joint Committee on Human Rights (uncorrected transcript)," March 15, 2011, 27, http://www.parliament.uk/documents/joint-committees/human-rights/HumanRightsJudgments/Transcript150311.pdf (accessed August 22, 2011).

13. *The Gender Recognition Bill*, House of Commons Research Paper 04/15 (London, 2004), on 17, http://www.parliament.uk/documents/commons/lib/research/rp2004/rp04-015.pdf (accessed August 25, 2011).

14. http://www.publications.parliament.uk/pa/cm200809/cmselect/cmfaff/memo/miscmatt/ucmi9202.htm (accessed August 25, 2011).

15. http://www.publications.parliament.uk/pa/cm/cmallparty/register/moldova.htm (accessed August 25, 2011).

16. http://www.publications.parliament.uk/pa/cm200708/cmhansrd/cm080717/text/80717w0039.htm#080717102000085 (accessed August 25, 2011).

17. Ana Anghel, "PEP Moldova: A Model of Diplomacy," *Peacekeeping English Project Newsletter*, no. 32 (October 2008): 7, http://www.britishcouncil.org/pep32.pdf (accessed August 26, 2011).

18. See the website of the Trust, http://www.johnsmithmemorialtrust.org/web/site/home/home.asp (accessed August 26, 2011).

19. Foreign and Commonwealth Office, "Chevening Scholarships," http://www.fco.gov.uk/en/about-us/what-we-do/scholarships/chevening (accessed August 25, 2011).

20. For an engaged account of this process, see Michael Hall and Joe Camplisson, *From Conflict Containment to Resolution: The Experiences of a Moldovan–Northern Ireland Self-help Initiative* (Newtownabbey, Northern Ireland: Island Publications, 2002).

21. The submission is available as Select Committee on International Development, "Appendices to the Minutes of Evidence – Sixth Report, Appendix 7," http://www.publications.parliament.uk/pa/cm199899/cmselect/cmintdev/55/55ap08.htm   (accessed August 25, 2011).

22. See *Routes across the Nistru: Transnistria: People's Peacemaking Perspectives* (London: Saferworld, 2011).

23. Expert Grup, *A Free Trade Area between the Republic of Moldova and the European Union: Feasibility, Perspectives and Potential Impact* (Chisinau, 2009), 17, http://www.expert-grup.org/library_upld/d51.pdf (accessed August 16, 2011).

24. Moldovan Embassy to the UK, "Bilateral relations."

25. Calculated from data compiled by the National Bureau of Statistics of the Republic of Moldova, "External trade," http://www.statistica.md/category.php?l=en&idc=336 (accessed September 29, 2011); figures for exports and imports are taken from this source.

26. See the relevant websites: http://www.laithwaites.co.uk and http://www.sunday-timeswineclub.co.uk (accessed September 2, 2011).

27. See the company's website: http://www.imperia-uk.com (accessed September 2, 2011).

28. Evghenia Sleptsova, "Shedding Light on the Ongoing EU-Moldova Trade Liberalisation," Eastern Partnership Community, January 27, 2011, http://www.eastern-partnership.org/community/debate/shedding-light-ongoing-eu-moldova-trade-liberalisation (accessed September 5, 2011).

29. See European Commission, "EU grants greater access to Moldova's exports from 1st July," July 1, 2011, http://trade.ec.europa.eu/doclib/press/index.cfm?id=722 (accessed September 5, 2011).

30. Flights into Chisinau arrived during the night in the Summer 2011 schedule.

31. Michael Palin, *New Europe* (London: Weidenfeld & Nicolson, 2007), 116–29.

32. Tony Hawks, *Playing the Moldovans at Tennis* (London: Ebury, 2000).

33. *Wikipedia*, s.v. "Hippocrates Centre," last modified June 30, 2011, http://en.wikipedia.org/wiki/Hippocrates_Centre; "Philantrophy," on Tony Hawks' official website, http://www.tony-hawks.com/philanthropy.php (accessed September 2, 2011); see also Tony Hawks, "I tried to show Moldovans as they are, and they are nice," interview with *Info-Prim Neo*, May 14, 2011, http://www.allmoldova.com/en/int/interview/tony-hawks-140511.html (accessed September 4, 2011).

34. British Embassy to Moldova, "British Volunteers," August 23, 2011, http://ukinmoldova.fco.gov.uk/en/about-us/working-with-moldova/british-volunteers (accessed September 4, 2011).

35. Misha Glenny, *McMafia: Seriously Organised Crime* (London: Bodley Head, 2008), 124–29.

36. The New Hope Trust, "Moldova," http://www.newhopetrust.org/index.php/about/moldova (accessed 16 Aug. 2011).

37. Amelia Gentleman, "Katya's Story: Trafficked to the UK, Sent Home to Torture," *The Guardian*, April 19, 2011, http://www.guardian.co.uk/law/2011/apr/19/sex-trafficking-uk-legal-reform (accessed August 16, 2011); this article evoked a widespread response.

38. Jason Lewis, "Now 80,000 Moldovans Eye UK Move," *Daily Mail*, September 16, 2006, http://www.dailymail.co.uk/news/article-405481; Macer Hall, "1m. Moldovans Head for Britain due to Loophole in EU Law," *Daily Express*, July 19, 2010, http://www.express.co.uk/posts/view/187747 (both accessed September 7, 2011).

39. *Daily Telegraph*, July 18, 2010, http://www.telegraph.co.uk/news/worldnews/europe/moldova/7897094/Romania-opens-back-door-for-thousands-of-Moldovans-to-claim-benefits-in-Britain.html (accessed September 7, 2011).

Chapter Seventeen

United States: Rewriting the Post-Soviet Narrative in Moldova

William Schreiber

In December 1991, the United States was quick to welcome Moldovan independence, recognizing the emergent state—along with the other former Soviet
republics. Yet in many ways, US foreign policy toward Moldova during the past
twenty years has continued to be defined, and often limited, by policy frameworks residual from the Cold War. Throughout the 1990s and early 2000s, experts and politicians noted a US foreign policy in Moldova afflicted by disconti-
nuity. This article argues that for the past twenty years, the US has repeatedly
demonstrated its appreciation for Moldova's potential as a strategic partner in
the region. Proportional to its size, Moldova commands enough attention and
spending from the United States to make it clear that the weaknesses in this
relationship stem from no simple case of neglect. Yet while the US presence in
Moldova has been replete with foreign aid and good intentions, it all too often
lacked a concrete, long-term political strategy.

Conversely, there is reason to believe that the relationship is headed in a
positive direction. Many former constraints on the bilateral relationship have
been removed. Since the elections of 2009, long-term ideological differences
between the US and previous Moldovan governments seem, at least for the
moment, a thing of the past. The bilateral trade relationship seems ready to benefit from the long-overdue repeal of irrelevant restrictions. Finally, changes in
global foreign policy style, a willingness on the part of the US to "lead from
behind" its European allies seem to have particularly promising applications in
Moldova.

The March 2011 visit of US Vice President Joseph Biden to Chisinau was
emblematic of the renewed hopes for US foreign policy in Moldova. Biden's
presence, as the highest ranking official to visit Moldova in the history of bilateral relations, indicated increased US interest in the country, and the large and
largely supportive audience show that many Moldovans maintain a positive
image of the United States and its ability to bring positive change.

Yet most tellingly, Biden's message was not exclusively one of unilateral
leadership. The vice president made it clear that the chief aim of the United
States in Moldova was supporting the country's path to the European Union.

Channeling American foreign aid and political clout through the stable policy structures of the European Union in Moldova could deliver promising results.

Yet US advocacy for EU membership is only the most recent example of how the US-Moldovan relationship is often somehow more than bilateral. The presence of third-party considerations well predates active EU policy in Moldova. At least in the first two decades of the relationship, it was Russia that played the primary role in determining the direction of US policy, whether in terms of an adversarial confrontation in Moscow's "sphere of privileged interests" or an uneasy cooperation in regional security. So finally, the relaxation of tensions with Russia, which the Obama administration titled Russian reset, is a final positive factor for US relations with the country.

US Strategic Interests in Moldova

Throughout the twentieth century, Moldova played a pivotal role in defining the geopolitical terms of Russia's often-confrontational relationship with the Western powers. In a protocol of the Molotov-Ribbentrop Pact, the Soviet Union claimed Bessarabia, Northern Bukovina, and Hertsa—a region strategically important because of the Dniester river, a convenient defensive line between the West and key Ukrainian objectives like Kiev and Odessa.[1]

The maintenance of Moldova as a buffer zone unaligned with Western powers only increased in importance with the 2004 NATO accession of Romania. Since that date, Moldova has been the only neutral barrier between the US-led alliance and the Russian Black Sea Fleet anchored in Sevastopol. Consideration of this strategic balance is enshrined in Moldova's constitutional neutrality, which at least in the short-term prevents it from joining NATO—or any other security alliance, whether led by CIS states or even the European Union.[2]

Of course, one of the Cold War's lessons was that ideas, not only geography, have the power to shape history. Moldova is also a strategic objective in the struggle for hearts and minds. As Damon Wilson, a former senior director for European affairs on the National Security Council noted, there is a prevailing narrative that democratic governance does not work in the post-Soviet Union. For the United States, Moldova is an opportunity to change that narrative, a country where a relatively small investment could make a large difference.[3]

Beyond its strategic position in the region, Moldova matters to the United States as a border country of Western institutions. In the context of a global war on terror, issues related to trafficking, border security and internal stability have brought US attention to Moldova. Thus, even while it lacks in relative terms many of the predictable drivers of US interest—a large diaspora, natural resources, significant investment or trade potential—Moldova has at least three compelling reasons for a global power concerned with stability in the international system to engage with it: geopolitics, ideology and international stability.

These interests have created clear but often generalized objectives for US policy in Moldova. The United States opened an embassy in Chisinau in March, 1992, and since the formal establishment of diplomatic relations, the aims of U.S. diplomacy in Moldova have been, if not concretely detailed, at least consistent. Former US Ambassador Asif Chaudhry (2008 to 2011) summarized four key pillars of US foreign policy in Moldova during a speech at the Carnegie Endowment: support for a democratic tradition, the preservation of Moldovan sovereignty within internationally recognized borders, the development of a robust market economy, and finally, Moldova's integration in European institutions.[4]

Political, Defense and Security Relations

Support for the democratic tradition in Moldova is an umbrella phrase for advocacy of fair and free elections, anti-corruption, the rule of law, and fair governance, particularly in its use of administrative resources and regulation of media, two areas of concern for the US throughout the late 1990s and early 2000s. Promotion of these objectives has been a constant in the US-Moldovan diplomatic discourse, and it remains an important condition of most US foreign aid to Moldova.

Since 2003, US government-funded organizations like the International Republican Institute, the National Endowment for Democracy and the National Democratic Institute have been active in promoting democracy, civil society and the reform of public institutions in Moldova.[5] These organizations conduct independent public opinion surveys, consult and train political actors, and fund NGO and grassroots-based initiatives. In the US, they play a role in shaping how policy makers in Congress and the State Department view Moldova. Republican Senator John McCain, chairman of the IRI, visited Moldova in June 2011.[6] The 2008 republican presidential candidate was the first American legislator to do so since 1999, when congressmen Curt Weldon and Dennis Kucinich visited.

McCain's arrival in Chisinau was a clear sign of support for the newly-elected Alliance for European Integration. McCain, like Vice President Joseph Biden, has only recently become an active Moldova advocate, telling audiences that "when we see little Moldova, now governed by democrats, but struggling against forces internal and external that want to drag it back into darkness, we must recognize the same challenges that Western Europe faced after the War."[7]

This recent influx of activism and unambiguous rhetoric from several prominent US politicians is a departure from US policy over the previous two decades. Until 2010, an important corollary to the support of democracy in Moldova was studied neutrality in the often schismatic landscape of Moldovan domestic politics. US embassy staff were emphatic during the 2010 elections, which pitted the incumbent Communists against the liberal AEI coalition that America was willing to work with either side.[8]

This attitude explains how even during the reign of the nominally Communist president, Vladimir Voronin, the US was able to maintain a cooperative and pragmatic relationship. This relationship functioned even though Voronin's counterpart, George W. Bush, placed a premium on ideological affinity. There could be no greater symbolic image of this neutrality than the meeting and joint press conference between Bush and Voronin in December 2002.[9]

In fact, US engagement in Moldova has a certain tradition of unlikely successes. US-Moldovan relations were born during the early 1990s, a time of public divide over the US role in the world at large, and specifically in the Balkans. The United States, after the Vietnam War and a disastrous 1982 peacekeeping mission in Beirut, was wary of long-lasting military commitments in Eastern European conflicts, especially the rapidly escalating conflict stemming from the breakup of Yugoslavia. Moldova, waging its own bloody civil war, was quickly conflated with its troubled Balkan neighbors.

The United States had only begun to engage in Bosnia in 1992, when Secretary of State James Baker visited Moldova in a July tour of the region, during which he dedicated the American embassy in Chisinau. In a press conference before the visit, Baker was asked by a reporter whether US involvement in Bosnia would set precedents for involvement in "many other areas like Moldova and other parts of the Soviet Union."[10] It was an obvious reference to the then still ongoing Transnistrian War. Baker replied that while the US could not be the world's policeman, it would not stand by and watch a "humanitarian nightmare" unfold. Fortunately, the violence of the Moldovan civil war ended the same month of Baker's visit; the US relationship with Moldova would not be defined by crisis intervention.

Nevertheless, US support for a Moldova whole and free within its internationally recognized borders quickly became another foreign policy priority. The tone of the US role in the conflict was not set by Baker's trip, but rather by the first public joint meeting at the executive level. In 1995, Moldovan President Mircea Snegur paid a visit to the United States, not long after an Organization for Security and Cooperation in Europe summit in Budapest. President Bill Clinton received Snegur, and the two discussed Moldova's economic progress toward a liberalized market system, increasing the levels of US aid and assistance, and the OSCE negotiations on the resolution of the Transnistrian conflict. Both presidents emphasized the importance of the withdrawal of the Russian Fourteenth Army according to the terms of a three-year withdrawal plan then on the table.[11]

From 1995 forward, all the OSCE heads of mission in Moldova have been US citizens.[12] Whether the Budapest summit or Clinton's public reception of Snegur played a role in deciding this arrangement is uncertain at best. William H. Hill, one former OSCE mission head, described a much more fundamental reason for the US appointment: The Moldovan side sought a natural and consistent counterweight to Russian influence.[13]

For the United States, its interest in cooperating with Moldova on security in Transnistria and defense issues more broadly was only intensified by the War on Terror.

Official defense cooperation at the high level began in January 1995, when Moldovan President Snegur and US Secretary of Defense William Perry signed the Joint Statement on Future US-Moldovan and Defense and Military Relations.[14] However, since it was constitutionally neutral, and since the NATO alliance is the primary framework for US defense cooperation in Europe, Moldova did not enjoy significant defense or security cooperation with the United States during the ten years following the joint statement.

Then in 2003, the Moldovan government passed a measure condemning the September 11 terrorist attacks on the United States. With parliamentary approval, Moldova joined Operation Iraqi Freedom. From 2003 to 2008, Moldova deployed six contingents to Iraq, each attached to a US brigade. Moldovans participated in routine duties like patrols, convoy security, and engineer reconnaissance. Their Explosive Ordinance Disposal teams were perhaps the most noted: Moldovan forces discovered and destroyed well over 540,000[15] articles of unexploded ordinance.[16] Moldovan Army Lt. Col. Alexandru Cebanu, Moldovan representative at US Central Command headquarters, credited de-mining expertise that Moldovan engineers and sappers had obtained during the Transnistrian War and its aftermath.[17] During Operation Iraqi Freedom, the US military provided Moldovan troops with significant training and equipment.

However, the joint defense cooperation was also the opening for greater US involvement in the Transnistrian conflict. In 2004, not long after Moldova joined Operation Iraqi Freedom, Secretary of Defense Donald Rumsfeld visited Chisinau. Rumsfeld, then the highest-ranking official to make the trip, nominally arrived to thank Moldova for its de-mining specialists—but he used the trip to address the problem of Russian troops in Transnistria, which after the 2004 NATO enlargement, were now stationed on the "border of NATO."[18]

The following year, Moldovan President Voronin signed an Individual Partnership Action Plan with the alliance during a 2005 visit to Brussels. No doubt in response to the same concerns Rumsfeld raised the previous year, NATO was now reaching out to Moldova. It assisted Moldova with defense reform and granted it interoperability with alliance partner nations, ostensibly with an eye to future Moldovan participation in regional peacekeeping missions.[19] Cooperation between Moldova and NATO increased throughout the mid-to-late 2000s, with Moldova becoming noticeably more active in the Partnership for Peace, NATO's outreach initiative with several post-Soviet states. In 2006, Moldova hosted interoperability exercises known as Cooperative Longbow/Lancer in Bulboaca.[20] In 2007, Moldova hosted the Medical Training Exercise for Central and East Europe according to an agreement with US European Command.[21]

Overall, US efforts to engage with Moldova bilaterally and via NATO have proved much more successful than efforts to rid Transnistria of Russian troops. Policy clashes between the US and Russia in the region have proved counter-

productive to the interests of both nations, for example in preventing cooperation through of the Treaty on Conventional Armed Forces in Europe.

Written in 1999 at an OSCE summit meeting in Istanbul, this adapted version of a Cold War treaty would have committed Russia to withdrawing its
troops by 2002. By 2004, Russia did indeed withdraw a considerable amount of
ordinance and heavy weapons, but some troops remained.[22] Due to Russia's
failure to withdraw its forces, the US, along with other NATO partner countries,
refused to ratify the treaty until the so-called Istanbul commitments (also including Russian troop withdrawals in Georgia) are satisfied. As a result, both sides
have lost access to common goods that would have accompanied the treaty's
implementation, including the right to inspect and monitor the troops deployed
by other parties in the region.

While prior engagement in the negotiations was usually accomplished
through the OSCE, since the establishment of the 5+2 format in 2005, with the
US and EU serving as permanent observers, the US role in solving the conflict
has become more official, but no more pronounced. The United States seems to
have deferred to the leadership of European partners like Germany in reopening
negotiations.

Outside the realm of conventional troop levels, the war on terror has intensified incentives for the US to help solve the Transnistrian conflict in a second
security-related dimension, since border security and anti-trafficking assumed a
new importance for the United States.

Transnistria, where it exists in US public perception, is portrayed as a dangerous trafficking region, particularly of trafficked weapons. The *Washington
Times* called it a "gunrunners' haven," claiming it had proof that several Alazan
rockets and "dirty bombs" had gone missing.[23] A most probably inauthentic
memoir by Nicholai Lilin, *A Siberian Education*, described organized crime,
including trafficking, in the Transnistrian town of Bendery. John Malkovich has
reportedly signed on to play in a film adaption of the novelistic account.[24]

The public's concerns are well reflected in political discourse. In July 2011,
Senator Richard Lugar, the ranking member of the Committee on Foreign Relations, ordered a delegation to travel to Moldova and assess the seizure of 9 kg of
highly enriched uranium by Moldovan authorities the previous month. The report found that the uranium likely originated at facilities in Russia and travelled
to Chisinau via Transnistria. It also noted that several individuals involved in the
sale were Transnistrian residents.[25]

The United States has provided Moldova with border security assistance
since the beginning of bilateral relations. In the mid-1990s, Congress purchased
Moldovan MiG fighter jets capable of nuclear strikes in order to prevent their
sale to hostile or rogue states like Iran. The Department of Energy has provided
radioactivity detectors and infrared cameras to the Ukrainian border. As the CFR
report noted, "Since 2005, ten interdictions of radioactive materials have occurred, and 587 illicit weapons shipments have been interrupted on the Ukrainian-Moldovan border," and it claimed further that several of the Moldovan agents

who intercepted the enriched uranium in June 2011 had only weeks before returned from training programs in the US.[26]

Border security will likely remain one area where the United States is not content to follow the European Union's lead. The congressional report pointed to two holes in the European Union Border Assistance Mission to Moldova and Ukraine, established by the EU in 2005: first, there is no screening for radioactive materials on flights. Second, EU personnel play only an advisory role and are not themselves involved in the screening process. The report concluded that limited US assistance to Moldova for border security did not seem to match the threat. Since the report was issued, the US government's Nuclear Smuggling Outreach Initiative signed a 2011 joint action plan with the Moldovan government.[27]

Some of the most innovative US strategies to promote Transnistria's reintegration into Moldova proper have been on economic terms. A case in point was the exploration of possible routes for highways funded by development funds from the US Millennium Corporation Challenge. Even though cost-benefit analysis revealed that highways spanning Transnistria and Moldova would not put the funds to optimal use, the US acquired extra funding to conduct feasibility studies on one of the Transnistrian routes, saving future investors time and significant expenditure.[28]

Another incidental contribution came from the Department of Commerce, which issued a 2001 anti-dumping order against steel from the Transnistria-based firms like Moldova Steel Works on the basis of less-than-fair value sales. Previously, the United States had provided a large market for Transnistrian steel, as firms would import steel wiring and rebar to create secondary products.[29] The decision to block Transnistrian imports was inspired not by government policy, but by a petition from a group of US steelmakers.[30] The anti-dumping order was upheld in 2007, against an appeal from Moldova Steel Works during the order's sunset clause.[31] As Moldova gradually integrates economically with the European Union, it may become clear that unification could provide Transnistrian industry with tempting new markets. Whether the modest incentives of new markets can outweigh the tens of millions to be made by elites smuggling everything from metal products to highly enriched uranium is another question.

Economic Relations

Moldova has consistently received a disproportionately high amount of foreign aid from the US when compared to other post-Soviet neighbors. Over the past decade, however, this allocation gradually declined, in keeping with regional trends. In 2000 the allocation was $106.82 million, for example; by 2009, it had shrunk to $20.17 million.[32] This was a consequence of shifting US attention to the Middle East and extensive development efforts in Afghanistan and Iraq.

Still, US aid spending spiked in 2010, when Moldova received the single largest investment of US aid to date in the form of the Millennium Challenge Corporation. The Millennium Fund was established by Congress to help the development of post-Soviet states. Following the successful implementation of a $24.7 million Threshold Country Program as a trial run, US Secretary of State Hillary Clinton and Moldovan Prime Minister Vlad Filat signed a new $262 million MCC compact in January 2010. Over a five-year period, the funds will go toward economic development and investment projects in irrigation infra-structure, high-value agricultural production, and road rehabilitation.

Some have linked the AEI election victory to the sudden influx of aid money. In reality, top US officials claim Moldova under Communist rule was at the top of its class when it came to engaging with the fund. Development of the compact took approximately two years, and MCC officials worked with Moldo-van Communist counterparts throughout these two years. In fact, there were some fears that the election of a new government would derail the compact.[33]

Yet the AEI was quick to agree to the terms that had been hammered out by their predecessors, and the newly elected government was able to cash in on the MCC compact early in their term. In another recent example of a US policy maker breaking from the tradition of neutrality, the US cashed in as well. Hillary Clinton spoke frankly about the Communist government: "We know it was not easy. We know that it came at political cost. But it was so important because it has established a democratic Moldova that has, for the first time, a democratical-ly elected prime minister in eight years."[34]

Foreign aid, combined with what may have been politically fortuitous cir-cumstances, is an example of US policy at its best. Unfortunately, other aspects of the economic relationship, particularly trade, display US foreign policy at its worst.

Despite its status as a full member of the World Trade Organization since 2001, Moldova is still subject to US trade restrictions under Title IV of the Trade Act of 1974, an arrangement better known as the Jackson-Vanik amend-ment. Designed in response to a Brezhnev-era policy that restricted Jewish emi-gration from the Soviet Union, Jackson-Vanik influences Most-Favored-Nation tariff status (now referred to in the US as Normal Trade Relation status) with regard to US trade with "Communist or formerly Communist countries that restrict emigration or other human rights."[35]

After the breakup of the Soviet Union, the legislation continued to apply to the twelve former Soviet Republics. During the 1990s, Congress signed a series of trade agreements with these countries, essentially providing waivers to the Title IV restriction.[36] The US signed such an agreement with Moldova in July 1992, thus providing the basis for reciprocal MFN status.[37] The problem is that the waiver agreement is not a permanent solution—it must be granted again each year by the US president. The uncertainty attached to Jackson-Vanik has been widely cited by both Moldovan diplomats and US experts on Moldova as ham-pering trade between the two countries, especially the development of Moldovan exports.[38] Some economic analysts suggest the effect on trade is mostly psycho-logical, since the actual risk of the waiver disappearing is minimal.

For whatever reason, the United States has maintained relatively low levels of trade with Moldova since the country's independence, particularly in compar-ison to the country's European and Eurasian partners. The US is also behind other global powers. In 2010, the United States was ranked ninth in Moldovan imports (directly behind Brazil), eighth for exports to Moldova (directly behind Kazakhstan) and ninth in overall trade volume (directly behind China). In each category, the US balance accounted for 1 percent or less of Moldova's trade volume.[39]

The top export category for both countries is agricultural goods. US exports to Moldova are dominated by animal and vegetable products, as well as pre-pared foodstuffs. Other significant US exports include mineral, chemical and plastic products. The composition of US exports has not changed significantly over the past ten years.[40]

Moldovan exports to the US are likewise mostly agricultural—vegetable products and textiles dominated the first decade of the partnership. US imports of prepared foodstuffs, a category which includes famous Moldovan products like wine, brandy, and vinegar slowly gained during the late 1990s and early 2000s. Then between 2005 and 2008, US imports of these products spiked dra-matically.[41]

Once again, these abnormalities can be attributed to US competition with Russia. In 2006, Russian imposed a ban on Moldovan wine. The official reason for the ban was consumer safety concerns, but it followed a 2005 recommenda-tion of the Russian Duma to stop the import of Moldovan wine and tobacco in response to Moldovan President Voronin's meetings with two regional leaders who came to power via color revolutions and who Moscow saw as especially pro-American: Ukrainian President Viktor Yushchenko and Georgian President Mikheil Saakashvili.[42]

Regardless of the Russian government's motives, Moldovan producers were abruptly forced to find new markets. The United States seems to have accom-modated part of that supply. Russia reopened its markets to Moldovan wine in late 2007. By 2009, the US figures registered a slight decrease, the first-ever decrease in imports of this category.[43]

Given that trade relations play a significant role in the post-Soviet power dynamic, the underdevelopment of US trade in Moldova is perhaps the weak point of economic relations, particularly when contrasted with the robust US aid, assistance, and foreign investment programs. The United States is not only out-distanced by Moldova's natural trading partners, large economies like the EU and Russia with geographic proximity, but it also trails other ascendant global powers like China and Brazil.

Jackson-Vanik is the quintessential example of how a policy framework left over from the Cold War continues to mitigate successful US policy in the re-gion.

During the Moscow stopover of his March 2011 trip, Vice President Joseph Biden promised to personally work with Congress to repeal Jackson-Vanik, stating at a roundtable with Russian and American business leaders that the Obama administration "strongly supports the lifting of Jackson-Vanik," and recognizes the "worldwide" benefits of doing so.[44] He again affirmed this position later in the same trip during a joint press conference with Moldovan Prime Minister Vlad Filat in Chisinau.[45] It was his second time discussing the issue with Filat, who brought up Jackson-Vanik when Biden received him at the White House in 2010.[46]

The full abolition of Jackson-Vanik and the issue of Russian ascension to the WTO remain politically contentious issues in US domestic politics. The administration has not hesitated to declare removal of Jackson-Vanik as one of the economically oriented "next steps" of Russian reset.[47]

Analysts have noted that some Congressional Republicans see the trade issues as an area of potential leverage over Moscow on issues of humanitarian rights in the region.[48] Both parties are quick to admit that Russia should meet the necessary minimum requirements for normal trade relations; the difference is in their interpretation of those minimum standards. During past attempts to lift Jackson-Vanik, Russia's lack of support for US operations in Iraq—as well as Russian trade barriers on US pork, chicken and beef have were also cited as stumbling blocks.[49]

The prominent Republican Senator John McCain is a strong proponent of abolishing Jackson-Vanik on a country-by-country basis. In a March 2011 speech, he called the Congressional repeal of Jackson-Vanik for Moldova the first step the US should take to tip the country's political balance toward liberty and democracy. When asked about repeal of Jackson-Vanik for Russia, however, McCain added a disclaimer that although the amendment was clearly irrelevant in many respects, there were certain norms that Russia did not adhere to which made them ineligible for such trade liberalization measures.[50]

Since the complete repeal of Jackson-Vanik faces political hurdles, a more likely answer to the problem is a permanent repeal for Moldova on the individual country basis. In fact, Congress and the president have already signed such measures for Albania, Armenia, Bulgaria, China, Czechoslovakia, Estonia, Georgia, Hungary, Kyrgyzstan, Latvia, Lithuania, Mongolia, Romania, Ukraine, and Vietnam, following each country's WTO accession. Moldova is currently the only country in the WTO that does not enjoy permanent normal trade relations with the US.[51]

The Moldovan Institute for Development and Social Initiatives "Viitorul" produced a report analyzing possible reasons for Moldovan exclusion. One issue cited was Holocaust history: In February 2007, the Moldovan parliament passed Law no. 17 on the protection of personal data, which prevented the movement of personal data across state lines, despite the Jewish community's interest in accessing records from the Holocaust in Bessarabia.

To address this problem, in January of 2010 Moldovan Prime Minister Vlad Filat met with the Jewish Community at the US Holocaust Memorial Museum, affirming Moldovan commitment to the protection of human rights. During the same visit, Deputy Prime Minister Iurie Leancă signed a memorandum of cooperation with the US Holocaust Memorial Museum, declaring "Moldova has nothing to hide, so it wants a full examination of archives in the country." Accordingly, Moldovan Acting President Marian Lupu issued a decree allowing for the transmission of personal data to the US Holocaust Memorial Museum.[52] Given the close tie between Jackson-Vanik and issues of Jewish and minority rights, it is very possible that these efforts helped the Moldovan cause.

A second issue possibly slowing the Jackson-Vanik repeal has been human rights abuse in Moldova. Throughout the 1990s and 2000s, the US Department of State's annual Human Rights Report on Moldova cited abuses in the legal system, disregards for fundamental human rights, and abuse of media rights and standards of democratic elections. However, the 2010 human rights report claims that Moldova under the Alliance for European Integration already has made some progress. Although the US State Department still has many concerns regarding human rights issues—especially the sensitive issue of human trafficking—some positive trends were observed, including growth of media freedom and fewer violent abuses in the criminal justice system.[53]

Both high-level Moldovan efforts to address the concerns of the Jewish community and the State Department's tentatively positive appraisal of the human rights in Moldova may have a positive impact on the passage of current legislation under consideration to repeal Jackson-Vanik for Moldova.

Several prominent congressmen have sponsored legislation excluding Moldova from Jackson-Vanik. Senator Richard Lugar, chairman of the foreign relations subcommittee, introduced a bill in 2008 "to extend permanent normal trade relations treatment to the products of Moldova" (S.334). In February 2011, the bill was reintroduced (as S.309) to the 112th Congress. It is interesting to note that Lugar simultaneously released a report on prospects of ending the Transnistrian conflict, which also mentioned Jackson-Vanik as an impediment to closer US engagement in Moldova. This implicit linkage between the amendment and security priorities in the region reflect a growing consensus.

Two months later, in April 2011, related legislation was introduced to the US House of Representatives (H.R.1463) by Representative David Reichert.[54] As of this writing, both bills remain in committee.

The biggest obstacle facing passage of this legislation may now be apathy. Moldovan diplomacy did not consider the abolition of Jackson-Vanik a priority until 2007.[55] Naturally, the US Congress was equally ambivalent. A Congressional Research Service report noted that "no congressional attempts have been made in the past to disapprove by joint resolution any initial extension or later renewal of the "no-violation" determination, which Moldova received in 1997. In other words, it is highly unlikely that Congress or the president would ever opt to discontinue the Moldovan waiver, and thus Jackson-Vanik has no substantial effect on US-Moldovan commercial relations. Nonetheless, abolition of the measure for Moldova could mean greater opportunities for exports to the US, and might translate into positive publicity for the Alliance government.

Conclusion

Departing from a long-standing policy of neutrality, high-level US politicians are clearly giving their support to the Alliance for European Integration. Because it prioritized Russian troop withdrawal from the Transnistrian breakaway region, the United States engaged with Communist partners for nearly a decade, despite ideological differences and official reservations about adherence to human rights and democratic norms under the Voronin regime.

The implementation of the MCC compact and the long-overdue repeal of Jackson-Vanik for Moldova may increase the ability of the US to further promote its values in the short term.

On the negotiation of the Transnistrian settlement, an area where the US has met with resistance from Russia and holds a mixed track record, the US now seems more willing to follow the lead of its European partners. The major exception to this trend is in border security and counter-proliferation issues, where the US has judged European initiatives, including the EUBAM program, wanting, and will continue to play an active leadership role.

Notes

1. For a more detailed historical analysis: George Friedman, "Geopolitical journey, part 4: Moldova," STRATFOR, November 19, 2010, http://www.stratfor.com/weekly /20101118_geopolitical_journey_part_4_moldova (accessed June 10, 2010).
2. Constitution of the Republic of Moldova (1994), art. 11.
3. Damon Wilson in an interview with the author, November 15, 2010.
4. Asif Chaudhry, "20 Years of Moldovan Independence: Looking Back and Forward," Carnegie Endowment for International Peace, Washington, DC, October 5, 2011, http://carnegieendowment.org/2011/10/05/20-years-of-moldovan-independence-looking-back-and-forward/5te0?solr_hilite=Moldova (accessed October 20, 2011).
5. House Committee on Foreign Affairs: Subcommittee on Europe and Eurasia, *Testimony of Stephen B. Nix, ESQ. Director, Eurasia Division International Republican Institute*, July 26, 2011.
6. "McCain backs demand for Russian troop withdrawal from Transdniester," *Radio Free Europe/Radio Liberty*, November 28, 2011.
7. John McCain, "Geremek Lecture" (lecture, Atlantic Council of the US, Washington, DC, March 1, 2011).
8. Marcus Merceli in an interview with the author, US Embassy Chisinau, November 2011.
9. George W. Bush and Vladimir Voronin, "Joint Statement by President George W. Bush and President Vladimir Voronin on U.S.-Moldovan Relations," December 17, 2002.
10. Christopher M. Gacek, *The Logic of Force: The Dilemma of Limited War in American Foreign Policy* (New York: Columbia University Press, 1994), 290.

11. William J. Clinton and Mircea Snegur, "Joint Statement With President Mircea Snegur of Moldova," January 30, 1995, http://www.presidency.ucsb.edu/ws/?pid=51856 (accessed June 12, 2010).

12. Vladimir Socor, "Vice-President Biden's Visit Can Reanimate US-Moldova Relations," *Eurasia Daily Monitor*, March 15, 2011, http://www.jamestown.org/programs /edm/single/?tx_ttnews[tt_news]=37649&cHash=98dc7500daf0c60ded357eaf35fa5cf5 (accessed June 5, 2010).

13. William H. Hill in an interview with the author, Washington, DC, March 2010.

14. US Department of Defense, "No. 017-P:01/27/95:Secretary of Defense William J. Perry wi," Press Advisories, No. 017-95, http://www.defense.gov/advisories/advisory .aspx?advisoryid=2333 (accessed June 5, 2011).

15. Author's own calculation from US Central Command figures.

16. US Central Command, "Moldova," http://www.centcom.mil/moldova/ (accessed June 5, 2011).

17. Lt. Col. Alexandru Cebanu interview with US Central Command. Ibid.

18. US Department of Defense, "Secretary Rumsfeld and Moldovan Minister of Defense Press Availability," June 26, 2004, http://www.defense.gov/transcripts/transcript .aspx?transcriptid=3358 (accessed August 12, 2011).

19. Individual Partnership Action Plan (IPAP) Republic of Moldova-NATO, http:// www.mfa.gov.md/img/docs/new_ipap_en.pdf (accessed August 12, 2011).

20. Oesterreichs Bundesheer, "NATO-PFP Exercises 'Cooperative Longbow and Lancer 2006,' " http://www.bmlv.gv.at/truppendienst/ausgaben/artikel.php?id=554 (accessed August 12, 2011).

21. "Memorandum of Understanding Between the Government of the Republic of Moldova and US European Command for the Execution of the Exercise Medceur-2007."

22. OSCE Mission to Moldova, "Arms control and disarmament," http://www.osce .org/moldova/43599 (accessed September 12, 2011).

23. "Hotbed of Weapons Deals," *The Washington Times*, January 18, 2004.

24. Scott Roxborough, "Transformers 3's John Malkovich Joins Gabriele Salvatores' 'Siberian Education,' " *The Hollywood Reporter*, May 7, 2011, http://www.holly-woodreporter.com/news/transformers-3-s-john-malkovich-207957 (accessed October 10, 2011).

25. US Congress. Senate. Committee on Foreign Relations, "Enhancing Non-Proliferation Partnerships in the Black Sea Region," 112th Cong., 1st sess., 2011, http:// lugar.senate.gov/issues/foreign/Moldova/blacksea.pdf (accessed September 30, 2011).

26. Ibid.

27. Nuclear Smuggling Outreach Initiative, "Bilateral Partners Engaged: Moldova," http://www.nsoi-state.net/bilateralpartnersengaged/moldova.asp (accessed October 5, 2011).

28. Millennium Challenge Account Moldova, "Componente posibile pentru Planul COMPACT," http://www.mca.gov.md/file/Microsoft%20PowerPoint%20-%20Prezentare %20privind%20componentele%20potentiale%20Compact.ppt%20%5BCompatibility%2 0M.pdf (accessed October 12, 2011).

29. For example, the welding firm Lincoln Electronics. See Paul C. Rosenthal, "Statement in Opposition to S. 1167, a bill to provide that certain wire rods shall not be subject to antidumping or countervailing duty order," http://finance.senate.gov/imo/media /doc/mtb_public_comments/S.%201167%20Comments.pdf (accessed August 1, 2011).

30. Department of Commerce. International Trade Administration, "Notice of Final Determination of Sales at Less Than Fair Value: Steel Concrete Reinforcing Bars from Moldova," http://ia.ita.doc.gov/frn/summary/moldova/01-15741.txt (accessed August 1, 2011)

31. David M. Spooner, "Steel Concrete Reinforcing Bars from Belarus, Indonesia, Latvia, Moldova, the People's Republic of China, Poland and Ukraine: Continuation of Antidumping Duty Orders," *govpulse*, August 2, 2007, http://govpulse.us/entries/2007 /08/09/E7-15572/steel-concrete-reinforcing-bars-from-belarus-indonesia-latvia-moldova-the-people-s-republic-of-china (accessed August 1, 2011).

32. US Department of State, "U.S. Government Assistance to and Cooperative Activities with Eurasia," http://www.state.gov/p/eur/rls/rpt/c10250.htm (accessed August 2, 2011).

33. Christopher Williams, "20 Years of Moldovan Independence: Looking Back and Forward," Carnegie Endowment for International Peace, Washington, DC, October 5, 2011, http://carnegieendowment.org/2011/10/05/20-years-of-moldovan-independence-looking-back-and-forward/5te0?solr_hilite=Moldova (accessed October 20, 2011).

34. Tom Junod, "Happy. Hillary," *Esquire*, May 12, 2010, http://www.esquire.com /women/women-issue/hillary-clinton-0510 (accessed August 2, 2011).

35. "Jackson-Vanik Amendment," http://www.cfr.org/trade/jackson-vanik-amendment /p18844 (accessed June 10, 2011).

36. Ernest Simone, ed., *Foreign Policy of the United States* (Huntington, NY: Nova Publishers, 2000), 1:68–69.

37. US Department of State, "US-Moldovan Relations: Background Note: Moldova," July 1, 2011, http://www.state.gov/r/pa/ei/bgn/5357.htm (accessed June 18, 2010).

38. *Testimony of Stephen B. Nix, ESQ*, under the section "Next Steps."

39. EUROSTAT, "Moldova: EU Bilateral Trade and Trade with the World," June 8, 2011, http://trade.ec.europa.eu/doclib/docs/2006/september/tradoc_113419.pdf (accessed August 16, 2011).

40. National Bureau of Statistics of the Republic of Moldova, "Imports by Sections and Chapters. United States of America," 2010, http://www.statistica.md/category.php?l =en&idc=336 (accessed August 16, 2011).

41. See ibid.

42. "Russian law-makers to outlaw Moldavian Wine," *Pravda.ru*, September 3, 2005, http://english.pravda.ru/russia/economics/09-03-2005/7852-wine-0/ (accessed May 2, 2010).

43. National Bureau of Statistics of the Republic of Moldova, "Imports by Sections."

44. Joseph R. Biden, "Remarks by Vice President Joseph R. Biden, Jr. at a Roundtable Discussion with American and Russian Business Leaders," March 9, 2011, http:// www.whitehouse.gov/the-press-office/2011/03/09/remarks-vice-president-joseph-r-biden -jr-roundtable-discussion-american- (accessed May 2, 2011).

45. Joseph R. Biden, "Joseph Biden's Declarations in Moldova," *Moldova.org*, March 11, 2011, http://politicom.moldova.org/news/live-bidens-declarations-in-moldova-video-218164-eng.html (accessed May 2, 2011).

46. "Conference Call on Vice President Biden's Upcoming Trip to Finland, Russia and Moldova," March 4, 2011, http://www.whitehouse.gov/the-press-office/2011/03/04 /conference-call-vice-president-bidens-upcoming-trip-finland-russia-and-m (accessed May 2, 2011).

47. Joseph R. Biden, "The Next Steps in the U.S.-Russia Reset," *The International Herald Tribune*, March 13, 2011, http://www.nytimes.com/2011/03/14/opinion/14iht -edbiden14.html (accessed May 2, 2011).

48. Ellen Barry, "Plain Speaking From Biden in Moscow Speech," *The New York Times*, March 10, 2011, http://www.nytimes.com/2011/03/11/world/europe/11biden.html (accessed May 2, 2011).

49. Julie Ginsberg, "Reassessing the Jackson-Vanik Amendment," Council on Foreign Relations, July 2, 2009, http://www.cfr.org/trade/reassessing-jackson-vanik-amendment/p19 734 (accessed August 1, 2011).

50. McCain, "Geremek Lecture."

51. Ginsberg, "Reassessing the Jackson-Vanik."

52. Ion Tăbîrţă, "Formal and Informal Aspects of Jackson-Vanik Amendment," *Moldova's Foreign Policy Statewatch*, no. 29 (June 2011), http://www.viitorul.org/public /3457/en/Policy%20Statewatch29_en.pdf (accessed August 12, 2011).

53. US Department of State, "2010 Human Rights Report: Moldova," April 8, 2011, http://www.state.gov/g/drl/rls/hrrpt/2010/eur/154439.htm (accessed September 28, 2010).

54. Library of Congress. US Congress, S.309, "Bill Summary & Status," 112th Congress, 1st sess. *Thomas.*

55. Tăbîrţă, "Formal and Informal."

Chapter Eighteen

Transnistria: A Policy of Denial, Containment and Separation from Moldova

Andrey Safonov

Twenty-one years after the dissolution of Soviet Moldavia, Transnistria's strategic vision of its relationship with Moldova is abundantly clear. First, it includes a Transnistrian nation-building project. Second, it does not recognize any conflict settlement according to the model, which stipulates the annexation of Transnistria by Moldova. Third, it seeks the active negation of anything related directly or indirectly to Romanian influence in Moldova, and it criticizes any evidence of the Romanian factor in Moldovan policy. Fourth, the Transnistrian authorities are objectively and subjectively disinterested in strong or consolidated Moldovan authorities.

In 1990s, when relatively little time had passed since dissolution of the USSR and the Moldavian Soviet Socialist Republic (1990–1991), Transnistria looked more favorably on a conflict settlement model for the Dniester region within the borders of the former MSSR than at present. The memory of Soviet Moldavia as a period of relative prosperity was alive in the minds of inhabitants on both banks of the Dniester River. Furthermore, some Transnistrians believed that the Commonwealth of Independent States would become not only an "institution of civilized divorce," but also a nexis for the integration of the former Soviet republics on a new basis.

At the turn of 1990s–2000s, it became clear that the republics of the former USSR were becoming increasingly estranged from one another, and that Chisinau and Tiraspol pursued policies in different directions. Even if propaganda is disregarded, it is still obvious that since 1991, Romanian influence within the Dniester's right bank has been strengthened, while the present-day Pridnestrovian Moldavian Republic is still oriented toward Russia and, to a lesser extent, toward Ukraine.

In Transnistria, Romania has traditionally been an antagonist. That is why symbols related to this country (the tricolored blue-yellow-red flag, Latin script, the demands of unionists to rename the Moldovan language to Romanian, etc.)

were rejected by Transnistria as far back as 1990, and became a harbinger of the cultural and political break-up.

Thus, after the war of 1992, Tiraspol focused on creating its own public institutions, and as mentioned earlier, on nation building. This is undoubtedly a lengthy process, one which will last for several decades, but the PMR has nevertheless already existed for twenty-one years without a fully shaped Transnistrian nation. Furthermore, by 2011, generations unable to remember the Soviet Union or the united Soviet Moldavia have grown up on both banks of the Dniester River. Today, both Moldova and the PMR have their own business elite, political parties, and government officials. These groups are unwilling to share their power.

With the strengthening of Transnistrian statehood, Tiraspol has proceeded to distance itself from the possibility of any settlement solution with Chisinau within the boundaries of the former MSSR. It was a generational change in the PMR, coupled with the approximately equal economic and military potentials of both Transnistria and Moldova that led Transnistrian leadership in this direction. In fact, regionalization existed even in Soviet Moldavia: The left bank of the Dniester River has never been a part of the Principality of Moldavia and it became a part of Russia in 1791. Bessarabia, on the other hand, was the part of the Moldovan state, with its capital at Iaşi; the segment of population living between the Prut and Dniester rivers was more loyal to Romania than the populations of Tiraspol, Rybnitsa and Dubossary. The territory on the right bank of the Dniester became part of the Russian Empire later, in 1812. Numerous and well-established enterprises were concentrated in Transnistria, while Bessarabia was traditionally an agrarian region, and in Soviet times food processing industry was created there.

In 1992, Chisinau lost the war: its primary objective of defeating Transnistrian forces was not achieved. Tiraspol had enlisted the support of Russia and the benevolent neutrality of Ukraine, which created the equilibrium of forces.

Currently, the official positions of the conflicting parties mutually exclude each other. Chisinau largely supports the renewal of a unified Moldova, as it existed prior to 1990. On July 22, 2005, the Moldovan Parliament unilaterally passed a law on the status of the settlement on the left bank of the Dniester River. First, it assumed that Bendery, located on the right bank, would not remain part of Transnistria after the settlement takes. Second, the Act envisioned the same old same unitary model of reconciliation between the parties. In response, on April 11, 2008, then-President of the PMR Igor Smirnov submitted a draft of the Treaty on Friendship and Cooperation between the Pridnestrovian Moldavian Republic and the Republic of Moldova to his Moldovan counterpart Vladimir Voronin at a meeting in Bendery. Since such treaties are usually concluded only between recognized states, Chisinau did not consider the proposal.

Despite the fact that on September 22, 2011, the decision was made to resume negotiations in the 5+2 format—which had been interrupted by Chisinau's diplomats in 2006—the distance between the respective positions of the PMR and Moldova has not diminished. Since 1990, any compromise on the settlement model is still not visible

However, one pattern became clear to Tiraspol over the past twenty-one years. Moldovan-Transnistrian relations improved (from the Transnistrian party's point of view) when Chisinau was embroiled with internal political struggles, and when there were multiple centers of power. Conversely, the most consistent pressure on Transnistria has come from a strong, consolidated Moldovan state. For example, from 1993–1996 there were three centers of power in Chisinau: the presidency with Mircea Snegur at its head; the government, headed by Prime Minister Andrei Sangheli; and the parliament with Petru Lucinschi at its head. According to many Transnistrian politicians and experts, it was the most positive period of the Moldovan-Transnistrian relationship. Internal political struggle in Moldova made the Transnistrian problem a side issue for Chisinau elite, and this stimulated the search for compromise approaches.

The period of 1997–2000, when Moldovan President Petru Lucinschi, who struggled with parliament shortly after winning the election of 1996, was also not a bad one for Transnistria. Political liaisons between Chisinau and Tiraspol were quite active, and there were no conflicts (at least, not any noticeable ones). Transnistrian businesses, especially exporters, functioned smoothly without Moldovan restraints.

Thus, the lack of concentrated power in Moldova guaranteed tranquility in Transnistria to some degree.

The situation changed in 2001, when the Party of Communists of the Republic of Moldova, headed by Vladimir Voronin, gained a majority in parliamentary elections in Moldova. The PCRM had its own man as president (Voronin); its own prime minister (Vasile Tarlev) and its own speaker (Eugenia Ostapciuc). With power concentrated in the hands of Voronin, Moldovan-Transnistrian relations were immediately affected: On August 31, 2001, the president of the Republic of Moldova stripped Transnistria of customs stamps granted in Tiraspol, which had been in place since the Snegur government.

The period of confrontation began, and remained de facto during the entirety of Voronin's tenure. This prompted Transnistrian leaders to actively influence the situation in Moldova, to prevent the concentration of power in the hands of any single political force in Chisinau. Of course, the opportunities of Tiraspol along these lines are not very extensive, but the tendency to do so is clear. The Moldovan parliamentary elections of 2005 were a good illustration. Then the PMR, along with Russia incidentally, provided PR for the Moldovan nationalist opposition in an attempt to defeat the Communists. This policy was provoked by incessant pressure from Voronin's administration on Transnistria and the Chisinau leader's attempts to become the "Moldovan Bismarck," a unifier of the Dniester River banks.

However, as far back as the presidential election of 1996, (when the election of the head of the Moldova state was a nationwide vote) Tiraspol was faced with a gamble. Publicly, it supported the "pro-Russian," but actually hopeless candidate, Premier Sangheli. But privately, Transnistrian leaders counted on the "pro-

Romanian" Snegur to win, as many mass media outlets predicted. The validity of this assessment of the Sangheli-Snegur election aside, let us consider the paradox: Why were PMR leaders interested in Snegur, who was associated in the mind of the average Transnistrian civilian with the nationalism of 1980s–1990s and the war of 1992?

The answer is clear. Snegur encouraged the continuation of policies aimed at the strengthening of Transnistrian independence. The question most frequently asked by the media and at negotiations became how Transnistria could negotiate with "pro-Romanian nationalists." And, conversely, Voronin's pro-Russian declarations were dangerous for PMR to the extent that they tempted the Kremlin to implement a scheme of consolidating its influence throughout the former MSSR by "pushing" Transnistria into Moldova.

The events of April 7, 2009, in Chisinau (civic unrest against alleged fraud in the Moldovan parliamentary elections), the fall of the Party of Communists, and the arrival of the Alliance for European Integration left Tiraspol with only ambivalent feelings.

On the one hand, the right wing, including undoubtedly pro-Romanian forces of Moldova (namely the Liberal Party, led by Mihai Ghimpu) came to power, and Transnistria once more had a reason to intensify community outreach programs aimed at bolstering support of pro-independence policies "in the context of the growing Romanian threat."

On the other hand, the Transnistrian authorities were concerned about the possibility of a real threat of increased pressure on PMR coming from Romania and the West, and even the possible threat of a new armed conflict. Nevertheless, official mass media expressed its satisfaction at the fall of Voronin.

As contradictions from within the ranks of the ruling AEI in Moldova have increased, it has become evident that the old Transnistrian tactic of encouraging Moldovan division is paying off. First of all, internal strife in the AEI has once again set Moldovan-Transnistrian relations back. Secondly, the possibility of negotiating with Chisinau on liberalization of Transnistria's foreign economic dealings, which was impossible under Voronin, has reappeared. Though it has not yet led to tangible results, the tension associated with the period of the PCRM's rule has declined.

At the same time, new risks and threats to the PMR have appeared. These include the increase in the resolve of Moldovan leadership to have Russia withdraw its troops from the banks of the Dniester River and to transform the peace-keeping operation—in which the Russian military forces play a key role—into a civilian observer mission under the auspices of the Organization for Security and Cooperation in Europe. Tiraspol's point of view is that the withdrawal of Russian troops will create a physical security threat to PMR and will provoke Chisinau and its potential allies to resolve a long-existing standoff by force.

However, the internal political instability from 2009–2011 in Moldova once again played into Transnistria's hand. The absence of a legitimate elected president in the Republic of Moldova indicates that the question of power in Chisinau is not resolved. The Party of Communists, which went into the opposition, strives to return to power, including via early parliamentary elections. Currently, Transnistrian leaders are interested in a scenario where the Communists preserve their strength and remain a threat to the Alliance authorities, preventing the AEI from consolidating power to a level that would endanger the PMR.

This old game of encouraging division in Chisinau justifies itself. But why does the PMR pursue a policy of containment toward Chisinau?

The fact of the matter is that both Moldova and Transnistria are characterized by a so-called "vacuum of prospects." It is clear that, despite loud declarations from Moldovan leaders on "Eurointegration," no one will admit Moldova into the European Union. At the same time, Transnistrian leaders have failed to achieve international recognition of PMR independence as of this writing. The two parties in the 21-year-old conflict simply have nothing to offer each other. Tiraspol is convinced that by retaining its independence, Transnistria will be able to keep at least partial control over its economic potential, as well as its linguistic and cultural environment.

Transnistria's policy of distancing itself from the possibility of a settlement is easily explained. The PMR's foreign policy is based on the assumption that time works in favor of Tiraspol. In recent years, it has become clear that the Helsinki Accords on the inviolability of frontiers has collapsed, and the political map of the world is quickly changing. Such states as Kosovo, East Timor, South Ossetia, Abkhazia, South Sudan, and Eritrea have been recognized by certain countries. Montenegro separated from Serbia. At the same time, Taiwan and Northern Cyprus, for example, have preserved their independence. Belgium is under the threat of dissolution—and this country is part of the EU. Transnistria certainly aspires to follow this rising global trend.

In conclusion, it seems likely that as Transnistria seeks to create favorable conditions for achieving its international recognition and preserving its de facto independence, Tiraspol will do everything in its power to prevent the Moldovan authorities from being strong enough to exert significant pressure on Tiraspol.

Index

273

About the Contributors

Andrea Ambrus studied international relations at Kodolányi János College, graduating as an international relations expert in 2011. Currently, she continues her studies in finance. Her thesis topic and main research interests are the Republic of Moldova and International Development Cooperation.

Jos Boonstra is a senior researcher at FRIDE, Madrid. Based in Brussels, he is also head of the Europe-Central Asia Monitoring (EUCAM) program. Before joining FRIDE, he was program manager at the Centre for European Security Studies, the Netherlands. His research focuses on Eurasian and transatlantic security issues (foremost EU, NATO and OSCE policy), as well as security and democratization in Eastern Europe, the South Caucasus and Central Asia.

Georgiy Byanov is deputy director of the South-Ukrainian Frontier Research Centre, Kherson, Ukraine.

Andrey Devyatkov, PhD, is a senior lecturer at the Institute of Human Sciences, Tyumen State University, Russia. He was a visiting fellow at the Institute for International and European Policy, Katholieke Universiteit Leuven, Belgium, and at New Europe College, Romania. His main research interests include Transnistria and Moldova, international relations in the post-Soviet space, and research methodology in international relations.

Vladislav V. Froltsov is an associate professor at Belarusian State University (Department of International Relations, Faculty of International Relations), Minsk, Belarus. He holds a PhD in history. His academic interests focus on topical issues of European and post-Soviet politics, trends in Germany's political development and foreign policy after 1990, and information policy and public diplomacy in modern states. He is the author of over seventy publications.

Ronald J. Hill is a fellow emeritus at Trinity College Dublin, Ireland, where he retired in 2007 as professor of comparative government. Born in the United Kingdom and educated at the Universities of Leeds and Essex, in 1967 he spent the academic year in Chisinau, moving to Dublin in 1969. His widely published work on the politics of the former Communist world includes *Soviet Political Elites: The Case of Tiraspol* (St. Martin's Press, 1977) and *Putin and Putinism* (Routledge, 2009).

Laura Kirvelytė is a Masters' lecturer at the Command and Junior Staff Officer Courses at the General Jonas Žemaitis Military Academy of Lithuania. Her field of academic research includes political processes in Eastern Europe and the South Caucasus. She is the author of several publications in academic journals and the press, both in Lithuania and abroad.

Vladimir Korobov is professor and head of the Department of Philosophy and Sociology at the Kherson National Technical University, and director of the South-Ukrainian Frontier Research Centre, Kherson, Ukraine.

Marcin Kosienkowski, PhD, is assistant professor at the Institute of Political Science of the John Paul II Catholic University of Lublin, Poland. His research focuses on the post-Soviet area. He has published extensively on Moldova and its breakaway region of Transnistria. Among other works, he is author of *The Pridnestrovian Moldavian Republic. Survival Determinants* [Polish] (2010).

Juraj Marušiak, PhD, is a senior research fellow at the Institute of Political Science of the Slovak Academy of Sciences in Bratislava, Slovakia. His research is focused on the contemporary history of Slovakia, the foreign policy of Slovakia and international relations in Central and East Europe. He is author of a monograph, *Slovak Literature and Power in the second half of 1950's* (Brno: Prius, 2001).

Lingqi Meng is a Chinese political scientist residing in Germany. He is currently executive director of the Confucius Institute in Munich. He studied political science at Peking University and at the Ludwig-Maximilians University of Munich. His research interests include theories of international relations as well as the foreign policy of the People's Republic of China.

Octavian Milevschi is a PhD candidate in international relations with the National School of Political Science and Public Administration, Bucharest. He recently completed a research fellowship with the New Europe College, Bucharest. His main research interests include Russian foreign and security policy, Black Sea regional studies, unsolved conflicts in the post-Soviet area, and EU's Eastern Neighbourhood Policy.

Florent Parmentier is a lecturer and academic adviser at Sciences Po (Paris, France). He has written two books on Moldova, *La Moldavie à la croisée des chemins* (2003), and *Moldavie. Les atouts de la francophonie* (Cartier, 2010 [Romanian edition 2010]). He has contributed to several books and articles on Moldova, and is co-founder of the web portal www.moldavie.fr. His research interests include the Eastern European partners and energy politics.

András Rácz is senior research fellow at the Hungarian Institute of International Affairs. He also lectures at the Department of International Studies, Péter

Pázmány Catholic University. He defended his PhD in modern history in 2008 at the Eötvös Loránd University. His research interests cover the post-Soviet region, EU Eastern Neighbourhood Policy, and the foreign and security policy of Hungary.

Andrey Safonov is president of the Association of Independent Political Scientists of Transnistria and editor-in-chief of the Transnistrian opposition newspaper *Novaya Gazeta.* He also served as a member of the parliament of the Moldavian Soviet Socialist Republic, was founder of the official Transnistrian news agency *Olvia-press,* and Transnistrian minister of education, science and culture.

William Schreiber is a Millar scholar at the Institute for European, Russian and Eurasian Studies, The George Washington University, Washington, DC. He has written about Central and Eastern Europe for *Newsweek International,* the *Wall Street Journal,* and others.

Özgehan Şenyuva is an assistant professor in the Department of International Relations and a researcher at the Center for European Studies, Middle East Technical University, Ankara, Turkey. He holds a PhD from the University of Siena. His work deals mainly with public and elite opinion, and the European Union. His recent publications include "Parliamentary elections in Moldova, April and July 2009," *Electoral Studies* 29, no.1 (2010): 190–95.

Natalia Shapovalova is a researcher at FRIDE, Madrid. Her research focuses on EU policies toward Eastern Europe, Russia and the Caucasus. Prior to joining FRIDE, she worked for the International Centre for Policy Studies in Kiev, Ukraine. She holds degrees from Maastricht University, the Netherlands; Maria Curie-Sklodowska University, Poland; and the National University of Kyiv-Mohyla Academy, Ukraine.

Nicolai Ţveatcov is a lecturer at the Faculty of International Relations, Political, and Administrative Studies, State University of Moldova, and a senior researcher at the Institute of European Integration and Political Sciences at the Academy of Sciences of Moldova. He holds a PhD in political science. His research contributions to the study of interethnic relations in Moldova are widely recognized.

Dareg A. Zabarah, PhD, studied political science, Slavonic studies, and the history of East and South-Eastern Europe at Ludwig-Maximilians University, Munich. He is an author of two monographs and various articles on language and national identity in Moldova and the Yugoslav successor states. Currently, he is working on a research project on the role of religion as a group boundary marker in Bosnia and Lebanon.

Davide Zaffi holds a degree in political science from Urbino University, Italy, and has held fellowships at the Central European University, the Európa Intézet (Budapest), and the Deutsch-Italienisches Geschichtsinstitut (Trento). He has published works on the history of the Habsburg Monarchy and Central Europe in several languages. Currently he is advisor for external relations of the Italian region Trentino-South Tyrol.

CPSIA information can be obtained at www.ICGtesting.com
Printed in the USA
BVOW031558300412

288979BV00004B/2/P